Novel Approaches to Urban Design and Architecture Education:

Design Studio Practice and Pedagogy

Pınar Dinç Kalaycı
Gazi University, Turkey

A volume in the Advances in Educational Technologies and Instructional Design (AETID) Book Series

Published in the United States of America by
IGI Global
Information Science Reference (an imprint of IGI Global)
701 E. Chocolate Avenue
Hershey PA, USA 17033
Tel: 717-533-8845
Fax: 717-533-8661
E-mail: cust@igi-global.com
Web site: http://www.igi-global.com

Copyright © 2024 by IGI Global. All rights reserved. No part of this publication may be reproduced, stored or distributed in any form or by any means, electronic or mechanical, including photocopying, without written permission from the publisher. Product or company names used in this set are for identification purposes only. Inclusion of the names of the products or companies does not indicate a claim of ownership by IGI Global of the trademark or registered trademark.

Library of Congress Cataloging-in-Publication Data

Names: Dinç Kalayci, Pinar, 1969- editor.
Title: Novel approaches to urban design and architecture education : design
   studio practice and pedagogy / edited by Pinar Dinç Kalayci.
Description: Hershey, PA : Information Science Reference, [2024] | Includes
   bibliographical references and index. | Summary: "The book collects the
   latest design studio practices as case studies. It seeks to cover the
   theoretical speculations that have the potential to form the design of
   future design studios"-- Provided by publisher.
Identifiers: LCCN 2024002079 (print) | LCCN 2024002080 (ebook) | ISBN
   9798369323298 (hardcover) | ISBN 9798369323304 (ebook)
Subjects: LCSH: City planning. | Architectural design--Study and teaching.
   | Educational innovations.
Classification: LCC HT166 .N6868 2024 (print) | LCC HT166 (ebook) | DDC
   307.1/16--dc23/eng/20240201
LC record available at https://lccn.loc.gov/2024002079
LC ebook record available at https://lccn.loc.gov/2024002080

British Cataloguing in Publication Data
A Cataloguing in Publication record for this book is available from the British Library.

The views expressed in this book are those of the authors, but not necessarily of the publisher.

For electronic access to this publication, please contact: eresources@igi-global.com.

Advances in Educational Technologies and Instructional Design (AETID) Book Series

Lawrence A. Tomei
Robert Morris University, USA

ISSN:2326-8905
EISSN:2326-8913

Mission

Education has undergone, and continues to undergo, immense changes in the way it is enacted and distributed to both child and adult learners. In modern education, the traditional classroom learning experience has evolved to include technological resources and to provide online classroom opportunities to students of all ages regardless of their geographical locations. From distance education, Massive-Open-Online-Courses (MOOCs), and electronic tablets in the classroom, technology is now an integral part of learning and is also affecting the way educators communicate information to students.

The **Advances in Educational Technologies & Instructional Design (AETID) Book Series** explores new research and theories for facilitating learning and improving educational performance utilizing technological processes and resources.

Coverage
- Bring-Your-Own-Device
- Curriculum Development
- Game-Based Learning
- Hybrid Learning
- Instructional Design
- Instructional Design Models
- Online Media in Classrooms
- Social Media Effects on Education

IGI Global is currently accepting manuscripts for publication within this series. To submit a proposal for a volume in this series, please contact our Acquisition Editors at Acquisitions@igi-global.com or visit: http://www.igi-global.com/publish/.

The Advances in Educational Technologies and Instructional Design (AETID) Book Series (ISSN 2326-8905) is published by IGI Global, 701 E. Chocolate Avenue, Hershey, PA 17033-1240, USA, www.igi-global.com. This series is composed of titles available for purchase individually; each title is edited to be contextually exclusive from any other title within the series. For pricing and ordering information please visit http://www.igi-global.com/book-series/advances-educational-technologies-instructional-design/73678. Postmaster: Send all address changes to above address. Copyright © 2024 IGI Global. All rights, including translation in other languages reserved by the publisher. No part of this series may be reproduced or used in any form or by any means – graphics, electronic, or mechanical, including photocopying, recording, taping, or information and retrieval systems – without written permission from the publisher, except for non commercial, educational use, including classroom teaching purposes. The views expressed in this series are those of the authors, but not necessarily of IGI Global.

Titles in this Series

For a list of additional titles in this series, please visit: www.igi-global.com/book-series

Augmented Reality and the Future of Education Technology
Rashmi Aggarwal (Chitkara Business School, Chitkara University, India) Prachi Gupta (Chitkara Business School, Chitkara University, India) Satinder Singh (Chitkara Business School, Chitkara University, India) and Rajni Bala (Chitkara Business School, Chitkara University, India)
Information Science Reference • copyright 2024 • 297pp • H/C (ISBN: 9798369330159) • US $175.00 (our price)

Integrating Generative AI in Education to Achieve Sustainable Development Goals
Ruchi Doshi (Universidad Azteca, Mexico) Manish Dadhich (Sir Padampat Singhania University, India) Sandeep Poddar (Lincoln University College, Malaysia) and Kamal Kant Hiran (Sir Padampat Singhania University, India & Lincoln University College, Malaysia)
Information Science Reference • copyright 2024 • 532pp • H/C (ISBN: 9798369324400) • US $295.00 (our price)

Considerations and Techniques for Applied Linguistics and Language Education Research
Hung Phu Bui (University of Economics, Ho Chi Minh City, Vietnam)
Information Science Reference • copyright 2024 • 241pp • H/C (ISBN: 9798369364826) • US $245.00 (our price)

Comprehensive Sexuality Education for Gender-Based Violence Prevention
Mariana Buenestado-Fernández (University of Cantabria, Spain) Azahara Jiménez-Millán (University of Córdoba, Spain) and Francisco Javier Palacios-Hidalgo (University of Córdoba, Spain)
Information Science Reference • copyright 2024 • 342pp • H/C (ISBN: 9798369320532) • US $245.00 (our price)

Enhancing Curricula with Service Learning Models
Sharon Valarmathi (Christ University, India) Jacqueline Kareem (Christ University, India) Veerta Tantia (Christ University, India) Kishore Selva Babu (Christ University, India) and Patrick Jude Lucas (Christ University, India)
Information Science Reference • copyright 2024 • 328pp • H/C (ISBN: 9798369359334) • US $265.00 (our price)

Encouraging Transnational Learning Through Virtual Exchange in Global Teacher Education
Alina Slapac (University of Missouri-St. Louis, USA) and Cristina A. Huertas-Abril (University of Córdoba, Spain)
Information Science Reference • copyright 2024 • 424pp • H/C (ISBN: 9781668478134) • US $215.00 (our price)

701 East Chocolate Avenue, Hershey, PA 17033, USA
Tel: 717-533-8845 x100 • Fax: 717-533-8661
E-Mail: cust@igi-global.com • www.igi-global.com

Table of Contents

Editorial Advisory Board xviii

Preface xix

Chapter 1
Being Earthian: Learning From Legendary Architects 1
    Nazan Kirci, Gazi University, Turkey

Chapter 2
Mura: A Practice-Based Design Curriculum for Future Creation in Rurual Japan 17
    Cihangir Istek, Center for Global Initiatives, Japan
    Andreas M. Schneider, Institute for Information Design, Japan

Chapter 3
UVIR: Unprecedented Virtual-Intellectual Representations Thought and Imagined 34
    Can Güngör, Gazi University, Turkey
    Gizem Özkan Üstün, Gazi University, Turkey

Chapter 4
Architecture as an Emancipating Ground: Emancipatory Architectural Designs of Atelier 1 61
    Zeynep Uludag, Gazi University, Turkey
    Gulsah Gulec, Gazi University, Turkey
    Neva Gercek Atalay, Gazi University, Turkey

Chapter 5
Learning by Doing at the Sapienza University of Rome: The Technological Design Studios'
Experiences Applied to Housing 78
    Eliana Cangelli, Sapienza University of Rome, Italy

Chapter 6
Feeling the Context 100
    Ayşegül İnce, Gazi University, Turkey
    Aysu Akalın, Gazi University, Turkey

Chapter 7
The CineArch Method in Architectural Education: Film Analysis and Filmmaking in the Design
Studio 114
    Gul Kacmaz Erk, Queen's University, Belfast, UK

Chapter 8
Waterfront Dynamics 132
    Zbigniew W. Paszkowski, Andrzej Frycz Modrzewski Kraków University, Poland
    Jakub I. Gołębiewski, West Pomeranian University of Technology in Szczecin, Poland

Chapter 9
Design Basics vs. Current Complexity: Studio 4 142
    M. Tayfun Yildirim, Gazi University, Turkey
    Özge Zenter, Gazi University, Turkey
    E. Fulya Özmen, Gazi University, Turkey

Chapter 10
Creative Experimental Architectural Design Teaching 156
    Bartosz Sliwecki, Bialystok University of Technology, Poland
    Adam Jakimowicz, Bialystok University of Technology, Poland
    Szymon Andrejczuk, Bialystok University of Technology, Poland
    Maciej Poplawski, Bialystok University of Technology, Poland

Chapter 11
Excessively Undisciplined Works: On Situating the Architectural Design Studio Off-Centre 178
    İrem Küçük, Gazi University, Turkey

Chapter 12
Active Learning Strategy for First-Year Design Studio: The ÖzU Case 192
    Derya Yorgancıoğlu, Özyeğin University, Turkey
    Semra Aydınlı, Özyeğin Univrsity, Turkey
    Beyza Şat, Özyeğin University, Turkey
    Doğa Dinemis Aman, Özyeğin University, Turkey
    Burçin Mızrak Bilen, Özyeğin University, Turkey
    Gizem Efendioğlu, Özyeğin University, Turkey
    Zümrüt Şahin, Özyeğin University, Turkey
    Mert Zafer Kara, Özyeğin University, Turkey

Chapter 13
Cultivating Sensibility: A Semester's Journey Through an Introductory Design Course 202
    Ece K. Açıkgöz, Ankara Bilim University, Turkey
    Mehmet İlhan Kesmez, Ankara Bilim University, Turkey

Chapter 14
Digital Explorers/Digitalized Explorations: A First-Year Architectural Design Studio Experiment
on Distant Urban Interventions 219
    Senem Yildirim, Gazi University, Turkey
    Arzu Özen Yavuz, Gazi University, Turkey

Chapter 15
On the Threshold: A Transitionary Architectural Design Studio 239
Esin Boyacıoğlu, Gazi University, Turkey
Hilal Aycı, Gazi University, Turkey
Bengi Su Erürkmen Aksoy, Gazi University, Turkey
Bilge Beril Kapusuz Balcı, Gazi University, Turkey

Chapter 16
Teaching Design Studios Face to Face and Online: Perspectives and Recommendations 255
Abdullah Al Mahmud, Swinburne University of Technology, Australia

Chapter 17
The Relationship Between Professional Practice and Architectural Education in Turkey 275
Mehmet Emre Arslan, Istanbul Kultur University, Turkey
Salih Ceylan, Bahcesehir University, Turkey

Chapter 18
Green Studio With Different Education Methodologies Based on Sustainability 292
Figen Beyhan, Gazi University, Turkey
Merve Ertosun Yildiz, Gazi University, Turkey

Chapter 19
The Multi Project as the First Encounter With the World of Integrated Design 312
Tom Veeger, University of Technology, Eindhoven, The Netherlands

Chapter 20
Beyond the Planetary Architecture 323
Lucija Ažman Momirski, University of Ljubljana, Slovenia

Compilation of References 335

About the Contributors 356

Index 362

Detailed Table of Contents

Editorial Advisory Board xviii

Preface xix

Chapter 1
Being Earthian: Learning From Legendary Architects... 1
   Nazan Kirci, Gazi University, Turkey

This chapter is about the studies being conducted in a6 Studio, one of the design studios of the Department of Architecture at Gazi University. A6 Studio has decided to get the theory of architecture to the center of its studies so that the unique knowledge of the field of architecture is getting carried from the theoretical courses to the practical area of the design studio. For this purpose, students are encouraged to take one of the legendary architects as their role models and learn from these masters. Being quite unrestrained in choosing the study area and subject, students enjoy the freedom of designing in any part of the world they wish; on the one hand, getting familiar with its responsibility, on the other hand, under the metaphorical guidance of the architects they have chosen to research. . So, in the A6 studio, the students experience being an earthling while learning from legendary architects to develop their vision and enhance their creativity.

Chapter 2
Mura: A Practice-Based Design Curriculum for Future Creation in Rurual Japan 17
   Cihangir Istek, Center for Global Initiatives, Japan
   Andreas M. Schneider, Institute for Information Design, Japan

Demonstrating the importance of Mura (a synonym for village or hamlet, also countryside, in Japanese) as a prototype for off-urban agglomerations and a place for design practice, this chapter presents a co-design studio practice as case studies that might contribute to community efforts for the future creation in Nose Town–a Satoyama (Japanese term applied to the border zone or fertile area between mountain foothills and arable flat land) in Osaka Prefecture, Japan. Students of Osaka University jointly discovered not only the charm of this region, but also the multiple problems and issues of building a sustainable future. Explorations providing fieldwork, micro-internships, and practical interventions have been particularly focused on how cross-disciplinary competences and project-based design learning can make a difference in solving the many problems of an aging community that faces the exodus of the younger generation to big cities.

Chapter 3
UVIR: Unprecedented Virtual-Intellectual Representations Thought and Imagined............................ 34
    Can Güngör, Gazi University, Turkey
    Gizem Özkan Üstün, Gazi University, Turkey

Design studios are the backbone of architectural education. At XXX University Faculty of Architecture, the vertical studio system allows 2nd, 3rd, and 4th-year students to work together in a design studio to learn from each other and contribute to the projects via primary literature research on design problems, project site analysis, and site model making. Group study also contributes to program generation, primary concept studies, sketch making, project generation, building model making, material research, 3d visualization studies, presentation works, and final submission CAD drafting. The retrospective evaluation of XXX's design studio practices from Spring 2016 to Spring 2022 showed various subjects and projects in different scales and programs in varying places and times. The students' projects produced within this period proved successful and gathered recognition and rewards from national/international student design competitions. That's the reason these projects are called "Unprecedented Virtual-Intellectual Representations: Thought and Imagined."

Chapter 4
Architecture as an Emancipating Ground: Emancipatory Architectural Designs of Atelier 1 61
    Zeynep Uludag, Gazi University, Turkey
    Gulsah Gulec, Gazi University, Turkey
    Neva Gercek Atalay, Gazi University, Turkey

This chapter is based on the design approach of Atelier 1, an architectural design studio at Gazi University Department of Architecture in Ankara. Atelier 1 aims to develop a critical understanding of design thinking, and promotes interdisciplinary approaches in the studio. The critical discourses in other disciplines indicate the developmental process of architectural concepts. As a critical design studio, Atelier 1 defined the main theme of fall and spring semesters of 2021 and 2022 as "Architecture as an Emancipating Ground." Students discussed the concept of emancipation in architecture from an interdisciplinary perspective including philosophical conceptions, social and ecological dimensions, and developed their own critical approaches. Due to the emancipatory approach of Atelier 1, students were encouraged to propose their own architectural scenarios and programs. The chapter presents a selection of the emancipatory design projects, as well as a cross-section of the educational model of Atelier 1 that involves interdisciplinary approaches.

Chapter 5
Learning by Doing at the Sapienza University of Rome: The Technological Design Studios' Experiences Applied to Housing 78
    Eliana Cangelli, Sapienza University of Rome, Italy

This chapter presents the Design Studios (DS) teaching method in technological and environmental design, applied in undergraduate and postgraduate courses in architecture at Sapienza University of Rome. Design Studios focuses on a comprehensive approach to the environmental sustainability of the architectural design process in the field of public social housing construction. Based on the teaching experiences, the chapter reports evidence of the teaching methods used for the design proposals submitted by the students of the different DSs for the regeneration of Rome's suburbs. Based on the results obtained, this approach could be seen as a way to develop students' ability to manage the project according to environmental sustainability criteria, from the initial analysis phase to the choice of construction techniques and materials. The article aims to contribute to a disciplinary approach that trains students to become competent architects to chapter contemporary issues of ecological transition, housing shortage, and suburban regeneration.

Chapter 6
Feeling the Context 100
    Ayşegül İnce, Gazi University, Turkey
    Aysu Akalın, Gazi University, Turkey

The contextual reasoning of place and subject dialog from a mimetic point of view has been central to this work. The chapter discusses modern mosque architecture, focusing on the studio project of the second-year students. The goal of each student in the design should be to reach the critical moment by seeing and expressing the spiritual feelings of the user in a place of worship. As designers, students are expected to feel the requirements of context by looking through the eyes of the users of the space, and the educators are expected to help this with the methods used. This chapter is written to convey the methodological details of feeling the context which is defined as contextual reasoning. According to the analysis, three different student approaches emerged at the end of the design process. These are inspired interpretation, imitation by partial interpretation, and exact imitation. In summary, the contextual attitudes that students develop by using the domain sources in a mimetic way help students empathically experience the space even at the superficial level of insideness.

Chapter 7
The CineArch Method in Architectural Education: Film Analysis and Filmmaking in the Design Studio 114
Gul Kacmaz Erk, Queen's University, Belfast, UK

This chapter reflects on an innovative design studio at Queen's University Belfast in Northern Ireland that unites architecture and cinema under the umbrella of design through cinematic analysis methods and filmmaking practices. By embracing film analysis and filmmaking as design and learning tools, CineArch studio focuses on questioning and redefining the boundaries of architectural creativity and spatial design. The fusion of cinematic analysis methods and architectural design processes takes a central role in the studio. Students explore methods such as storyboard, montage/collage, cinematic plan/model, poster, and moodPaint to analyse film scenes but also to design buildings, structures, and film sets. In parallel, filmmaking practices, such as concept film, site film, city film, model film, animation as well as AR/VR, are utilised to test and articulate architectural ideas through dynamic audio-visual means. The spatial outcomes of this multidisciplinary collaboration are a series of atmospheric and experiential projects that exceed conventional architectural boundaries.

Chapter 8
Waterfront Dynamics 132
Zbigniew W. Paszkowski, Andrzej Frycz Modrzewski Kraków University, Poland
Jakub I. Gołębiewski, West Pomeranian University of Technology in Szczecin, Poland

The practice of The Architectural Design Studio's "Waterfront Dynamics" focuses on the processes of spatial and functional transformation in modern cities. They are particularly interested in the changes affecting post-industrial areas and historic centers of port cities. Their students deal with various issues related to transforming the riverside landscape. The subject of design interventions is their hometown of Szczecin (Poland), where many spatial problems focus and where many demanding design topics can be found. The results are projects to restore the historic riverside district and bold visions of the new development of degraded post-industrial areas. This studio is trying to teach students methods of creating new architecture in a historical setting and considering strong exposure in the waterside zone - landscape analysis, the composition of the principles of domination and subordination, scale, and continuity of development.

Chapter 9
Design Basics vs. Current Complexity: Studio 4 142
    M. Tayfun Yildirim, Gazi University, Turkey
    Özge Zenter, Gazi University, Turkey
    E. Fulya Özmen, Gazi University, Turkey

During history, architectural design education was based on typological patterns and local styles such as vernacular architectures, Greek, Roman, Gothic, Ottoman, Baroc, etc. Professional guilds have carried out these types by repetition of their iconic styles. However, developing technologies and changing materials over time also affected this local architectural design education. Architectural education, like other branches of education, includes many complex processes from the first stage to the last stage. In this process, the student's experiences, knowledge and the method followed are very important. The method taught in architectural design studios guides the design and plays a major role in the formation of the design. In this context, the study covers the design process and student studies of "AAAA University Faculty of Architecture, Department of Architecture - Studio 4." Considering the pros and cons of the design method used in Studio 4, it is clear that it is an important method in terms of providing students with analytical thinking and problem-solving skills.

Chapter 10
Creative Experimental Architectural Design Teaching 156
    Bartosz Sliwecki, Bialystok University of Technology, Poland
    Adam Jakimowicz, Bialystok University of Technology, Poland
    Szymon Andrejczuk, Bialystok University of Technology, Poland
    Maciej Poplawski, Bialystok University of Technology, Poland

This chapter explores computer-aided architectural design (CAAD) in architectural education, focusing on innovative tools in design studios. A collaboration between AAAA University of Technology's Architecture Faculty and AuReLa Laboratory, it investigates form-finding through emotions, particularly fear's impact on design. The chapter demonstrates 3D tools' versatility for various design aspects, from abstract to more technically feasible. Additionally, it presents an approach integrating AI-generated images into architectural design, highlighting AI's potential in creating almost real time concept designs. Findings show a dichotomy in architectural education: students using abstract tools in their third semester struggle technically later, while those focusing on technical skills initially limit their creative expression. This emphasises the need for balance in architectural curricula between abstract and technical skills, but also challenges the academic community into using novel tools to constantly modernise their design teaching methods.

Chapter 11
Excessively Undisciplined Works: On Situating the Architectural Design Studio Off-Centre............ 178
    İrem Küçük, Gazi University, Turkey

This study deals with the pedagogy of architectural design studios. By analyzing atelierz as a case study, it builds a discussion on situating the architectural design studio off-center, implementing experimental pedagogy, and producing excessively undisciplined work. Dealing with such a subject is crucial in exploring and discussing how architectural knowledge and skills, which cannot be fully accommodated within the scope of architectural education, are made accessible, used, and produced in the studio. The first part of the study, divided into three parts, explains what is off-center in architecture. The second part discusses the need to adopt an experimental pedagogic approach to situate the studio off-center and explains the experimental fiction of atelierz. The third part exemplifies the fictions and works of atelierz, discussing the excessively undisciplined nature of the knowledge and skills they lead to. Considering the conceptualizations, pedagogic fiction descriptions, and experiences presented, the opportunities and risks of situating the studio off-center are discussed.

Chapter 12
Active Learning Strategy for First-Year Design Studio: The ÖzU Case.. 192
    Derya Yorgancıoğlu, Özyeğin University, Turkey
    Semra Aydınlı, Özyeğin Univrsity, Turkey
    Beyza Şat, Özyeğin University, Turkey
    Doğa Dinemis Aman, Özyeğin University, Turkey
    Burçin Mızrak Bilen, Özyeğin University, Turkey
    Gizem Efendioğlu, Özyeğin University, Turkey
    Zümrüt Şahin, Özyeğin University, Turkey
    Mert Zafer Kara, Özyeğin University, Turkey

This study aims to examine the active learning strategy applied in the first-semester design studio, the 2023-2024 fall semester, in the Department of Architecture at Özyeğin University in Türkiye. The ÖzU Case differed from traditional basic design pedagogy, where the design problem is divided into its components and the basic elements and principles of design are discussed through a part-to-whole approach. Methodologically based on a case study analysis, the examination dwells on the following themes: (1) Student engagement in learning process, (2) cooperative learning, (3) role of the tutor, (4) multiplicity of teaching and learning activities, and (5) flexibility and adaptability of space. The study revealed that the active learning strategy enabled ARCH 101 Design students to grasp a holistic approach to design and develop ways of seeing with the mind's eyes, through the integration of the learning by experiencing and learning by doing activities.

Chapter 13
Cultivating Sensibility: A Semester's Journey Through an Introductory Design Course 202
   Ece K. Açıkgöz, Ankara Bilim University, Turkey
   Mehmet İlhan Kesmez, Ankara Bilim University, Turkey

This chapter explores an introductory design course for architectural education, emphasizing the importance of transcending conventional standards and embracing uncertainty. Rooted in objectivism and existentialism, it encourages students to question assumptions and explore beyond the visible. Through a semester's experience of carefully curated assignments and iterative processes, it showcases how design principles are culminated in the synthesis of accumulated knowledge into visionary design solutions. It highlights the transformative journey of preparing students to navigate the complexities of creative challenges and contribute meaningfully to the design profession. Through comprehensive exploration of curriculum development and student learning experiences, it offers insights into the interplay between theoretical principles and practical application in design education, providing practical implications for educators, curriculum developers, and policymakers aiming to foster the next generation of creative thinkers and innovative problem solvers in design and architecture.

Chapter 14
Digital Explorers/Digitalized Explorations: A First-Year Architectural Design Studio Experiment on Distant Urban Interventions 219
   Senem Yildirim, Gazi University, Turkey
   Arzu Özen Yavuz, Gazi University, Turkey

First year design education is one of the most challenging stages of architectural education. Although first-year architectural design studio mainly follows the footsteps of Bauhaus Ecole in many institutions focusing on establishing an abstract way of thinking while preparing students for upcoming architectural design studios, some institutions design their curriculum to address the fundamentals of architectural design in the first year. Gazi University's Department of Architecture follows this path where first year education is treated as a stage where abstract thinking is introduced, while also acting as an intermediary step to use basic design thinking to design habitable units. Focusing on Architectural Project II, the chapter explores the teaching methodologies of first-year design studio taught at Gazi University and aims to present the specific pedagogies, design strategies, and students' approaches to first-year education on the project conducted during Spring semester of 2021 titled Digital Explorers/Digitalized Explorations: Distant Urban Interventions to Istanbul's Kadikoy.

Chapter 15
On the Threshold: A Transitionary Architectural Design Studio 239
    Esin Boyacıoğlu, Gazi University, Turkey
    Hilal Aycı, Gazi University, Turkey
    Bengi Su Erürkmen Aksoy, Gazi University, Turkey
    Bilge Beril Kapusuz Balcı, Gazi University, Turkey

Architectural education, rooted in historical models like Beaux-Arts and Bauhaus, has long shaped pedagogical practices focusing on formalism and functionality. However, contemporary discourse suggests a need for a paradigm shift towards addressing social and cultural dimensions in architectural education. This chapter explores the evolution of architectural pedagogy through the lens of Studio 201 (atölyeikiyüzbir), a design studio experience spanning over two decades at the Gazi University Department of Architecture.

Chapter 16
Teaching Design Studios Face to Face and Online: Perspectives and Recommendations 255
    Abdullah Al Mahmud, Swinburne University of Technology, Australia

This chapter presents reflections on teaching an introductory design studio to first-year industrial design and architecture students. The unit was taught online in 2020 and face-to-face in 2021. To improve online delivery, student feedback was gathered and analyzed thematically. Along with personal teaching reflections, the feedback was used to identify challenges and facilitating factors in online delivery. Findings showed that students appreciated having live support from the lecturer throughout the online class, rather than relying on recorded lectures, and benefitted from seeing each other's finished work. However, students expressed dissatisfaction with the limited options for developing the course's required prototypes. The experience suggests that design studios can be partially offered online successfully. However, students must have access to design workshops for specific weeks. This chapter documents the challenges of adapting a design subject for online delivery, with recommendations for academics who intend to develop engaging online design courses.

Chapter 17
The Relationship Between Professional Practice and Architectural Education in Turkey 275
    Mehmet Emre Arslan, Istanbul Kultur University, Turkey
    Salih Ceylan, Bahcesehir University, Turkey

One of the biggest challenges in architectural education is its necessity to adapt to a continuously evolving professional environment. In many countries, professional organizations such as chambers of architects and educational institutions work together to come up with various strategies and formulae that strengthen the bond between the two. However, the rigid system imposed to the higher education institutions in Turkey hinders architecture schools to propose effective strategies for creating such bonds. Historical research on the topic indicates that this bond has become weaker in time. Currently, concerns reflect on the opinions of various stakeholders. As a result, there are various comments on architectural education to become more sufficient for the professional environment. This chapter aims to draw a framework for the relationship between education and practice in Turkey. It elaborates on the past, present and the future of the relationship from local and global perspectives.

Chapter 18
Green Studio With Different Education Methodologies Based on Sustainability 292
    Figen Beyhan, Gazi University, Turkey
    Merve Ertosun Yildiz, Gazi University, Turkey

Design studios have great importance for architecture education because they consist of an interactive process carrying out theory and practice together. In design studios, many discussions about design processes focus on different approaches, and many alternative design methods are produced. Studio V, one of the architectural design studios at AAA University, offers students design practice both inside the school and on out-of-school technical trips. Studio V determines sustainability as the basic concept and experiences the spirit of the place with knowledge from the past. It aims to develop the student's ability to analyze, perceive, construct, criticize, question, and design. This chapter explains the concept and execution style of Studio V and illustrates the end-of-term products through a few student projects. It ends with an evaluation of the scope of the studio and its teaching methods.

Chapter 19
The Multi Project as the First Encounter With the World of Integrated Design 312
    Tom Veeger, University of Technology, Eindhoven, The Netherlands

The Multi is a project in the third year of the bachelor of the department of Built Environment (AAAA) and the first encounter with the world of integrated design. Today's building demands have become increasingly complex which necessitates the preparation of students for a practice in which they are ready to cooperate in design teams in close interaction with all disciplines. The multidisciplinary assignment is a practical assignment designed to train students in solving problems with a high level of complexity. An additional goal is teaching students how to cooperate in a team in which every student takes responsibility for a specific domain.

Chapter 20
Beyond the Planetary Architecture 323
Lucija Ažman Momirski, University of Ljubljana, Slovenia

The design studio is an enjoyable experience and a creative atmosphere in a community of young students and their supervisors, where new ideas and imaginative design proposals emerge. The design studio can be complemented by workshops in the form of short-term courses, which are a dynamic component bringing students and practice together. In general, workshops are a quality-control tool to evaluate the themes and processes of a design studio. The design studio topics are very diverse, and the students had to discover all the fundamental questions of dwelling from scratch; they had to question every detail of the starting point of the design. Working beyond planetary architecture offered students the opportunity not only to develop innovative designs, but also to address the essential reasons for habitation. A critical review of the projects was offered to the students at the end of the design studio course by external students and supervisors, and some projects were refined by more precisely defining the values they represent or carry.

Compilation of References 335

About the Contributors 356

Index 362

Editorial Advisory Board

Eliana Cangelli, *Sapienza University of Rome, Italy*
Michele Conteduca, *Sapienza University of Rome, Italy*
Neslihan Dostoğlu, *İstanbul Kültür University, Turkey*
Carola Hein, *Delft University of Technology, Netherlands*
Nazan Kırcı, *Gazi University, Turkey*
Hare Kılıçaslan, *Karadeniz Technical University, Turkey*
Lucija Ažman Momirski, *University of Ljubljana, Slovenia*
Zeynep Uludağ, *Gazi University, Turkey*

Preface

The evolving spatial needs of humanity continuously challenge and transform our existing environments, design processes, and related educational systems. Design studios, as the cornerstone of architectural education, serve as crucibles for the exploration and response to these ongoing and emerging changes. Each urban or architectural design studio, through its unique curriculum, offers a theoretical and practical structure for understanding and solving the world's issues. Some studios excel in formulating new questions and fields of research, while others focus on crafting direct solutions. The varied approaches to learning and teaching across (under)graduate educational levels all contribute to the enhancement of our physical environments.

Being the backbone of urban design and architectural education, design studios always seek new ways of teaching. Conventional components and processes that continue in studios and the confrontations with various new (and mostly diverse) fluctuations of the world put design studios in a very specific position that requires deeper concern. Each studio is a conceptual and physical microcosm that has a unique way(s) of contact with the universe. Therefore, collecting different approaches and decoding the dynamics behind the uniqueness of studio environments was considered to be necessary for constructing effective methods of dealing with the global/universal problems of time and for reconsidering the habits of vocational education in general.

The design of Design Studios, including the pedagogies used, varies depending on time, society, region, culture of institutes, national/international expectations of the profession, student backgrounds, teacher preferences, topics chosen, and a very large variety of other considerations. All of the above constituents might be considered as the design studio variables because they all serve architecture/city directly and the architectural/urban education in general, as well as the formation of the individual architect/urban designer.

Numerous scientific journals, popular magazines, and even single books have been curated and published; they depict the history of studio education, the most recent studio trends, and noteworthy studio practices. Some studios, on the other hand, continue to operate within their institutes' well-established values and procedural traditions as they continue to put one brick on another. Though these conventional studio practices consist of the majority of modern design studio instruction, many of them remain out of sight. In the realm of this relatively quiet and relatively novel design education, the diversity of contemporary studio pedagogies necessitates reinforcement via the new collections of original cases and research.

This book aims to compile the latest practices in design studios, presenting them as case studies while also exploring speculations that could shape the future of studio education. The studios in this collection were conceived of and treated as if they were in purgatory, residing on a threshold position. They were discovered to be retaining institutional values while attempting to restructure these values around the universe's new problematic challenges and utilizing the most recent pedagogical advancements. Each studio was acknowledged as a microcosm in practice, a philosophy, an operation, a unique entity, and a form of existence on its own. Studios were considered to be the miniature, ephemeral and collective

Preface

societies in charge of molding students into architects from whom innovative solutions to the problems of the world/universe have been expected. Studios were thought to be most impacted by the institutional policies and the day-to-day changing issues of the society/humanity they belong to.

The present inquiry focuses on single/unique studios and their works by showcasing the diversity in design studio teaching/learning. In addressing the multifaceted nature of design studios, the book encompasses a large range of themes: Retrospective stories of single studio practices, comprehensive stories of single semesters in studios, architecture education-studio relationships from a historical perspective, the role of arts in studios, step-by-step involvement of AI in the studio, online teaching and its effects on the studio, studios devoted to rising water levels and the development of coastal lines, learning from the works of living legends in the studio, digitalization of the studio, scientific approaches to data and its direct use in design in the studio, cooperative learning exercises in the studio, engaging with local people and designing accordingly in and out of the studio, experimenting imitation-context clashes in the studio, designing for place-sustainability framework through the studio, redesigning the studio curriculum as an enlarged workshop and the architectural transformation of existing urban-residential textures within the studio. Via these themes, the book explores the studio's possible responses to both local and global problems, displays the diversifying variables of studio environments, and delves into the curriculum design issues specific to studios. The significant themes within this comprehensive exploration are the knowledge used and produced in the studio, learning paradigms, studio principles or manifests, critical pedagogies, collaborations, and the multidisciplinarity of design studios. For the curious reader, it is possible to dive into chapters and be carried away with the adventure of each studio and each theoretical background introduced by the tutors, whereas some possible answers that might occur in the minds of the audience might need inference.

A careful reader may notice that the design studios presented here are not equivalent to each other in terms of student compositions and studio objectives. As one studio is devoted to basic design education in architecture, another is designed for vertical groups that consist of students from 2nd, 3rd and 4th-year levels. Also, it should be noted that, due to the curricular differences between countries, 4th-year 2nd-semester education, for instance, can refer to the diploma project in architectural design undergraduate education in some countries, whereas the same level might mean different for the other. Also, some studios in this collection are special for undergraduate education and certain topics in architecture, whereas some are devoted to graduate-level interdisciplinary groups aiming at architectural designers of the future to be more equipt in solving the problems that go beyond the responsibility of a single profession. Each approach adds different dimensions and discussion to the total practice of teaching. Therefore, each approach embodies promises and associations that can guide one another despite the level and objective differences.

The compilation within this book is intended to provide design teaching professionals with examples and ideas for structuring their studio practice and pedagogy. The primary focus will be on current studio practices and methodologies, while theoretical discussions of papers will pave the way for new experiences and innovations. The book is also crafted for professionals seeking to deepen their understanding of the essential elements, actors, processes, topics, and missions—essentially, the pedagogical ingredients—of individual and unique design studios. The target audience for this book includes teaching professionals and researchers in the field of urban and architectural design studios, who play a crucial role in shaping our built environment. Additionally, the book will offer valuable insights to executives involved in education and the culture of professional education, as well as authorities governing cities and institutions at both local and global levels that deal with urban development and architecture.

Preface

Collecting different practices and approaches in design teaching was very meaningful for me in terms of refreshing my professional network and developing new collaborations around the ongoing experiences. All these became possible with the help of participant eminent teachers and their sincere interest in taking place in this book. I am so thankful to those who responded to the first call, who showed great patience and collaboration in the development process of the book, and to those who reviewed the chapters in detail. The intellectual contributions of the advisory board members and the very accurate assistance of the publisher created an atmosphere that made this voluminous book possible.

We are living in a critical time in which most practices need revision/readjustment, and this book stems from such a quest. I hope this book can present a non-conventional collection of ongoing practices in design studio teaching in architecture and urban design and become a basis for further research and collaboration by adding new studios and institutions to its discussion. Also, I want to express my sincere wishes for this book to go beyond the limits of conventional methodologies and their well-known outcomes. I believe the genuine nature of each design studio presented in this book deserves an innovative, unconditioned, creative, and demanding approach from the reader. This comprehensive exploration aims to inspire and guide those dedicated to the advancement of design education, fostering a better understanding and application of the dynamic practices within design studios. Through the shared experiences and theoretical insights presented in this book, we hope to contribute to the continuous evolution of urban design and architecture education, ultimately enhancing the environments we inhabit.

Pınar Dinç Kalaycı
Gazi University, Turkey

Chapter 1
Being Earthian:
Learning From Legendary Architects

Nazan Kirci
Gazi University, Turkey

ABSTRACT

This chapter is about the studies being conducted in a6 Studio, one of the design studios of the Department of Architecture at Gazi University. A6 Studio has decided to get the theory of architecture to the center of its studies so that the unique knowledge of the field of architecture is getting carried from the theoretical courses to the practical area of the design studio. For this purpose, students are encouraged to take one of the legendary architects as their role models and learn from these masters. Being quite unrestrained in choosing the study area and subject, students enjoy the freedom of designing in any part of the world they wish; on the one hand, getting familiar with its responsibility, on the other hand, under the metaphorical guidance of the architects they have chosen to research. . So, in the A6 studio, the students experience being an earthling while learning from legendary architects to develop their vision and enhance their creativity.

INTRODUCTION

A consensus has been acquired as an outcome of long studies conducted at the international level on what architectural education should comprise and what it should bring to students. It would be appropriate to make an excerpt to the Objectives of Architectural Education in UNESCO/UIA Charter For Architectural Education:

> The main purpose of architectural education is to develop the capacity in students to be able to conceptualize, design, understand, and realize the act of building within a context of the practice of architecture which balances the tensions between emotion, reason, and intuition, and which gives physical form to the needs of society and the individual.
> During the education process, students gain the ability to reconcile divergent factors, integrate knowledge and apply skills in the creation of a design solution. (UNESCO/UIA)

The directives on architectural education are clear in this case. The main question is how are the students supposed to achieve all of this knowledge, skills, and understanding? Design studios play a crucial role in integrating them. Consequently, they are pretty challenging, creative, and joyful environments in the architectural education system.

As tutors, we all see the world from our own perspectives; therefore, thousands of brilliant ideas have been developed to increase creativity in design education. Related researchs can be found through articles and published conference papers. A6 is one of the architectural design studios of the Department of Architecture in Gazi University, which takes students on a round trip on earth together with star architects. Being Earthian: Learning from Legendary Architects is a warm invitation to our students.

DESIGN OF a6 STUDIO TRAINING

This study attempts to present the thought system on which the work carried out in the a6 Design Studio is based. The human brain gives easier and more familiar answers to the problems it recognizes. Scientists have a saying that goes, "The change takes people off autopilot." Removing the usual boundaries allows people to change their minds and opens up the path to innovations. Changing a familiar environment can bring not only exciting and challenging experiences, but also creative results. *From this perspective, we can think of problems as learning opportunities. To put it another way, "The more diverse the problems to be considered, the more enriched the learning experience."* Therefore, providing an enriched learning experience is one of our studio's goals. The design studio work is a system in which a close relationship is established between students and instructors despite the hierarchical structure between them. In addition to the flow of information, there is a reciprocal transfer of emotions, just like with other people with whom we interact in daily life, during this intimate relationship. It is possible to see a projection of life in the design studio. What we learned from them, and how we constructed analogies for design studio operations. Let us share some daily-life situations, even if it seems a little contradictory

Table 1. Analogies from daily life to the design studio operations

Daily life situations	Estimation for studio
If our life is monotonous	How to keep the interest of the students alive in design studio.
- we get bored.	
We want life to offer us lots of experiences	How to ensure that students are not lost in uncertainty in their assignment while giving them a variety of options
-meanwhile we want to stay on the safe side.	
We want to make our own decision	How to ensure that students prefer to be free but still be able to consult when they would like to
- we also want to hear a reliable, wise voice we can consult.	
We want to travel	Let's travel in the comfort of home then.
-bye the way, we are homesick	

We aimed to excite and attract the students and make them feel comfortable and free the whole time. We asked the following questions:

Question 1: Which knowledge, experience, and skills would you like to acquire without spending a lifetime of effort?
Question 1 is addressed to role model.

Question 2: If you were to have even a fraction of the knowledge, skills, and experience of that architect you admire so much, how would this affect your design?
Question 2 is addressed to receiving contribution.

Question 3: If you had the opportunity to ask for their help whenever you needed or wanted, to what extent and how would your decisions change?
Question 3 is addressed to gaining confidence.

Question 4: As an architect, where would you like to make your presence known with your design proposal?
Question 4 is addressed to success.

Based on these questions in a6, we gave our students the chance to choose three important issues that will affect their design process as a three-item protocol.

The first is about the architect they will take as a *Role Model*.
The second is related to the *Subject Of Their Design*.
The third is about the choice of *The Design Place*.

Role Modeling

We all continue to evolve, with the guidance of our parents, teachers, and other people whom we find interesting and valuable. People love to read inspirational stories and biographies of celebrities to gain insight into how successful people handle crises and solve complex problems. Biographical narratives are important because they reveal how people experience transitions and changes throughout their lives (Hallqvist et al. 2012; Biesta et al. 2011). Higher education itself can be seen as a biographical learning experience, where students undergo significant transitions and learn to cope with them. The concept of biographical learning suggests that education isn't confined to classrooms. We learn continuously as we navigate through life. Alheit and Dausien (2002) summarizing this concept: "without biography there can be no learning, without learning there is no biography" This emphasizes the interwoven nature of our experiences and how they shape our understanding of the world (Merrill B 2015).

The quote "Learn from other people's mistakes. Life is too short to make them all yourself," is attributed to author Sam Levenson. Reading biographies allows us to learn from the experiences, successes, and failures of others, which aligns perfectly with Levenson's wise advice. By absorbing these lessons, we can potentially avoid repeating their mistakes and pave a smoother path for ourselves.

Figure 1. Inspirational stories and biographies

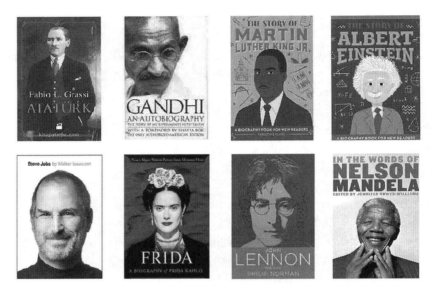

We can learn how to overcome some obstacles, even if we have not experienced them personally. We also develop the strength and courage to realize our ideals thanks to these inspiring stories. Learning from others' lives is a great experience for the entire lifetime of a human. One could of course take a biography of someone with a strong motivational character, such as Atatürk, and examine the development of his remarkable resolve, drawn from the ideals of democracy and freedom.

Educational studies that require reading biographies aim to make people think of the famous person being studied as a role model. Ahn JN. et al., (2016) argued that content-focused instruction is important for student learning, but even the best content instruction does not guarantee that students will engage deeply with the material. Instead, students' motivation ultimately prepares them to better interact with content knowledge to improve their learning (Ahn J N., et al., 2016). According to Benton, biography is a hybrid. It is the history crossed with narratives. The biographer has to present the available facts of the life yet shape their arbitrariness, untidiness, and incompleteness into an engaging whole. The readerly appeal lies in the prospect both of gaining documentary information, scrupulously researched and plausibly interpreted, and of experiencing the aesthetic pleasure of reading a well-made work of art with a continuous life story and a satisfying closure (Benton, M., 2007).

Nowadays, the visibility and audibility of everything have dramatically increased. Products and ideas are rapidly exchanged through the media. As a result, we are very susceptible to interactions and influences. Indeed, we may no longer even be aware of what we learned from where. Inspiration from examples and learning through repetition is a very common method. Therefore, it would be helpful to mention the definitions associated with the subject.

Imitation is such a well-understood concept and means "a novel action that replicates both the processes and outcomes of a model". Learning by imitation is a primary way children learn during their early years. Children acquire the ability to use various learning tools and instruments. Meltzoff and Moore (1977, 1989), Want and Harris (2001) declared that observational learning may be an important factor in children's learning. Although the capacity of children to use imitative tools has been neglected, the existence of such observational learning among primates has become an essential matter of investigation (Want S. C. and Harris P. L. 2001) What is the role of mimesis in creating 'the new'? Mimesis refers to the activity of mim ing, copying or imitating. Taussig (1993) suggests that human beings are inescapably both mimetic and social; they learn by imitating others (both as a part of childhood learning and through professional training); they participate (for better or worse) in the nature of their models. Slutskaya, in her article Creativity and Repetition (2006), while explaining the relationship between dance and mimesis, cites Taussig (1993) as a reference for achieving creativity. The process of mimesis is a dual game between copying an 'original' and more bodily and sensory contact with the original. In order to participate in this mimetic game of copying and contact, one has to imitate something other than oneself. 'Pulling you this way and that, mimesis plays this trick of dancing between the very same and the very different,' (Taussig, 1993).

There are several words in an approximate descending order of resemblance that are often used synonymously: copying, emulation, mimicry, simulation, modeling, and exemplification. Imitation is an essential educational ingredient in schooling and also in many fields of social science and the arts. For example, students learn to play their chosen instruments by copying the physical techniques and sound quality of their teachers' playing in music education. This activity can easily be applied to other arts, where the student is asked to mimic the style of an acknowledged master.

An ongoing debate in primate research has concerned the nature of the information an observer extracts from a display. Tomasello and colleagues (Nagell et al 1993; Tomasello, 1990, 1996) distinguish between imitation and emulation. In principle, an observer can learn how to use a tool by understanding the demonstrator's purpose and then producing a relatively faithful copy of the actions seen to achieve that purpose. Tomasello and colleagues describe this type of learning as imitation (Tomasello, 1990, 1996; Tomasello, et al. 1993). Such faithful imitation can be an effective strategy even when the causal effect of the tool is invisible or difficult to infer from observation An observer can also learn to use a tool by observing the causal effect of the tool and trying to reproduce this effect through his/her own action. Tomasello and colleagues describe this type of learning as emulation (Tomasello, 1990, 1996; Tomasello and Call, 1997). Under these conditions, the observer may not produce a faithful copy of the actions he or she sees, but instead a causally efficient version. Tomasello and colleagues emphasised that many acts of apparent imitation (learning to reproduce a goal-directed action) among non-human primates could equally well be characterised as emulation (Want S. C. and Harris P. L. 2001).

Apprenticeship as a mode of learning has been the most widely used method of development throughout human history. Like its counterpart the lecture method, role-modeling is a popular training method and allows organizations to readily control trainee completion of the training program. As with the lecture method, there is no expectation of interaction suggesting a lack of support for learners to overcome challenges (Martin, B. O. et al. 2013).

John Dewey's concept of learning by doing has established a teaching methodology supported by adult learning scholars who argue that social and intellectual skills are acquired through situations characterised by interaction, not isolation (Carr, 1992). Of course, it is possible to " learning by doing" by participating in real assessments. However, when teaching a course in assessment procedures or theory that takes place over a limited as an academic semester, the approach of participating in assessments has limitations. Therefore, Alkin M. C. and Christie C. A., (2002) consider role-playing to be an appropriate and efficient method for "learning by doing".

To better explain the definition of role-playing, a distinction can be made between role-playing and simulation. The use of role-playing as an educational or training technique is considered part of a broader set of techniques collectively known as simulation. Simulations are complex, lengthy, and relatively inflexible activities, but they always include an element of role-play. Role-play, on the other hand, can be a simple, short technique that can be easily organised. Role-playing is highly flexible and allows much more room for individual variation, initiative and imagination (Ladousse, 1987). Livingstone, (1983) claimed that role-playing encourages interaction and peer learning in the classroom, which increases motivation (Alkin M. C. and Christie C. A., 2002).

Role Modelling Learning is a method used in many fields such as literature, language learning, computer, nursing, etc. and has been found to increase achievement through various studies. Hou (2011) emphasized that the use of role-playing enhances students' level of focus by allowing the student to assume a role in a specific simulated situation and training the student to concentrate on the task. (Yen-Chen Yen, et al. 2015).

It is often claimed that role models are a way of motivating individuals to set and achieve ambitious goals, especially for members of group stigmatised in achievement settings. However, it has been found by (Morgenroth, T., et al. (2015) that the literature on role models tends not to draw on the motivational literature to explain how role models can help role candidates achieve these outcomes.

Ahn JN, et al. (2019) indicated that an effective role model should demonstrate competence and attainable success in the desired or relevant domain. Competence matters because role models are those who exhibit skills that others lack and are subsequently motivated to learn from them (e.g., Kemper, 1968; Marx & Ko, 2012; Marx & Roman, 2002).

Primarily it is necessary to define what is meant by role-playing. Ladousse (1987) suggests that we look at the words themselves. Participants assume a "role", i.e. they play a role (their own or someone else's) in each scenario. "Play" means that the role is assumed in a safe environment where participants can express their views in creative ways.

As mentioned above, role playing / role modelling learning system has been applied in many fields and it has been observed that it accelerates learning, increases motivation and helps students to realise their own creativity.

Role Modelling Learning in Architecture

Although role modelling practices are not encountered with this name in the literature on architectural education, this method finds a place in the field of architecture with another concept, namely master apprentice training. The oldest learning method in architecture has been the master-apprentice relationship since the tradition of the Beaux Arts school. When we open ourselves up as apprentices, we look for masters in our lifelong learning project. Therefore, architects love to take long, inspirational trips with the motivation to learn from what others did. Today, architectural media and literature searches have made it much easier for architects to learn from the architectural experiences of others. Legendary Architects, an international practice, has designed some iconic buildings all over the world, which later inspired other architects and student work. The history of architecture is full of such inspirations.

Figure 2. Role Modelling (a6 poster by Ümit Şimşek) and some a6 students with their role model architects

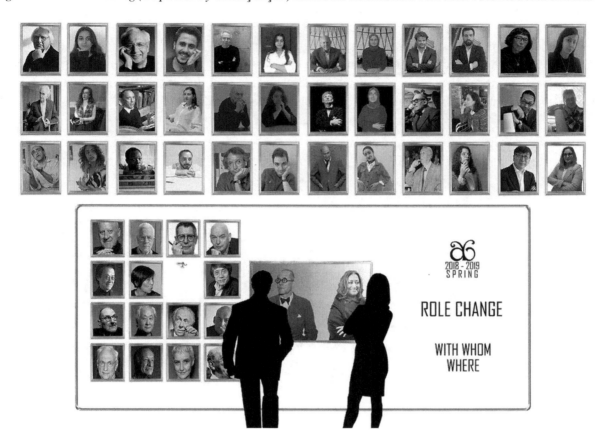

As we have seen, people - students, artists and architects - need the guidance of masters in order to learn, to be inspired and to find encouragement in their achievements. We have planned the design studio work of a6 to take this significant need into account. We invited the Star Team of the architectural world into our studio as role models for the students. and we are very pleased to have been working with these legendary architects.

Selection of Design Subject and Place

Based on their research about architects, they become ready to make their own inferences on a design topic. This is a kind of knowledge transfer, adaptation, and transformation process. Students start to consider what kind of design subject would be appropriate for the corresponding special qualities. Later, the subject proposal step comes, an essentially bargaining step. At the end, while students act, think, and design like a legendary architect, they gain slightly more self-confidence. The next task is deciding where to place this design.

The design is made for the place. - In an urban context, in distinct climate conditions, within a certain economy, available technological resources, for known or unknown users, in the specific culture and way of thinking, and the conditions of the time.- All these parameters constrain design problems, and there are design studios being carried out by getting either of these parameters into their centers. There are always possibilities hidden within the limitations of the design program for the studio work. In our opinion, the task of design studios is to teach students to find the possibilities within the constraints of the given design problems. As problems change, solutions will also change, the ways of making appropriate designs will change too. It is known that "The change takes people off autopilot." To change the memorized truths and discover new truths we need to change our pilots. Discovering new places, at the same time, ensures that the excitement in the design studio game does not fade.

Figure 3. Earth is our place to design

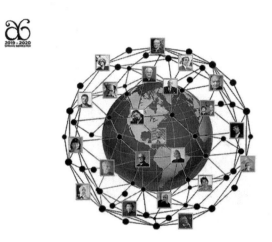

(a6 posters by Ümit Şimşek)

Today's technology offers us opportunities in this regard; for instance, Google Earth, which takes us to unknown places. Since 2018, we have been virtually exploring various parts of the world. Traveling is free of charge, secure, and easy-to-use. Traveling in the comfort of your home is a big change and a chance. What is going on outside our borders? How the rules change, what other needs exist? What is possible? And how people change. This will assist in obtaining a better understanding of the differences in life and, thus, improve the design experience. We let our students freely choose their design fields on earth and make appropriate design topics for the chosen place.

There are around 10–14 students in our studio in each academic term. Each of them chooses a different working area in which they complete their design project. The USA, Japan, Kenya, Egypt, Australia, Singapore, Switzerland, Spain, France, Bangladesh, Brazil, Canada, Italy, Switzerland are some of the selected countries. It can be imagined that students' contributions to sharing information about their fields with our studio culture. Our studio hours had become quite similar to the United Nations meeting. They began to experience being Earthian. Thus, their paradigm shifted.

Depending on their choices regarding the design field, design parameters like the weather, economy, in a urban setting, culture, as well as the users' day-to-day lives. That began to change from what they were used to.

Learning From Legendary Architects to Students Work

Sir Francis Bacon has defined knowledge as power (Azamfirei, L. 2016). At the beginning of the semester, our students spend a few weeks doing architectural literature research. Students will read biographies of the architects they have chosen, various articles written about them, analyse their projects, of course they will work hard, but in the end they will learn from successful people and be inspired by their various ideas. After this experience, they will have an inner drive to learn new things and discover new ideas. After reading about the legendary architects, our students find out the qualifications that make them what they are. Surfing through tens of design projects students started to have a clearer insight into what makes architects special, the fine details of design among many other benefits. Thus, they wrote new biographical stories to tell it to both other students in the studio and to the members of the jury. Through this informative process, they recognise and learn a lot about the design priorities and thinking of the architects who are their Role Models. This may be called an abstraction of the design ideas. Table 2. Created by referring to Kırcı's (2013) book 20th Century Architecture.

Table 2. Inferences from design ideas of architects

Architects	Ideas
Mies	Open plan, purism, structural refinement
Wright	Open plan, organic architecture, destruction of the box, visibility
Corbusier	Purism, 5 golden rules of modern architecture, brutalism, mannerism
Kahn	Monumentalism, distriction between service space, power of shadow
Ando	Brutalism, minimalism, "ma" of zen budhism, light
Sejima	Minimalist living and office spaces
Libeskind	Memorial spaces and contradictions between new and old, sharp geometries
Nouvel	Transparency, flexibility
Hadid	Fluid forms, defy gravity, tectonic expression
Gehry	Structural complexity, sculptural forms
BIG	Yes to all, anti-cubic, graphic expression
Piano	Sustainability, green architecture, lighting
Foster	Sustainability, green architecture, lighting
Safdie	Modularity, structuralism
Eisenman	Deconstruct of the boxes, reinterpretation of topography, questioning of traditional forms
Tange	Metabolism, structural challenges, settlement alternatives
Graves	Post Modernism, sign, meaning
Venturi	Post Modernism, complexity and contradiction
Pei	Transparency and triangle variations.
Chiperfield	Classism and modernism, urban context sensitisation
Neutra	Interior and exterior transmission,
Barragain	Combination of landscape and architecture, love of colors
Aalto	Regionalism, orientation to light

continued on following page

Table 2. Continued

Architects	Ideas
Kuma	Wooden structures
Niemeyer	Social and state architecture, sculptural forms
Bahn	Simplicity temporariness and flexibility
Kurokawa	Impermanence and change
Maki	experimental with materials and fusing east and west culture.
Koolhaas	Programmatic complexity, generic and Flexible Architecture

Students are expected to continue their studies by adapting the design principles they have deduced as a result of analysing the works of the architect they have chosen as a role model to the conditions of their own design field. Fifteen of the works carried out in A6 are presented in Figure 4 and brief explanations about the projects arranged in alphabetical order are given below.

In the early stages of the semester, for example, one of our students might come up with a design proposal to use Jean Nouvel's (a) successful use of literal and phenomenal transparency in a business school in Singapore. Another might want to use Adolf Loos' (b) raumplan to make the exhibition hall in the cultural centre in San Francisco more visible. Norman Foster's (c) hi-tech design approach, which is aware of the physical environment has been tried out by our student in the stadium project in Lyon.

The children university, which allows children to work experimentally, is designed as a hi-tech building in harmony with nature in accordance with the principles of Renzo Piano (d) in the neighbourhood of Tilburg University. The children university, which allows children to work experimentally, is designed as a hi-tech building in harmony with nature in accordance with the principles of Renzo Piano (d) in the neighbourhood of Tilburg University. Two students designed neighbouring buildings with a common courtyard accross to Frank Gehry's Jewish Memorial Space in Berlin. Interesting cultural centres with elegant white elevations offering different degrees of transparency might be expected from Richard Meier as in his museums-and a light-structured exhibition centre design by Shigeru Bahn (e) can be proposed adjacent to this building A student thought that Kengo Kuma's (f) hotel, which attracts attention with its use of wood materials on a parcel between two iconic buildings of Gaudi in Barcelona, such as Casa Battlo and Casa Mila, famous for its use of materials and unimaginable forms, could be interesting for tourists.

One student might experiment the design of a new Ferrari museum by reinterpreting the topography in the Eisenman (g) style in Modena, to replace existing Enzo Ferrari Museum. Richard Neutra's (h) calm and serene design style, which invites nature into the interior, was considered appropriate for the design of a special education centre that would enable children to feel outdoors in the Santa Barbara climate. The design of a figure skating ice centre is proposed with the graphic design and programme creation skills of Bijarke Ingels (i).

A craft centre and bazaar in Rio de Jenario could be designed by David Chipperfield (j), known for his simple designs that respect the urban context. The design for fluid and flexible office spaces at Rivershore Chicago could be proposed by a male student who wants to represent Zaha Hadid (k) despite the large number of female students in the studio. Kisho Kurokawa (l), as an architect who cares for the public good and invites trance in his spaces, can design a memorial hall for the victims of the atomic bomb in Nagasaki.

Jorn Uutzon (m) could design an iconic and innovative museum in the neighbourhood of Eero Sarinen's auditorium and Alvar Aalto's dormitory building on the MIT campus in Boston. If Rem Koolhaas (n) designs a sports school in Belgrad in accordance with the L scale of the SMLXL grouping, it is possible

Being Earthian

to have volumetric and graphic differences that express the types of sports. To design a mountain resort in Revelstork, British Colombia, it was thought that Ma Yansong (o) would set a good example in his designs, reflecting the balancing of the natural environment, urban landscape and community in new ways.

Figure 4. Some studio works

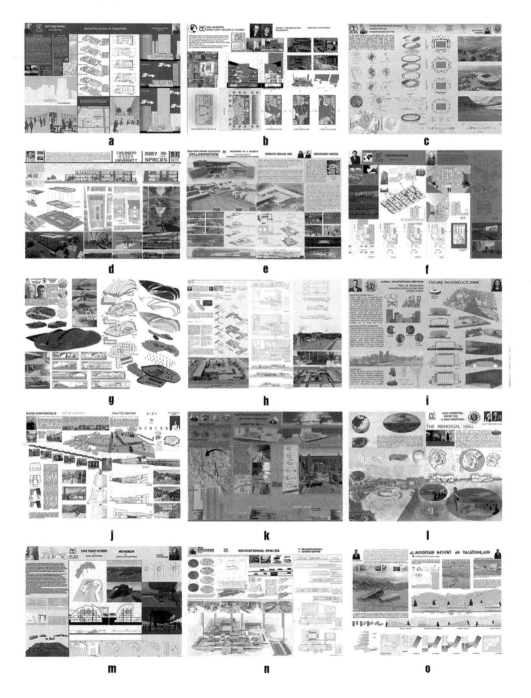

This becomes a new "challenge" for the studio work that motivates students pretty well. The last weeks of the semester are allocated to the presentation rehearsals. In this way, we are making sure that they also understand the importance of finishing a project after starting it. At the end of the semester, it provides students with great convenience. Students traditionally present their work to the jury at the end of the semester. Before the end of term jury, a group video is shot with a6 students explaining their work. This video can be interpreted as both creating a memory for them and as a farewell ceremony. The video published on the a6 YouTube channel also serves as a reference for new students. Let's examine the aforementioned design studio strategies with an example.

Student name: Betül Şayir - a 4th semester student in 2023 autumn term.
Role Modelling Architect: Thom Mayne.
Design principles inspirations: Thom Mayne is the architect that Şayir analysed in his study to be inspired by his design principles. Mayne is known for his brave designs that strike a balance between sculptural and monolithic forms and differentiate themselves from the surrounding built environment. The buildings designed by Thom Mayne do not respond harmoniously to context. In his designs, Mayne uses screening materials that provide different degrees of transparency on the facades that serve as sunshades and shades, depending on the climate zone in which the building is located, and transforms them into symbols that enable the building to be recognized. He utilises an intricate approach by combining multiple spatial functions in his designs. Şayir also tried to direct her design by considering these principles.
Design subject: Social housing
Design Place: Şayir decided to work for the Latina district of Madrid by researching the places with social housing deficit in Europe. She made a Swot analysis of the region and identified its strengths and weaknesses.

How the student handled her project is described below in her own words.

My primary goal when initiating the design was to create a complex that combines housing and culture-art functions. realising the lack of cultural buildings in the region, I thought that Mayne could not design only a social housing in this area.

Initially, I designed two courtyards for the project. The courtyard formed by the social housing mass and the cultural complex and forming a barrier to the main street was open to the use of not only residential users but also outsiders.

When creating the courtyards, instead of the traditional "O" or "U" shaped courtyard form that exists in most of the Spanish urban fabric, I formed sharp lines in the courtyards as Mayne would do.

I designed the courtyard formed by the social housing mass and the cultural complex, which forms a barrier to the main street, to be open not only to residential users but also to outsiders. On the ground floor of the cultural complex, which forms a barrier to the street, I designed open commercial spaces and a library, and on the upper floor I designed exhibition spaces and a café.

I autonomised the courtyard surrounded by my social housing mass, which I orientated towards the pine forest view in the south of the land, so that it belongs only to the residential users. I created the landscape of the courtyard with a children's playground, basketball court and common seating areas.

On the ground floor of the mass, I allocated spaces such as gymnasium, kindergarten, educational workshops for socialising and meeting various needs of the users. On the other floors, I produced various plan types to meet the needs of different users. I designed all these in a monoblock and dynamic mass that curves and draws sharp lines. At the same time, on the facades of the mass facing the courtyard, I created spaces with different degrees of transparency. By extending the terraces outwards from the facade, I achieved a dynamic appearance for different directions. In both masses, I designed a roof that rises following the elevations of the building. I hope that I have designed a social housing like Mayne can do. and unites the whole system. On the top floors, I designed common terraces covered by the roof. (Url 1)

Figure 5. A social housing design with Thom Mayne as a role model

As it can be clearly seen from the student's own statement above, Tom Mayne's opposing attitude to the urban texture in terms of mass and form, the reconsideration of the urban living environment, the differences in the degree of transparency of the elevations, the use of shades have been taken as guiding ideas, and the project has been reinterpreted based on the subject and site requirements.

DISCUSSION

In these days when everything started to become independent of time and space, we also made a6 studies independent of space. There are competencies and capabilities we want to deliver to our students, in addition to the distinctive instructive aspects of designing in a field in a subject. A6 students are encouraged to take one of the legendary architects, especially those who have taken a significant position in the history of architecture through their work in the 20th and 21st centuries, as their role models and learn from these masters. When we put researching architectural literature at the centre of studio education, the sources become limitless. Through this informative process, they learn a lot about the design priorities and thinking of the architects who are their Role Models. Students are inspired by the architects they take as role models by researching their characteristics that are both successful and recognizable. This can sometimes be in the form of the use of a mega structure, the choice of lightweight structure, the way of handling topography, the degree of transparency, screened spaces, interspatial voids, fluid spaces, total space, raumplan design or mass clusters. The use of the masters' ideas by the students creates a familiar but new production, as it requires a process of adaptation by reconsideration.

In role modelling studies, increased motivation and self-confidence in students were reported in many studies. Similarly we observe that the self-confidence of our students, who started to work with questions on how to think, act and design like a legendary architect, increased significantly at the end of the semester.

Moreover, through the method we use, we aim to provide opportunities for them to develop their decision-making skills. Without opportunities and possibilities, choices cannot be made, and the practice of making decisions cannot be acquired adequately. Different cultures, geographies, economic opportunities, and physical conditions can change people's perspectives and expectations of life. We teach our students how to make people happy and to be humane. How to integrate it into the world we experience when they analyze a new city, transportation, neighboring settlements, and buildings; how to be an earthian as a result of these factors. It is the mission of our studio to enable students to step into their professional life with the self-confidence of overcoming problems.

The success of a studio study that intends to use this method will primarily depend on a good theoretical background. In addition to good research by the student, it is important for the jury members to be familiar with the architectural literature in order for the criticisms to be reciprocated. While struggling with the functional requirements of the subject after the literature research, it has been observed that the theoretical research is sometimes pushed to the background, albeit for a short time, in this case, it is reminded to reassemble the broken pieces of information in the studio criticism.

If a discussion is to be conducted between whether the students' design is an imitation or emulation, it should be remembered that both are learning methods that start from childhood. It should be realised that there is a significant difference in experience between them and the architect taken as a role model, and that due to the difference in the project subject and design area, the memorisation learned is disrupted and the way for an adaptation process and self-actualisation is opened. In this way, students were able to reflect their interpretations to their projects in creative ways. As Ladousse (1987) emphasises, role-playing is highly flexible and provides opportunities for individual diversity, initiative and imagination. As mentioned in Ross and Glăveanu's (2023) work explaining the idea of creativity through repetition, a process based on repetition produces creative results.

REFERENCES

Ahn, J. N., Hu, D., & Vega, M. (2019). "Do as I do, not as I say": Using social learning theory to unpack the impact of role models on students' outcomes in education. *Soc Personal Psychol Compass*. 10.1111/spc3.12517

Ahn, J. N., Luna-Lucero, M., Lamnina, M., Nightingale, M., Novak, D., & Lin-Siegler, X. (2016). Motivating Students'. *Stem Learning Using Biographical Information, IJDL*, 7(1), 71–85.

Alkin, M. C., & Christie, C. A. (2002). Teaching Evaluation, The Use Of Role-Play in Teaching Evaluation. *The American Journal of Evaluation*, 23(2), 209–218. 10.1177/109821400202300210

Azamfirei, L. (2016). Knowledge Is Power. *The Journal of Critical Care Medicine*, 2(2), 65-66. 10.1515/jccm-2016-0014

Benton, M. (2007). Reading Biograph. *Journal of Aesthetic Education*, 41(3), 77–88. 10.2307/25160239

Hou, H. T. (2011). A case study of online instructional collaborative discussion activities for problem-solving using situated scenarios: An examination of content and behavior cluster analysis. *Computers & Education*, 56(3), 712–719. 10.1016/j.compedu.2010.10.013

Kemper, T. D. (1968). Reference groups, socialization and achievement. *American Sociological Review*, 33(1), 31–45. 10.2307/20922385644338

Kirci, N. (2013). *20. Yüzyıl Mimarlığı, Nobel Yayın Dağıtım, Ankara, TR. 20th Century Architecture*. Nobel Publication.

Ladousse, G. P. (1987). *Role-play*. Oxford University Press.

Martin, B. O., Kolomitro, K., & Lam, T. (2013). Training Methods: A Review and Analysis. *Human Resource Development Review*, 13(1), 11–35. 10.1177/1534484313497947

Marx, D. M., & Ko, S. J. (2012). Superstars "like" me: The effect of role model similarity on performance under threat. *European Journal of Social Psychology*, 42(7), 807–812. 10.1002/ejsp.1907

Marx, D. M., & Roman, J. S. (2002). Female role models: Protecting women's math test performance. *Personality and Social Psychology Bulletin*, 28(9), 1183–1193. 10.1177/014616722022812004

Merrill, B. (2015). Determined to stay or determined to leave? A tale of learner identities, biographies and adult students in higher education. *Studies in Higher Education*, 40(10), 1859–1871. 10.1080/03075079.2014.914918

Morgenroth, T., Ryan, M. K., & Peters, K. (2015). The motivational theory of role modeling: How role models influence role aspirants' goals. *Review of General Psychology*, 19(4), 465–483. 10.1037/gpr0000059

Ross, W., & Glăveanu, V. (2023). *The constraints of habit: craft, repetition, and creativity*. Phenom Cogn Sci., 10.1007/s11097-023-09902-5

Slutskaya, N. (2006), Creativity and Repetition. Creativity and Innovation Management, 15: 150 156. 10.1111/j.1467-8691.2006.00384.x

Taussig, M. (1993) Mimesis and Alterity. Routledge, London. In Slutskaya, N. (2006)

UNESCO/UIA. (2011). *Charter For Architectural Education Revised Edition*. UIA General Assembly, Tokyo. www. uia-architectes.org

Want, S. C., & Harris, P. L. (2001). Learning from Other People's Mistakes: Causal Understanding in Learning to Use a Tool. *Child Development*, 72(2), 431–443. 10.1111/1467-8624.0028811333076

Yen, Y.-C., Hou, H.-T., & Chang, K. E. (2015). Applying role-playing strategy to enhance learners' writing and speaking skills in EFL courses using Facebook and Skype as learning tools: A case study in Taiwan. *Computer Assisted Language Learning*, 28(5), 383–406. 10.1080/09588221.2013.839568

Chapter 2
Mura:
A Practice-Based Design Curriculum for Future Creation in Rurual Japan

Cihangir Istek
Center for Global Initiatives, Japan

Andreas M. Schneider
Institute for Information Design, Japan

ABSTRACT

Demonstrating the importance of Mura (a synonym for village or hamlet, also countryside, in Japanese) as a prototype for off-urban agglomerations and a place for design practice, this chapter presents a co-design studio practice as case studies that might contribute to community efforts for the future creation in Nose Town–a Satoyama (Japanese term applied to the border zone or fertile area between mountain foothills and arable flat land) in Osaka Prefecture, Japan. Students of Osaka University jointly discovered not only the charm of this region, but also the multiple problems and issues of building a sustainable future. Explorations providing fieldwork, micro-internships, and practical interventions have been particularly focused on how cross-disciplinary competences and project-based design learning can make a difference in solving the many problems of an aging community that faces the exodus of the younger generation to big cities.

INTRODUCTION

In 2017, the rural town of Nose at the northern tip of Osaka Prefecture (Figure 1) and Osaka University signed a comprehensive agreement on education, research, culture, and planning (Nose Town Office, 2017). Both parties pledged to promote cooperation within the local community and to contribute to development and revitalization by using their respective resources. The agreement was (a) part of the "Osaka University Vision 2021" calling for openness – internally among departments in the university, and externally through open dialogue and interaction with society (OPEN 2021, 2016). This openness would also be the unifying principle of the university's improvements in the next five years leading to the 90th anniversary in 2021.

DOI: 10.4018/979-8-3693-2329-8.ch002

Figure 1. Nose Town, Toyono District, Osaka

A year after the launch of this agreement, Osaka University's Center for the Study of Co*Design and IIDj, Institute for Information Design Japan, began working on a community-oriented, collaborative design project called *MURA*, exploring the role of design and its learning in social contexts (Istek & Schneider, 2020). The project focused specifically on the impacts of Japan's aging society in rural communities, villages – *Mura* in Japanese.

Throughout the three years of the project, three concerns were followed: *Planning and Building, Cultivating and Harvesting, Learning and Mentoring*. Each year had also its specific focus: *A Place for Design Practice, On-Site Opportunities, Power to the Community*.

This chapter focusses on the first year only, *A Place for Design Practice*, for learning practice-based collaborative design methods, co-design, in Nose. Students jointly discovered not only the charm of the region while expanding their cross-disciplinary competences, but also the multiple issues and challenges of building a sustainable future.

Co-design is an approach to designing solutions and action with people (Sanders, 2002; Sanders & Stappers, 2008; Burkett, 2012; McKercher, 2021). In the project, this approach was supported by an interactive thinking tool, *DesignFactors* (IIDj – Institute for Information Design Japan) to help create a structured framework for assessment, development, and implementation. Through informal meetings, workshops, micro-internships, and presentations, the project team engaged and collaborated with the community of long-time residents, *U-Turners* (those who return to their hometown), new-comers such as the so-called *I-Turners* (those who decide to quit big city life), and the occasional visitors.

According to Bickford and Wright (2006), communities accelerate deep learning, hence should be considered as a critical driving factor when planning for physical and virtual learning environments. Our collaboration in Nose, where the community and society at large are active participants, was aimed not only to enhance the learning experience, but also to create positive social impact.

The remainder of the chapter examines where – *the Places*, who was involved - *the Actors*, and what - *the Activities*, the co-design studio actually did. The chapter argues that a practice-based curriculum consisting of personal encounters, physical experiences, and the recognition of holistic relationships are necessary factors for planners and decision-makers at all levels, working towards a truly meaningful and sustainable future. Suggesting follow-up activities, the chapter concludes with lessons learned and an agenda of nine actions that reflects both the expectations of the community as well as the demands of students for a practice-based curriculum.

MURA, a Place for Design Practice

Launched in Fall 2019, the main concern of the MURA Project was how, at Osaka University's Center for the Study of Co*Design, a practice-based learning and teaching approach involving a broad scope of cross-disciplinary competencies, could help address the many issues that rural communities are facing.

The complexity of the social problems and challenges of such communities can only be meaningfully understood if their socioeconomic, cultural, and political contexts - past, present, and future - are examined in greater detail. Thus, from the beginning, an important principle has been not only to observe people, but *to engage with them* in their everyday activities. Only through such immersive research would we be able to recognize the motivations, constraints, and opportunities that shape life in Nose, by the following three steps:

- Seeking innovative solutions through contextualization
- Modeling relationships through the identification of patterns
- Prototyping, implementing, and testing of proposals through situated design interventions

Schedule and Planning

Our curriculum planning consisted of four main activities:

- *Context and Connections,* First Hands-On Field Research (19-26 October)
- *Models and Prototypes,* Preparatory Workshops (27 October - 21 November)
- *Interventions and Change,* Second Hands-On Field Research (22 November - 24 January)
- *Lessons Learned and Agenda,* Open Public Presentation (25 January)

Our aim was not only to provide rich learning opportunities for the students, but also to catalyze relationships between community members, which we hoped that would stimulate further developments.

Relationships and Networks

In the planning phase it was important for us to seek contact with locals who could collaborate as anchors in the community. Through preparatory visits and meetings with many people in Nose who had a record of successful initiatives and whom we referred to as actors, we identified a small group that could become an anchor in the community for our collaborations.

Later, during our various on site activities, we partnered with other locals to organize and negotiate relationships, roles, and responsibilities in a variety of ways. These were designed and implemented in coordination with local collaborators. Visualizing these relationships that emerged not only helped uncover hidden possibilities, but also affirmed local identities and triggered new associations (Figure 2).

Figure 2. Participants, roles, and responsibilities

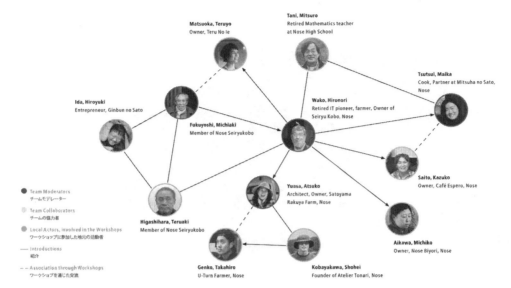

Roles and Responsibilities

24 students with different backgrounds and expertise, including engineering, economics, physics, industrial design, anthropology, cultural studies and linguistics, responded to a major call within Osaka University for participation in the project. After a careful recruitment process, a total of 12 students (10 international and 2 Japanese), evenly distributed between graduate and bachelor, agreed to participate.

The students were divided into three teams with complementary missions of the MURA Project:

- *Helping Hands,* engaging with old abandoned houses, *Akiya*
- *Making Commitments,* looking into natural resources
- *Building Competencies,* investigating specific crafts

This division allowed for a diverse approach to change that considered short-, medium-, and long-term developments. Each team also included one or two faculty members and a local facilitator who represented a particular aspect of the MURA Project and introduced the group to other community stakeholders.

Figure 3. Communities participating in the MURA project

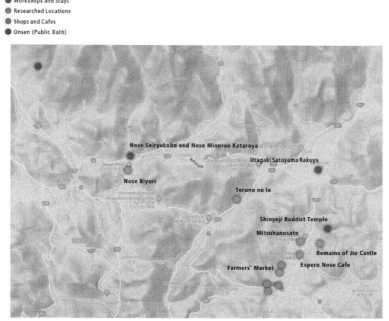

CONTEXT AND CONNECTIONS

The vitality of rural areas and villages is critical to ensuring long-term prosperous and sustainable communities. Cultural, environmental, and economic factors determine how natural resources, people, and practices interact. National land policies and processes in Japan have focused on quantitative rather than qualitative development by providing significant financial support to rural areas (Odagiri, 2016). The greatest challenge, however, is to explore solutions for creating value that benefit communities' continuing existence.

Among the challenges facing Japan today, the aging population and the declining birthrate are high on the list (Pasick, 2014; Christopher, 2015; Rowan, 2016; Human Mortality Database, 2024). According to Hiroya Masuda (2014), former governor of Iwate Prefecture and head of a government committee on local revitalization, their effects are particularly acute in rural Japan, where the female population of 20- to 40-year olds is declining by 50 percent and young people are migrating to cities.

Nose is one of those rural places deemed unsuitable by the government to remain as a municipality by 2040 due to expected population loss. As of the end of March 2021, the population of Nose is 9,598 people (male 4,652 and female 4,946; see also Table 1 for populations by age groups), the number of households 4,557 in the area of 98.75 km^2 (Nose Town Office, March 31, 2021). Although Masuda's projections for Nose predicted a population decline of 7% from 2014 levels over the next 10 to 14 years, that number already doubled by 2020, and the decline in the young female population is projected to be more than 30 percent, higher than the Japanese average by 2040.

Table 1. Male and female populations by age groups (as of March 31, 2021, Nose Town Office)

Ages	Males	Females
0-19	502	487
20-40	745	704
41-59	1,197	1,183
60+	2,208	2,572

While the many problems associated with an aging society and declining birth rates are in urgent need of answers, there are currently only a limited number of studies examining the expertise that design can contribute. Since Japan is one of the countries at the forefront of such demographic changes, it is well positioned to take a leading role in addressing them. Recognizing the importance of the context in which communities live, creative design processes can reveal new opportunities for wide-ranging development.

In 2019, a local activist invited us to Nose to see what could be done to reverse this grim prediction by the statistics which ignore the many lives that produced such data without realizing it.

> Nose is in danger of being abandoned and there are fewer and fewer people. It's not just Nose in Japan —many villages in outlying areas have the same problem —but Nose is at the top of that list. (H. Wako, Nose local and collaborator, personal communication, February 4, 2019).

Although we passed many abandoned houses, *Akiya,* we also met a large number of extremely enthusiastic people – young and old – who are committed to preserving the land and continuing the diverse community life that makes up the long and rich history of this welcoming *Satoyama,* Nose (Figure 3).

Nose retains a truly natural environment surrounded by the mountains *Mikusa, Myōken, Miyama, Kenpi,* and *Utagaki*. The district around the Mikusa mountain is a particularly quintessential Nose landscape, dotted with some charming traditional houses. On Myōken mountain, a well-known sanctuary of Myōken Bodhisattva worship, one can enjoy a panoramic view (see Figure 1, image). Utagaki mountain is one of Japan's three most representative Utagaki sites – where an ancient ritual exchange of love songs and poems as part of spirit worship and courtship were made. Here, unlike in urban areas, it is still possible to feel the distinctive four seasons of Japan.

The foothills of this landscape have gradually developed through moderate intervention by farming villagers contributing to the age-old *Satoyama* landscape with chestnut orchards and Japanese beech trees.

> The population is shrinking, and regional and local authorities have no sense of urgency about agriculture. (Y. Yuasa, I-Turn farmer, personal communication, February 4, 2021)

Nose has always been an active rice growing area. The clean water and the great differences between day and night temperatures, which are typical of a mountainous area, contribute to high quality cultivation.

Mura

>Nose has good soil which is ideal for organic farming. Finding a convenient location in nearby Toyonaka or downtown Osaka, its products could be easily brought to city folks. (D. N. Nguyen, Intern, Doctoral student in Biotechnology, Osaka University, personal communication, December 8, 2021)

Above all, Nose is known for its chestnuts. It is home to *Ginyose*, the chestnut variety which is considered the King of Chestnuts because of its light sweetness and large size. In autumn, many visitors visit the village for this natural delicacy.

>I noticed that people were visiting Nose to experience nature. Most of them were city dwellers. (M. Suzuki, Intern, Master's student in Geography, Osaka University, personal communication, December 12, 2021)

The Nose Town Office (2018) and the Nose Town Tourism Association (n.d.) are working hard to promote and support migration of those who return to their hometown, the *U-Turners,* and those who leave big city life behind, the *I-Turners.*

Like most towns and villages in Japan, Nose has dilapidated farms and abandoned houses. Japan's inheritance laws are partly to blame for this situation, where over 8 million homes are vacant across the country (Barrett, 2018). Fixed asset taxes on empty lots are six times higher, so it makes sense not to demolish old houses or farmsteads. The number of forsaken buildings in Nose is expected to increase significantly over the next years.

While some local nonprofits offer advice and assistance in finding a new place, such as an Akiya vacant house, moving to a small rural community can be challenging. Because the local community is very tight-knit, it is difficult for newcomers to be accepted. If they do not understand and respect local traditions and norms, they run the risk of being excluded.

>It is not difficult to get information about Akiya if you talk to the locals. Sometimes these houses are even let for free. However, there are still the typical problems of traditional agrarian societies. People are reluctant to abandon their inherited property. The main concern of rural communities is the conservation of the land. (M. Tani, Nose native and retired Mathematics teacher, personal communication, February 22, 2022)

Models and Prototypes

The First Hands-On Field Research, *Context and Connections*, was an opportunity for the teams to explore Nose and to meet local moderators, collaborators, actors, and stakeholders; intentionally, each of the teams started to explore their tasks without any prior briefing on methodological framework nor conceptual models.

A week later, the next iteration, Preparatory Workshops, took place at the Co* Design Center of Osaka University focusing on *Models and Prototypes*. Each of the teams consulted with the invited experts both in groups and in plenary sessions to identify the core issues, to brainstorm on possible solutions, and to set priorities. The moderators introduced a range of design methods and models to expand what has been practiced in the first workshop; experiences of *Doing* should lead to the construction of models and prototypes that would inform and guide the Second Hands-On Field Research of the third activity, roughly one month later.

Figure 4. Contributors brainstorming

Helping Hands

In their research, Team *Helping Hands* discovered the role and potential of Akiya in Nose, which are representative of the problems that many other towns in the country face in a similar way. There are about 8.5 million such properties nationwide that are various stages of disrepair.

The place in Nose that became a hub for the team's activities is not an Akiya in the strict sense, a small run-down former farmhouse with a neglected but charming chestnut grove at the back (Figure 4). Following *Yui* – the concept of mutual assistance, currently, this house is repurposed by a mixed group of locals and people from the surrounding area under two different identities: *Nose Seiryūkōbo - Nose Pure Flow Atelier* and *Nose Minōran Kataroya - Nose Conversation Salon*.

Figure 5. Team Making Commitments working

Making Commitments

Team *Making Commitments* concentrated on Nose's famous Ginyose chestnuts and their plantations. The chestnut orchards are not only a cultural heritage, but also important for its biodiversity, as they provide habitat for many species of animals such as insects, butterflies, and birds. Maintaining chestnut cultivation is also one of the symptomatic challenges Nose faces, as the hard work requires the vigor and commitment of young farmers who are so lacking.

The team worked with a diversified group of chestnut farmers (Figure 5); some of them were newcomers to the agricultural business, others saw their agricultural work as part of nature conservation, and others have been practicing professional farming for many years.

Figure 6. Team Building Competencies

Building Competencies

Team *Building Competencies* investigated community-based initiatives and small businesses, some of which were started by people from other parts of the country and all of which had different backgrounds and agenda. One of them, *Mitsuhanosato*, is a grassroots community organization that seeks to create a space for children and families through educational activities related to agriculture and cooking. Two other small businesses, *Nose Biyori* and *Café Espero*, which produce delicacies based on the Ginyose chestnuts in various forms (Figure 6).

Through site visits, interviews, and participation in chestnut processing operations, the team members learned about the workload, the problems arising from the short shelf life of these natural products, and the issues arising in marketing from consumers' conservative attitude towards culinary innovations.

INTERVENTIONS AND CHANGE

The Second Hands-On Fieldwork consisted of two consecutive parts, *Action One* and *Action Two*. *Action One* focused on designing solutions, for which some of the teams had to pay additional visits to Nose, meeting local collaborators and stakeholders for further brainstorming and preparing of next actions. *Action Two* concentrated on planning implementation and determining what works and what does not by seeking quick results from prototyping.

Figure 7. Helping Hands

Helping Hands

The many interactions Team *Helping Hands* had with the local stakeholders and related sites led to the realization that hosting volunteers interested in agriculture and environmental activities could help overcome endemic local constraints. By giving these visitors the opportunity to participate in work where their hands are urgently needed and inviting them to village events and community activities, the two identities of *Nose Seiryūkōbo* and *Nose Minōran Kataroya* would gradually merge into one.

This in turn would strengthen the perception and brand of this place as an attractive destination with many incentives – from short-term solutions to long-term strategies. Some of the passing guests would eventually make life-changing decisions, settle down, start a new existence, and become a new member of the ongoing cycle of Satoyama.

Experiencing the age-old practice of *Yui,* or mutual assistance. that is disappearing in many urban areas of Japan, transformed Team *Helping Hands'* understanding of planning and implementation. The team had to review and readjust their previously set options and goals to focus on the usability of the house as a venue for indoor and outdoor events, such as workshops and community meetings.

To validate their proposals, the team successfully organized two small prototypical events: a workshop that brought all the teams together and a dinner party with staff and neighbors on site. The building was thoroughly cleaned inside and out, and the entire site was transformed into an exemplary open house. More than 20 guests attended the dinner party. The team had prepared a large bonfire from wood scraps found all over the property and set up props in unexpected combinations so that the guests could enjoy a fantastic view of the orchard (Figure 7). After dinner, everyone went outside and enjoyed the warmth of the fire while sharing stories from the past, the present and the future.

Figure 8. Team Making Commitments

Making Commitments

While working in the chestnut orchards, Team *Making Commitments* became aware of the physical demands of maintaining this sustainable asset of Nose. The team also learned firsthand that there was a shortage of labour. Through several brainstorming sessions with local farmers, the idea emerged to establish the 'Adopt-a-Tree' Program as a means of creating commitment, addressing not only volunteers and short-term visitors from outside the area, but also the locals and the owners of the chestnut plantations.

Rather than relying on traditional means of recruiting seasonal workers, the transfer of ownership would not only promote a sense of stewardship, but also provide recurring returns on the investment made.

In order to validate the potential of tree adopters and better understand the profile of the target audience, Team *Making Commitments* decided to conduct a survey at the Farmers' Market. Questions addressed demographics, interest and knowledge about chestnuts, and some details about the proposed program. Local residents provided the space and helped the team set up a photo wall to attract participants for the survey (Figure 8).

Analyzing the result of the 22 submissions the team found:

- 45% expressed interest in the 'Adopt-a-Tree Program and are willing to visit the chestnut orchards 4-5 times a year to care for their trees
- 60% would be happy to receive support on request
- 30% see no need for support
- 10% expect constant advice and help from a professional farmer

About half of the respondents were willing to share a tree with other families to reduce labor and make the product cheaper.

Figure 9. Team Building Competencies

Building Competencies

Given the great potential of young people to do amazing things with minimal adult support, Team *Building Competencies* decided to harness the power of school-age children to facilitate intergenerational problem solving.

A visit and separate joint brainstorming workshop at Osaka Prefecture's Nose Senior High School confirmed the team's belief that the Ginyose has much more potential than a nut collected only once a year, in autumn. Further research into the nut's health benefits, its importance in a gluten-free diet, and unorthodox processing such as *Nose Biyori's* carbonated chestnut drink led the team to propose a number of ideas: *Chestnut Cookbook* – a compilation of recipes by local experts; *Superfood* – highlighting the benefits of chestnut as a nutritional supplement; *Ginyose Cafe* – a place for locals and visitors to sample Nose brand delicacies.

After researching local ingredients and trying out different recipes, Team *Building Competencies* thought that branding Nose as a source and destination of high-quality chestnuts could address many of the village's economic and socio-demographic challenges. A vibrant chestnut industry creates employment opportunities, and highly visible products would put Nose on the map of attractive destinations.

Determined to increase appreciation for chestnut dishes and recipes, the team decided put some of its ideas into practice (Figure 9). They organized a family and child-oriented cooking workshop using *Nose Biyori* brand chestnut powder in collaboration with *Mitsuha no Sato*. A total of 7 families with 12 children from Osaka and the suburbs worked hard in mixed teams to make cream soup, tea and doughnuts whose main ingredient was chestnut powder. Their appetizing creations were taken to *Café Espero*, where they were tasted by both local residents and visitors. The collected impressions and suggestions clearly showed that there is a great potential for a profitable business around this local resource.

LESSONS LEARNED AND AGENDA

These activities concluded with a summary of lessons learned and an agenda discussed and confirmed with locals. An open public presentation was held at Ikeda Daigaku, a local NPO and open kitchen café, which pursues a range of community-based development activities in the immediate vicinity of the Center for the Study of Co*Design at the Toyonaka campus of Osaka University.

Together with local actors from Nose, each team presented the process, results, and proposals developed over the past three months. Problems that show up in communities like Nose as a result of changes in demographics, social values, and also politics, can only be solved by involving their structural complement, the city. Following these assumptions, it was important for us to interact with an urban audience.

We were able to demonstrate the importance of *Mura*, the off-urban agglomeration, as a place for design practice. Personal encounters, physical experiences, and the recognition of holistic relationships are necessary factors for planners and decision-makers at all levels, working towards a truly meaningful and sustainable future.

To guide the next steps – both for visiting collaborators as well as the people at *Mura*, the village community, we have summarized a list of actionable conclusions in the form of a matrix (Figure 10) to avoid premature prioritization and to support the discovery and establishment of connections across the field.

Figure 10. Actionable conclusions

	Context and Connections	Models and Prototypes	Intervention and Change
Helping Hands	Create a platform where local expertise can be shared, used, rewarded, and developed	Publish open-source blueprints for the restoration of unused properties	Identify a pilot facility that can initiate, drive, and symbolize communal efforts and achievements
Making Commitments	Engage parents and children off-site to become responsible patrons and symbolic owners of local public goods	Develop financial vehicles where the return of investments in publicly traded social capital leads to direct benefits for the local community	Release a local currency and issue certificates that document the acceptance of responsibility over selected natural resources
Building Competencies	Build curricula together with different levels of local schools and in initiatives for lifelong learning in domains that advance local needs and oportunities	Partner with institutions of formal higher education and governments to assure compatibility of competences and credentials across domains, demographies, and geographies	Through diversified branding and marketing, local initiatives can inspire the world

CONCLUSION

This chapter presented the efforts of a practice-based curriculum through co-design carried out together with local partners in Nose and students and faculty from Osaka University.

The foundation of the MURA Project was to explore the role that planning and design can play in helping individuals and communities become more resilient, sustainable, and productive – not just to survive, but to thrive.

We believe that our efforts show how socially- and environmentally-conscious design thinking and the practice of co-design can inform social progress. Out of the 17 UN's Sustainable Development Goals that call for action, the MURA Project relates to at least 6 of them, including *Goal 3 (Health and Well-Being For All)*, *Goal 4 (Quality Education for All)*, *Goal 8 (Decent Work and Economic Growth)*, *Goal 11 (Sustainable City and Communities)*, *Goal 15 (Life On Land)*, and *Goal 17 (Partnerships For The Goals)*.

Our place-based activities with collaborative approaches involving local actors are expected to have a lasting impact on the evolution of Nose as a prototype of a community where aging has become a trigger for thriving – inspiring a new generation of creative leaders and change makers who can bring innovative ideas to the development of local communities and society as a whole.

REFERENCES

Barrett, B. (2018). When a country's towns and villages face extinction. *The Conversations.*https://theconversation.com/when-a-countrys-towns-and-villages-face-extinction-88398

Bickford, D. J., & Wright, D. J. (2006). Community: The Hidden Context for Learning. In Oblinger, D. G. (Ed.), *Learning Spaces.* Educause. https://www.educause.edu/ir/library/pdf/pub7102.Pdf

Burkett, I. (2012). *An Introduction to Co-Design.* Knode: Sydney. https://www.yacwa.org.au/wp-content/uploads/2016/09/An-Introduction-to-Co-Design-by-Ingrid-Burkett.pdf

Christopher, M. J. L. (2015). Global, regional, and national disability-adjusted life years (DALYs) for 306 diseases and injuries and healthy life expectancy (HALE) for 188 countries, 1990-2013: quantifying the epidemiological transition. *The Lancet.* https://www.thelancet.com/journals/lancet/article/PIIS0140-6736(15)61340-X/fulltext

IIDj. (n.d.). *DesignFactors.* Institute for Information Design Japan. https://www.designfactors.com/DesignAtCommunities

Istek, C., & Schneider, A. (2020). *MURA - A Place for Design Practice: CO-Design Workshop 2019-2020.* Osaka University, CiNii Books. https://ci.nii.ac.jp/ncid/BC04874273?I=en

Masuda, H. (2014). *Chihō shōmetsu – Tōkyō ikkyoku shūchū ga maneku jinkō kyūgen* [Local extinctions: Rapid population decline due to the concentration in Tokyo]. Chuokoron-Shinsha Publishers.

McKercher, K. A. (2021). *Beyond sticky notes. Doing co-design for Real: Mindsets.* Methods, and Movements, Kindle Edition.

Nose Town Office. (2018). *Asoberu Nose: Nose Town Promotion Project.* [Video]. Youtube. https://www.youtube.com/watch?v=miuwLbHeuP8

Nose Town Office. (2021). *Reiwa 3 nen jūmin kihon daichō jinkō [2021 Basic Registered Resident Population].* Nose Town Office. http://www.town.nose.osaka.jp/material/files/group/7/202103.pdf

Nose Town Office. (n.d.). *Ōsakadaigaku to hōkatsu kyōtei o teiketsu shimashita [Nose Town has concluded a comprehensive cooperative agreement with Osaka University].* Nose Town Office. http://www.town.nose.osaka.jp/kurashi/kyodo_machi/daigaku/1700.html

Nose Town Tourism Association. (n.d.). *Nose Note: Nose Town Tourism and Local Products.* Nose Town Tourism Association. https://www.town-of-nose.jp/

Odagiri, T. (2016). *Atarashī kokudo keisei keikaku no tokuchō [Characteristics of the new national land formation plan]. Tochi Sōgō Kenkyū [Comprehensive Land Research].* Land Institute of Japan.

OPEN. (2021). *Osaka University Vision 2021.* OPEN. https://www.osaka-u.ac.jp/en/guide/strategy/OUvision2021/open2021/top

Pasick, A. (2014). Japan is rapidly losing population and half the world is about to join it. *Quartz.*https://www.qz.com/162788/japan-is-rapidly-losing-population-and-half-the-world-is-aboutto-join-it/

Rowan, H. (2016). Rethinking the age-old question of youth. *The Japan Times.*https://www.japantimes.co.jp/news/2016/07/16/national/science-health/rethinking-age-old-question-youth/

Sanders, E. B. N. (2002). From user-centered to participatory design approaches. In Frascara, J. (Ed.), *Design and the Social Sciences*. Taylor & Francis. 10.1201/9780203301302.ch1

Sanders, E. B. N., & Stappers, P. J. (2008). Co-creation and the new landscapes of design. *CoDesign*, 4(1), 5–18. 10.1080/15710880701875068

The Human Mortality Database. (2002). The University of California, Berkeley, USA and the Max Planck Institute for Demographic Research, Germany. https://www.mortality.org

Chapter 3
UVIR:
Unprecedented Virtual-Intellectual Representations Thought and Imagined

Can Güngör
http://orcid.org/0000-0002-0393-4293
Gazi University, Turkey

Gizem Özkan Üstün
Gazi University, Turkey

ABSTRACT

Design studios are the backbone of architectural education. At XXX University Faculty of Architecture, the vertical studio system allows 2nd, 3rd, and 4th-year students to work together in a design studio to learn from each other and contribute to the projects via primary literature research on design problems, project site analysis, and site model making. Group study also contributes to program generation, primary concept studies, sketch making, project generation, building model making, material research, 3d visualization studies, presentation works, and final submission CAD drafting. The retrospective evaluation of XXX's design studio practices from Spring 2016 to Spring 2022 showed various subjects and projects in different scales and programs in varying places and times. The students' projects produced within this period proved successful and gathered recognition and rewards from national/international student design competitions. That's the reason these projects are called "Unprecedented Virtual-Intellectual Representations: Thought and Imagined."

LITERATURE REVIEW

Design studios are a prominent indicator of architectural pedagogy. Different approaches are observed in a broad spectrum beyond traditional architectural design studios in this context. Kuhn (2001), in her research, describes the features of the design studio as follows;
1. Student work is organized primarily into semester-length projects, responding to complex, open-ended assignments.
2. Students' design solutions undergo multiple and rapid iterations.
3. Critique is frequent and occurs formally and informally from faculty, peers, and visiting experts.

DOI: doi

4. Heterogeneous issues, ranging from structural integrity to the design's social impact, are often considered in the same conversation.
5. Students study precedents (past designs) and are encouraged to consider the big picture.
6. Faculty help students impose appropriate constraints on their design process to navigate a complex, open-ended problem and find a satisfactory design solution (Kuhn, 2001).

Conventional studio teaching has numerous advantages due to face-to-face interactions between students and teachers. However, knowledge acquisition is centered on personal experiences, which may benefit only specific individuals. There are also concerns regarding excessive abstraction and disconnection from real design problems (Rodriguez, et.al., 2018).

Ciravoğlu A. (2014) describes an architectural studio: The studio becomes the primary medium of architectural design education, and the conversation (mainly attributed as critique) between the student and the tutor becomes the means of this education. Here, the student is expected to learn by doing. However, the conversation, which may be in one of the following forms: one-on-one, desk, or jury critique, is very fragile. It also states that the execution of the architectural design studio has many disadvantages today. The most important one is that it is still building on the traditional master-apprentice relationship with the teacher in a master and the student in an apprentice position (Ciravoğlu, (2014). Glasser (2000) also underlines this situation and states that the master-apprentice relationship still influences the way of thinking in design studios in most architecture schools. According to him, critical thinking should be encouraged to address today's agenda, but instead, architectural ideologies and beliefs are transmitted to students either explicitly or implicitly. Creating an environment of competition instead of co-operation also holds students back in confronting current world problems (Glasser, 2000).

It may be appropriate for the 21st century for design studios to address issues adapted to today's problems and to make their methods suitable for today's agenda. In this context, when design studios are investigated, it is seen that similar concerns have started to emerge in different schools of the world, and innovations are followed. For example, Ibrahim and Utaberta (2012) state that in the University of Tasmania and the University of Sydney, creativity in the first and second years, pragmatic thinking in the third and fourth years are transferred to students and sustainability and innovation issues are integrated into traditional architectural education (Ibrahim and Utaberta, 2012). Hacihasanoglu (2019) emphasizes that the design studio culture in schools in the United States was formed in the late 1990s. As a requirement of the 21st century, the article investigates the design studios of 10 architecture schools in the U.S.A. with the parameters of cooperation instead of competition and innovation in creating alternative learning and teaching methodologies. It emphasizes that intellectual diversity is given importance, the interaction between studios is determined as a policy, and students are equipped with skills such as time management, design process, and recycling of design materials (Hacihasanoglu, 2019).

Masdéu, M., & Fuses, J. (2017) in their research state that, In order to adapt to the changes in the professional practice that architecture students will face after graduation, There is a need for the schools of architecture, to revise their programmes to develop teaching methods that enable them to adapt to the current situation. Thus, the Design Studio -considered as the core of education in architecture- needs a reconceptualization in order to change the way architects should learn. Pedagogical approaches such as distance learning and blended learning can help update the concept of the Design Studio and transform it into a new participatory and delocalized learning space. The study suggests a generic Blended Design Studio where the students have to acquire the ability to be more critical, curious and autonomous (Masdéu, M., & Fuses, J. 2017).

It is understandable that, even before the Covid-19 Pandemic- where the design studio practices were altered and changed significantly due to precautions, in a mandatory manner- proposals for change and restructuring of design education were being considered and theorized as the previous research indicates.

In Casakin and Wodehouse's (2021) research paper, make a systematic evaluation of 17 research papers on the design studio practices and their effects on design creativity. Their evaluation classifies those results in 5 categories (and subcategories) of which student outcomes are evaluated:
1. Pedagogy (Training for Creativity and Structuring design Process and Problems)
2. Cognitive Approach (Reflection, Design Strategies and Methods and Information Processing)
3. Interaction and Socialization (Collaboration and Shared Mental Models)
4. Information representation (Tools for Information Representation and Manipulation of Information
5. Measuring Ideation and Creativity (Assessment of Creative Processes and Outcomes and Assessment of Personal Abilities)

The discussion of these categories contributed to the comparison and connections between the selected papers, and the identification of critical issues and directions for promoting creativity in the architectural design studio were concluded in the study as follows: the architectural design studio it is highly collaborative while inviting individual expression; it invites the use of a wide range of stimuli within a context of established typographies; it is well-suited to the use of advanced visualization technologies, but relies on conventional sketching and drawing practices; and increasing structure is recommended to support activities despite the recognition for individual reflection and metacognition (Casakin, H., & Wodehouse, A. 2021).

Kılıçaslan and Kalaycı (2021) state that architectural studio education encompasses different approaches from past to present; it is continuously researched and is both vocational and personality training. An updated manifesto for the current era is essential to ensure that the design approaches and tools updated by the boundless opportunities presented by the 21st century do not overwhelm the proven principles from the past (Kılıçaslan & Kalaycı, 2021).

As a matter of fact, Yurtsever and Polatoğlu (2020) emphasize that the current environment requires an environment where the studio instructors are not the focus in architectural design studios and where the sharing cycle is essential. They underline that pure knowledge transfer is insufficient for this age. Therefore, they propose a blended studio understanding in which the individual is developed to make sense of the knowledge. In this 'active studio' environment, where not only the students but also the instructors are in active learning, there is a fiction adapted to the day and can be transformed according to the flow of change of the day (Yurtsever and Polatoğlu, 2020). Lekesiz and Gürer's (2022) proposal is to evaluate the design studio from a complex system perspective, which is different from traditional understandings. In the new pedagogical approach they put forward, self-organization, criticality among students, spatial openness to be in contact with the environment, simultaneous activities, connectivity with other studios and other departments, group work, strengthening the flow of information in the complexity of interaction networks, systematic studio construction are prominent qualities. In their approach to increase studio efficiency, they see the studio as a multivocal, complex process that is not linear and hierarchical (Lekesiz & Gürer, 2022).

In addition to all these studio models and understandings, there are also the following approaches that have come to the fore in recent years: Ersine Masatlıoğlu and Balaban (2024) developed a model in which they added architectural discipline literacy training and peer-assessment exercises to the traditional studio curriculum. Grennan and Lus Arana (2024) propose a studio design that addresses the graphic and historical nature of the comic book and uses it as a design tool. They construct a dialectical process that starts with a simple comic book layout but uses its sequential, simultaneous structure to highlight the narrative role of architecture. Ceylan, Şahin, et al. (2024) emphasize the importance of using digital tools, artificial intelligence, and parametric, generative design in architectural design studios. They underline that digital tools have also changed the studio setup regarding energy performance simulations, structural behavior, construction costs, visualization, and representation.

To summarise, architectural design studios are open to transforming according to the changing world and various parameters and moving away from their traditional structure as architectural education continues. The standard and different qualities of the studios followed in different geographies arise from the structure of architecture that allows for originality and creativity. Like architectural design, designing architectural design studios also stems from the nature of the act of designing.

MATERIALS AND METHOD

Gazi University Faculty of Architecture Department of Architecture has a vertical Studio system. The vertical Studio system enables students at different stages of their education to work in the same design studio with the same design problem. With this system, inexperienced students from the M2022 project and final project students from the ARCH4022 project can work together at the beginning of the semester on primary stages of the project generation, such as understanding the design problem, searching literature on the given subject, finding examples on the previously built buildings on that subject, understanding the site via SWOT analyses and mock-up making of the site. If the given problem enables the students to work together, this collaboration can extend from the initial design proposal until the final submission.

Studio Think-Imagine is one of the eight design studios of the Gazi University Faculty of Architecture Department of Architecture. All these design studios are responsible for the "Architectural Project" lessons of the second year-second semester (M2022) to final semester (ARCH4042) students. Students from 2nd, 3rd, and 4th years choose from these design studios regarding the subject proposed for that semester by the studio and enroll in the one they want. All the studios prepare posters of their semester subject before the selection and explain how they will apply the lesson throughout the semester.

Students' choices of studio mainly dwell on the subject proposed, the lecturers they want to work with, the past studios they have attended, and mostly, the possible success they would achieve at the end of the semester. Studio Think-Imagine encourages students to achieve their goals and be successful in their projects by providing an initial manifesto describing how the studio lessons will be conducted and what is expected of them. Also, the project subject declaration poster explains the semester's focus and the essential hints on how the work will be applied. This information helps students clarify what intensity of work they will handle and eliminates some students.

The primary purpose of Studio Think-Imagine has always been to make all of its students accomplish the best performance they can and achieve maximum success at the end of their semester. This chapter includes the structure, content, design approach and retrospective analysis of Studio Think-Imagine. In this way, Think-Imagine's approach to architectural design education is revealed.

What We Do

The manifesto of our design studio suggests that the design studio is based on the individual and supports the development of his or her imagination and expressive power individual dreams and fantasies are evaluated and sharpened by the studio's interactive environment. While doing these, contemporary architectural practices, theories, and scientific knowledge are the thinking tools of the design studio; also, history and contemporary architecture refer to the design studio. Design begins with the exploration of the place. The individual who determines his design is considered to have drawn the first line of his design. The studio's task is to make students comprehend that each line in the design is an instant interpretation of human life. The design studio uses all communication possibilities in which the individual expresses himself in writing, architectural drawings, model making, and other driving products. The design is trying to grasp the face-to-face evaluation of the student's studies that have brought him, and it has to be understood by the student what can be done and what cannot be realized by a Project.

Furthermore, the studio is responsible for developing and testing the knowledge and skills at all stages.

Another critical point in our studio's manifestation and also in the application is that the design studio has to offer an outside eye to the student's studies so that the student can test his work with some other Professional so that he or she can get feedback and develop it for a better project and these products are of course. The product of all semesters is evaluated together comparatively at the end of the semester. Of course, the other eye introduced in the previous stage is also invited to the last meeting so that the student can feel the evaluation is like a competition within itself.

How We Do It

In the introduction week, our students come together at a meeting in the first week and talk about the project. They talk about the manifestation of the studio, the term's project, and what they will do to achieve success. They talk about what they will do to research the project subject, the past and present of the project site, and what they will find there. Then they think and comment on what they are going to put as a new project as a new function to that place, how it will answer the problems stated in the project subject, and how they will answer the problem within the existing surrounding environment.

The design process starts within a few weeks of research, and maybe some statistical analysis of the site, and the next stage of the process are called the "thing" study. The designer starts off the design process with the "thing" study, which is what the initial design idea a project can improve from but not only a sheet of drawing or a fast plunge into the plans and section drawings or elevation drawings, but it can be as simple as a wire mesh a cardboard pile cut into an installation a foam board on the mock-up of the place. Anything that will turn into a project later in the design process can start as the "thing" they put on the mock-up. The students must first understand what the "thing" is and let the instructors understand what the "thing" is. After that, they can turn this "thing" into a building, or it can turn out to be just an element on the facade of the building. It must make a starting or ending point in the design; not only can the "thing" become the project, but the project cannot be the "thing" itself.

Another unique experience in the Studio Think-Imagine's application of architectural project design studios is the "critical day. "It is the most essential stage after day-to-day critiques with the students. They are told to prepare up to four copies of the projects they have been designing throughout the semester, complete with plans, sections, elevations, and, if necessary, 3D models. The Studio Think-Imagine then invites other architectural professionals from municipalities, architectural offices, and academics from other universities to evaluate the students' projects. Students are told to make at least four presentations to these newcomers/ total strangers and get their feedback on their projects. This one-time engagement of the designer and the critic on the "critical day" is crucial for our students. They get at least four critiques from four different professionals from different areas of expertise on what they see on their projects, and the essential point is that they must evaluate what is suitable for their project and what is doable for their project at the end of the semester. The students must choose from the feedback and apply it to their projects for the course's last three or four weeks. Their Projects are not supposed to change completely, but they are altered positively after the "critical day."

As a final stage, the studio focuses on the presentations of the student projects at the end of the semester. The students study the presentation posters, which the Studio Think-Imagine gives the outline. However, they must fill it in with proper and qualified quantitative and qualitative drawings. The posters are supposed to be able to tell the jury in the final presentation what the project is, what the initial problems were, and what the answers to those problems are without the designer being present. Everything should be understandable for them. This final presentation in our studio is the final day. It is called "the project bazaar," and all the projects are hung on the walls. The jury that the studio has invited to the "critical day" is also invited to the "project bazaar." At the final gathering, the jury gives "first place," "second place," and "third place" awards to the students' projects. "Honorable mention" and "jury's choice" awards are also presented to the students.

What We Did

Studio Think-Imagine had been challenging for architecture project students to reflect on the intellectual accumulations of their education and visualize them via different media on varying subjects at alternating places and times. This chapter lists some projects the Studio Think-Imagine defines as Unprecedented Virtual-Intellectual Representations: Thought and imagined. The content of this chapter has been presented in the "International Exhibitions & Webinars of Design Studios" webinar that was coordinated by the Studio Think-Imagine of Gazi University, Faculty of Architecture, Department of Architecture for the "Gazitr-towards100" program. The first of eight Webinars took place on 15th October 2021.

THE STUDIO CONTENT

Pavilion Space(s) Kınalıada / İstanbul (2016 Fall)

In the Fall of 2016, Studio Think-Imagine went to Kınalıada Istanbul, an island in the Sea of Marmara. It is the closest of the Prince Islands to Istanbul for a Project. The main design challenge was the generation of pavilion spaces within the existing historical fabric of this beautiful island. The design problem was the production of pavilion spaces within the existing historical texture of Kınalıada, which will be a landmark of the 21st century. The Unique and one-off nature of a pavilion building had to bring a Vibrant touch to its context and gave its designer a chance to Improvise and Realize a utopian yet functioning building.

Firstly, the pavilion structures in the international and national literature were examined. In each example, how the spaces where people can meet, interact, and share are created were discussed through the pavilion architecture. It was emphasized how each example is fed from its immediate environment and what it added to it. It was discussed how special groups such as the elderly, people with disabilities, and children, for whom design-based solutions are not offered in our society, are included in the design.

One of the students responded to this with an expanding structure in a single plot of land (Demirhan). At the same time, another one attached his pavilion to an existing historical building on the island (Aytaç). One student designed a stand-alone monumental orb on the seashore, easily recognizable from the city of Istanbul (Ateş), while another took her chances on the sea surface (Arıkan) (Figure 1).

Figure 1. A) Telescopic workshops; B) Pavilion thoughts; C) For seasons Pavilion; D) Marina camp

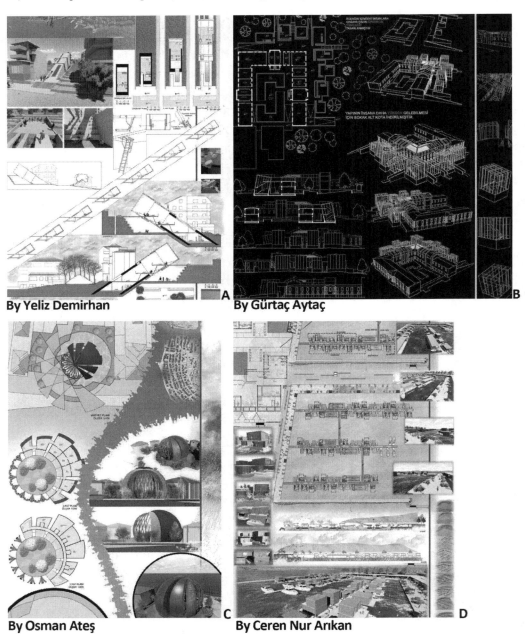

Topography(s) Cappadocia / Nevşehir (2017 Spring)

In Spring 2017, we did not abstain from going to the beautiful Cappadocia / Nevşehir, a historical region in Central Anatolia, famous for its volcanic peaks and touristic hot-air balloon rides. The design problem for our students was the generation of architecture faculty campus as a landmark of the 21st century on the rural-historical topography of Cappadocia. The Untouchable natural environment has provided challenging areas, yet, Virtuous design solutions have been provided by the Ingenuity of our students, who were highly attentive to Rural and tourist areas.

At the beginning of the project, each student discovered his/her place. The studio could have offered a fixed place to the participants. They were encouraged to search and find suitable physical conditions for his/her dream design. The studio finds it essential to gain sensitivity to the place and to feel it and recognizes that design starts with understanding the sense of the place. Developing his/her senses for the environment, the student chose a unique and singular place for his/her design. Where is appropriate if a place is chosen for the design? Why? What are the near and far connections of this place?

One of the students chose a plot of land overlooking the Peri Bacaları "Fairy Chimneys" rock formation near Göreme, in Cappadocia, and resided on it within her organic forms (Yalçın). Another student decided to build her Uçhisar Castle in the shape of a Pyramid and occupy it with the architecture faculty campus (Bilgi).

Another Student took the semi-underground approach to design a faculty campus, most probably influenced by the Derinkuyu Underground city that we visited (Kulaklı), and another one chose to resemble slightly pressed down chimney formations and blend into the natural environment (Karabulut) (Figure 2).

Figure 2. A) Design universe; B) Dynamic process; C) Life; D) The universe of architecture

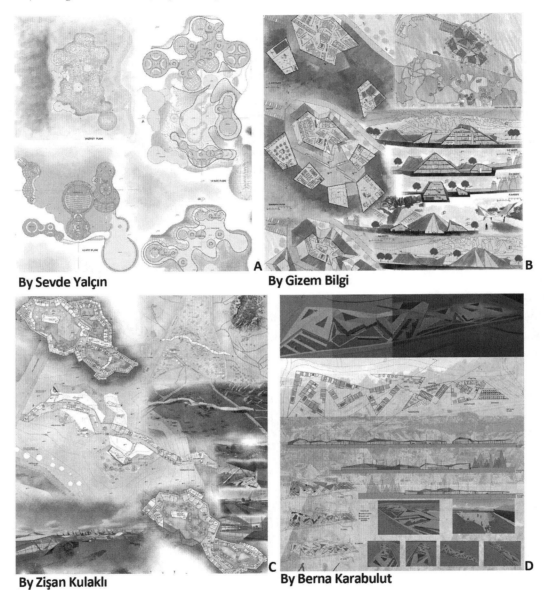

Transformation(s) Kaleiçi / Antalya (2017 Fall)

In the fall of 2017, we went to Kaleiçi / Antalya, the historic city center of Antalya, Türkiye, where buildings dating back to the late 18th and 19th centuries. Traditional Turkish homes, many of which have been converted into boutique hotels, restaurants, and shops, serve as a Tourist area and are fronted by the yacht harbor that dates to the Roman era. The project design problem was the transformations of these historical buildings and sites within architectural approaches representing 21st-century Architecture.

The Unequivocal Value of the Kaleiçi area and The Antalya Harbor, aging back hundreds of years, had to be Imagined with Riveting new functions and professionally designed buildings within the historical context. "Technology" and "ecology" were among the most critical inputs of the project and had to be a common concern for all designs. Summer heat humidity was also a necessary input that required precautions. Whether in housing or port management, the fact that the building parts were mobile/transformable/autonomous units and could be controlled by intelligent systems affects usage and life positively. Suggestions were expected to include such content and represent the present and even the near future.

One of our students rose to the challenge by providing a protective institution to the endemic plants of the region (Taş), and another one re-functioned the existing walls of Kaleiçi to be used with both touristic and cultural and educational attractions (Coşkun).

Others focused on the existing harbor area, which is today filled with touristic ferry rides, and transformed it to alternating cultural and bazaar functions without neglecting the human proportions (Kutun, Solak) (Figure 3).

Figure 3. A) *Endemic;* B) *No transformation;* C) *Cooperation;* D) *Enhanced perception;* E) *Cavity;* F) *Threshold port*

Mall Transformation Akköprü / Ankara (2018 Spring)

In Spring 2018, Studio Think İmagine approached a growing problem for our city of Ankara and sampled it in the Akköprü region of Ankara, which takes its name from a historical bridge in Yenimahalle district. It crosses the Ankara River in front of Varlık neighborhood. It is the oldest bridge in Ankara and is still in good condition. The design problem was the realization of transformations to be created with a new architectural approach on a shopping mall site and create an urban landmark of the 21st century. The Unsustainable growth in size and number of shopping malls in a city should be controlled with Viable design Interventions for the Regeneration of better and more functional public gathering areas. Functional selection/program/framework was free for all project groups. Depending on the scenario of the transformation of the region/place, it was expected to be proposed by the designer and based on a clear discourse / architectural theory. Observing the place, reading the texts suggested by the workshop as references, and following the classroom sharing were told to contribute to creating the transformation scenario. Irrational scenarios were not desired. The originality and suitability of the scenarios were among the primary evaluation criteria.

Some students re-structured and transformed the enormous land of an old shopping mall and turned it into a park with artificial hills covered with green spaces, gathering areas, sports fields, and hobby structures, and also open-air concert areas and bicycle routes and jogging parkour (Sarı, Kılıç).

One other student approached the area as an opportunity for an international fairground that would enrich the city of Ankara and host many inviting events throughout the year. Another one combined water and greenery with a cultural center and a library where University students across Ankara would benefit (Figure 4).

Figure 4. A) City museum; B) Park C); Non-Space; D) Green library

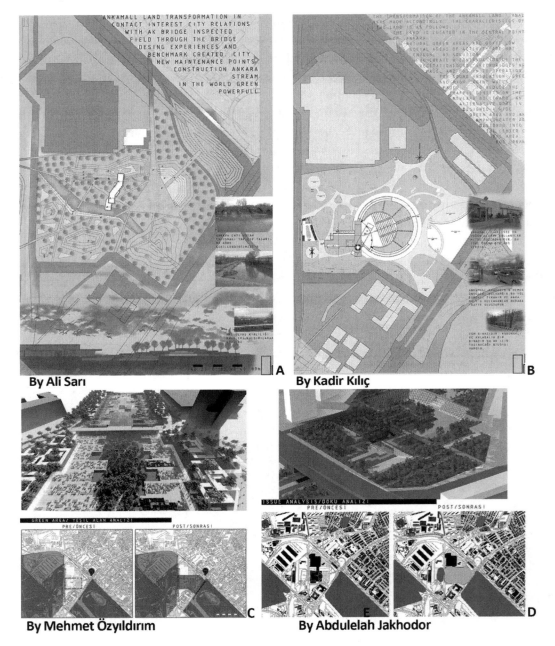

Flow Space and Time / Various Riversides (2018 Fall)

In the Fall of 2018, we chose to be apart from space, place, and time. The design problem was today's architectural production embracing the place instead of design. Where designing in time can be a flow-oriented interpretation. Seasonal spaces had to be developed on a riverside in danger of overflow.

These spaces would stand functionless in times of overflow and would be reopened to use in times of normal flow. Music, with choreography, program, narration, and scenario, can be a reference to obtain a flow-oriented interpretation in architecture. There are places where nature, sometimes society, and other changes require the rapid disappearance and re-existence of the place. More is needed for the designer to offer a single space/architecture proposal for such places. Future scenarios, update proposals, alternatives, additions, demolition-build-(again)destroy-(again) plans must be realized with attention to the current architecture paradigms… The architect depends on space, and time depends on space or vice versa. It has to design the space. Now, "time" is an architectural component that needs to be designed, one of the functions of space… Time and its design can mean owning a "place."

Our students chose a place near a riverside from their hometowns or cities if they thought that their projects would benefit from and came up with solutions integrating technology, science, and cultural development of those areas and reflected them on their projects with at least four time-spatial solutions (Figure 5).

Figure 5. A) The maze; B) Hypercube; C) Walls; D) Boomerang

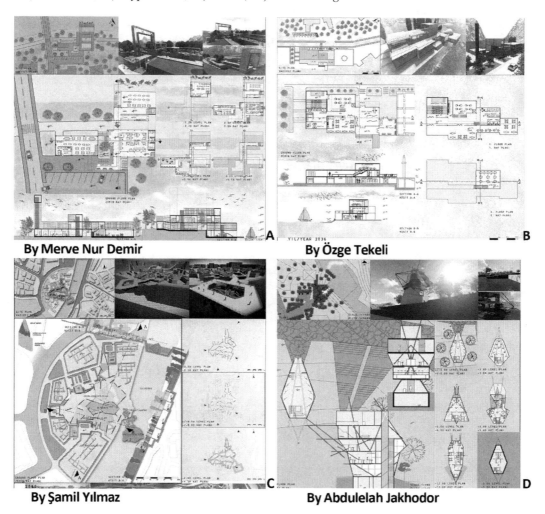

(Im)Migrant-Space GMK Blvd. / Ankara (2019 Spring)

In Spring 2019, a growing situation emerged as immigration was increasingly felt around Ankara. The design problem was the production of a migration museum and related spaces for the immigrants within the existing context of Gazi Mustafa Kemal Boulevard, where temporary accommodation of the immigrants was felt intensely. The Unpredictable flow of immigrants to a city can cause Vagaries in social behaviors and test the Infrastructure in Residential areas. In the frame of the two poles of the social structure (the migration-migrating), the students had to propose time-space scenarios subjected to meaningful sustainability by considering Industry 4.0-Society 5.0 and its meaning for architectural design. Different forms and with different content in cases of new developments regarding migration can keep an urban place alive/daily/architectural all the time; in place's existence adventure, discovering the potentials of architecture as a product that can flow with social realities instead of considering it as a fixed activity.

Our students responded to the situation in varying ways. One of them solved the museum function within a single plot of land, whereas another chose to turn to a high-rise development where accommodation and other functions take place along with the museum. They also provided solutions to the surrounding environment. They chose to integrate other functions into the museum, elevate their design over existing parks, and keep ground level as a public space (Figure 6).

Figure 6. A) Rotation; B) Green utopia; C) Space migration museum; D) Flowing museum

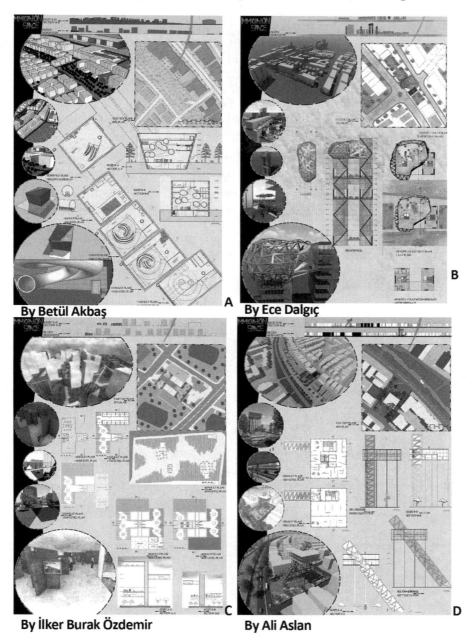

Memory to Dream / Zafer Square / Ankara (2019 Fall)

In Fall 2019, the existing usage of the Zafer Square in Ankara. Although traditionally called a square, it is no longer a junction point today. The design problem was the reconstruction of Zafer Square and the ground floors of its surrounding buildings with at least two time-spatial solutions addressing today and future problems by new functions and revitalizing old uses of existing spaces. The Unintentionally occupied Zafer Square should be Valuated via the Intentional Refunctioning of the Square with new approaches. Studio Think-Imagine is experienced in generating flow-driven scenarios over time. Although the subject and place have historical meanings, the following concepts that shape the present and future world should also be used as inputs in the design: Flow, fluidity, fluid architecture, Industry 4.0, Society 5.0, Life 3.0, cyberspace, virtual reality, augmented reality, artificial intelligence, collective intelligence, collective memory, digital archive, interface, software etc.

Our students were to solve two different timelines at the selected place. After intensive research on the history of Zafer Square, they tried to design alternating solutions for the development of the square as of today and approximately 50 years from today. The solutions in today's designs mainly focus on the area's existing usage and the square's functioning. However, some future predictions went on to foresee vast changes in the height and function of surrounding buildings. Nevertheless, the square remained intact and provided its users with open public areas and green spaces (Figure 7).

Figure 7. A) *Gastro art;* B) *Memory revolution;* C) *Libr-Art;* D) *Social square;* E) *Explosion;* F) *Rising space*

Fantasy to Rule G.M.K. Blvd. / Ankara (2020 Spring)

In Spring 2020, we were struck by the disrupted education semester as the Universities were shut down due to the COVID-19 pandemic. The initial design problem was to learn the rules and regulations governing the city of Ankara and transfer both these rules and our students' imagination into designing a 3-star hotel within the context of giving a green and ecology-oriented facade to the Boulevard. A Vibrant and Improvised hotel solution should enrich the Unimpressive facades of Gazi Mustafa Kemal Boulevard. Regarding regulatory restrictions. After three weeks of face-to-face education, we went online and distantly continued our project critiques.

As Studio Think-Imagine, we were not profoundly frustrated by the situation, as our online platforms were already installed for one-to-one evaluation of uploaded projects, and we started using them more effectively. We managed to go on to finish our students' designs before the end of June. The results were satisfying and complete but lacked the touch of a mock-up (Güngör & Özkan Üstün, 2022) and replaced it all with detailed computer models as seen here (Figure 8).

Figure 8. A) The Canyon hotel; B) Rising levels; C) Contrast; D) Diffusion; E) Spiral; F) Uniform response

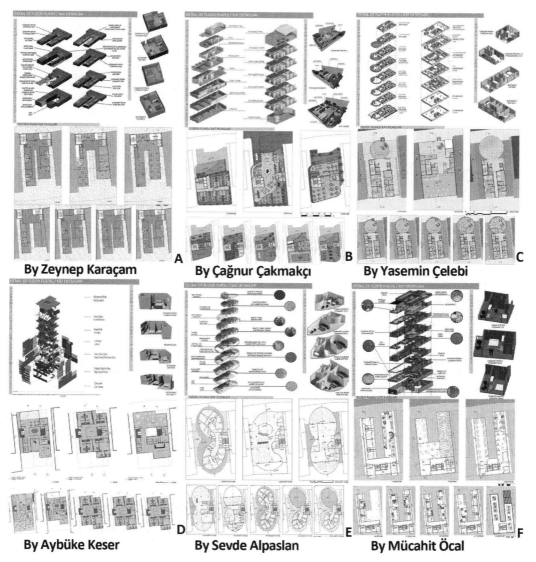

Choose and Compete I, II, III and IV (2020 Fall / 2021 Spring / Fall 2021 / Spring 2022)

From 2020 Fall to Spring 2022, Spring Studio Think-Imagine went on to design with students online and chose another platform to conquer—online national and international student competitions. The challenge proposed for the students was to select and participate in an international/national competition that they thought would address the problems of a changing world where their ideas and designs could effectively solve a specific problem. The Ubiquitous solutions to design problems in Various subjects are Inadequate and should be Revamped by fresh approaches via architectural competitions. The students went on to attend student competitions in varying subjects all around the world, such as student dorm for the poor, an innovative approach to vertical university, a new cultural center proposal for an oasis in the middle of the desert, a religious / non-religious center by the walls of Chinese town, a new approach to justice for humanity and a competition about the shoreline of a Black Sea town in Türkiye.

As results came in, we proudly announced that they gained recognition from the jurors of those competitions as they received honorable mentions, Equivalent 1st place awards, and editor's choice lists. And those awards are just one of many reasons these projects are called: "Unprecedented Virtual-Intellectual Representations: Thought and Imagined" by all of those valuable, clever, and hardworking students of Studio Think-Imagine (Figure 9, 10, 11, 12).

As a final word, Studio Think-Imagine believes that:

The Universities should be the Vanguard of using Information technology in vie for Restructuring architectural education. They should also be prepared for unexpected situations and powerfully respond to the challenges.

ACKNOWLEDGMENT

The writers would like to thank Prof.Dr. Pınar DİNÇ KALAYCI for allowing presenting the Works of Studio Think-Imagine in this International Webinar. Also, the writers would like to acknowledge the Contributions of Part-time teacher Bolkar AÇIKKOL for his full hearted guidance and support to the Studio and the Research Assistants Yusuf Bera BİLİCİ and Mehmet Özyıldırım in preparation for the online virtual Exhibition. The virtual exhibition of all the projects can be found on the following link:

URL-6: https://www.artsteps.com/view/602a1bec9cb19b786ac5bb26/

All these valuable work became possible with the participation of the following students of the Studio and of the many that exceeds the limits of this chapter: Abit Dedeyurt, Abdulelah Jokhodar, Ali Aslan, Ali Sarı, Alihan Aktaş, Aybüke Keser, Ayşenur Haldan, Bade Eloğlu, Berfin Kangal, Berna Karabulut, Beste Eser, Betül Akbaş, Beyza Nur Kotanak, Buket Demir, Buse Cini, Cerennur Arıkan, Çağnur Çakmakçı, Ece Dalgıç, Ecra Güngör, Eda Buse Usta, Elif Seda Koz, Emrah Ökten, Emre Koç, Erol Üresin, Fatma Gündoğan, Feyza Gül Ekim, Furkan Iskar, Furkan Karakuş, Furkan Taş, Gizem Bilgi, Gülnur Betül Tuncer, Gürtaç Aytaç, Hilal Yılmaztürk, İlker Burak Özdemir, Kadir Kılıç, Kübra Cambaz, Kübra Harmankaya, Kübra Mutlu, Medina Karimova, Mehmet Özyıldırım, Merve Akça, Merve Nur Demir, Nejla Altom, Onur Gültekin, Osman Ateş, Ömer Faruk Karatepe, Özge Kutun, Özge Tekeli, Özlem Esra Polat, Rümeysa Coşkun, Sait Kızıl, Saranda Pelingu, Sevde Yalçın, Semih Solak, Sena Bulut, Sevde Alparslan, Sıddıka Türkmen, Sümeyye Atasayar, Şamil Yılmaz, Tuğba Kalem, Tuğçe Sevinç, Yeliz Demirhan, Yasemin Çelebi, Yaşa Nur Çil, Yunus Emre Akdemir, Yusuf Bera Bilici, Zeynep Aybüke Saçlı, Zeynep Coskuner, Zeynep Dinktepe, Zeynep Karaçam, Zişan Kulaklı

CONFLICTS OF INTEREST

The authors declare that there is no conflict of interest regarding the publication of this article.

Figure 9. A) Microcosmos; B) Vtc; C) The Elysium; D) Living Layers

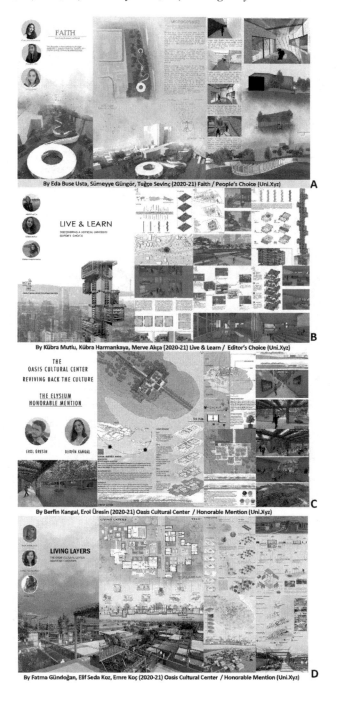

Figure 10. A) The slit; B) Lifting boundaries: Getting together; C) Piece-Full; D) The aesthesis

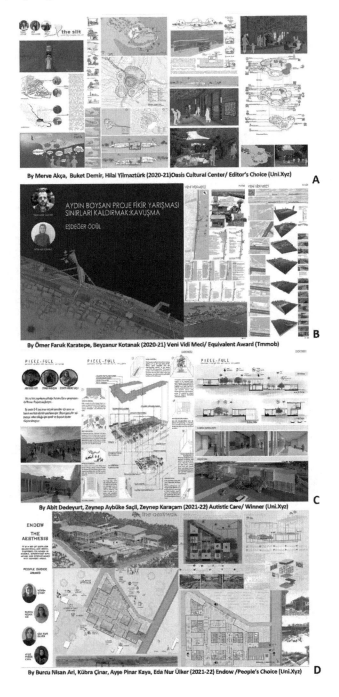

Figure 11. A) Symbio-Farm; B) The Fusion; C) Artwind; D) The Oasis of Gardens

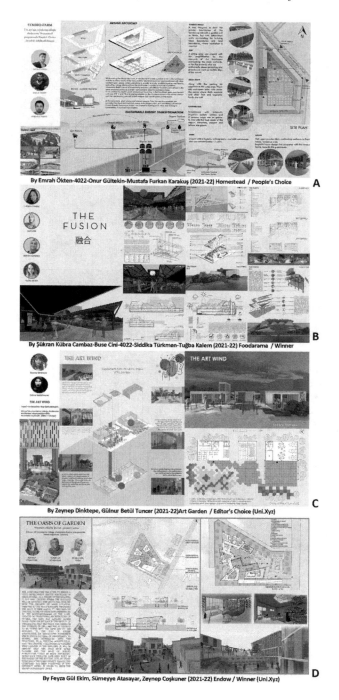

Figure 12. A) Orphic; B) Yellow trumpet; C) Rhythm-Hub; D) Re-Nkra

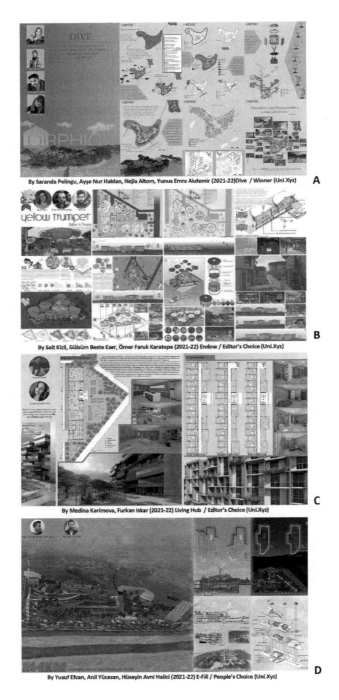

REFERENCES

Casakin, H., & Wodehouse, A. (2021). A systematic review of design creativity in the architectural design studio. *Buildings*, 11(1), 31. 10.3390/buildings11010031

Ceylan, S., Şahin, P. et al. (2024). The contribution of digital tools to architectural design studio: A case study. *Ain Shams Engineering Journal.*

Ciravoğlu, A. (2014). Notes on architectural education: An experimental approach to design studio. *Procedia: Social and Behavioral Sciences*, 152, 7–12. 10.1016/j.sbspro.2014.09.146

Ersine Masatlıoğlu C. S. and Balaban, Ö. C. (2024). Reflective thinking and self-assessment: A model for the architectural design studio. *Journal of Design for Resilience in Architecture and Planning, 5.*

Glasser, D. E. Reflections on Architectural Education. *Journal of Architectural Education, 53*(4).

Grennan, S., & Lus Arana, L. M. (2024). Comics in the design studio. On the use of graphic narrative as a tool to represent, narrate, and rethink architectural space. In Colonnese, F., Grancho, N., & Schaevebeke, R. (Eds.), *Approaches to Drawing in Architecture and Urban Design.* Cambridge Scholars.

Güngör, C., & Özkan Üstün, G. (2022). *The Importance of Working with Architectural Mock-Ups in Architectural Project Atelier Lessons: Comparison of Applications During and After the Pandemic Period.* 7th International "Başkent" Congress on Physical, Social, and Health Sciences, Ankara, Turkey

Hacihasanoglu, O. (2019). Architectural Design Studio Culture. *Journal of Design Studio*, 1(1), 5–15.

Ibrahim, N. L. N., & Utaberta, N. (2012). Learning in Architecture Design Studio. *Procedia: Social and Behavioral Sciences*, 60, 30–35. 10.1016/j.sbspro.2012.09.342

Kılıçaslan, H., & Kalaycı, P. D. (2021). A Joint Manifesto for Design Studios Based on Residuals and Experiences. *Periodica Polytechnica Architecture*, 52(1), 66–74. 10.3311/PPar.16758

Kuhn, S. (2001). Learning from the architecture studio: Implications for project-based pedagogy. *International Journal of Engineering Education*, 17(4/5), 349–352.

Lekesiz, G., & Gürer, E. (2022). An overview of the architectural design studio in the conceptual framework of complex systems. JCoDe. *Journal of Computational Design*, 3(2), 1–26. 10.53710/jcode.1135984

Masdéu, M., & Fuses, J. (2017). Reconceptualizing the design studio in architectural education: Distance learning and blended learning as transformation factors. *Archnet-IJAR*, 11(2), 6. 10.26687/archnet-ijar.v11i2.1156

Onur, D., & Zorlu, T. (2017). Tasarım Stüdyolarında Uygulanan Eğitim Metotları ve Yaratıcılık İlişkisi. *The Turkish Online Journal of Design, Art and Communication, 7*(4).

Rodriguez, C., Hudson, R., & Niblock, C. (2018). Collaborative learning in architectural education: Benefits of combining conventional studio, virtual design studio, and live projects. *British Journal of Educational Technology*, 49(3), 337–353. 10.1111/bjet.12535

Uluoğlu, B. (1990). *Mimari Tasarım Eğitimi:Tasarım Bilgisi Bağlamında Stüdyo Eleştirileri*, [Doctoral dissertation, Istanbul Technical University].

Yurtsever, B., & Polatoğlu, Ç. (2020). Mimari Tasarım Eğitiminde 'Aktif Stüdyo' Deneyimleri. *Megaron, 14*(3). https://www.artsteps.com/view/602a1bec9cb19b786ac5bb26/

Chapter 4
Architecture as an Emancipating Ground:
Emancipatory Architectural Designs of Atelier 1

Zeynep Uludag
Gazi University, Turkey

Gulsah Gulec
https://orcid.org/0000-0002-8041-2018
Gazi University, Turkey

Neva Gercek Atalay
Gazi University, Turkey

ABSTRACT

This chapter is based on the design approach of Atelier 1, an architectural design studio at Gazi University Department of Architecture in Ankara. Atelier 1 aims to develop a critical understanding of design thinking, and promotes interdisciplinary approaches in the studio. The critical discourses in other disciplines indicate the developmental process of architectural concepts. As a critical design studio, Atelier 1 defined the main theme of fall and spring semesters of 2021 and 2022 as "Architecture as an Emancipating Ground." Students discussed the concept of emancipation in architecture from an interdisciplinary perspective including philosophical conceptions, social and ecological dimensions, and developed their own critical approaches. Due to the emancipatory approach of Atelier 1, students were encouraged to propose their own architectural scenarios and programs. The chapter presents a selection of the emancipatory design projects, as well as a cross-section of the educational model of Atelier 1 that involves interdisciplinary approaches.

DOI: 10.4018/979-8-3693-2329-8.ch004

INTRODUCTION

Architecture as a challenging discipline in between social and physical sciences, continuously questions and renews its relationship to society, and intends to stimulate change. Critical thinking offers a new path to interrogate and a new ground to build changing practices in the discipline of architecture. In that sense, criticism has been an emerging method in architectural education as well as in architectural theory and design. It leads to new discussions in the field of architectural theory, and enhances multidimensional design thinking and knowledge in architecture. It has a potential to change not only theoretical, but also educational and design methods. Particularly in architectural education, criticism helps to enhance the conceptual process tied to architectural theory. It helps to release from the formal norms and concerns of design which are dominant in the schools of architecture that unfortunately reduce architecture to a form finding process (Uludağ, Güleç, Gerçek Atalay, 2018).

The architectural design studio as being the basis of architectural education is where students first come face to face with the complexities of the discipline, including the combination of cultural and social issues, and the functional relationships to be unraveled between the cultural configuration and technological constraints. They are expected to be able to understand the design problem and develop their own design strategies within a conceptual framework while negotiating programmatic needs and demands. This is the architectural cognition process that paves the way for concept formation in the students' minds. As a part of this process, the critical discussions in the studio help in the formation of thematic concepts that are related to the site, program and environment. This knowledge-based process that finds its expression in the design process may be referred to as a process of 'creativity', and is very much related to the student's cultural and social background, national identity, intellectual background, and other competencies. The richness of this variety in the studio makes the introduction of new methods and educational practices even more challenging. The architectural design studio creates a common ground from which the students explore their own paths to the achievement of creativity and aesthetic decision-making in architectural design.

In the architectural studio, the process of creativity is supported simultaneously by practical and theoretical knowledge. Students are expected to re-conceptualize the theoretical knowledge that they have gained from their theoretical courses, and relate them to the sophisticated production of their design projects. This process is structured by relating it to the academic program of the school, the academic and professional background of the tutors, the academic background of the student, and finally, the technology chosen during education.

Theoretical courses and architectural research are significant components of the architectural curriculum. They broaden the students' understanding of the architectural problem and help them to develop a critical understanding of it. Theoretical knowledge serves as the ground for the comprehension of architecture, and the architectural studio is the only milieu in which this knowledge is integrated with practical knowledge where they can develop a design strategy of their own.

This article provides a cross-section of the design method and approach that was experienced within the scope of the architectural project course in the fall and spring semesters of 2021, under the theme of 'Architecture as an Emancipating Ground' of Atelier 1, which has a unique place in the architectural design education and tradition of Gazi University Faculty of Architecture, and encourages its students with innovative and liberating design approaches. The design approach experienced in Atelier 1, leads the students to justify their designs by opening their minds during the design processes with interactive discussions in theoretical courses, and the aim of the article is to share this approach with architecture

Architecture as an Emancipating Ground

students and tutors on an international platform, and to improve it by discussing in the following processes. Because the architectural design studio involves difficult processes in which students are left alone with complex design problems together with cultural, social, technological, psychological, environmental, social, functional and contextual inputs. By observing students' confusion and difficulties in these processes, Atelier 1 believes that it facilitates the design process by questioning the liberating potential of architecture and architectural education for students in the context of design through its fictional structure, critical thinking and critical design strategies that it experiences in the studio. Successfully transforming this difficult, complex and yet enjoyable design activity into an architectural product, depends on building and managing the architectural design process in a multidimensional way.

Among the schools of architecture, the richness and strength of Gazi University Faculty of Architecture lie in its hosting of different design studios introducing different design strategies and conceptual approaches that aim to encourage students to discover their own design methods.

Briefly, design education at Gazi University is conducted in four phases, with the first phase being the basic design studio, covering the first two semesters of the first year. Basic design education helps students in using their imagination and develops their understanding of architecture. It is the first stage and is where students first encounter architectural knowledge, terminology, and media. In this stage, they learn how to enhance abstract design thinking and conceptualizing during the studio hours. They design abstract models in relation with abstract design concepts and methods such as cutting, subtracting, adding, intersecting, overlapping, etc. These concepts enable the students to find their own ways to be able to design three dimensional relations and intersections in an architectural model. But they mostly do not use their skills of abstract design thinking, conceptualizing and modelling after they complete the basic design studio education, whereas these skills and the basic design knowledge in general lead them to free the design process particularly from the reductive programmatic and contextualistic constraints, and think this process more freely and emancipatory.

The second phase covering the first semester of second-grade students, has a threshold quality, and aims to instil in students an awareness of architectonics, the problems of small-scale buildings, the natural and cultural context and user requirements.

The third and fourth phases of design education continue with vertically structured studios. In the design studios, the tutors, who have experienced in the field of theoretical sciences (academic praxis), applied sciences (interdisciplinary praxis), and design applications (professional praxis), come together with students from a range of different grades (Caglar, Uludag, 2014), creating an interactive, dynamic and productive medium both for the students and for the academicians. So, a good synergy is created by bringing together second-, third- and fourth-grade students. Each studio follows a different educational and conceptual approach, with projects characterized by programmatic complexity requiring technical research and innovation such as for large-span structures, building control systems, buildings with acoustic concerns, etc., and unique design strategies, and serves also for the development of environmental consciousness in the students.

The unique conceptual approach of Atelier 1 focuses on the development of critical concepts related to the conceptualization and organization of social spaces. We motivate students to discover their own design methods based on their understanding of different lifestyle patterns, cultural diversity, traditions, beliefs and values – in short, all tangible and intangible values – supported by discussions of conceptual, perceptual and cognitive issues in the studio.

During the design process, we are always in search of new approaches to design and new methods of abstraction that manifest in art, as well as new techniques of representation in our explorations of different ways of communication in architecture (Uludag, 2016). So, we actually try to enhance the abstract thinking, designing and conceptualizing skills of the students which they already developed in the basic design studio. We believe that they need to use the abstracting skills also in the next studios to design their projects in an emancipatory and interdisciplinary way. That's why; we adopt tools and methods in an interdisciplinary field that eventually leads us to focus on the concept of emancipation in the fall and spring semesters of 2020–2021, during the pandemic and the associated lockdowns (Figure 1).

Figure 1. Screenshot from online studio critics during the pandemic in 2021. With contributions of invited tutor Hakan Evkaya – an award-winning professional architect who graduated from the Department of Architecture of Gazi University and Inst. Barış Yaglı from the Department of Architecture of Middle East Technical University.

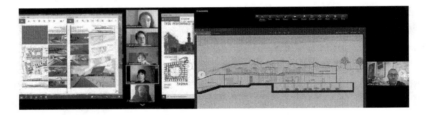

THE CONCEPT OF EMANCIPATION

The concept of emancipation has been defined in many ways and from many perspectives since the times of the ancient philosophers, however it is generally defined as an idea or activity that is free from restraint, control, or power. In one sense, humans can be considered emancipatory beings only in their minds, which implies a mental emancipation process (Nancy, 2006), while others suggest that emancipation is more than a mere idea, being rather an activity (Arendt, 2012). The opportunities for emancipation in the mental and real world have been broadly discussed in the field of philosophy, although these discussions have significance also for other fields, and particularly for art and architecture, which have been in search of emancipation throughout their histories. This search is about being freed from the restrictions of materiality, functionality, technology, society, history, politics and economy for the sake of creativity, and while this may be possible for art, which needs to be neither ethical nor functional in any case, it is certainly impossible for architecture to find an entirely emancipating ground, either in design or in production. It is not only the programmatic demands that architects have to understand and negotiate, but also technological requirements, rules and regulations, building and climate control systems, sustainability issues and ergonomic problems. Despite these constraints, architects strive to be creative and innovative in this discipline.

With this in mind, we ask our students how they can conceptualize architecture on an 'emancipating ground'. By changing their points of view, releasing them from programmatic constraints, using unconventional design tools or by introducing different presentation techniques?

Just as art, architecture also seeks to produce order out of chaos. The principles of art help architecture not to portray, but to evoke the ideas lost within the chaos of daily life. Hence, it focuses on the abstract world of art to realize the truth. In this regard, architecture is about combining the rational and the irrational (Uludag, 2016), although it is challenging for architects to design an emancipatory space when there are so many worldly restrictions and responsibilities.

So, Then, What is Emancipation?

As mentioned above, the concept of emancipation has been defined and discussed in many ways in the discipline of architecture. Akcan discusses this concept by relating it with the emancipatory design process. She suggests that emancipatory is basically evoking the concept of autonomy. For her, architecture creates emancipatory designs, if it becomes an autonomous field emancipated itself from formal and functional facts. She also suggests that such an autonomy is impossible for the disciplinary field of architecture, since this field mainly depends on facts. These are formal, functional, technological, political, social and financial facts which eventually create architectural designs. She thus claims that architecture is a relatively autonomous field that can, at least, emancipate itself from the architects' desires, fantasies or ideologies. But it cannot be an absolutely autonomous field as art (Akcan, 1994). However, emancipation was frequently identified with modern architecture being practiced as an interdisciplinary field of art and design in the 20th century. It is discussed that modern architects emancipated architecture from its norms and traditions. That said, emancipation was only restricted by material and structural technologies in modern architecture (Tanyeli, 2017). Technological restrictions are almost irrelevant within the context of the post-, neo- or super-modern architecture of the 21st century. As such, emancipation is re-defined in line with the developments in technology, particularly in the computer technology. Computers present architects an emancipatory ground where almost everything is imaginable and designable. Architectural images are even more emancipative and seductive in this century, so it is argued that the main controlling system in today's society is not suppression, but seduction (Bauman, 2015). Images seduce humans and transform them into consumers – or 'consumans' according to the theory of consumer society (Baudrillard, 1998). Nonetheless, architecture is neither an object for consumption nor a seductive image, being rather spatial and experiential, as well as visual and imaginal. This is the critical fact that should be conceived not only in the field of architectural design, but also in the field of architectural education.

EMANCIPATORY ARCHITECTURAL DESIGNS OF ATELIER 1

Atelier 1 as a critical studio in Gazi University Faculty of Architecture Department of Architecture, encourages students to think and design critically. You can find some of our publications in the International Journal of Art and Design Education (IJADE) that are explaining the critical design approach adopted and internalized in Atelier 1 since the year of 2014 in which the design studio was re-structured by the tutors. We, as the tutors, designed various architectural projects with our students under the main theme of the studio defined as 'City as a Critical Ground'. This theme led us to criticize urban ground within the interdisciplinary theoretical field of architecture. Atelier 1 studied with the second, third- and fourth-year undergraduate students, re-interpreted and re-designed the urban ground of Ankara with a critical approach to reveal its unique identities and implicit values. Ground accepted as the main critical material in the design process, was criticized not only in its physical sense, but also its social, cultural, political, economic, technological and even psychological aspects. The students were able to discover their own design methods from their criticisms of the urban ground, which also allowed them to determine their sites and programs. In this way, Atelier 1 promoted freedom and flexibility as well as criticality in the design process, and pointed out that the relationship of architecture with city, ground and criticism should be discussed from a new theoretical perspective, particularly in the architectural design studio as being the basis of architectural education. Atelier 1, as a theory-based architectural design studio, motivated the students to develop a critical approach to the urban ground of Ankara so as to replace the rising formalism with criticism in architecture (Uludağ, Güleç, 2018). However, the main theme of the atelier was re-defined as 'Architecture as an Emancipating Ground' for the fall and spring semesters of 2021. We critically discussed the possibilities and potentials of designing an emancipative space under this theme, and these critical discussions were enhanced by online seminars, juries, workshops and collaborations.

The critical discussions on the theme of 'Architecture as an Emancipating Ground' established a ground from which we made a deep search of the anarchist designs of Gordon Matta-Clark, who adopted such methods as destructing, cutting, and splitting to reveal the potential of existing space and building, and creating huge voids throughout buildings by destructing. It is called an-architecture (anarchist + architecture) or anti-architecture, since it rather promotes destruction than construction in architecture (Bal, 2017; Can, 2017). It inspired us to use some specific architectural methods to design an emancipative space and structure.

We discussed the concept of emancipation in the studio both as an idea and an activity, as it has been discussed in philosophy. Students were free to design the activities and functions of their architectural projects, and find their own design methods and concepts. They worked on different areas and activities for the design of emancipatory spaces, and determine the problems and potentials of those areas, seeking to enhance them through emancipatory spatial, structural, and functional relations. We adopted a specific design process in Atelier 1 so as to lead students to design emancipative spaces and structures. At the beginning of this process, students designed abstract models as they usually designed and practiced in the basic design studio, by using methods discovered during the thematic readings and discussions including such processes as destructing, deforming, metamorphosing, carving, overlapping, superposing, articulating, intersecting, integrating, etc. (Figures 2, 4, and 6). They made use of these methods and models as three-dimensional tools for the design of emancipative spaces and spatial experiences (Figures 3, 5, and 7). We did not only motivate them to develop their designs spatially, structurally, and experientially, but also conceptually, methodologically and critically (Figures 8, 9, and 10), in the studio process through which they understood that our main concern was not designing a seductive architectural image; instead, this process was involving to propose critical concepts and methods served to contextualize the design projects.

Figure 2. M3022 Beyza Demircan, Abstract Poster, 2020-21

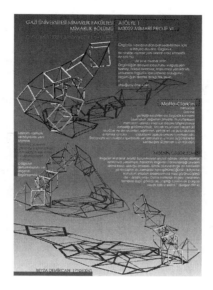

Methods: Deforming, Overlapping, Superposing, Articulating

Beyza criticized the concept of prototyping in architecture. While developing this criticism, she was inspired by Gordon-Matta Clark's criticism of prototyping. The intellectual production that emerged by combining Clark and Beyza's criticism, was reflected in the abstract model, as the breaking of prototyping with new borders that were created by exceeding the boundaries. Through this abstract model, Beyza emancipated the image, or shadow of the object from the object itself. She photographed the architectural object created out of deformed, overlapped, superposed and articulated cubes, from diverse angles to reveal that its images were very different, even though the object did not change.

Figure 3. M3022 Beyza Demircan, Final Posters, 2020-21

Methods: Deforming, Overlapping, Superposing, Articulating
Function: Science and Technology Centre
Area: Maltepe, Ankara

While Beyza was designing her abstract model in line with her critical approach to prototyping, she made a research on the possible design methods, which were suitable for her criticism so that her model could transcend prototyping and imply liberation. As a result of her research, she discovered the design methods of deforming, overlapping, superposing and articulating. She designed a similar building image to the one captured in the abstract model. The image here showed us the deformed, overlapped, superposed and articulated prismatic spaces and structures spread across the project area in Maltepe, in order to design the Science and Technology Centre of Ankara. Accompanied by the atelier's approach of freeing the students in program design, Beyza argued that prototyping in architecture and uniformity in society could be overcome through more education, science and technology, and she developed her architectural program in this direction. She chose the site as Maltepe-Ankara, a route where high school and university campuses are dense, arguing that the students and all the city-dwellers would benefit from the Science and Technology Centre. The elevational and perspectival views of the centre differed considerably in this project, as the shadows of the abstract model photographed at the beginning of the design process.

Figure 4. M3022 Feyza Gül Ekim, Abstract Poster, 2020–21

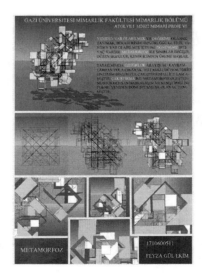

Methods: Metamorphosing, Intersecting, Superposing, Rotating

Feyza created a metamorphic structure in the abstract design process by using the methods of overlapping and intersecting. In this way, she discovered that the boundaries and the shapes of the structure were changing. So, she conceived metamorphosing as a means of breaking free from one's individual, environmental and mental limits. In her abstract model, she developed her critical approach through

Architecture as an Emancipating Ground

grid structures by intersecting and superposing them rotationally. The rigid form of the grid structure was therefore metamorphosed by creating an emancipatory formal entity.

Figure 5. M3022 Feyza Gül Ekim, Final Posters, 2020–21

Methods: Metamorphosing, Intersecting, Superposing, Rotating
Function: Social and Educational Centre for Children with Down Syndrome
Area: Sorgun, Yozgat

Feyza argued that individual and environmental boundaries could be overcome, and even people with limited mental and physical levels could be liberated through education, and she designed the Social and Educational Centre for Children with Down Syndrome by using the methods of metamorphosing, intersecting, superposing and rotating, which she discovered in the abstract model process. Since we were in the pandemic conditions and online education period, Feyza chose Sorgun in Yozgat as the site of her design project, where there is a lack of structures with such functions for people with Down Syndrome. As in her abstract model, she proposed a metamorphic structure for a new social and educational centre in Sorgun designed specifically for the children with Down Syndrome, so as to integrate them with the city and society. The social and educational spaces within the structure were rotated, intersected and superposed to reflect the main design idea defined as integrity.

Figure 6. M3022 Saranda Pelingu, Abstract Poster, 2020–21

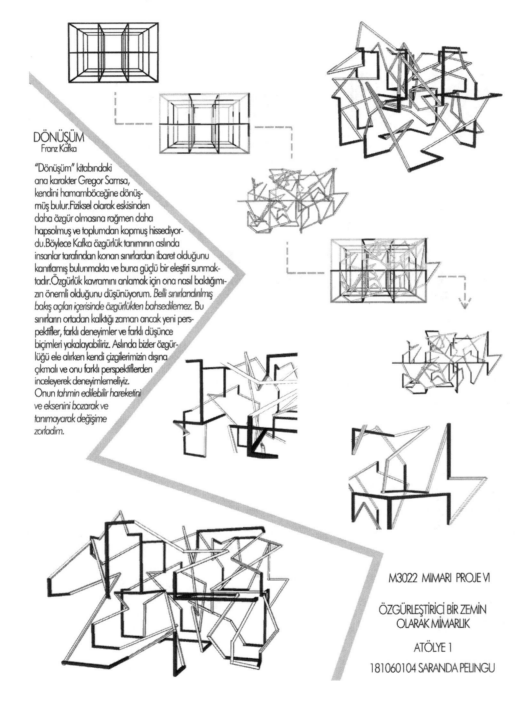

Methods: Metamorphosing, Deforming, Destructing

Inspired by Kafka's novel of 'The Metamorphosis', Saranda argued that what limits freedom in fact was the limited perspectives of individuals. She believed that when these boundaries were eliminated, new perspectives, experiences and systems of thoughts could be developed. While designing the abstract model in line with this critical approach, she interrogated the stable borders of the grids by deforming and destructing them to form an unstable model.

Figure 7. M3022 Saranda Pelingu, Final Posters, 2020–21

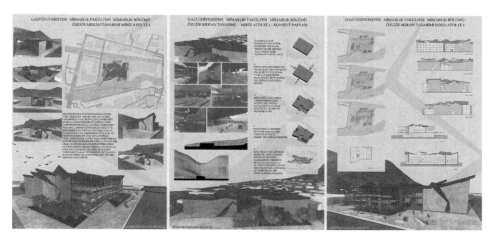

Methods: Metamorphosing, Deforming, Destructing
Function: Contemporary Arts Centre
Area: Kotor, Montenegro

Saranda suggested that when the limited perspectives of individuals were eliminated, the metamorphosis in individuals and the transformation in society would begin in favour of liberation. According to her, one of the powerful tools that could achieve transformation and liberation in society is art. So, she designed the Contemporary Arts Centre with the methods of metamorphosing, deforming and destructing, which she discovered while designing the abstract model project in line with her critical approach. The project site of Kotor is the city that attracts tourists all around the world to her home country of Montenegro. Saranda aimed to reach more people, and enable the Contemporary Arts Centre to be experienced by a wider range of users. She focused on her abstract model for the design of a metamorphic structure. This structure was characterised by the metamorphic, deformed and destructed spaces, surfaces and roof plates. It was contextualized in Kotor particularly by these characteristic roof plates, which imitate both the silhouettes of the mountains and the buildings in the site of the project. In this way, she created a new building silhouette for the new Contemporary Art Centre located in Montenegro.

However, the site of the final projects was chosen by collaborating with the tutors of Ondokuz Mayıs University Faculty of Architecture in Samsun. The site is one of the historically important urban spaces which is very close to the city of Samsun located in the Black See district of Turkey. The students studying in this site were also free to design their projects programmatically, but the main theme was determined as 'A Cultural Hub for Merzifon' by the tutors in Gazi University Faculty of Architecture and Ondokuz Mayıs University Faculty of Architecture. In this context, they designed a cultural hub relating to their critical discourses and approaches to the daily life practices in Merzifon. The students in the final project course were not responsible for designing an abstract model at the beginning of the process. They designed the project site and program according to their critical approaches.

Figure 8. ARCH4022 Rumeysa Çelik, Final Posters, 2020–21

Methods: Layering, Integrating, Intersecting
Function: CULTURAL HUB: Agricultural and Social Centre
Area: Merzifon, Amasya

Rumeysa critically discussed the limited freedom in the public life of Merzifon, and she proposed to design more open and flexible spaces that could enhance public gatherings and sharings in the city. She designed an agricultural and social centre in Merzifon, where one of the main sources of income was agriculture. By dealing with the possible scenario of the future that the agricultural continuity would be disrupted, she focused on the freedom of the public spaces, and sought agricultural continuity in the program of CULTURAL HUB: Agricultural and Social Centre. She designed her project by using the common lines and axes that she discovered during the design process. And she discussed that agriculture constitutes a common ground in the city. The centre was therefore designed by her as a structure of integrated and intersected lines and layers, evoking the social and historical layers of the city, and the integration of the agricultural activity to the city.

Figure 9. ARCH4022 İrem Sütçü, Final Posters, 2020–21

Methods: Deforming, Elevating, Intersecting, Integrating
Function: CULTURAL HUB: Performance Arts Center
Area: Merzifon, Amasya

İrem sought freedom by criticizing the unique historical and social structure of Merzifon. According to her, Merzifon needed a threshold space where people could practice their daily lives in a different way, and engage in the new public activities in the city. In this context, İrem designed the architectural program as CULTURAL HUB: Performance Arts Centre by which people could encounter and come together, engage in the art and performative activities freely. She proposed a singular building structure in her final project that was deformed and elevated to represent the unique historical and social structure of Merzifon. She actually designed this structure by influencing from the diverse migrations throughout the history of the city. İrem elevated the deformed structure to create an area of intersection and integration in the city. This open area was connected to the other open areas, halls and the huge amphi-space of the performance arts centre. It was discussed through the project that the building structure was itself a performer depending on its creative formal and functional character, which was explicitly in contrast to the historical urban structure of the city centre.

Figure 10. ARCH4022 Hatice Arslanoğlu, Final Posters, 2020–21

Methods: Intersecting, Interacting, Landscaping
Function: CULTURAL HUB: Urban Gardens
Area: Merzifon, Amasya

Hatice discussed freedom in terms of designing multi-purpose spaces where people of all ages, genders and socio-economic levels could find a space for themselves according to their daily needs and routines. Since it was challenging to design such a multi-purpose complex on the scale of a small district as Merzifon, she declared that one of the possible ways to bring people together at this scale was creating agricultural and green areas in this district. In her final project, she designed a structure characterised with urban gardens, agricultural and open spaces for all people. These spaces were critically discussed by Hatice as the manifestation of the agricultural activities in the city, and they would serve to motivate the public to cultivate and be a part of this activity. She therefore considered urban gardens and terraces as the open spaces for enhancing the intersections and interactions of people in the city. So, the project was actually a huge landscape mostly reserved for the agricultural activities in the city.

The critical design approach of Atelier 1 and its main design theme of emancipation adopted in the 2020-21 academic year encouraged the students to think in an alternative way, and to explore the critical concepts and strategies during the design process. By this approach, Atelier 1 focused on the liberating potential of architecture and architectural education. As the tutors of the atelier, what we experienced in this process is that giving the opportunity to the students to make a research on diverse disciplinary fields particularly such as art and philosophy, were freeing them from the conventional norms, restrictions and obligations in architecture. They were able to design their projects without being restricted to design a building form with the ordinary spatial and sectional organizations of the ordinary buildings such as multi-storey apartment blocks. They were free to design emancipatory structures criticized and characterized by presenting new spatial experiences to the users. That's why; they were also free to design the programmatic needs and limits to design innovative, creative and emancipative spatial relations. The abstract models and practices at the beginning of the semesters paved the way for the students to discover their own critical concepts and methods that would eventually been used as the design tools in their architectural projects. It was important for us to develop the reciprocal relations between the abstract models and the final models in the projects. But it could not be a physical relation; instead, it could be a non-physical relation, that means a conceptual and critical relation as well.

In this context, we believe that what distinguishes Atelier 1's design approach from the other design studios is that it instrumentalizes criticism in the design process. This method allows students to realize abstract design models in line with their criticisms of the main theme, to discover the design concepts and methods at this stage, and to develop the site and the site-specific architectural program at the stage of the architectural project. So, Atelier 1's students do not follow a form-finding process in the studio; they learn to enhance the process not only formally but also critically, conceptually and methodologically. This is the unique design approach adopted both by the tutors and students of the atelier since the year of 2014.

IN LIEU OF CONCLUSION

As discussed throughout the article, Atelier 1 as an architectural design studio promotes a critical design approach in the field of architectural education. Criticality leads the atelier to develop its approach within an interdisciplinary field including the fields of art and philosophy that paves the way for the concept of criticism to be discussed in a broader theoretical framework in architecture. Through the interdisciplinary discussions and readings in the design studio, the students engage in critical thinking, and put forward their critical approaches both for problem-solving and decision-making. Discussing the concept of emancipation in an interdisciplinary field has helped us to develop criteria from the other disciplines, taking into account, for example, philosophical approaches, social issues, ecological aspects and new technical achievements.

In this process, the inclusion of information technologies in the studio is of prime importance. Instead of providing students with technological knowledge related to the representation of architecture or the exchange of information, we give importance to expanding the limits of creativity learned and enhanced with the aid of technology. Hence, the education model of Atelier 1 is based on interdisciplinary approaches, digital technologies and social and cultural networking. The invited professional guests from different fields of art and architecture give added colour to the studio. During the days of lockdown, the richness of the invited quests including architects, artists, social scientists and engineers, supported the studio drawing upon the benefits of online communications. The students were able to benefit from the critics of different experts and develop different methodological approaches. Each student laid their own unique methodological path leading to a unique project, developing two- and three-dimensional investigations. They developed a critical approach to the concept of emancipation after the theoretical discussions, abstract design practices and workshop exercises, and decided how, and to what extent, they could free themselves from the architectural restrictions. They also came to understand what aspects of the design process are negotiable.

To conclude, we can say that Atelier 1 provides the students with the opportunity to understand and find their own design methods and approaches based on their experiences. Moreover, they learn how to design in a theory-based architectural studio and to be a part of the theoretical discussions. We believe this alternative educational model would pave way for them to develop their own professional identities in the future.

CONFLICTS OF INTEREST

The authors declare that there is no conflict of interest regarding the publication of this article.

REFERENCES

Akcan, E. (1994). Sanatın ve mimarlığın göreli özerkliği / özgürlüğü üzerine. *Mimarlık*, 257, 21–22.

Arendt, H. (1961). *Between past and present*. The Viking Press.

Bal, B. (2017). Gordon Matta-Clark'ın kadavralarında mimari tanı[mlama]lar. *XXI, 2*. https://xxi.com.tr/i/gordon-matta-clarkin-kadavralarinda-mimari-tanimlamalar

Baudrillard, J. (1998). *The Consumer society*. SAGE Publications.

Bauman, Z. (1988). *Freedom*. University of Minnesota Press.

Caglar, N., & Uludag, Z. (2004). Vertically structured design studio: Developing critical concepts on conceptualization and organization of social space in urban context. In S. Constantin & M. Voyatzaki (Eds.), *Monitoring architectural design education in European schools of architecture* (pp. 211-223). EAAE Transactions on Architectural Education Series.

Can, A. (2017). Gordon Matta-Clark. *Manifold, 8*. https://manifold.press/gordon-matta-clark

Nancy, J. L. (1993). *The Experience of freedom*. Stanford University Press.

Tanyeli, U. (2017). *Yıkarak yapmak: Anarşist bir mimarlık kuramı için altlık*. Metis Yayınları.

Uludağ, Z. (2016). Re-Thinking art and architecture: An Interdisciplinary experience. In Uludağ, Z., & Güleç, G. (Eds.), *Rethinking art & architecture: A Challenging interdisciplinary ground* (pp. 2–11). Nobel Academic Press.

Uludağ, Z., & Güleç, G. (2018). Reinterpreting city as a critical ground in atelier 1 projects: Some prospects and projections on Ankara. [IJADE]. *International Journal of Art & Design Education*, 37(3), 413–425. 10.1111/jade.12144

Uludağ, Z., Güleç, G., & Gerçek Atalay, N. (2018). *Criticism as a Design Method in Architectural Education: Criticizing City and Culture in Atelier 1. Architectural episodes 01: Educational pursuits and experiences*. İstanbul Kültür University Publications.

Chapter 5
Learning by Doing at the Sapienza University of Rome:
The Technological Design Studios' Experiences Applied to Housing

Eliana Cangelli
https://orcid.org/0000-0003-0736-2488
Sapienza University of Rome, Italy

ABSTRACT

This chapter presents the Design Studios (DS) teaching method in technological and environmental design, applied in undergraduate and postgraduate courses in architecture at Sapienza University of Rome. Design Studios focuses on a comprehensive approach to the environmental sustainability of the architectural design process in the field of public social housing construction. Based on the teaching experiences, the chapter reports evidence of the teaching methods used for the design proposals submitted by the students of the different DSs for the regeneration of Rome's suburbs. Based on the results obtained, this approach could be seen as a way to develop students' ability to manage the project according to environmental sustainability criteria, from the initial analysis phase to the choice of construction techniques and materials. The article aims to contribute to a disciplinary approach that trains students to become competent architects to chapter contemporary issues of ecological transition, housing shortage, and suburban regeneration.

INTRODUCTION: ENVIRONMENTAL DESIGN APPROACH TO THE DSS

Architectural technology is a fundamental subject in the training of architects in Italy. It aims to equip students with the skills required for constructing architecture. This is done by examining the regulatory context within which the construction process takes place, and by imparting knowledge of building techniques and materials. In the first two years of their architectural studies, students take theoretical

DOI: doi

courses that teach them about construction systems, building components, and materials. These courses provide a basic understanding of the construction process.

In the third year of their studies, students take a Technological Design Studio, where they apply the theoretical knowledge gained from previous courses to architectural projects. During their studies, students can have a final Technological Design Study, which allows them to further apply their knowledge of architectural projects from a constructive point of view, and possibly support their final thesis for the achievement of the Master's Degree in Architecture.

Technological DS play a pivotal role in the architect's training. They develop critical thinking skills necessary for making constructive choices that achieve the objectives of the project from both technical and aesthetic perspectives. The design studios delve into the contents of Environmental Design and the Technological Culture of Architecture, areas of knowledge relating to the theoretical principles and operational practices necessary to control the technical and construction aspects of building systems.

The scientific-disciplinary contents of the design studios concern theories, tools, and methods aimed at experimental architecture at different scales. They also cover the evolution of settlement uses, construction and environmental conception, as well as techniques for the transformation and maintenance of the built environment. These design approaches and strategies are useful for balancing the complex relationship between man, environment, and technology.

The primary objective of the design studios is to provide students with the knowledge necessary for the technological and environmental control of the design, construction, and management process of architecture, highlighting the dialectic between the environmental setting of the project, technical choices, and expressive purposes of architecture. Through in-depth analysis and application of methods, tools, and techniques of the "integrated project," students are exposed to a unitary design process capable of managing the many specialisms of contemporary design.

At the end of the DS in Technological Design, students must have acquired the ability to control the project from the initial phase to that of defining the construction solutions concerning the entire life cycle of the building. They must have also refined their basic knowledge, which comes from previous architectural technology courses, useful for understanding the close interdependence between structure and form, matter and figuration, and for governing the relationship between the conceptual and realization activities of architecture according to environmental sustainability criteria.

Over the years, I have coordinated two DSs for Master's Degree in Architecture - the Laboratory of Technological Design (third year) and the Laboratory of Synthesis in Environmental Design (fifth year) - as well as a Laboratory of Technological and Environmental Design in Master's Degree in Architecture – Construction (second year).

The Technological Design Studios that I develop follow a learning-by-doing approach. This means that students acquire the skills of design thinking and apply the design process to projects, making it the most effective way to transfer knowledge. The Studio courses are practice-based, and under the monitoring of the teaching team, students explore a variety of architectural issues. They learn how to control the complexity of the project and solve real-world problems through a highly interdisciplinary learning process of design by research and practice.

To make the project themes more relevant and familiar, I propose real project cases, almost always located in the city of Rome, with the support and discussion of public bodies dealing with land planning. These courses involve teachers from other disciplines such as Systems, Structures, and Estimation.

The courses are programmed with a focus on environmental sustainability in architectural design. It aims to adopt a comprehensive and sustainable design process in the built environment by reducing the ecological footprint of transformations and resource consumption. It also aims to improve the well-being and optimize the indoor and outdoor environmental quality by introducing an interdisciplinary perspective on how the built environment interacts with the natural environment and impacts people and communities.

The courses are designed to prioritize environmental sustainability in architectural design. The objective is to establish a holistic and sustainable design process in the built environment by minimizing the ecological impact of transformations and reducing resource consumption. Additionally, the design process utilised aims to promote well-being and optimize both indoor and outdoor environmental quality by incorporating an interdisciplinary perspective on how the built environment interacts with the natural environment and affects people and communities.

The design approach follows the natural process, taking the ecological cycle as an analogical reference. This process begins with the recycling of any organic material, including water, and applies technologies that interact with the external climatic environment and the internal requirements of users to make interventions more efficient and sustainable. In this regard, the students should emphasize the environmental aspects of the project by focusing on bioclimatic and bioecological factors, technical aspects, eco-compatibility of building materials and life cycle, vegetation and green infrastructure, energy efficiency, use of renewable energy, and reduction of active systems.

The pedagogical approach used to teaching environmental sustainability is based on a European research project called EDUCATE (Altomonte et alt., 2012). The project was coordinated by the University of Nottingham and included partners such as the Sapienza University of Rome, the Architectural Association School of Architecture, the Catholic University of Leuven, the Technical University of Munich, the Seminar of Architecture and Environment - SAMA and the Budapest University of Technology and Economics. The White Paper on Sustainable Architectural Education produced by the project partners (EDUCATE Project Partners, 2012) underlines the importance of design at universities as a means of producing knowledge and exploring the complex relationships between the various aspects involved in modeling the built environment.

By using real design themes, involving local administrations and municipalities, and comparing them with teachers from other disciplines, a real design process can be simulated. In this way, students can critically apply theoretical knowledge about the sustainability of architecture. Using simple climate modeling software such as Ecotect and Envimet or applying the results of environmental analysis to the project areas helps students to understand how buildings and structures interact with the sun, wind and geography of the site. This knowledge can then be critically applied to the project.

It is a "pedagogy based on learning by doing, with investigative "hands-on" coursework given at the same time of delivery of knowledge, can engage students in their learning, instigate passion and enthusiasm for sustainability, and target the sensitization of students towards the development of an architectural language informed by sustainable environmental design" (ibidem, 2012).

HOUSING AS AN EXCELLENT TOPIC FOR DSs

The DSs tackle with the theme of the housing as one of the most crucial themes in architecture and urban design. The current state of housing emergency in Italy and the experience of the pandemic have drawn a renewed attention on this issue and the "home" has emerged again as a central topic of the Italian architectural debate. The communities of suburb neighbourhoods suffered more from the pandemic and are subject to economic and environmental crisis. In this regard, the design projects are mostly based on the intervention in the public social housing, considering both developing new constructions, and recovering of existing housing estates. In the recent years, according to the objectives of Next Generation EU (European Commission, 2020), the focus of DSs is on the regeneration projects in suburbs, and in particular recovery of the large scale Affordable Public Housing estates, built between the 70s and the 90s, in the suburbs of Rome.

These peripheral districts are mostly designed by some of the skilled modernist architects and are characterized by: a predefined urban layout; high population density; different types of buildings (linear, tower, court); allocated large area to public services and open spaces; and built with heavy industrialised techniques that today manifest a significant degradation in terms of performance (Cangelli et al., 2021).

TEACHING AND LEARNING METHODS

Through scientific knowledge of technological and environmental design, the DS provides an introduction to theoretical principles, technological tools and design methods. There are introductory lectures, seminars, tutorials focusing on specific issues. The DSs are organized in a way to bridge theoretical content and practical application of the environmental design in a project work and it is expected that students participate in the live sessions on campus and work in groups.

Students should provide a design proposal for a public affordable housing estate in suburbs of Rome by investigating various social, technological and environmental solutions that help to define a new living model, new typologies consistent with current lifestyles, meanwhile increasing the accommodation capacity of existing buildings. The project work should also propose a new image of peripheral districts, which is integrated and complementary to the city.

According to the theme of the year, the design project can range from a new construction to renewing of existing housing estates. The design work should be developed from the macro-scale of urban design (the relationship between residential buildings and open spaces, and surrounding area), to the micro-scale of specific technological solutions and details. This helps students to understand how the varied scales connect and interrelate with each other.

Lectures

Applying an integrated method of developing the design project, during the DS there are several experts invited from different disciplines and local authorises to participate in lectures and seminars. This helps the students to achieve a comprehensive understanding of how the complexity of project should be managed by integrating various expertise. These are weekly lectures and presentations or online sessions in environmental design, architectural technology, energy efficiency in building, best practices and etc.

Exercise

The project work activity starts with an exercise crucial for understanding the level of knowledge of students and to calibrate subsequent activities.

The exercise includes studying and critiquing a specific case study assigned by the course coordinator and in coherence with the theme of the year. The students redesign the case study highlighting its typological, morphological, technological, structural, bioclimatic, energy and environmental characteristics (Figure 1).

After the completion of the exercise there is an introduction to the theme of the year through seminars and lectures. Then students will start working on the project.

Figure 1. Example of the work that a group of students presented in the classroom for exercise

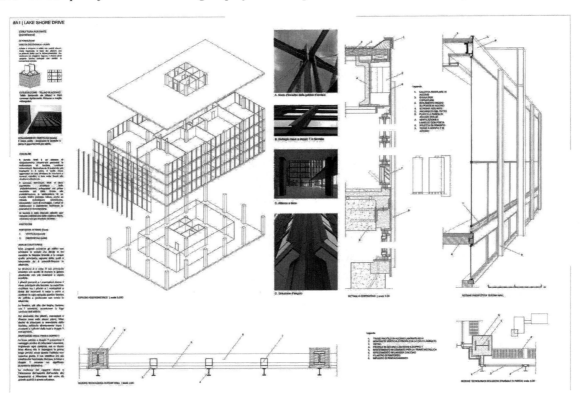

The exercise was elaborated by students Chiara Cristini, Pietro Paolo Di Franco, Chiara Di Giorno in the Laboratory of Technological Design in 2019-2020

Learning by Doing at the Sapienza University of Rome

Site Visit

There is a collective site visit where the students and lecturers attend together with some other actors involved in the project.

The site visit is a crucial activity and provides an opportunity for students to investigate the social and physical characteristics of the project area and match theory with practice. There is also the opportunity to discuss various issues with community inhabitants, social activists and municipality actors.

Project Work and Weekly Tutorials

The project work activity consists of live activities developing the design proposal. The students are divided in groups of three. They are expected to present and discuss group's 'work in progress' in the weekly tutorials, which will be face-to-face sessions.

The teaching method provides a preliminary phase of analysis of the context and a comprehensive understanding of the intervention area. The aim of this phase is to highlight the opportunities, and critical issues from an environmental, social, bioclimatic, morphological, technological, and energy point of view.

The projects vary at different scales from the neighbourhood scale to the single building. Different building typologies like towers, linear residential building, single-family houses, villas are considered. Project design should be developed considering residential buildings and community facilities and surrounding open spaces.

The focus is on creating opportunities for the students to work on a real case study by involving different stakeholders and local authorities from Municipality of Rome in lectures and tutorial sessions and through different phases of project design. This helps students to understand the complexity of issues.

Based on the preliminary analysis, in the next step students should also outline the strategies of interventions.

The project must respond to the following criteria:

- The increase and/or improvement of the housing offer and the quality of living taking into consideration the change in the composition of households and lifestyles over the last thirty years;
- The provision of new collective services capable of increasing the sense of community;
- The redevelopment of public spaces according to criteria that favour their safety, comfort and usability by different age groups;
- The improvement of the technological, energy and environmental performance of buildings by promoting an appropriate use of natural resources and renewable energy.

Students are also encouraged to provide the architectural models during different phases for getting a physical feel for how a design project will develop.

Critiques

During the DS there are different sessions of Critiques and collective discussions. The students publicly present the progress of the project, providing the related design drawings according to a predefined layout. The Critiques help to monitor and review the students' work and comment on group work, giving them a different perspective. They also help the teaching team to coordinate and monitor the progress of the course's objectives.

The DSs Learning Outcomes

The DSs aim at developing the ability of students to control the project (progressing with project design process) from the preliminary phase of analysis to the selection of construction solutions considering the entire life cycle of the building.

By the end of the DSs, it is expected that students will be able to understand the correlation between structure and form, between technological choices and aesthetic of architecture.

The students should also acquire the critical tools to manage the relationship between the conceptual activities and the construction of architecture according to criteria of environmental sustainability.

TECHNOLOGICAL AND ENVIRONMENTAL DSS AND EXAMPLES OF STUDENTS' WORKS

In the following pages, various DSs are introduced with objectives, themes and practices that took place in the past 10 years, dealing with different building typologies and different types of intervention: from construction of new single-family houses to the construction of new social housing, to the refurbishment of large-scale public housing complexes developed between the 60s and 80s in Rome's suburbs (Figure 2).

The selection of objectives and project areas is based on national and local strategies to tackle the urgent housing crisis. The main objective is to create new homes for the disadvantaged population or renovate the existing public residential stock. These objectives have different design themes, each addressing a specific issue. The proposed designs range from constructing new buildings for public housing, which can be used to accommodate a large number of individuals, to redeveloping and densifying living areas built spontaneously by inhabitants without a building permit.

In addition, the construction of new flywheel residential buildings using prefabrication techniques has been proposed. These buildings can be used to temporarily accommodate inhabitants during the renovation period of public houses. Moreover, deep recovery interventions of large public residential buildings carried out in the 1980s have also been proposed. These interventions will aim to improve the existing infrastructure and amenities in the buildings, which will, in turn, improve the living conditions of its inhabitants.

All the proposed project cases are located in areas affected by serious social hardship selected with the goals of trying to provide relief to vulnerable populations and help uplift their living standards. Each of the presented DS has a brief description of the political context and the social objectives of the projects proposed to the students. This information will help the students understand the underlying principles of the proposed designs and their relevance in the given context.

Figure 2. The location of DSs' case studies in the city of Rome

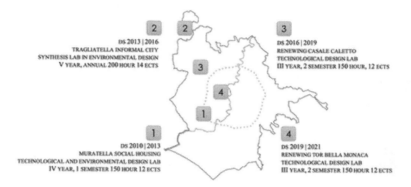

Laboratory of Technological and Environmental Design[1]

The focus of this DS was on the regeneration of abandoned areas and the construction of social housing complexes. Through an applied experimentation to a specific case study, the students investigated various social, technological and environmental solutions for defining a new affordable residential building and improving the image of residential district in suburbs.

Theme of DS: Urban Regeneration of Abandoned Areas Through Development of New Social Housing

The site is located in *Collina Muratella*, in the XI Municipality in the western outskirts of Rome. The intervention should be developed through a new social housing project in accordance with the development plan of the former Alitalia complex (piano di assetto del complesso ex Alitalia). The project should also follow the environmental, social and economic sustainability criteria, as part of the *Millennium Project* developed by Richard Rogers.

In this DS, the students developed a design proposal for the construction of one or more buildings with linear typology for social housing use. The design project was articulated from masterplan to construction details.

In the project work a particular attention put on the energy efficiency of the buildings and choosing the materials and technologies that increase the life span of buildings aiming at minimizing the construction costs (Figure 3).

The design project should include community services for enhancing liveability of the residential area. The student should also provide a proposal for open spaces which should be able to guarantee the landscape continuity, in order to reorganize the different levels of belonging to the place - from public to private and vice versa - without creating any barriers.

Figure 3. In the design project particular attention has been put on the energy efficiency of the buildings

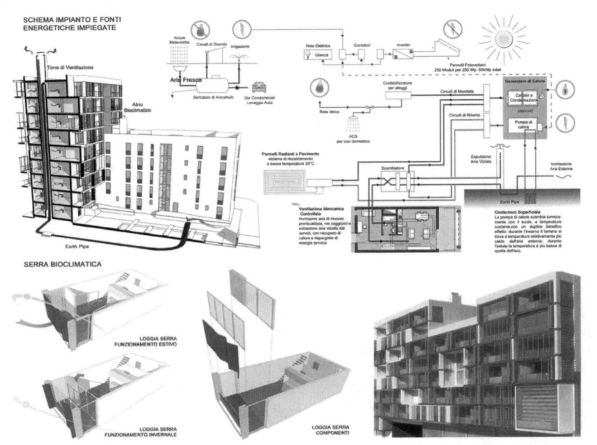

Students: Viola Albino, Francesco Antinori, Michele Conteduca

The design theme proposed was part of a political moment in which the Italian State implemented new policies for building public houses, in response to the previous regulations that had led to a significant public housing stock from the second post-war to the end of '90. The new social housing law mandated that private companies participate in constructing homes for the underprivileged segments of society. This was achieved by granting these companies tax breaks and volume bonuses, allowing them to build more square meters than the planning instruments had originally foreseen. As a result, new public residential buildings were constructed to cater to the housing needs of disadvantaged communities.

Despite the government's efforts, these policies were not widely implemented due to various reasons such as lack of interest from private companies, bureaucratic hurdles, and other socio-economic factors. Over time, the government shifted its focus to redeveloping existing public housing assets instead of building new ones. The main advantage of this approach was that it allowed for the optimization of existing land resources while catering to the housing needs of disadvantaged communities. Overall, the government's approach to public housing has undergone significant changes over the years, reflecting the country's evolving socio-economic conditions and political priorities.

Learning by Doing at the Sapienza University of Rome

Laboratory of Synthesis in Environmental Design[2]

This DS addressed to the issue of regeneration of peripheral areas of Rome. The informal suburban and the urban fabrics with spontaneous growth areas due to their fragmented urban textures were identified as potential for practical learning activities. It aimed at densification and completing degraded and fragmented urban fabrics and enhancement of buildings in terms of technological and environmental point of view (Cangelli, 2018). Through an experimentation applied to a specific case study, the students were asked to provide a design proposal for enhancing the urban fabric performance through different technological and environmental solutions. Not focusing only on formal aspects, but also physical and plant engineering, especially from an energy point of view.

The students who participated in this Design Studio are in their final year of Architectural studies and have already completed the Technological Design Studio in their third year. Therefore, they have already developed strong skills in design and construction, as well as in urban studies and the history of modern and contemporary architecture.

Theme of the years 2014 – 2015 | 2015 – 2016: Theme: regeneration and recovery of the informal city and spontaneous urban fabric in suburban area of Tragliatella, through densification, technological, energy and environmental enhancement

The goal of the DS is to densify and complete degraded urban fabrics. Specifically, the former "Zone O" and the areas called "Toponimi" have been identified as potential experimentation areas for laboratory activities. The "Toponyms" are areas with high potential for design quality, environmental, social and economic sustainability of urban planning interventions. Due to their fragmentation and notable diffusion within the urban fabric, they lend themselves to the application of urban regeneration strategies that systematize them with the urban fabrics and adjacent portions of Roman countryside.

The toponym that was worked on in the laboratory is Tragliatella [Toponym 19.08][3] located in the north-west suburb of Rome.

During the DS, the students developed urban and building level design solutions for the regeneration of the Tragliatella toponym with the aim of improving the functionality of the urban habitat, the architectural quality of buildings and open spaces, and the energy efficiency and ecological effectiveness of the proposed urban layout. At an urban level, the students worked to define an innovative settlement model that would draw resources for its development from the rural context. The students explored widespread and renewable energy production technologies, innovative methods of economic development linked to the specificities of the context, and solutions for sustainable mobility and management of resources. In the first semester, the students provided an urban and environmental masterplan working in a group of 6.

At the building level, the DS defined the project of a Low T.E.C. housing model as its focus (Low Technology _ Low Energy _ Low Cost) combinable for the completion of the residential fabric of the Tragliatella toponym. The housing model project had to clearly define the architectural and technological character of the new construction interventions, to allow the densification of the area in a non-invasive way and with the clear recognition of the new buildings. The design models were developed according to criteria of social, economic, and environmental sustainability, from the urban scale to that of technological detail. In the second semester they individually designed a Low TEC (Technology Energy Cost) single-family / two-family homes. They should develop the design proposal from the building scale to the architectural detail scale (Figure4).

The objective of the course was to promote the formation of an eco-sustainable community by defining an architectural identity linked to the context. The projects must be developed by meeting the following criteria: designing a building that would make good use of the climatic conditions of the area, following orientation and bioclimatic criteria in placing the building in a sector identified by the teaching staff within the "Tragliatella" implementation plan.

The choice to work on a new building intervention rather than on a characteristic recovery/reuse intervention derived not only from the indications of the executive plan of the Toponym but also from the analysis of Tragliatella as a whole. It is a former abusive nucleus, which therefore insisting on an already compromised territory, with very low architectural quality, but equipped, or in any case in the process of being equipped, with primary urbanization works. For this reason, its completion through its densification seems to constitute the path to effective sustainable urban regeneration that does not involve further land consumption.

The Laboratory's theme in the Tragliata area was supported by both the Department of Urban Transformation of Rome Capital and the Self-Recovery Consortia. Throughout the project, the students engaged in meetings and debates with various individuals. Additionally, public events were held to discuss the project's outcomes on different scales. These events aimed to expose the students to real-world problems and provide them with a better understanding of the professional reality.

The complexity and multiple design objectives assigned to the students are due to the nature of this specific Technological Design Studio. It serves as the basis for the students' degree thesis and is carried out throughout the academic year, spanning two semesters.

Learning by Doing at the Sapienza University of Rome

Figure 4. Design proposal for a Low TEC single-family / two-family homes in Tragliatella

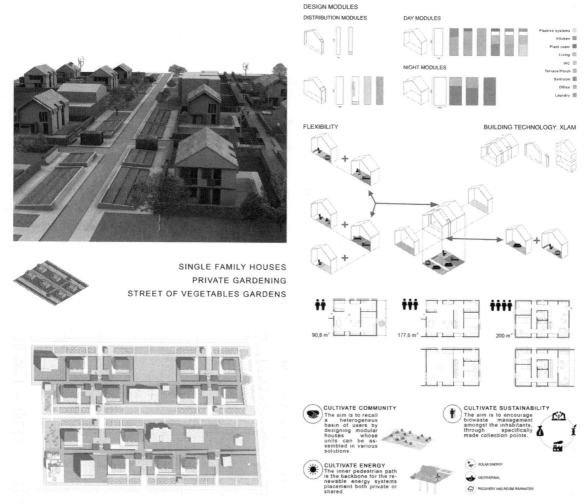

Students: *Michael Emiliano, Vincenzo Guarini, Pasquale Iaconantonio, Valentina Iaquinandi, Antonietta Innella, Fabio Lamanna, Marco Lucci, Giuseppe Lucisano, Giulia Menditto*

Laboratory of Technological Design[4]

This Technological Design Studio is a part of the third year of the study course and focuses on addressing the issue of housing emergency. The main objective of the studio is to recover, transform, and construct new public residential neighborhoods in the Roman hinterland. The students participating in the studio have been experimenting with various design themes to investigate different social, technological, and environmental solutions. Through these experiments, they aim to define a new housing model, new typologies that align with current lifestyles, and increase the number of accommodations in the areas that are part of the design experimentation.

The students attending this Technological Design Studio have already acquired fundamental skills in design and construction, along with knowledge about the urban characteristics of a city and the history of modern and contemporary architecture.

Theme of the years 2018 – 2019 | 2017 – 2018 | 2016 – 2017: recovery of public social housing estates (ERS) through developing new housing project in Casale Caletto

The goal of the design theme proposed from 2017 to 2019 is to densify and complete the fragmented urban fabrics in the small public housing district of *Casale Caletto* in the V Municipality of the eastern outskirts of Rome.

The Casale Caletto neighborhood, which was mostly built with public housing, presents an opportunity to densify, recover, and requalify the architecture and energy of its buildings. This is due to its nature as a socially-intervened area and the dense network of multi-scalar relationships it possesses, which involves different thematic areas within the same complex. The aim of the proposed laboratory work is to explore the possibility of densification by working on existing buildings and creating a new building with high functional flexibility. The new building will initially serve as accommodation for the inhabitants during the 'deep retrofitting' process of existing buildings. Afterward, it will serve as a home for new families and collective services. So, the students developed a new linear type building for mix of housing and neighbourhood's services in order to stimulate the regeneration of the existing urban fabrics and enhancing the integrity of the neighbourhood. The design proposals included from the building scale to the architectural details. The students also provided technological solutions for the energy efficiency of the building through the choice of innovative techniques and materials and also integrating solar shading, improving of lighting access (Figure 5).

Learning by Doing at the Sapienza University of Rome

Figure 5. Example of the design proposal for new linear type building for mix of housing and community facilities in the Casale Caletto

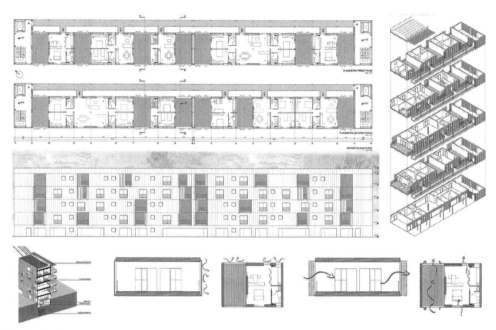

Student: Valentina De Caro

This project involves the densification, redevelopment, and energy retrofitting of the residential complex. It will promote an innovative concept of the culture of living and a review of how the neighborhood is enjoyed and used, leading to an evolved concept of functional mix.

The new building will have a simple typological layout and will accommodate approximately 30 minimum accommodations (from 38 to 76 m2) and spaces for collective services. The building will be constructed using light dry construction techniques and prefabricated elements and systems available on the market.

The project aims to investigate the performance implications that can affect the project in its methodological and instrumental contents. It will examine the complex relationship between the construction system, production, and environmental factors to guarantee sustainability requirements. These requirements are determined by the functional organization of physical-spatial variables that define the "internal" structures of the constituent parts and the "external" macro-environmental components that have a direct and significant impact on the quality of living.

The newly constructed building will be configured as a Low TEC (Low Technology _ Low Energy _ Low Cost) housing model. It will complete the residential fabric of the Casale Caletto neighborhood. The design model will be developed according to criteria of social and economic environmental sustainability, from the neighborhood scale to that of technological detail.

The students were given a set of criteria to follow during the design process, which included a bioclimatic approach, flexible and aggregable typological accommodation solutions, the use of prefabricated construction systems with high-performance standards, attention to the life cycle of the building and its associated operating and management costs, optimization of energy efficiency, minimizing indoor and outdoor pollution, water and waste management, use of innovative components, and controlling costs and implementation times. The building design had to be in line with the climatic conditions of Rome.

The decision to construct a new building was made to address the increasing demand for social housing and the need to adapt existing public residential heritage. The building will be located in a public housing district that will undergo extensive redevelopment interventions, including deep retrofitting, which necessitate the movement of residents. By offering accommodation to current inhabitants in the same area, the eviction process can be facilitated, and residents can monitor the progress of the recovery operations of the homes assigned to them.

One of the main challenges of adapting public residential stock in Italy is the difficulty of temporarily relocating residents to different homes due to their fear of losing their accommodation. Once the redevelopment of existing buildings is complete and accommodation is returned to assignees, the homes created for them can be used to accommodate new beneficiaries, thereby increasing the neighborhood's reception capacity. The proposed operation is based on the Lazio Region's Housing Plan, which allows a 30% increase in existing volumes for social housing.

Theme of the years 2019 – 2020 | 2021 – 2022: recovery of residential towers in the public housing estate in the Tor Bella Monaca

The proposed design theme from 2020 to 2022 aims to address the refurbishment of residential towers in the public housing estate of the Tor Bella Monaca neighbourhood. This will be achieved through deep-retrofitting while increasing the accommodation potential of the public residential building (ERS) in the Roman suburbs.

The Tor Bella Monaca neighbourhood was constructed in the 80s in the eastern suburb of Rome as part of the first Plan for Public Housing (PEEP), which was approved in 1964. This plan allowed for the construction of 48 Area Plans and 379,547 rooms to cope with the housing emergency at that time. However, these public housing estates have since become vast and highly degraded urban areas with severe social degradation.

The Tor Bella Monaca district was designed by skilled modernist architects with a predefined urban layout, high population density, different types of buildings (linear, tower, court), and standard square meters intended for services and public spaces. However, the heavy industrialization techniques used at the time have led to significant deterioration in terms of performance.

The regeneration of the M4 sector aims to identify architectural and energy recovery and redevelopment strategies in different areas of the city. The lab will verify the possibility of proceeding with a 'deep retrofit' of the buildings, promoting an innovative culture of living, energy self-sufficiency, and an evolved functional mix for the neighbourhood.

Figure 6. Project works illustrating the intervention strategies

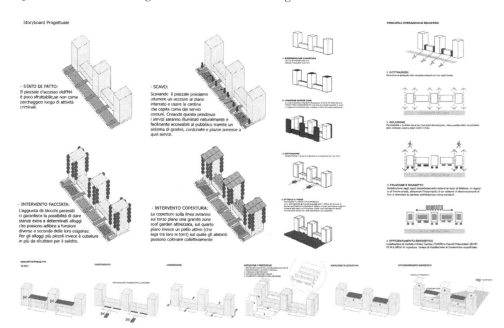

Students: Lisa Elena Costantini, Alessia De Sanctis, Matteo Fanicchia, Alessia Feruglio, Gianmarco Fiaschetti, Gianmarco Di Nucci

The proposed refurbishment project in this DS aims to adapt the apartment layouts based on the contemporary lifestyle and the needs of the inhabitants. Increasing the number of apartments is also an important task that needs to be considered. Students are required to provide solutions for the possibilities of fractioning and reducing the size, rearrangement of the apartment's layout (Figures 7 and 8), and modification of the buildings' skin.

Thus, students should adapt housing cuts and typologies to the current composition of family units and new lifestyles, while also proposing the reorganization of public and semi-public spaces and open areas. They should also design urban services for the neighbourhood and community, and effective and innovative functional mixes.

The proposed technology solutions should prioritize low cost of works, work time control, and inhabitant's ability to occupy the accommodation during the entire redevelopment phase.

Regeneration should increase and/or improve the housing offer and quality of living, provide new collective services, redevelop public spaces, and promote safety, comfort, and usability for all age groups. It should also improve building's technological, energy, and environmental performance by promoting appropriate use of natural resources and proposing innovative methods of energy production.

The theme provides an opportunity to investigate the performance implications that can affect the project methodologically and instrumentally. This includes the complex relationship between the construction system, production, and environmental factors to guarantee sustainability requirements. This involves both the functional organization of physical-spatial variables that define the "internal" structures of the constituent parts, and the "external" macro-environmental components. The design proposals included from the building scale to the architectural details. The students proposed various interventions in the building envelope by adding an external layer or subtracting spaces from the building (Figure 9). These interventions included thermal performance enhancement through the choice of innovative techniques and materials and also integrating solar shading, improving lighting access, and providing external terraces or balconies (Figure 10).

Figure 7. The spatial configuration of a typical housing unit before and after the refurbishment

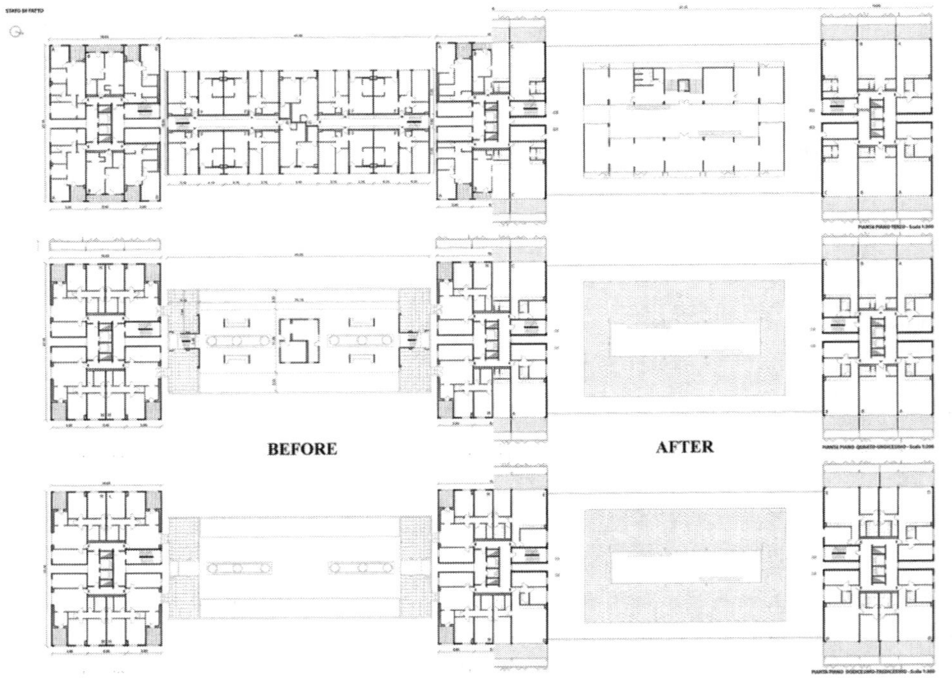

Student: Alessia De Sanctis

Learning by Doing at the Sapienza University of Rome

Figure 8. Reconfiguration of a duplex apartment's layout, inspired by the solution of Le Corbusier's Unité d' habitation

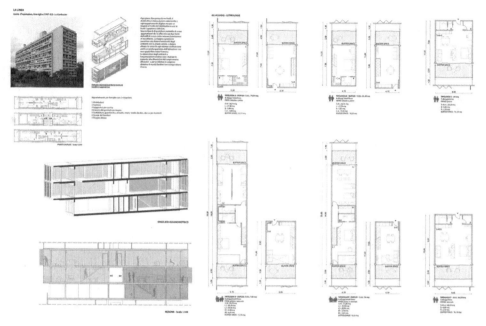

Student: Alessia De Sanctis

Figure 9. Various solutions for building envelope and façade refurbishment. The project was developed by Lisa Elena Costantini.

Figure 10. The technological solutions are developed in detail in a scale of 1:10. The project was developed by students Chiara Cristini, Pietro Paolo Di Franco, Chiara Di Giorno.

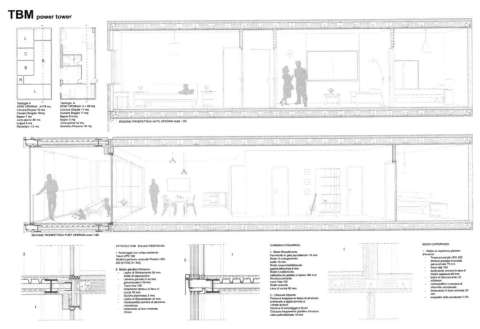

The proposed recovery operation of the Tor Bella Monaca Towers is based on the Law on Urban Regeneration of the Lazio Region. The Municipality of Rome plans to increase the population of Tor Bella in the PdZ Monaca by 284 inhabitants, bringing the population from the current 27,947 with a density of 149 inhabitants/ha to 28,231 inhabitants. This housing need will be localized in interventions to be carried out on surfaces currently intended for public green areas for 7,111 m2.

CONCLUSION

This paper discusses the effectiveness of the Design Studio (DS) approach in engaging students with contemporary issues such as climate change, housing emergencies, and the regeneration of suburbs. The DS approach provides an educational platform for students to gain practical experience in managing multifaceted projects with a focus on environmental sustainability.

Through the DS approach, students can apply theoretical knowledge to real-world projects and create sustainable solutions. The approach serves as an opportunity for students to practice the theoretical contents related to environmental sustainability.

Moreover, the paper highlights the potential replicability of the methodology used for architectural, technological, and energy refurbishment of large-scale public housing complexes developed between the 1970s and 1990s in not just Italy, but across Europe. By using modernist public housing estates as DS case studies, we can propose different ways of improving the image of residential districts in suburbs and present a new integrated and complementary image of peripheral districts to the city.

The paper concludes that the Design Studio approach is an effective educational tool that provides students with the skills and knowledge necessary to address complex issues related to built architecture, architectural technologies and environmental sustainability.

ACKNOWLEDGMENT

General: I am grateful to all of those with whom I have had the pleasure to work during the DSs experiences. I am especially grateful to my colleague Prof. PhD Michele Conteduca and my teaching team, PhD Elnaz Behnam Kia, Arch. Massimiliano Coccia, Arch. Valerio Fonti, Arch. Gabriele Vitiello and PhD Caterina Reccia for their valuable collaboration and contribution to the DSs.

REFERENCES

Altomonte, S., Cadima, P., Yannas, S., De Herde, A., Riemer, H., Cangelli, E., Lopez De Asiain, M., & Horvath, S. (2012) *Educate!Sustainable Environmental Design in Architectural Education and Practice*. Proceedings of PLEA2012 - 28th Conference. Research Gate.

American Institute of Architects (2006). Ecological Literacy in Architecture Education. *COTE Report and Proposal*. AIA.

Cangelli, E. (2018). Work on the informal city. Restoring the environmental balance of cities from their outskirts. *Journal of TECHNE vol. 01 (Special Issue)*, 150-157. FU Press. https://oaj.fupress.net/index.php/techne/article/view/5098/5098

Cangelli, E., Arbizzani, E., Daglio, L., Baratta, A., Ottone, F., & Radogna, D. (2021). *Architettura e Tecnologia per l'Abitare. Upcycling degli edifici ERP di Tor Bella Monaca a Roma*. Santarcangelo di Romagna, Maggioli Editore.

De Graaf, R. (2020). Padroni dell'Universo. *Journal of Domus*, 1042, 9–13.

EDUCATE Project Partners. (2012) *Sustainable Architectural Education*. (White Paper). EDUCATE Press/University of Nottingham.

European Commission. (2020). EU Recovery Instrument Next Generation EU. EC. https://eur-lex.europa.eu/EN/legal-content/summary/eu-recovery-instrument-nextgenerationeu.html

Maldonado, T. (1970). *La speranza progettuale*. Einaudi Torino.

Marvin, S., Luque-Ayala, A., & McFarlane, C. (2016). *Smart Urbanism, Utopian Vision or False Dawn?* Routledge.

Morin, E. (1986). *La Connaissance de la connaissance. Anthropologie de la connaissance* (Vol. 3). Seuil.

ENDNOTES

[1] Laboratorio di Progettazione Tecnologica e Ambientale: Master's Degree in Architecture – Construction, II year | 8 cfu | SSD ICAR/12, 150 hours in the classroom. The course is scheduled for the second semester | starting from October to early January. The theme of Year 2011 – 2012 / 2010 – 2011

[2] Laboratorio di sintesi in Progettazione Ambientale: Master's Degree in Architecture, V year | 14 cfu | SSD ICAR/12, 175 hours in the classroom. The course is scheduled for the first and the second semester | starting from October to early June. Year: 2015-2016 / 2014 - 2015

[3] Tragliatella is a small settlement covering an area of 147.04 hectares, situated on the border between the Municipality of Rome and Anguillara Sabazia. The urban recovery plan for this area aims to add residential buildings on approximately 50% of the available lots, amounting to a total of 400,000 cubic meters or 133,000 square meters. Additionally, the plan proposes the creation of green areas and construction of public service buildings integrated into public green spaces on the outskirts of the area.

[4] Laboratorio di Progettazione Tecnologica: Master's Degree in Architecture, III anno | 12 cfu | SSD ICAR/12, 150 hours in the classroom

Chapter 6
Feeling the Context

Ayşegül İnce
Gazi University, Turkey

Aysu Akalın
Gazi University, Turkey

ABSTRACT

The contextual reasoning of place and subject dialog from a mimetic point of view has been central to this work. The chapter discusses modern mosque architecture, focusing on the studio project of the second-year students. The goal of each student in the design should be to reach the critical moment by seeing and expressing the spiritual feelings of the user in a place of worship. As designers, students are expected to feel the requirements of context by looking through the eyes of the users of the space, and the educators are expected to help this with the methods used. This chapter is written to convey the methodological details of feeling the context which is defined as contextual reasoning. According to the analysis, three different student approaches emerged at the end of the design process. These are inspired interpretation, imitation by partial interpretation, and exact imitation. In summary, the contextual attitudes that students develop by using the domain sources in a mimetic way help students empathically experience the space even at the superficial level of insideness.

INTRODUCTION

Context is a crucial concept in architecture, despite the frequent ambiguity around its use. Because architecture cannot detach itself from its *context,* and because *context* is never the same, it is essential that knowledge and insight be gained. The technique of gaining insight into an environment involves both research into the context of place, and in-depth investigation of the context of the subject, both have tangible and intangible values. The design activity always deals with the unknown and the unknown is discovered through 'visual thinking' which is established mostly through *mimetic* behavior. As Hilde Heynen argues, *mimesis* refers to certain patterns of similarity or resemblance. It has to do with copying, but a specific form of copying that implies a critical moment (Heynen 1999: 6). The goal in design

DOI: doi

should be to reach that critical moment by seeing and expressing the difference between the feelings of the user in a nursing home or the spiritual feelings of the user in a place of worship as the house of God.

According to Zarzar (2008) *mimetic approach* represents transference of specific characteristics from the source to the target object. It involves the transfer of relational information from a domain that already exists in memory (usually referred to as the source or base domain) to the domain to be explained (referred to as the target domain) (Vosniadou and Ortony 1989). In terms of the mimetic approach, a design can be context related (*within domain sources*) or it has its own context (*other domain sources*) which is more likely to be applied somewhere else. In the design process, some of the students would be more likely to relate with the existing context creating strong connection with the place (Özkan and Akalın, 2019a; Özkan and Akalın, 2019b). According to Casakin, mostly the experts relate *between domain sources* which are more difficult to access (Casakin 2004), but when accessed, they are supposed to lead to a successful analogy (Vosniadou and Ortony 1989).

In these within domain and other domain sources, the contextual reasoning of place & subject dialog from a *mimetic* point of view has been central to our work. Both context of place and context of subject might have tangible and intangible values. Throughout architectural design education, students are expected to discover and feel intangible values (*soft data*) as well as tangible values (*hard data*) of the context. As the derivation of the word means "weave together" (Porter, 2004: 30), the spirit of its meaning denotes an interdependence—"weaving" or "knitting" values into existing site conditions and the striving for a sense of fit. In this sense, the design problem faced by the students during the education process can be defined as how tangible and intangible contextual values can be transformed into an architectural product. It is shown that, in both tangible and intangible contextual values of place is mainly based on *deep structures* and *surface features* (Akalın 2018; Özkan and Akalın, 2019a; Özkan and Akalın, 2019b). The tangible *deep structures* cover environment/nature (such as the topography, nature, climate, and the neighbourhood), urban setting, material /construction technique, etc. On the other hand, the tangible *surface features* include object(s) and highlighted item(s) of the settings. The intangible *deep structures* cover historical past /site origin and cultural / human values, while the intangible *surface features* include an event related with the context.

The context of the subject is the core of contextual reasoning. Just as every place may contain different contextual values, every subject also includes tangible and intangible, in other words, perceptual - psychological requirements. When designing, designers have to concentrate both on the concrete requirements (such as hospital beds, supermarket shelves, etc.) and the spiritual requirements of the subject which can only be managed by feelings. Besides, there needs to be a technique of systematic investigation to find out superposed information that might be hidden in the context of place. The non-negotiable and more subjective issues of a place might be awaiting to be discovered.

Owing to the more concrete and subjective aspects of this analysis, the question of how the features of a context may impinge upon a design holds no clear-cut solution. In fact, context analysis requires the evaluation of these phenomenon's that appear independent from each other. This is under the control of the student designer; it is subject to ideas on which he or she has to make a stand (Porter, 2004: 31). Therefore, the main concern of design students is to feel the context in general but getting it to the student should be the main concern of the instructors. While working with our students, our job as instructors is to remind them to be aware of the mysterious existence of the place with both detailed place analysis and subject analysis.

By concentrating Gazi University 2020–2021 / 2nd term the second-year students' studio projects of Atelier Two, Gazi University, this paper discusses the contextual reasoning of the students. A total of 17 students, 10 males and 7 females, took the course in Atelier Two. In this article, the projects of 10 students are included, 7 of them are female and 3 of them are male. Since the design environment and its surroundings are a new residential area, there is no historical cultural background, and intangible values of the place have been almost non-existent. The students were asked to design a modern mosque. The goal of each student was to reach the critical moment by expressing the spiritual feelings of the user in a place of worship. The insideness is at "the superficial level" because the space could not be experienced bodily / haptically, only through the digital screen (online training due to the pandemic). Most of the students were miles away from Ankara and unfortunately, none got a chance to see the design environment. As shown by Özkan Yazgan, & Akalın, (2019b) low place awareness is based on analogy, which is the transposition of the conceptual structures based on tangible/concrete and objective features, and high place awareness is based on abstraction, which is related to mental concepts and actions based on intangible and conceptual/subjective features.

By analyzing a studio process, the paper discusses how second-year architectural students might sense the space in which a "nexus of ideas" (Brook, 2001) captured from the subject to implement into a design process. In this work it is assumed that the students who are inspired by the images, they found could perfectly feel both intangible and tangible values of the context of the subject. On the other hand, those who cannot fully feel the context of the subject and place are more likely to imitate exactly what is given to them and mostly from other domain sources. Despite all the limitations of the pandemic, our role as educators is to help students feel this place and subject mixed contextual reasoning even from a far distance and not experiencing the project site physically. The details of this study are presented below.

TEMPLE IN ISLAM

All religions have their own words, concepts, and understanding of the temple. In Islam, the temple stands out as the place where people worship Allah (Eşmeli, 2018). According to the Quran, the Kaaba, the first temple on earth, is also the first temple of Muslims. The term "masjid" is preferred in the Quran and hadiths to refer to places established for the worship of Allah. The word masjid is derived from the Arabic word "sujud" (   ), which means "to bow down, to put the forehead on the ground with humility," and it translates to "place of prostration" (Önkal and Bozkurt, 1993). Based on the following hadith, it is understood that there is no limitation regarding the location; "...the earth has been made for me clean and a place of worship (masjid)" (Imam Muslim, Sahih Muslim, Vol. 1). In this respect, it can be said that, unlike other divine religions, there is no requirement for a specific 'temple' for worship in Islam. Although one meaning of the masjid is a place of worship without borders, in the Quran, the concept of the masjid is also used to describe a concrete temple site (Hajj, 22/40; Tawbah, 9/18; Tawbah, 9/107). Thus, it can be said that the term masjid signifies both 'a clean place on earth' and a 'temple structure' (İnce, 2021: 11). In fact, Islamic decrees such as recommending daily prayers to be performed in congregation and the requirement to perform Friday and Eid prayers in a congregation necessitated the establishment of a specialized place for Muslims. Since it means a place of prostration, it is possible to associate this place with the act of worship called 'salaah'. In this context, when we associate mosques with the act of salaah, salaah appears as worship performed with standard acts. If there is a standard for a behavior, the space surrounding that behavior must conform to the standard of that behavior and complement it (Cansever, 2010: 17).

In this context, the primary determining factor for mosque construction is 'orientation.' According to Islamic belief, although Allah transcends physical space, the concept of direction is deemed necessary in certain prayers that involve symbolic physical movements. This necessity is rooted in the discipline of worship and the integration of the individual with a spiritual center (Özel, 2002). This direction is referred to as the 'qibla.' The Quran states that every ummah has a qibla to which they turn, and for Muslims, this qibla is the Kaaba (Al-Baqarah, 2/144). Because it is essential to face the qibla during prayer, mosques are constructed so that their qibla walls or the entire building is oriented towards the Kaaba.

The second determining factor in the construction of mosques is the 'row order' of prayer. The term 'row' refers to the proper alignment of the congregation side by side (Öğüt, 2008). Adhering to the row order is obligatory when performing prayers in congregation. Pekdemir (2016) has delineated the key aspects of the row order, considering the words, actions, and approvals of the Prophet Muhammad (pbuh) on this matter;

1. The rows should not be interrupted (Ebû Dâvûd, Salât, 93).
2. The rows should not be crossed (Buhari, Salât, 101).
3. Being in the first row is encouraged (for men). (Buhârî, Ezân, 9; Müslim, Salât, 28).
4. Privacy must be respected in rows (Müslim, Salât, 132).

The issues to be considered regarding the row order have been effective in shaping mosque architecture. Due to the necessity of not interrupting the rows and not passing in front of the praying person, the entrances in mosques are usually given either from the back or from the sides. Regarding the virtue of the first rows, it is known that the width of many mosques is kept longer in order to ensure that more congregations take place in the front rows (Öğüt, 2008) (such as Diyarbakır Grand Mosque (1092), Siirt Grand Mosque (1150), Diyarbakır Silvan Grand Mosque (1157)). If women pray in the same place, the rows should be in the form of men, then children, and then women, respectively (Apaydın, 1998: 273). In the following periods, special places such as women's galleries were built in the main prayer area.

As briefly demonstrated, there are no specific requirements regarding the shape of mosques in Islam. However, certain conditions for congregational prayer have influenced architectural design. Consequently, each society has shaped mosques according to their geographical conditions, needs, and cultures.

THE METHOD USED BY *ATELIER TWO* VIA THE DIGITAL SCREEN

- At the beginning of the term, considering that the second-year students of the project group had deficiencies in the use of any drawing program, external support was received for the Sketchup (educational version) training in the first two weeks. Instructor CCC CCC CCC (PhD candidate supervised by Prof. Dr. GGG GGG) is the person who provided the support all through the semester.
- After the Sketchup training, the history of mosque architecture is given with its conceptual foundations, and the limitations of the context of the subject were introduced. Then the students were asked to design a mosque mass to cover min 1/3 and max 1/2 of the given land.

- After the presentation about the historical process of mosque architecture, examples of modern mosques in Turkey were shown, and examples of modern mosques including applied and proposed competition projects, were introduced to the students. Afterwards, students were asked to bring their favourite modern mosque design image(s) (national or international) and redesign a mosque on the site.
- After the presentations on the subject, the information about the land and its surroundings was shown to the students with videos, pictures, and maps by the article writer, who has been residing in this region since 2015.
- Since the pre-architects had to experience the space through the digital screen, "other domain sources" were adopted as a method to make them feel the context of the subject as well as the sloping context of the site. Thus, the students were asked to bring domain examples that affected them by considering the context of the subject and the place. In the following weeks, they were also requested to bring their domain examples focusing only the use of topography.
- Almost one month after the beginning of the term, students were asked to present their modern mosque design proposals, taking into account the environmental data of the land. Until the students reach this stage; they got to know the context of the land + they learned the essentials by taking the contextual data of the program + they learned how to draw in a digital environment. When these stages were completed, the land was ready in their hands, and they could now use the drawing program quite well. And they even had some ideas about how they could more or less interpret the subject by feeling the context of the place.

ANALYSIS OF THE PROJECTS THROUGH CONTEXTUAL ATTITUDES

When we examined the projects, we encountered three different attitudes of students. These; inspired interpretation, imitation by partial interpretation and exact imitation.

Inspired Interpretation

The students in this group were inspired by the images they found during the semester. These students, who can research, perceive and feel, have chosen to be inspired and interpreted instead of imitating what they see. They felt the spiritual values of the subject very intensely and accepted the place of worship as the house of God, and emphasized this not only with their form, but also with the material, light and scale they used. For them, the qibla wall is not just any orthogonal wall parallel to the Kaaba, but the most basic element interpreted in the plastic of the form. These students, who have overcome the difficulty of modelling the 18 m elevation difference in the topography without being afraid of digital modelling, have a strong sense of not only the context of the subject but also the context of the place. The students paid attention to the value of accessibility in this steep topography by connecting the different levels of the area with shortcut / bypass transitions. These students, who are all female can be described as a self-confident creative group capable of interpreting the tangible values of the place quite well and feeling both the intangible and tangible values of the context of the subject.

Feeling the Context

Figure 1. Student A: a) Fangshan Tangshan National Geopark Museum (URL-1); b) Roosendaal Pavilion Building (URL-2)

Figure 2. Student B: a) Tod's Building (URL-3); b) Bird's Nest (URL-4)

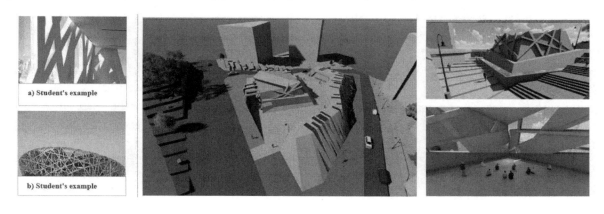

Figure 3. Student C: a) Musée Atelier Audemars Piguet (URL-5); b) (URL-6) c) (URL7)

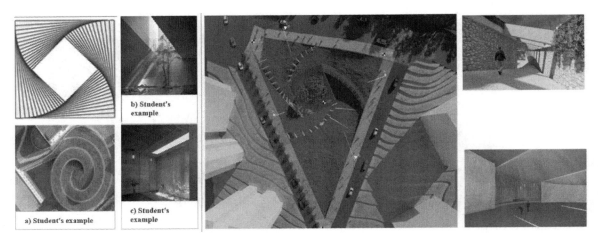

Imitation by Partial Interpretation

Some of the students in this group, consisting of two female and one male, were impressed by the visuals they found or were shown to them during the semester, and they tried to improve their projects by interpreting what they saw and imitating them to some extent. Most of these images were not even religious buildings. The balances between the concern for the contextual data of the place and the spiritual feelings for the context of the subject differ for each student. In the examples below, out-of-context images are partially imitated and interpreted.

Figure 4. Student D: a) Halide Edip Adıvar Complex Competition, 3. Prize (URL-8); b) Halide Edip Adıvar Complex Competition, participant (URL-9)

Feeling the Context

Figure 5. Student E: a) Community Center on Behance (URL-10); b) Centro Clínico Champalimaud (URL-11)

Figure 6. Student F: a) 'Nine Dragon' Housing Complex (URL-12); b) (URL-13)

Exact Imitation

Students in this group, consisting of two male and one female, are generally those who cannot fully feel the context of the subject and place. These students focused on the adaptation of a project to the challenging topography of the area. This project was either proposed by us in parallel with what they wanted to do (although it was undesirable, this was used as a design method during the pandemic so that the students could better feel the context), or a project that they were impressed by the examples shown in the presentations at the beginning of the semester. It would be a mistake to describe these students as unsuccessful, who have difficulties even when adapting them to the land by looking at the visuals. These students were hardworking but had a basic problem of perceiving what they see in general, which prevents them from feeling the context. In general, all the students exemplified below adopted the idea they imitated and tried their best for a perfect delivery. Some of these projects have adapted quite well to their new context. All the student projects below are designed by imitating out-of-context images, which were other domain sources.

Figure 7. Student G: a) Yiwu Cultural Center (URL-17); b) Louvre Abu Dhabi (URL-18)

Figure 8. Student H: a) Gymnasium in Qatar (URL-19)

Figure 9. Student I: a) Idea Competition on Mosque Architecture, participant (URL-20)

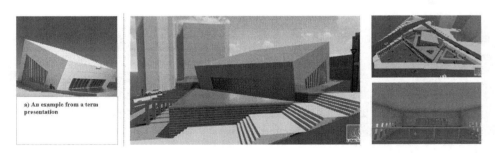

Feeling the Context

Figure 10. Student J: a) Westwerplatte Memorial Museum (URL-21)

DISCUSSION AND CONCLUSION

As Norberg-Schulz defines, the task of architecture is to transform a site into a place, *"to uncover the meanings potentially present in the given environment"* (Norberg-Schulz, 1980, 18). The meanings can be uncovered with the help of *mimetics* and the context of place can be transformed into creative design (Özkan and Akalın, 2019a; Özkan and Akalın, 2019b). The architectural design teaching involves organizing situations that furnish students with experiences in which helpful *mimetics* emerge (Coyne et al., 1994). Thus, *mimesis* can help novices to significantly improve their performance (Casakin and Goldschmidt, 1999) and thinking through mimesis enables them to explain and understand an unknown situation in reference to a familiar one (Ortony, 1993). The *mimetics* used in architectural design studios, however, are rarely concerned with the place awareness[1], which is the main theme of *Atelier Two* where the students are asked to work on different subjects that require different contextual parameters in each semester. Each student is free to choose the advantage of the context to create a strong connection with the place (context related) or create his/her own story regardless of the existing context. Whatever they choose, however, the students are expected to understand the current context of the place where they design and to generate designs that can be integrated with this context.

The challenge of online education is helping the student empathically experience the space through mimetics in a situation where insideness is at a superficial level. According to the results, despite that *insideness*, the students tried to understand contextual possibilities while designing and many of them managed to capture the critical moment by blending contextual values with powerful domain sources in a *mimetic* way. Among the three different contextual approaches of students that emerged at the end of the design process, the students of "inspired interpretation" had a high sense of authentic space and almost never applied the other domain sources. The exact imitation students, on the other hand, heavily resorted to outside domain resource(s), but were able to locate outside domain(s) into its new existence after a lot of hard work and effort made. According to the results, since these students could not bodily experience the place, they ignored some of the values in their designs. For example, only a few students were able to see the large green park area right next to the area as a project data. The other thing is that the more the domain belonged to the student, the more he/she has embraced his/her project.

The information dialogue between the studio educator and student can be listed under the five headings: perception, thinking, analysis, guidance, association. In this dialogue, the educator is the person who questions what, why and how (Uluoğlu, 2000), and her role in the process is limited. As a matter of fact, in the study of Aybek Özdemir and Akalın (2024), who researched the connection between changes in learning styles and the components of creativity, it was revealed that the change in learning styles is related to the level of creativity exhibited in the design process and the final product (Aybek Özdemir and Akalın, 2024). Thus, depending on the subjective qualities such as the perspective, skill, personal background of the student accessing the information, and the information pattern needed in the design problem, the information belonging to the architectural reference is imitated with a new story. Therefore, each outside domain used in the atelier has a new existence and a new story in its new location.

According to some theoreticians, repetitive designs are an activity that encourages creativity and does not obstruct originality. Gilles Deleuze, as one of them, defends the necessity of repetition to achieve perfection and see repetition as an option for difference (Deleuze, 1994). He argues that difference arises through repetition and believes that when we encounter difference, there is repetition here. According to Deleuze, the difference itself is already repetition, and the difference will emerge only through repetitions. What we believe is that difference arises in repetition but only in mutation. This resembles a gene that undergoes repetitions with mutations and through each repetition, it changes and develops.

Future studies can investigate whether there will be a difference in face-to-face education after students are provided with the opportunity to experience the context more deeply, rather than at a superficial level. This deeper experience can be achieved not by visiting the place once, but by visiting it multiple times, across different seasons and at various times in a day.

ACKNOWLEDGMENT

Thanks to Şükran ALPDEMİR for proofreading the article.

CONFLICTS OF INTEREST

The authors declare that there is no conflict of interest regarding the publication of this article.

REFERENCES

Akalın, A. (2018). Architectural Design Education as a Context Related Mimetic Discipline, *Dicle University 1st International Architecture Symposium: From Environment to Space*. Dicle Üniversitesi.

Apaydın, Y. (1998). In *İlmihal: İman ve İbadetler* (v.1). İstanbul: DİVANTAŞ, 273.

Aybek Özdemir, D., & Akalın, A. (2024). Mimetic Teaching Strategy in Design Education: Relationship Between Students' Learning Style and Creativity. *DEPARCH Journal of Design Planning and Aesthetics Research*, 3(1), 24–55. 10.55755/DepArch.2024.26

Brook, I. (2001). In Warwick, F. (Ed.), *Can 'Spirit of Place' Be a Guide to Ethical Building? Ethics and the Built Environment* (pp. 139–151). Routledge.

Cansever, T. (2010). *Kubbeyi Yere Koymamak. İstanbul:Timaş Yayınları*, 17.

Casakin, H. (2004). Assessing the use of metaphors in the design process. *Environment and Planning. B, Planning & Design*, 33(2), 253–268. 10.1068/b3196

Casakin, H., & Goldschmidt, G. (1999). Expertise and the use of visual analogy: Implications for design education. *Design Studies*, 20(2), 153–175. 10.1016/S0142-694X(98)00032-5

Coyne, R., Snodgrass, A., & Martin, D. (1994). Metaphors in the Design Studio. *Journal of Architectural Education*, 48(2), 113–125. 10.1080/10464883.1994.10734630

Deleuze, G. (1994). *Difference and Repetition, Trans*. Columbia University Press.

Eşmeli, İ. (2018). Dinlerde mabed-ibadet ilişkisi (yahudilik örneği). *Pamukkale Üniversitesi İlahiyat Fakültesi Dergisi*, 6(11), 24–43.

Heynen, H. (1999). *Architecture and modernity; a critique*. Massachusetts Institute of Technology Press.

Ince, A. (2021). *Understanding contemporary contextualism: the relationship between designer approach and user perception in sancaklar mosque*. [Master Thesis, Gazi University, Ankara].

Alyn Griffiths (2014). *Hospital for rural chinese community fetureas a ramp that slopes up to the roof*. Dezeen. https://www.dezeen.com/2014/09/29/angdong-rural-hospital-rural-urban-framework-china/

Internet Arkiv. (2012). *Katılımcı (Manço Mimarlık), Şişli Halide Edip Adıvar Külliyesi Ulusal Mimari Proje Yarışması*. Internet Arkiv. https://www.arkiv.com.tr/proje/katilimci-manco-mimarlik-sisli-halide-edip-adivar-kulliyesi-ulusal-mimari-proje-yarismasi/2386?lang=en,

Arkiv. Katılımcı, Cami Mimarisi Üzerine Fikir Projesi Yarışması. Internet Arkiv. https://www.arkiv.com.tr/proje/katilimci-cami-mimarisi-uzerine-fikir-yarismasi-projesi/2380?lang=en, Last accesed: 03.08.2022.

Azzurra Ferraris (2019). *Fantastic Greenhouse Challenge*. URL-6: https://www.cgboost.com/challenges/fantastic-greenhouse-challenge, Last accesed: 03.08.2022.

Christian Richters (2010). *Roosendaal Pavilion*. URL-2: https://www.e-architect.com/holland/roosendaal-pavilion, Last accesed: 03.08.2022.

David Pereira (2011). *More Photographs of Champalimaud Centre for the Unknown.* URL-11: https://www.archdaily.com/147761/more-photographs-of-champalimaud-centre-for-the-unknown-charles-correa-associates, Last accesed: 03.08.2022.

Derya Gursel (2012). 3. Ödül, Halide Edip Adıvar Külliyesi Ulusal Mimari Proje Yarışması. URL-8: https://www.arkitera.com/proje/3-odul-halide-edip-adivar-kulliyesi-ulusal-mimari-proje-yarismasi/, Last accesed: 03.08.2022.

Distance Studio Consultant (2014). *Gymnasium.* URL-19: https://www.behance.net/gallery/69481259/Gymnasium, Last accesed: 03.08.2022.

Gallardo Architects Design Firm (2015). *Beijing National Stadium.* URL-4: http://gallardoarchitects.com/beijing-national-stadium/, Last accesed: 03.08.2022.

Homeworlddesign. *House with Panoramic Ocean View in Okinawa.* URL-7: http://homeworlddesign.com/house-panoramic-ocean-view-okinawa-clair-archi-lab/, Last accesed: 03.08.2022.

Iwan Baan (2020). *Musee Atelier Audemars Piguet.* URL-5: https://www.archdaily.com/938537/atelier-audemars-piguet-museum-big, Last accesed: 03.08.2022.

Market And Music School In Son Servera. URL-14: http://www.matoscastillo.com/index.php?/proyectos/mercado-y-escuela-de-musica-en-son-servera/, Last accesed: 03.08.2022.

Matthieu Gafsou. *Barozzi veiga clad monolithic art museum in lausanne with vertical brick fins.* URL-15: https://www.designboom.com/architecture/barozzi-veiga-mcba-art-museum-lausanne-switzerland-06-14-2019/, Last accesed: 03.08.2022.

Navasa & Partners (2021). Tod's Omotesando Building. URL-3: https://www.archdaily.com/966848/i-am-always-inside-the-architecture-that-i-design-in-conversation-with-toyo-ito?ad_medium=gallery, Last accesed: 03.08.2022.

Odile Decq (2014). *Fangshan Tangshan National Geopark Museum / Studio Odile Decq* [digital image]. URL-1: https://www.archdaily.com/771367/fangshan-tangshan-national-geopark-museum-studio-odile-decq, Last accesed: 03.08.2022.

Özüm İtez (2020). Yiwu Kültür Merkezi. URL 17: https://www.arkitera.com/proje/yiwu-kultur-merkezi/, Last accesed: 03.08.2022.

Pavlo Kryvozub (2012). *Community Center.* URL-10: https://www.behance.net/gallery/5272859/Community-Center, Last accesed: 03.08.2022.

Piotr Zelaznowski. Westerplatte Memorial Museum. URL-21: https://www.behance.net/gallery/25547309/Westerplatte-Memorial-Museum-Gdansk

Roland Halbe. Louvre Abu Dhabi's giant dome creats a 'rain of light'. URL-18: https://thespaces.com/louvre-abu-dhabis-giant-dome-creates-a-rain-of-light/, Last accesed: 03.08.2022.

Theories of Architecture. URL-13: https://kfynm.wordpress.com/2017/09/26/context-vs-building/, Last accesed: 03.08.2022.

Norberg-Schulz, C. (1980). *Genius Loci: Towards a Phenomenology of Architecture.* Rizzoli.

Norberg-Schulz, C. (1996). In Nesbitt, K. (Ed.), *The Phenomenon of Place, Theorizing a New Agenda for Architecture: An Anthology of Architectural Theory 1965-1995* (pp. 414–428). Princeton Architectural Press.

Öğüt, S. (2008). Saf. In *TDV İslâm Ansiklopedisi* (c. 35, s. 435-436). Ankara: TDV İslâm Araştırmaları Merkezi.

Önkal, A. ve Bozkurt, N. (1993). Cami. In *TDV İslâm Ansiklopedisi* (c. 7, s. 46-56). Ankara: TDV İslâm Araştırmaları Merkezi.

Ortony, A. (1993). *Metaphor and thought.* Cambridge University Press. 10.1017/CBO9781139173865

Özel, A. (2002). Kıble. In *TDV İslâm Ansiklopedisi* (c. 25, p. 365-369). Ankara: TDV İslâm Araştırmaları Merkezi.

Özkan Yazgan, E., & Akalın, A. (2019a). Metaphorical reasoning and the design behavior of "pre-architects". *International Journal of Technology and Design Education*, 29(5), 1193–1206. 10.1007/s10798-018-9485-9

Özkan Yazgan, E., & Akalın, A. (2019b). The comprehension of place awareness in a historical context: Metaphors in architectural design education. *METU Journal of The Faculty of Architecture*, 36(1), 183–202. 10.4305/METU.JFA.2019.1.7

Pekdemir, Ş. (2016). In *Fıkhın Cami Mimarisine Etkisi. Çağımızda Cami Mimarisinde Arayışlar Sempozyumu bildiriler kitabı* (p. 187-195). Giresun: Giresun Üniversitesi İslami İlimler Fakültesi Yayinlari.

Porter, T. (2004). *Archispeak: an illustrated guide to architectural terms.* London: Spon Press (an imprint of the Taylor & Francis Group). 10.4324/9780203643150

Uluoğlu, B. (2000). Design knowledge communicated in studio critiques. *Design Studies*, 21(1), 33–58. 10.1016/S0142-694X(99)00002-2

Vosniadou, S., & Ortony, A. (1989). Similarity and analogical reasoning: A synthesis. In Vosniadou, S., & Ortony, A. (Eds.), *Similarity and analogical reasoning* (pp. 1–18). Cambridge University Press.

Zarzar, K. M. (2008). The use of architectural precedents in creative design. In Zarzar, K. M., & Guney, A. (Eds.), *Understanding meaningful environments, architectural precedents and the question of identity in creative design* (pp. 7–21). Delft University Press.

ENDNOTE

[1] This awareness has also been defined as familiarity with "*the spirit (essence) of a place*" by Norberg-Schulz (1996), sometimes also called "*genius loci*" or used for "sensing" place to denote an effort to sensitively come to know the nature of a place.

Chapter 7
The CineArch Method in Architectural Education:
Film Analysis and Filmmaking in the Design Studio

Gul Kacmaz Erk
Queen's University, Belfast, UK

ABSTRACT

This chapter reflects on an innovative design studio at Queen's University Belfast in Northern Ireland that unites architecture and cinema under the umbrella of design through cinematic analysis methods and filmmaking practices. By embracing film analysis and filmmaking as design and learning tools, CineArch studio focuses on questioning and redefining the boundaries of architectural creativity and spatial design. The fusion of cinematic analysis methods and architectural design processes takes a central role in the studio. Students explore methods such as storyboard, montage/collage, cinematic plan/model, poster, and moodPaint to analyse film scenes but also to design buildings, structures, and film sets. In parallel, filmmaking practices, such as concept film, site film, city film, model film, animation as well as AR/VR, are utilised to test and articulate architectural ideas through dynamic audio-visual means. The spatial outcomes of this multidisciplinary collaboration are a series of atmospheric and experiential projects that exceed conventional architectural boundaries.

EMPHASIS OF CINEARCH STUDIO

Architecture is a pragmatic profession that does not shy away from borrowing theories and practices from other disciplines including philosophy, art, culture, design, science, technology, and media. Design tutors have been experimenting with multidisciplinary approaches to promote learning in the studio environment for decades. Though not much has changed since Bauhaus (1919-1933) revolutionised the master-pupil system of Beaux Art a century ago, technological advancements (computer aided design and manufacturing), ecological changes (climate emergency) and communication shifts (from real to virtual, from local to global) have transformed architecture and its education considerably (Salama 1995,

DOI: doi

Pallasmaa 2009 and 2011, ArchNet-IJAR 2010, and, for unusual data analyses, Hettithanthri and Hansen 2022). Architect and writer Juhani Pallasmaa (2009, p. 109) positions the architectural designer as follows:

> Architecture needs to build a better world, and this projection of an idealized human dimension calls for an existential wisdom rather than professional expertise, skill and experience. In fact, a design task is an existential exploration in which the architect's professional knowledge, life experiences, ethical and aesthetic sensibilities, mind and body, eye and hand, as well as his/her entire persona and existential wisdom eventually merge.

Figure 1. Stuart Petticrew, Weddings and Funerals Project, AAD 2021-22, Semester 1

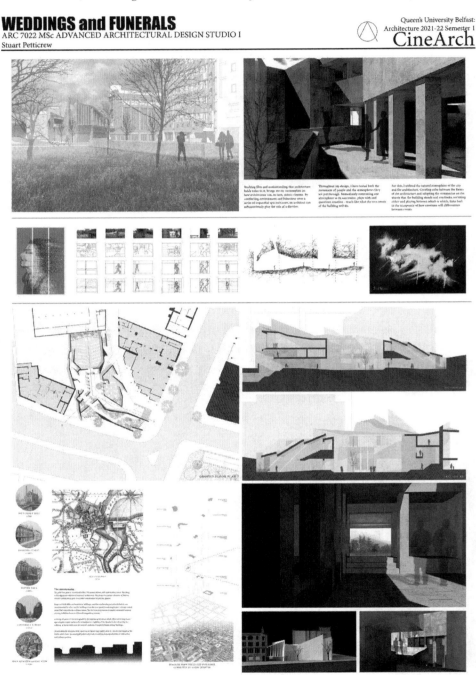

Pallasmaa's insight implies that conventional studio education might not be the best instrument for design tutors to promote the development of this kind of existential wisdom and the implementation of such maturity. In this context, this chapter reflects on an innovative studio at Queen's University Belfast that unites the territories of architecture and cinema under the umbrella of design through cinematic analysis methods and filmmaking practices. By embracing film analysis and filmmaking as design and learning tools, CineArch studio focuses on questioning and redefining the boundaries of architectural creativity and spatial design.

Architectural educator Semra Aydinli (2007, p. 113) refers to motivating design students "to transform creative thinking into critical thinking" that is highly embraced in CineArch. Students' creative outputs are used as vessels to analyse and discuss space-making and spatial experience both in cinema and the built environment. To boost existential wisdom, or to discover the persona and the designer in oneself, a constant flow from ideas and theories to practice and making towards further theory is encouraged throughout students' education via curricular and extra-curricular activities. This is a methodology partly 'learned', experienced and developed through the lessons of architectural educator Necdet Teymur in the 1990s in Middle East Technical University (Teymur, 1992 and 2002).

Within the CineArch studio that is collaboratively experienced by architects, artists, designers, and filmmakers in two separate semesters, the fusion of cinematic analysis methods and architectural design processes takes a central role. Students explore methods such as storyboard, montage/collage, cinematic plan/section/model, poster/abstraction, moodPaint, and spatial layering to analyse film scenes but also to design buildings, structures, and film sets. In parallel, filmmaking practices, such as concept film, site film, city film, model film, animation as well as AR/VR, are utilised to test and articulate architectural ideas through dynamic audio-visual means. Filmmaking empowers CineArch students and graduates to explore and communicate intricate design proposals.

There is a deliberate choice in this studio to 'force' students to look at the world through a different lens and perspective to expend their horizons as designers – a lesson learned from the writings of art critic John Berger. CineArch studio as a pedagogical vehicle is highly inspired by Berger's theories discussed in their BBC documentaries and books, particularly *Ways of Seeing* (1972). Among other commendable arguments, Berger writes: "The way we see things is affected by what we know or what we believe. […] We only see what we look at. To look is an act of choice" (1972, p. 8). In this context, CineArch expends students' knowledge and horizon through innovative multidisciplinary practices. But why cinematic architecture, not a different pedagogical approach, is chosen to enable this intellectual shift? As Pallasmaa who is an advocate of the concept of 'lived space' suggests (2020, p. 57):

> The ground of both artforms is lived space, in which the inner space of the mind and the external space of the world fuse into each other forming a chiasmatic bind. The lived space of cinema offers a great lesson for us architects, who tend to see our craft through a formal bias.

Though when she was a young Architecture student, the author was not able to see it in the complexity Pallasma expresses above, she was intuitively aware that creating a relation of representation between architecture and cinema based on space was essential for discovering the designer in her. The fact that films are extremely spatial in a different way than physical space is crucial here. In addition, some parallels between the two artforms were/are harder to find in other disciplines. These include, for instance, 'selling' the design idea, long design process, long making process, collaboration of various professional teams, and requiring clients for large budgets. Architects and filmmakers not only design lived spaces but also create them via similar practices.

Going back to Pallasmaa, the methodology below intents to enable a move away from the emphasis of form towards embodiment, presence, existence, and perception. The outcomes of this multidisciplinary collaboration are a series of outside-the-box projects that exceed conventional architectural boundaries. Architectural spaces are transformed into immersive narratives, and cinematic techniques advance the atmosphere and experience of these environments. Highlighting the profound impact of cinematic analysis methods and filmmaking on architectural theory and practice, CineArch studio pilots a new system of montaged architecture designed bottom up.

The CineArch Method in Architectural Education

Figure 2. Amy Cross, Transforming Carrickfergus Project, CA 2022-23, Semester 2

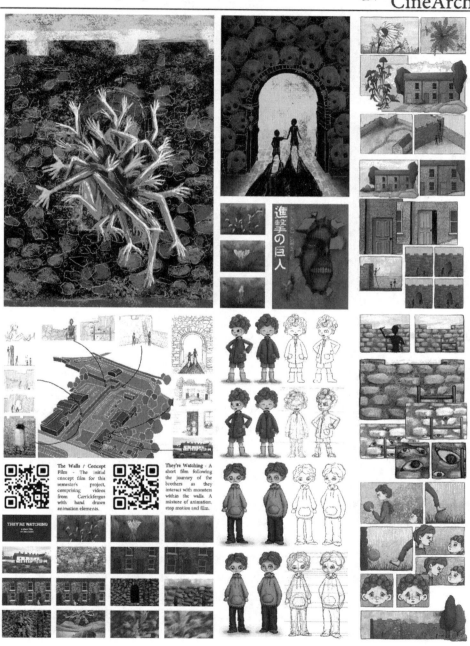

Evolution of CineArch Studio

Though the author has often benefitted from her research on architecture and cinema (since 1994) in her teaching in several Schools of Architecture in Ireland, Netherlands, Turkey, UK and USA (since 2002), via elective modules, assignments, and master dissertations, she has developed a full studio in this area at Queen's University[1] in Northern Ireland. Queen's Department of Architecture[2] was founded in 1965 and has medium size studios in UK standards in each year group in the undergraduate programme (60-70 students) and about half of that number in the year groups of the master's programme. Being new, the CineArch studio at postgraduate level is much smaller (up to 15 students).

The CineArch studio, established in 2017, started as a vertical studio in the three-year undergraduate course (BSc Architecture, RIBA Part 1). Several vertical studios are offered every year to students from second and third year of the programme, and Year 2 students are allocated to while Year 3 students choose one of these thematic studios (15-20 students each). The majority of the cinematic analysis methods and some of the films discussed below were tested and developed in this vertical studio. This undergraduate studio ran as a single semester module from January to May for three years in academic years 2017-18 and 2018-19 in person, and in 2020-21 fully online using Teams and Miro.

Until 2021, the only postgraduate taught course in Queen's Architecture was the two-year Master of Architecture programme (RIBA Part 2). Both the BSc Arch and MArch are established courses in which about one third of the students are international. When the author was asked to develop a new PgT course, the team decided to differentiate the new yearlong master's using the cinematic emphasis of the CineArch studio. In 2021-22, the new MSc Advanced Architectural Design programme started running partly online and continued with masked faces because of the Covid19 pandemic.

Full-time AAD students have 5 modules running from September to September: CineArch Studio 1 (Semester 1), CineArch Studio 2 (Semester 2), Technical Dissertation (Semesters 1 and 2), Humanities Dissertation (Semesters 1 and 2), and finally Thesis Project (Semester 3). CineArch1 in which new skills are explored is a highly structured studio, CineArch2 is semi-structured, and Thesis Project is student-led and research-heavy to prepare students to personal career goals. Contact time lasts 12 weeks that is followed by an assessment period. As in BSc and MArch, there are no exams; all assessment is through coursework. Each student submits a digital A2 design portfolio (including their films) at the end of the semester.

CineArch has recently expanded with students who have a creative background such as art, film, and design. In 2022-23, a part-time postgraduate certificate course was added to AAD. This is called PgCert Cinematic Architecture and is open to all creative backgrounds, not just architecture. The few art and film students who joined CA have made a significant difference to the studio dynamics and a significant contribution to the studio culture. Their interests, ideas, skills, and needs were different from architecture students, which improved the learning curve of the students and design tutors. CA students usually work part-time or full-time and join CineArch solely on Tuesdays. They need to complete CineArch Studio 1 (Semester 1) and CineArch Studio 2 (Semester 2) to finish the course.

With the confidence and know-how that is gained by establishing the PgCert, AAD will be open to non-architects in 2024-25. People with any creative background; architects, designers, artists, and filmmakers will be able to do the full masters. For that reason, AAD is renamed as Applied Architecture and Design to be inclusive for 'the creatives'. Students with diverse backgrounds look at the projects differently and their perspectives enrich the studio environment. The certificate course is preferred among local students mainly because their tuition is covered through the Skill Up Fund of the Department for

The CineArch Method in Architectural Education

the Economy. The DfE in Northern Ireland funds several programmes in Queen's University and other higher and further education institutions to upskill professionals in the workforce. Dissimilar to CA, mostly international students prefer AAD, and the symbiosis of the two courses in the same studio, one mostly local, the other global, creates a rich learning environment.

The multidisciplinary nature of the studio is strengthened by various external collaborations. Students have worked as the client of Software Engineering students who have taken their 3D models to create AR and VR experiences of the design proposals. They collaborate with Mid and East Antrim Borough Council to propose improvements to the historical town of Carrickfergus. Students have made documentaries with Media and Broadcast Production students in Carrickfergus. Every spring CineArch curates a student exhibition at Queen's Film Theatre open to cinemagoers and the public. They visit other universities (like the University of Liverpool) and present student work. There are 8 project reviews live streamed publicly per year, and esteemed architects, filmmakers, and academics are invited as guest reviewers to give feedback to students. A joint film/set design project with Belfast Met is being planned for next year. The list goes on.

Figure 3. Alice Poole, Building Peace Project, AAD 2022-23, Semester 1

Education of CineArch Studio

Two main trends have been shaping the characteristics of CineArch, cinematic analysis methods and to-the-point filmmaking practices.

Cinematic Analysis Methods

The first studio starts in a very specific, structured way that is new to *all* students. There are multiple film stills in the project brief from fiction films/series/animations in which architecture plays a prominent role like *Grant Budapest Hotel, Blade Runner, Inception, Squid Game, Spirited Away* and *Arcane*. Put into groups of three, students are asked to choose one still as a group to analyse the related film scene individually in the order identified below. Different approaches of the three to the same film scene create a prolific discussion around perception, thought processes, ways of seeing, representation, and space-making. As architectural theorist Diana Agrest states "representation as part of the production of architecture is one of the most important operations that articulates theory and practice" (2000, p. 164). Students do this exercise in each studio.

Cinematic Analysis Methods in CineArch Studio

Cinematic Plan + Section
↓
Cinematic moodPaint (atmosphere of the scene)
↓
Cinematic Rendering + Spatial Layering (of a film still)
↓
Poster/Abstraction
↓
Cinematic Storyboard
↓
Cinematic Collage/Montage
↓
Cinematic Model (as a group) + 10 Second Film (individually)
↓
Architectural Collage (for a building/space/film set)
↓
Architectural Storyboard
↓
Poster/Abstraction
↓
Architectural Rendering + Spatial Layering (of a key space)
↓
Architectural moodPaint
↓

Architectural Plan + Section + Model + 10 Second Film
↓
Site Film (as a group) + Concept Film (individually)

These methods deliberately bring hand drawing/physical modelmaking/painting and digital production together. Referring to education, Pallasmaa says, "The intelligence, thinking and skills of the hand also need to be re-discovered" (2020, p. 89). Cinematic analysis methods are described in the project brief as follows:

Cinematic Plan + Section: Draw a plan and section of the main space in the scene. Include furniture, lighting and the choreography of the camera and actors. You may try to draw also a cinematic axonometric. The medium is up to you; this could be by hand or digital. Line drawings usually work better. If you have not studied architecture, you can sketch the plan.

Cinematic moodPaint: This will be a painting expressing the mood/atmosphere/ambience of your chosen scene based on sound and image. It could be an abstract painting, but it is by hand - not digital. Acrylic paint is preferrable, but you can use other media (like watercolour, oil pastels or felt tip pens). If you have not used acrylic before, give it a go. You might like it.

Cinematic Rendering + Spatial Layering: Re-draw (recreate) your film still using CAD, SketchUp or another software (if you are not familiar with such apps, do it by hand). Pay attention to contrasts, light, colour, and texture. Try to capture the still's composition closely. Then, keeping in mind all the layers withing the frame (usually foreground, middle-ground, and background), explode the frame into 3-4 layers and show them in an axonometric drawing or (digital or physical) model. You can use laser-cut layers, for instance.

Poster/Abstraction: Make a poster or an abstraction of your film scene to capture its essence - its meaning to you. This could for instance be a digital illustration.

Cinematic Storyboard: Watch the scene that the film still is from again and make a storyboard of your scene (like Gordon Cullen's serial vision). Generate 6 frames using hand sketching (this is not an exercise of bringing actual film stills together. Draw each frame by hand on paper or screen). Try to use varied shot scales (close-up, medium and long shot). Keep it as a line drawing or add shade and shadow, or colour.

Cinematic Collage/Montage: This technique has similarities to moodPaint and poster, they all try to capture the essence of the scene, but at the same time, the differences in the medium (acrylic, digital and mixed media) make them dissimilar. For your collage/montage, you can mix any medium to create a whole with 'bits and pieces'. The collage will show how you perceive the film scene.

Cinematic Model + 10 Second Film: In your small group, make one scale model of your film space using any materials. Monochromatic models are preferable, but it depends on the film scene. Then make 10 second films of this model/space individually. You may try unusual camera angles/ techniques.

In time, students prefer using certain methods more than the others. Storyboard, collage and -to their surprise- moodPaint are highly utilised throughout the year. When the project started with these methods followed by architectural design, the students were forgetting all the excitement and creative work they produced in the first month of the studio. They were going back to the comfort of designing the way they are used to. A shift in the methodology resolved this huge problem and was revolutionary. Students are now asked to start architectural design using the same methods in reverse order. This not only provided a new way to initiate a design project but also moved designers away from a solely top-down design process towards a bottom-up approach - that is similar to Adolf Loos' concept of *raumplan*. Students were 'forced' to design spaces and then montage them together, the way they edit film scenes after shooting. They knew how to design a whole and then 'divide' it up but not the opposite. As Pallasmaa (2009, p. 108) reminds architects, "The design process simultaneously scans the inner and outer worlds and intertwines the two universes."

Figure 4. Madi Whiteside, Building Peace Project, CA 2022-23, Semester 1

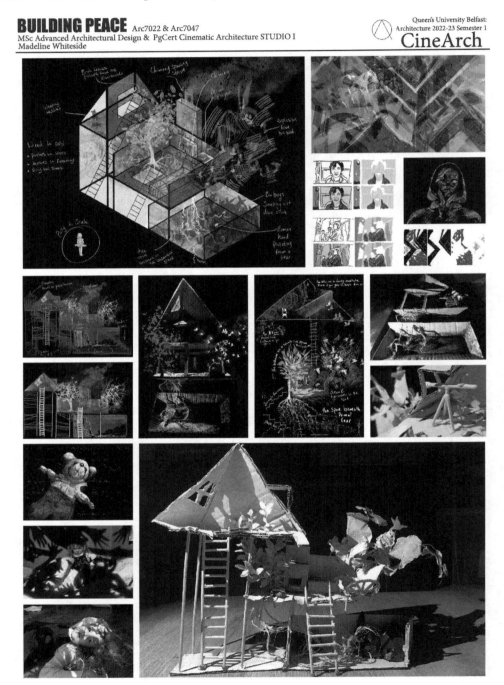

Filmmaking Practices

The author has been experimenting with various filmmaking assignments in practice-based (studio), theory-based (dissertation/thesis), and lecture-based (history/theory) modules in several countries, mainly the UK and Turkey, since 2005. Film is used to see, to feel, to study, to analyse, to understand, to map, to frame, to explore, to experiment, to process, to conceptualise, to develop, to animate, to present, to communicate and to critique urban, architectural and design issues. In the CineArch studio, these may take the form of a city film, site film, urban analysis film, concept film, model film, and animation. Some of these film typologies are more important that the others in the CineArch method; all students make concept and site films each semester. Architects are also expected to provide a walkthrough of the 3D digital model of their buildings/spaces using animation. Films are made individually or in groups.

In recent years, students are given the option to make a comprehensive film as their final project of the semester. This is a preferred choice among part-time PgCert Cinematic Architecture students. AAD students usually prefer using film as a tool for the exploration of design ideas and/or for architectural representation. Students may also create their own film typology like moodFilm (Esraa Hamido, 2024) and animated section (Hollie Hamilton, 2023). Students can do the design project, or any part of it, in pairs if they wish.

What do these films do or mean? A site film is made right at the beginning of the semester following the site visit in Week 1 as an intuitive spatial analysis tool before starting the research. Because conventional *and* high-tech urban analysis techniques like mapping, drawing, laser cutting, and 3D modelling are mixed in the studio, urban analysis film can be used, for instance, to explore light and shadow changes on the site in motion and to layer historical maps in a stop-motion format. The design process does not start with a preliminary sketch or model but a concept film; this captures designer's preliminary idea(s) that they would like to conceptually explore in the project. Concept films can be highly abstract, experimental, artistic, or critical.

Alongside 3D/digital models, physical modelmaking is highly encouraged in CineArch. These process/design development and final presentation models are then carefully photographed and filmed to add a new layer to the information they may reveal. Various forms of animation (stop-motion, shadow puppetry, walkthrough, etc.) are also used at different stages but usually in the final presentation. A city film is made in study trips to capture the unique perspective of the student as an 'outsider' when we go to Berlin, Naples, Liverpool, Derry, etc. The variety of films made and the reasons behind their making prove that cinema has a substantial potential to enrich the design experience and the quality of the outputs in studio.

CineArch Projects

Educator Hulya Yurekli writes, "one of the bases of architectural education is architectural design, which is not something to be taught but something to be experienced" (2007, p. 31). Over the years, many projects are tested in the CineArch studio. In the form of buildings, usually more 'performative' briefs are chosen because atmosphere and experience in these buildings, for instance, in a theatre or cinema, are more in the foreground compared to, say, a factory or hospital. The first CineArch project at master's level was an inclusive Weddings and Funeral building for all people in Belfast. Students also conducted urban design for Carrickfergus followed by each student's chosen site and project for the town. They designed a peace museum/ exhibition as well as a film studio in Belfast. As mentioned earlier,

The CineArch Method in Architectural Education

designing film sets and making films as the final output of the studio is encouraged. Posters of selected projects are included to this chapter to give the reader a deeper insight about CineArch studio's content (Figures 1-5). Not a selection of but all student work is exhibited in this format once or twice a year.

Figure 5. Kaarthick Ravichandran, Transforming Carrickfergus Project, AAD 2022-23, Semester 2

Effects of CineArch Studio

CineArch Studio will continue to be the core pedagogical backbone of the AAD programme that is now open to all creative backgrounds. It is worth asking what is learned from running this studio between 2017 and 2024 as an alternative way of design education:

1. Design learning is based on practice (learning by doing) and triggered when students are out of their comfort zone. A cyclist does not think about riding their bike unless they need to ride it in an uncommon way (maybe backwards), or they are given an unusual bike that needs to be operated differently (for instance a unicycle). Multidisciplinary projects provide this opportunity.
2. Bringing cinema into design in higher education is beneficial. As a temporal audio-visual medium, film can communicate, and shape, design ideas in a way drawing and/or modelling cannot. As a way of perspectival, narrative, and sequential thinking, film can also help learners see design in new light.
3. Educating creative people with diverse backgrounds together is worth the effort since their varied perspectives boost peer-learning on an intellectual level. Besides, it is said that the best way to learn is to teach. On a practical level, teaching each other skills helps students to look at this familiar tool, be it modelmaking, video editing, collage, etc., in a new way.
4. Montage can be an effective tool to design buildings and spaces. A bottom-up approach can be beneficial to educate young designers further. This also helps them to learn to shift between scales and various media as they design.

In *Future Practice* (2012), Rory Hyde shows that the career path of an Architecture student is not straight forward. In the twenty-first century, architects not only design and/or construct buildings but may choose to be urbanists, project managers, entrepreneurs, educators, activists, artists, and designers of all sorts. The professional and transferable skill set that is gained via multidisciplinary architectural education can creatively be applied to many practices from building industry to business, urbanism to government, technology to communications, and education to civil society (Hyde 2012, p. 25); for them, the sky is the limit.

ACKNOWLEDGMENT

I would like to thank Rory Caithness of Caithness Architects, Pat Wheeler of ALW Architects, Marie Curie Researcher Ece Sila Bora at Queen's Architecture, and Jamie Campbell of EnTOP Architects for co-tutoring CineArch studios between 2017 and 2024 and for contributing to the evolution of the CineArch Method. My gratitude extends to our external examiner Professor Francois Penz of University of Cambridge for his guidance and constructive feedback.

REFERENCES

Agrest, D. (2000). Representation as Articulation between Theory and Practice. In Stan Allen, *Practice: Architecture, Technique and Representation* (pp. 163-178). Routledge.

Aydinli, S. (2007). "Awareness" as a Design Paradigm. In Gulsun Saglamer (Ed.), *The Design Studio: A Black Hole* (pp. 113-136). Yem.

Berger, J. (1972). *Ways of Seeing*. Penguin.

Hettithanthri, U., & Hansen, P. (2022). Design Studio Practice in the Context of Architectural Education: A Narrative Literature Review. *International Journal of Technology and Design Education*, 32(4), 2343–2364. 10.1007/s10798-021-09694-2

Higher Education Widening Participation. (n.d.). Department for the Economy online. https://www.economy-ni.gov.uk/articles/higher-education-widening-participation

Hyde, R. (2012). *Future Practice*. Routledge. 10.4324/9780203100226

Pallasmaa, J. (2009). *The Thinking Hand: Embodied and Existential Wisdom in Architecture*. Wiley and Sons.

Pallasmaa, J. (2011). *The Embodied Image: Imagination and Imagery in Architecture*. John Wiley and Sons.

Pallasmaa, J., & Zambelli, M. (2020). *Inseminations: Seeds for Architectural Thought*. Wiley.

QUB. (n.d.). A Timeline of the Queen's Story. *QUB 175 Celebration online*. https://www.qub.ac.uk/about/175-celebration/timeline/

Salma, A. (2010). Design Education. *ArchNet-IJAR: International Journal of Architectural Research*, 4(2).

Salama, A. (1995). *New Trends in Architectural Education: Designing the Design Studio*. Arti-arch.

Teymur, N. (1992). *Architectural Education: Issues in Educationl Practice and Policy*. ?uestion Press.

Teymur, N. (2002). *Re-Architecture: themes and Variations*. ?uestion Press.

Yurekli, H. (2007). The Design Studio: A Black Hole. In Gulsun Saglamer (Ed.), *The Design Studio: A Black Hole* (pp. 17-34). Yem.

NOTES

[1] Founded by Queen Victoria in 1845, QUB is an independent higher education institution governed by its own Senate and a Russell Group university based in Northern Ireland, UK. Its growth from 90 students to 24,000 in 180 years is noteworthy: "the Queen's University in Ireland was designed to be a non-denominational alternative to Trinity College Dublin" and had three Queen's colleges in Belfast, Cork, and Galway. At the time, the island of Ireland was a colony of Britain and was not divided. "Although it was the first University in the north of Ireland, Queen's drew on a tradition of learning which goes back to 1810 and the foundation of the Belfast Academical Institution."

In 1908, the college in NI was replaced by the Queen's University of Belfast (QUB History and Heritage, 2024).

2   Queen's Department of Architecture is currently in the School of Natural and Built Environment. Out of the three faculties in the university, SNBE is in the Faculty of Engineering and Physical Sciences.

Chapter 8
Waterfront Dynamics

Zbigniew W. Paszkowski
https://orcid.org/0000-0002-7506-0185
Andrzej Frycz Modrzewski Kraków University, Poland

Jakub I. Gołębiewski
https://orcid.org/0000-0002-4314-6769
West Pomeranian University of Technology in Szczecin, Poland

ABSTRACT

The practice of The Architectural Design Studio's "Waterfront Dynamics" focuses on the processes of spatial and functional transformation in modern cities. They are particularly interested in the changes affecting post-industrial areas and historic centers of port cities. Their students deal with various issues related to transforming the riverside landscape. The subject of design interventions is their hometown of Szczecin (Poland), where many spatial problems focus and where many demanding design topics can be found. The results are projects to restore the historic riverside district and bold visions of the new development of degraded post-industrial areas. This studio is trying to teach students methods of creating new architecture in a historical setting and considering strong exposure in the waterside zone - landscape analysis, the composition of the principles of domination and subordination, scale, and continuity of development.

INTRODUCTION

Architectural design within a cultural, historic or landscape-protected area is an important component of teaching architecture and urban planning in Poland. Transforming existing facilities or degraded areas, while recognizing, analyzing and preserving their historical value, is a growing challenge for graduates (The HUL Guidebook, 2016). The new standards introduced for the higher education in architecture and urban planning in Poland, are specifying the number of teaching hours for subjects and the proportion to be shared between lectures and practical exercises (Paszkowski & Gołębiewski, 2020). The practical tasks of architectural design and spatial planning referring to acute problems are therefore more welcome.

The Architectural Design Studio „Waterfront Dynamics" concept emerged due to the necessity of an advanced discussion about the waterfronts in Szczecin (Paszkowski, 2004, 2005). The City of Szczecin is located at the Odra River estuary, where the interconnection of the city with water is obvious, but in fact not fully developed in the formal sense in comparison to other seaport cities development in Europe (Paszkowski, 2003). Our Studio deals with developing design methods and principles in the historical environment - urban conservation and revitalization of neglected post-industrial areas. Waterfront areas related to the city's industrial past are of particular interest.

The goal of the Architectural Design Studio is to show architecture as the game of architectural form and function with different factors, typologies, points of view, and the range of possibilities to achieve the sustainable spatial solutions composed within the existing multilayered and changing environments.

THE STUDIO CONTENT

The XX century historical processes in the Pomerania Region are the main issue to understand the chain of changes affecting the city of Szczecin. Mentioning them briefly, there was the change of the national belonging of Szczecin and Western Pomerania from German to the Polish state, as a result of World War II, demolition of a large part of the historic city as a result of the British air raids in 1943 and 1944 on at that time German Szczecin, the demolitions done by the Russian army going to conquer Berlin in 1945 (Białecki, 1992), the period of rebuilding the city in the form of a socialist city during Poland's dependence on Soviet Russia (1945-1989), and finally, contemporary changes in the structure of the shipbuilding industry and how to port transshipments operate, as well as symptoms of climate change - constitute a transformational conglomerate that especially affects Szczecin (Januszkiewicz et al., 2021).

Figure 1. Past and present: On the left, the historical view of the Old Town quay in Szczecin before the war damage. On the right, the current view. Despite the destruction of buildings, the boulevards in Szczecin still remain an important space visited by residents, which defines the city's identity.

The intertwining of historical processes, industrial development, and taking root of Polish society in Western Pomerania is awaking its cultural awareness and the search for the identity of the places where they live (Paszkowski, 2008). The new global trends in the relocation of port and shipyard areas from urban locations towards river mouths, to the periphery of the agglomeration (Rudewicz, 2021; Schubert, 2001), created an excellent platform for considering the new waterfront related development of the city, what constitutes the process, which could be named "the waterfront dynamics". This process can be seen both in functional and formal aspects. Its leading motif is the interface between the city and the river with wide exposure from the water side and with an appreciation of the architecture that is being developed in this area in the past and in present times (AIVP, 2004).

Figure 2. Transformation of port areas in Szczecin. As in Hamburg and London, the areas used for centuries for the port transshipments are now empty due to the relocation of the main port activities.

The riverside exposition contributes to the emblematic character of the architectural landscape, and its form tends to symbolize the city (Bal, et. al., 2023). This process can already be seen in the preserved historic waterside structures of Szczecin, such as Wały Chrobrego, designed to open a view toward the wide landscape of the valley of the Odra River (Czałczyńska -Podolska, Sochacka-Sutkowska 2016; Paszkowski, 2015). Therefore the link between the processes of transformation of the waterfront area going on in the city of Szczecin and the field of education in architecture and spatial planning, which is performed at the University is very interesting for all parties involved: students, teachers, the city, and its inhabitants.

The educational novelty of the architectural design in our Studio is to see the designed objects as a part of the ongoing process of transformative changes in the city, using the time factor as a similarly important feature as the existing context of the surroundings and contemporary trends in the architectural design and functional needs (Paszkowski, 2011). Before the beginning of the designing process, students are obliged to analyze the historic development of the site in the wider city context, find out the illustrations of previous arrangements of the area, valorize the past architecture, and advice about the direction of further development of the site. To consider among other issues, whether the reconstruction of the past architectural forms can be a justified solution, or a new arrangement should replace the previous forms of use. In the case of applications of modern, contemporary architectural styles, some reflection on past uses is recommended, but not always justified.

The presented examples of architectural design proposed by the students along the scope of urban ideas developed at the waterfronts had to illustrate the results of programming, analytical, and designing processes in which the students are playing the main role, having the tutors, and teachers as supporting and criticizing specialists (Paszkowski & Gołębiewski, 2020). A notion of a need for transformative processes to create the important interface between the city's built environment, the water, and the natural landscape, opened the discussion on waterfronts and gave students a chance to create architecture

Waterfront Dynamics

in a very interesting and challenging environment (Ryce-Paul, 2004). It is also to mention, that not only just geographic and topographic features of this city led to statements on the need for the introduction of dynamic transformative changes.

The city of Szczecin, located at different waterfronts of rivers estuary of the Odra River, and Dąbie lake, constitute a diversity of connections and barriers between the city and the waterfronts. The waterfront landscape of the city is therefore a challenging subject for urbanization purposes and the creation of new landscapes and cityscapes (Gołębiewski, 2018). These emerging chances to prepare academic projects in prime riverfront locations have been undertaken by several students of architecture. They have prepared the project at different levels of architectural education, but the most advanced has been a performer at the II stage of architectural education, Master Studies, workshops organized by the Faculty of Architecture, and final design projects. A selection of projects has been presented below, to illustrate the variety of concepts possible and the complexity of the topic of waterfront development.

One of the important design issues undertaken by students during the course is the reconstruction of the silhouette of the historic waterfront in Szczecin. The riverside buildings were destroyed during the war and never rebuilt. Additionally, in line with the urban planning strategy popular in the post-war period, a wide communication artery was built along the waterfront, cutting off the city and its inhabitants from the river (Zaremba, Orlińska, 1965). There has been an ongoing discussion in the city for several years regarding the need to restore the natural relationship between the urban fabric and the waterfront. At the same time, the architectural form of the new buildings is a widely discussed issue. The project presented below is a voice in this discussion. The concept restores the layout of the waterfront buildings, referring to their historical dimensions and the gable form of the façade, typical of Hanseatic cities. At the same time, faithful reconstruction of historical forms is abandoned in favor of a contemporary interpretation of pre-war buildings.

Figure 3. Sample student work, Architectural design – conservation / Semester II / Analytical study.

Authors: Jan Piotrowski, Klaudia Walukiewicz, leading teacher: PhD Arch. Jakub Gołębiewski

Another category of projects is interventions within existing, historical structures in the waterside space. An example of this type of activity is the revitalization project of a former port boiler house for the needs of the Maritime Museum. The historic building with an attractive architectural form is currently awaiting new development (Kotla, 2008). In this case, the design intervention consisted of adapting the historic part of the building and expanding it. The main design challenge was to combine the historic and newly designed forms. The project was preceded by extensive archival research and studies of the existing building. The result is a contemporary form that draws creatively from history. In its facades, we will find a reference to the proportions and decorations of the historic building. The main leitmotif visible in the facades is the multiplied form of architectural detail taken from the existing building. The above example shows that a thorough analysis can lead to finding interesting inspirations and creating a form that simultaneously manifests its modernity and is rooted in the identity of the place.

Figure 4. Diploma design: Conservation. Adaptation of a port boiler room into a maritime museum.

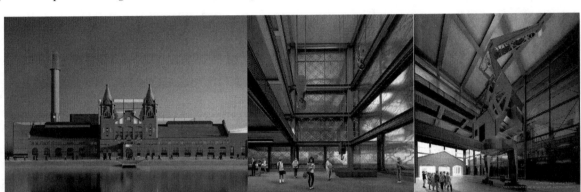

Author: Krystian Bąkowski, promoter: Prof. PhD Arch. Zbigniew Paszkowski

The last of the presented objects can be described as an attempt to introduce an attractive, contemporary architectural form in a waterside context. This trend is visible in many port cities, where iconic buildings were built in the immediate vicinity of water bodies, including the most famous examples of the Opera House in Sydney and Oslo, the Museum of Contemporary Art in Bilbao, and the Philharmonic Hall in Hamburg (Kłosek-Kozłowska 2010; Skivko et. al., 2023). The system of waterways and port basins in the center of Szczecin is so diverse that it is possible to identify several attractive locations for important public facilities. As part of our design studio, students test various locations and solutions, which often constitute important analytical material for city authorities. The presented project of the film center has a dynamic form that successfully fits into the landscape of the headland at the junction of the Odra River and the Green Canal. For the author of the project, in addition to its expressive form, the public character of the building was also important. The public space on the waterfront is expanded by a publicly accessible roof terrace, which takes advantage of the unique scenic values of the place.

Figure 5. Diploma design: Conservation. The film center as a new architectural icon of the riverside landscape.

Author: Aleksandra Kmieć, promoter: Prof. PhD Arch. Zbigniew Paszkowski

DISCUSSION

The process of transformation, as the multilateral city development task, causes a lot of intertwined problems which should be identified and solved (Paszkowski, 2008). The urban and architectural design can be seen in this aspect as the basic regulation for the urban layouts, defining the directions of city urban transformation, as the form-giving activity and cultural action, a performer to strengthen the identity of the place and the whole city (Paszkowski, 1997). Waterfront is becoming a very challenging development area, allowing it to present architecture created in a modern language of architecture (Paszkowska, 2014). Some student projects present a new architecture placed in a very challenging context, showing that not only reconstruction but also modern thinking, with the use of contemporary design tools, can bring interesting results. At the same time, each intervention should be carried out in relation to the broader urban context. Waterfronts are open spaces with great exhibition value, so we should always pay attention to the impact of its individual elements on the entire composition.

The conclusions concerning waterfront planning as a perfect base for students' architectural considerations, discussions, and design projects, are the following:

- The processes of transformation of waterside areas are multi-wave, long-term and complex;
- Waterfronts are an area suitable for the location of significant culture-forming objects;
- The use of areas equipped with infrastructure and centrally located in the city structure is the implementation of the idea of a compact city, although large expenditure is required on additional communication infrastructure - bridges, and anti-flood infrastructure;
- Adaptive reuse of existing port buildings is an expression of environmental responsibility and reduces the potential carbon footprint. At the same time, it makes it possible to preserve examples of historic port architecture for future generations, which is an important element of the urban landscape and cultural heritage.
- Revitalization of the riverside areas is conducive to building the identity of the port city;

- The attractiveness of the waterside space for center-forming and housing purposes as well as for recreation is conducive to building the well-being of residents, as evidenced by the high level of acceptance of already completed waterfront revitalization projects;
- In the case of Szczecin, the connection of the city center structure with sea waters creates a unique situation with the presence of large sailing ships and related urban (social) events.

CONCLUSION

Many years of experience in working on the issue of waterfront transformation during design classes in our Studio revealed three main topics taken up by students. These are: the issues of restoration of degraded Old Town areas - destroyed during the war; adaptations of historical objects - mainly post-industrial ones, and contemporary architectural creations in the built environment. All these topics have their own specificity, however, they allow the use of a common methodology for working on each of the issues. Work on each of the projects begins with site visit; queries in the archives; historical studies; analysis of contemporary conditions and compositional studies. All these activities, taken in the first phase of the design process, translate into the individual contribution of our Studio to the development of students' competences and skills. We can say that our Studio's specific contribution to architectural education is:

- Building awareness of the complexity and comprehensiveness of activities undertaken in the historical area;
- Learning to use various information sources (e.g. libraries, archives, map resources, geodetic resources, archeology, specialist studies, etc.);
- Linking the functional and spatial programs of the design of the facilities with the planning requirements and development trends of the city (critical discussion with the provisions of local plans);
- Developing methods for creating new architecture in a historical setting and taking into account strong exposure in the waterside zone - landscape analysis, the composition of the principles of domination and subordination, scale and continuity of development.

The issues raised during the preparation of master's projects also contribute to further specialized research (doctoral theses) related to the topics of revitalization of the waterfronts. Our studio's specific consideration of 21st century and 21st-century architecture is the need to be aware of the history, to consider the remains of the past in the area of planning by possibilities of adaptive reuse, to design architecture with the contemporary parametric tools, to adjust the functions to future needs, to see the new projects as a continuation of the city development (both in terms of time and space) and finally – to contribute to the building of the local identity of the city and its society.

ACKNOWLEDGMENT

Author Contributions: All authors contributed equally to the writing of the manuscript.
Conflicts of Interest: The authors declare that there is no conflict of interest regarding the publication of this article.

REFERENCES

Bal, W., Całczyńska-Podolska, M., & Nieścior, M. (2023). The Importance of Architectural Icons of the City of Szczecin for the Transformation of Landscape Identity and Promotion of the City's Image. *Sustainability (Basel)*, 15(11), 8648. 10.3390/su15118648

Białecki, T. (1992). *Historia Szczecina*.

Całczyńska-Podolska, M., & Sochacka-Sutkowska, E. (2016). *Landscape values of the embankment of the Odra River in Szczecin and the degree of their use for building the city's identity*. Space & Form.

Gołębiewski, J. I. (2018). Perspektywy rewitalizacji Międzyodrza w Szczecinie przy zastosowaniu tymczasowych interwencji przestrzennych, Teka Zachodniopomorska 5/2018, Szczecin.

Januszkiewicz, K., Paszkowska-Kaczmarek, N., Aduna Duguma, F., & Kowalski, K. G. (2020). *Living in the "Age of Humans". Envisioning CAD Architecture for the Challenges of the Anthropocene—Energy, Environment, and Well-Being*, MDPI Energies.

Kłosek-Kozłowska, D. (2010). Strategiczny plan rewitalizacji Bilbao, gdzie architektura podąża za urbanistyką, [in:] Walczak B. M. (red.), *Modele rewitalizacji i ich zastosowanie w miastach dziedzictwa europejskiego*. Łódź.

Kotla, R. (2008). *Rozwój techniczny i przestrzenny zespołu portowego Szczecin-Świnoujście na tle stosunków handlowych*.

Paszkowska N. E. (2014). Muzeum Tadeusza Kantora. Nowa Cricoteka w Krakowie. *Archivolta*, 4(64).

Paszkowski, Z. (1997). *Tradycja i innowacja w twórczości architektonicznej*. Politechnika Szczecińska.

Paszkowski, Z. (2003). *Transformacja przestrzeni śródmiejskich na przykładach miast europejskich*. Walkowska Wydawnictwo.

Paszkowski, Z. (2004). *City planned in the city without the masterplan*. Wydawnictwo Politechniki Krakowskiej.

Paszkowski, Z. (2005). *Wizja rozwoju przestrzennego Szczecina*. Space & Form.

Paszkowski, Z. (2008). Restrukturalizacja miasta historycznego jako metoda jego współczesnego kształtowania na przykładzie Starego Miasta w Szczecinie. hogben, Szczecin.

Paszkowski, Z. (2011). Miasto idealne w perspektywie Europejskiej i jego związki z urbanistyką współczesną. Universitas Kraków.

Paszkowski, Z. (2015). *Is there any sense of Port landscape protection in Szczecin?* Space & Form.

Paszkowski, Z., & Gołębiewski, J. I. (2020). International design workshops as an intensive form of architectural education. *World Transactions on Engineering and Technology Education*. World Institute for Engineering and Technology Education.

Paszkowski Z. & Gołebiewski J. I. (2020). Heritage protection in the education of the modern architect. *World Transactions on Engineering and Technology Education*. World Institute for Engineering and Technology Education.

Rudewicz J. (2021). *Spatial and functional transformations of post-port areas in Szczecin in the context of classical city-port models.* Studies of the Industrial Geography Commission of the Polish Geographical Society.

Ryce-Paul, R. *Waterfront revitalisation: profitability vs social equity strategies shaping the urban waterfront*, [Thesis at Columbia State University, USA]. https://www.academia.edu/27040058/WATERFRONT_REVITALISATION_PROFITABILITY_VS_SOCIAL_EQUITY_STRATEGIES_SHAPING_THE_URBAN_WATERFRONT?email_work_card=view-paper

Schubert, D. (2001). *Hafen und Uferzonen im Wandel.* Leue Verlag.

) Skivko M., Korneeva E., & Bisakayeva N. (2023). City ports as a place for iconic architecture and the meeting point for sustainable ideas: the cases of Antwerp and Hamburg. *E3S Web of Conferences 458*, 07028.

Zaremba, P., & Orlińska, H. (1965). *Urbanistyczny rozwój Szczecina.* Wydawnictwo Poznańskie, Poznań 1965.

Chapter 9
Design Basics vs. Current Complexity:
Studio 4

M. Tayfun Yildirim
Gazi University, Turkey

Özge Zenter
https://orcid.org/0000-0002-7785-3218
Gazi University, Turkey

E. Fulya Özmen
Gazi University, Turkey

ABSTRACT

During history, architectural design education was based on typological patterns and local styles such as vernacular architectures, Greek, Roman, Gothic, Ottoman, Baroc, etc. Professional guilds have carried out these types by repetition of their iconic styles. However, developing technologies and changing materials over time also affected this local architectural design education. Architectural education, like other branches of education, includes many complex processes from the first stage to the last stage. In this process, the student's experiences, knowledge and the method followed are very important. The method taught in architectural design studios guides the design and plays a major role in the formation of the design. In this context, the study covers the design process and student studies of "AAAA University Faculty of Architecture, Department of Architecture - Studio 4." Considering the pros and cons of the design method used in Studio 4, it is clear that it is an important method in terms of providing students with analytical thinking and problem-solving skills.

INTRODUCTION

During history, architectural design education was based on typological patterns and local styles such as vernacular architectures, greek, roman, gothic, ottoman, and baroc types. Professional guilds have carried out these types by repetition of their iconic styles. Local materials, technologies, and culture

DOI: doi

influenced these local architectural differences. It is seen that some mass education institutions appeared at the end of medieval times by the push of enlightenment, trade, and industrialization. Colbert's Cite Universitaire (1671), Academy Beaux-Arts (17th cent.) in France, Chicago school in the US (19th cent.), Bauhaus school in Germany (1930's) are samples that aimed universal information-based mass education for people (Bayazıt, 1994).

Architectural designs have mostly gone on typologies and reshaping those types depending on capacity, scale, and place in architectural history. After Bauhuse, in this approach, design problems were divided into functional classes, and plan types and morphologies were produced. These function types are educational, health, office, tourism- leisure, industrial, transportation buildings, housing types. This concept still goes in most buildings today to shorten architectural, and engineering design periods, construction duration, and also for less costs. Choosing the commonly used main iconic shape (type) according to building function, and adapting that form to the design area are current common design ways for modern architects. That pre-acceptance of the main form can be an easy way but also an obstacle to creativity and architectural progress. For this reason, it is best to determine the design process and apply it step by step and with feedback to reach the final form.

Norbert Wiener's system theory "Cybernetics" affected all science and production branches such as system engineering, aviation, defense, and industrial products after the '40s. Architectural design and building production sectors also used this concept to shorten production periods, low cost, and correct decision-making. Architectural designs, which were accepted in the black box through the work of talented artists, turned into a step-by-step progress called the transparent box after this paradigm chance (Lawson, 1990).

In the black box approach, the design process takes place inside the designer's head, and what goes on inside the mind is unknown (Bayazıt, 2004). For this reason, it has intuitive features and the formation of a rational perspective is prevented (Terzidis, 2006). In the transparent box approach, the designer's mental activities while designing are externalized. For architectural design to be transparent like a transparent box, the design process should be systematically divided into parts and the relationship between the parts should be defined. Following a systematic approach in the design process, provides a transparent space (Ünal, 2013).

Algorithmic and intuitive methods have been created and used for that purpose. The algorithmic way is inductive (from data parts to complete design) and the intuitive approach is deductive (from complete to detail) (Christopher, 1970). Louis Kahn (1974) states that design is a form produced within order. In fact, design needs to have a certain order and be intuitive. Every idea starts with sketches in design. Algorithmic methods use exact parts and go on toward complete form by using linear thinking. However, intuitive methods use more holistic forms toward detailed design by using lateral thinking (Uraz,1993). There is no clear distinction between these forms of creative thinking. During the process, the designer can emphasise both ways of thinking at different times. While the intuitive approach enables finding original and innovative solutions, the systematic approach assesses the feasibility and sustainability of these solutions in a systematic way. Both ways of thinking (Figure 1) can be used in the development of design (Zenter, Özmen & Yıldırım, 2024).

Figure 1. Psychological thinking types

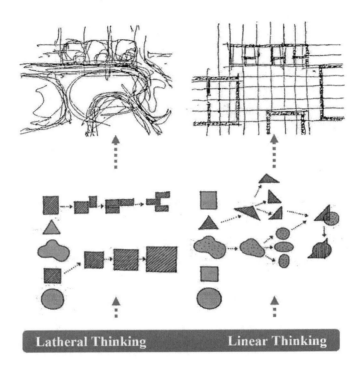

(Uraz, 1993)

All this information about the design process and creativity is acquired from instructors in design education. Architectural education, like other branches of education, includes many complex processes from the first stage to the last stage; therefore, the experiences, knowledge of students and instructors, and the tools and methods used to teach design are essential at this stage. The method taught in architectural design studios guides the design and plays a major role in the formation of the design (Farelly, 2011).

In this context, the study covers the design process and student studies of "Gazi University Faculty of Architecture, Department of Architecture - Studio 4". This study proposes a method to systematize the current complexity in architectural education. It aims to convey the effects of using the proposed method on students. To express and analyze the design approach of "Studio 4", student projects from different semesters were evaluated with qualitative research methods through different design problems.

The Studio Content: Studio 4

After an overview of to design history and design process, the "Studio 4" design education approach has been described below (Figure 2):

- Data analysis and listing them under the titles of environmental and building functions,
- Classifying data according to their weight in the design problem,
- Choosing one or couple of inputs as a "primary generator idea" and "main shape",

Design Basics vs. Current Complexity

- Developing and detailing the main shape with additional inputs with the guidance of the main idea.

Figure 2. The design process used in Studio 4

This method has been used in "Studio 4" for many years to complete the education and design process within the exact time. The aim is to equalize students by means of design ability. This algorithmic thinking is usable for all grade students. This analytic and step-by-step method is also usable for architectural criticism.

Data Analysis / Classifing Data

The most important and challenging step in architectural design is the decision-making upon the main shape called the "primary generator, first sketch, main idea or starting node" in design science. This decision needs experience, more information about previous solutions, expectations, and data analysis in professional life. Due to the amount of this data, decision-making about the main idea as a threshold to start shaping architectural design is complex today. Because of that data analysis and listing data sets according to their importance is necessary as a timesaver method in architectural education. In addition to that, Architectural design is always open to experimental approaches. However, these new ideas should provide functional, technological, and formal programming expectations.

The creating idea period must be given to students step-by-step, in an algorithmic-inductive way in design education because of their experience level. However, this does not mean that intuitionism should be completely abandoned. A systematic approach can also provide a structured environment for students to develop their intuitive thinking skills. Intuition is not a skill that can be taught, but it is also not something that arises by chance. In the design process, certain situations can be prepared and intuition can be given the opportunity to emerge (Cornell, 1997).

The design process applied in "Studio 4" begins with the data analysis phase. Analyses are classified as site analyses and design needs analyses. In site analyses, analyses of the natural and artificial environment and climatic analyses are carried out (Zenter, Özmen & Yıldırım, 2024). Pre-design period data collection and analysis are classified under two main titles. Natural environmental data (climate, topography, daylight, and wind) and artificial environmental data (surrounding city texture, cultural behaviours, codes- regulations, and transportation). Data about building type consists of previous building typology, inner space lists, and their volume/area requirements, space-environment relations, connections between spaces, structural and material requests, and semantic messages.

Idea Generation Period / Detailing Main Shape by Inputs

In data analysis, after examining and making meaning of the data, the period of generating ideas starts with creative thinking techniques. Different approaches need to be synthesized and combined to find appropriate solutions to the problem. Throughout the process, alternatives should be evaluated until there is harmony between the problem and the solution. While the early stages in the design process develop ways of thinking about the problem, the final stages require focusing on a specific design solution (Ching, 2011).

How successful the design is depends as much on the approaches to design as on the good management of the design process. These approaches can be defined as the basic principles necessary for building design. The first step in "Studio 4" is to identify the approaches to be used and establish their relationship with form. Each semester, current approaches are used, one or more of them are chosen as a focus point, and students are expected to use them in their projects. These approaches can be listed as follows: Aesthetic and artistic authenticity, sustainability, contextual facts, technology-driven architecture, and kinetic and biomimetic architecture.

Aesthetic and Artistic Authenticity

Architecture is defined as a structure that reaches the level of art and cannot be a construction that only provides for certain needs. As a field of plastic arts, architecture is both an art of expression and an art of thinking with symbolic meaning. For a building to be an architectural design, it must have some aesthetic values, utility, and strength (Aydınlı, 1993). Aesthetic success in architectural design is based on the formation of plastic form with concepts and elements such as dimension-scale, integrity, continuity, balance, light and shadow, and color and texture (Şentürer, 1995).

Architecture as art is realized as a result of the creation of a functional form; this form provides visual satisfaction and carries symbolic value. (Aydınlı, 1993).

Focusing on aesthetic authenticity in architectural education is vital in encouraging creativity in students, identifying aesthetic values, and the ability to create aesthetics along with functionality (Figure 3).

Contextual Facts

Contextual thinking is a way of evaluating the building, its surroundings, and the conditions in which it exists in the design process. According to Frampton and Smith, contextualism means maintaining the art of building with a character appropriate to the urban fabric. Context is not only related to the natural or artificial environment, but also to social, economic, and cultural factors (Kuloğlu, 2014).

Grahame Shane (1976) mentions that the language of context contains dualities such as order-disorder, formal-informal, and center-border. Designs that relate to the context can take either a harmonious approach that utilizes the data of the existing fabric or an oppositional approach that is contrary to the environment.

Evaluating the context, and experiencing the building's relationship with the existing environment should be indispensable for studios in architectural education. Students need to gain cultural sensitivity and environmental awareness (Figure 6, Figure 7).

Design Basics vs. Current Complexity

Technology-Driven Architecture

In architectural design, technology is an essential element that develops imagination and directs the designer to new ways of thinking. The practice of architecture, which progresses with technological developments, enables the appearance of different forms and extraordinary structures (Hasol, 2004; Vural-Cutts, 2018). In technology-oriented building design, criteria such as materials used, strength, ecological design, space organization, and sustainable energy use are taken into consideration. In addition to the use of technological developments and new materials in design, the integration of computer technologies into design facilitates the construction of complex buildings (Vural-Cutts, 2018).

In architectural education, following the technology of the age and applying it in design is important for students to be able to make creative and innovative designs that are compatible with contemporary architectural practice, produce extraordinary designs, and solve complex problems. The integration of computer technologies into design contributes to the strengthening of students' visualization and presentation skills and their ability to produce fast and practical solutions (Figure 5, Figure 8).

Sustainability

Williamson et al. (2003) mention that sustainable architecture is the consciousness of building design that is energy efficient, suitable for physical environmental conditions, and respectful to the social, cultural, and economic structure of the place (Williamson, Radford, and Bennetts, 2003).

Ventilation systems that can provide the fresh air needs of the space, openings that allow sufficient daylight to be taken into the space, heating systems, the use of materials that affect human psychology, and building envelope design that is sufficient in thermal insulation are necessary regulations of sustainable design (Filiz, 2010).

Emphasizing the importance of sustainable design in architectural education in terms of social, cultural, and economic aspects is important in creating awareness in students, developing a sustainable approach and producing solutions, and integrating sustainability principles into their designs (Figure 4).

Kinetic and Biomimetic Architecture

It is necessary not to freeze architecture in the various and constantly changing modes of life. On the contrary, architecture should be fluid and changeable with life. The concept of kinetics has entered architecture as a solution to these reasons. Kinetic architecture is architecture that can adapt to the changes in the set of forces acting on the structure consisting of many environmental data, and the technology of the tool that can interpret and apply these data (Zuk & Clark, 1970).

Biomimetic design can be defined as the imitation of the functional foundations of biological forms, processes, and systems to produce flexible solutions in architecture. Developing new systems by imitating the systems in nature is also crucial in terms of not wearing down the environmental conditions and increasing the benefit from the environment (Zenter, 2018).

The use of both approaches in the design process in architectural education helps students to think dynamically, to provide aesthetic experience with moving elements, produce solutions that can be adapted to changing needs, and make designs that allow physical environmental control (Figure 9, Figure 10).

STUDENT PROJECT DESIGNS OF STUDIO 4

The design process applied in "Studio 4" architectural design education and the selection of approaches to detail the main shape are shown through examples. Examples are detailed under the titles of design, prior data, and main idea.

Figure 3. 3rd class student studio work

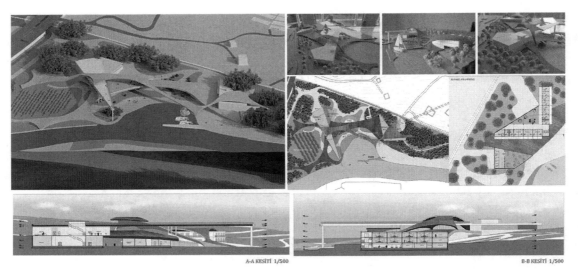

Design Title: Students' Village for a weekend in Kalecik
Prior Data: Vinery farms by the river, Natural, non-urbanised environment.
Main Idea: Using organic forms to obtain nature adaptive village (Figure 3).

Design Basics vs. Current Complexity

Figure 4. 2nd class student studio work

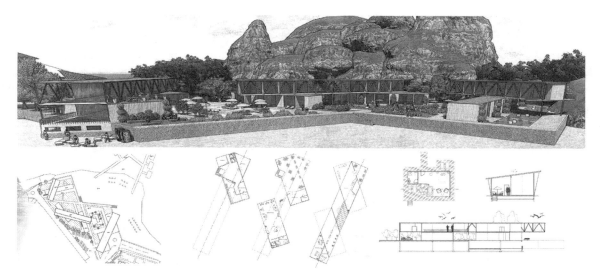

Design Title: Beach Hotel and Bungalows in Amasra
Prior Data: Vernacular architecture, Domain (single and double storey houses), Citta slow character (slow city).
Main Idea: Using scale, proportion and material of vernacular architecture (Figure 4).

Figure 5. 3rd class student studio work

Design Title: Gazi University Faculty of Architecture Proposal
Prior Data: Architectonics and expression of contemporary structures, technical demonstration.
Main Idea: Using long-span 3D steel structures to obtain that technological expression (Figure 5).

Figure 6. 3rd class student studio work

Design Title: Agriculture Institute and Seed Storage in Hasanoglan
Prior Data: Attaching to old early republic period buildings, reuse them with new buildings, and connection to Experimental plantation areas.
Main Idea: The student created a connection between old buildings and plantation areas by using the street in her new building, used organic roof form for nature-adaptive building (Figure 6).

Figure 7. 4th class student studio work

Design Title: Beyşehir Ecological Youth and Water Sports Village
Prior Data: Context, and Sports village by the lake.
Main Idea: Using geometric forms to obtain nature-adaptive village (Figure 7).

Figure 8. 4th class student studio work

Design Title: Agriculture Institute and Seed Storage in Hasanoglan
Prior Data: Attaching to old early republic period buildings, reuse them with new buildings, and technical demonstration.
Main Idea: Using long-span 3D steel structures to obtain that technological expression (Figure 8).

Figure 9. Post graduate M.Sc. student work

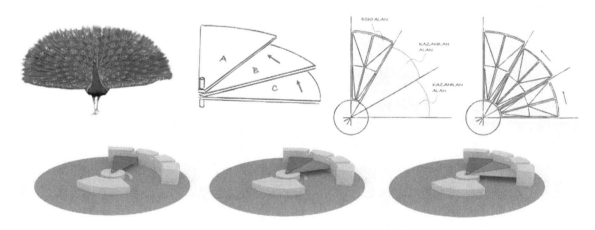

(Zenter, 2018)
Design Title: Multi-use Elementary School (and can be used as shelter for earthquake victims and temporary hospital)
Prior Data: Flexible use for different purposes, and mobile structural elements for different types.
Main Idea: Creating movable building parts inspired by Peacock tails (Figure 9).

Figure 10. Post graduate M.Sc. student work

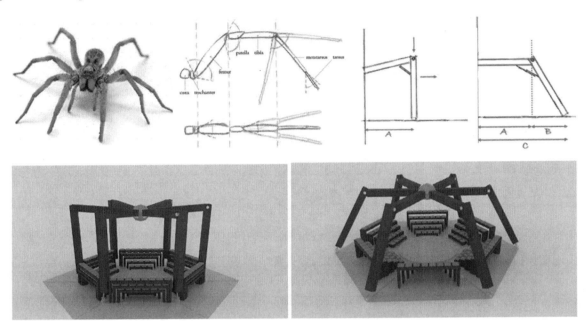

(Zenter, 2018)
Design Title: Flexible auiditorium
Prior Data: Obtaining different scale auditorium according to audience quantity.
Main Idea: Movement of Spider legs was selected for Kinetic structural parts of the hall (Figure 10).

CONCLUSION

In traditional architectural education, design was seen as an intuitive way of solving a problem, whereas after the 1960s design began to be seen as a scientific way. In the scientific approach, design is seen as designing the process. It is crucial to determine the process to reach the right results from the right design approaches (Uraz, 1993).

Architectural education, like other branches of education, includes many complex processes from the first stage to the last stage. Systematizing these processes, and determining the methods and approaches to be used in the process is one of the important steps in providing students with design and creativity skills. In this way, students acquire knowledge about how the act of designing should be realized and how it should progress step by step.

The design method used in "Studio 4" consists of data analysis/data classification and idea generation process/elaboration of the main shape according to the inputs. In the early stages of the design process, there is a tendency to start with analyzing data and then classify it. Data analysis and listing data sets according to their importance is necessary as a timesaver method in architectural education. There is a progression in the design process from considering the necessary functions, the structure of potential solutions, and then the behavior of these solutions (Cross, 2001). In the stages following the data analysis, the final design is created by applying the approaches determined as contemporary approaches to the architecture.

The use of this method in the architectural education process helps students to develop both creative/intuitive and analytical skills. This method is necessary for students to look at various design problems from a wider perspective. It also enables them to adapt to changing conditions and new information quickly and effectively.

As a conclusion, the advantages and disadvantages of this method can be listed as follows, based on the student examples described under the titles of design, prior data, and main idea:

Advantages:

- Method is a timesaver on decision making. This is usable in limited-time semesters. It also equalizes different thinking and working student types in exact education duration.
- It also gives analytic thinking and problem-solving ability to students in various design problems, even in different places, scales, and functions.

Disadvantages:

- Method needs to save time (nearly one month) for research and data collection. During analysis and listing of these inputs, lecturer guidance is necessary. Thus instructor should be informed to explain previous solutions of each input.

CONFLICTS OF INTEREST

No conflict of interest was declared by the authors.

ACKNOWLEDGMENT

The authors would like to thank Gazi University Academic Writing Application and Research Center for proofreading the article.

REFERENCES

Aydınlı, S. (1993). *Mimarlıkta Estetik Değerler*. İTÜ Mimarlık Fakültesi Baskı Atölyesi.

Bayazıt, N. (1994). *Endüstri Ürünlerinde ve Mimarlıkta Tasarlama Metodlarına Giriş*. Literatür Yayıncılık.

Bayazıt, N. (2004). *Endüstriyel Tasarımcılar için Tasarlama Kuramları ve Metotları*. Birsen Yayınevi.

Ching, F. (2011). *İç Mekan Tasarımı* (Çev: B. Elçioğlu), Yem Yayınevi, İstanbul.

Christopher, J. J. (1970). *Design Methods; seeds of human futures*. John Wiley and Sons.

Connell, E. (1997). *Teaching Intuition: Ways of Knowing for Begining Design Students*, the 14th Conference on the Begining Design Students, Pittsburgh, Pennsylvania, April 3-6.

Farrelly, L. (2011). *Mimarlığın Temelleri* (Çev. Neslihan Şık). Literatür Yayınları, Akademik Temeller Dizisi 01, İstanbul.

Filiz, S. (2010). *Konut Tasarımına Yönelik Sürdürülebilirlik ve Teknoloji Bağlamında Bir Gelecek Tahmin Modeli*. Doktora Tezi, İstanbul Teknik Üniversitesi Fen Bilimleri Enstitüsü.

Hasol, D. (2004). *Mimarlık ve Teknoloji*. Cumhuriyet Gazetesi Mimarlık Eki, Web Sitesi. https://xxi.com.tr/i/teknoloji-etkisi

Kuloğlu, N. (2014). Mevcut Çevrede Tasarım: Stüdyo Deneyimleri. Mimari Güncellemeler, Şengül Öymen Gür (Editör), Nobel Yayın Dağıtım, İstanbul,.

Lawson, B. (1990). *How Designers Think, The Design Process Demystified*. The Architectural Press Ltd.

Şentürer, A. (1995). *Mimaride Estetik Olgusu: Bağımsız-Değişmez ve Bağımlı-Değişken Özellikler Açısından Kavramsal, Kuramsal ve Deneysel Bir İnceleme*. İTÜ Mimarlık Fakültesi Baskı Atölyesi.

Shane, G. (1976). Contextualism. *Architectural Design*, 46(11), 676–679.

Terzidis, K. (2006). *Algorithmic Architecture*. Architectural Press. 10.4324/9780080461298

Ünal, F. C. (2013). Tasarım Sürecinin Saydamlaştırılmasında Hesaplamalı Tasarım Yöntemlerinin Kullanılması. In *VII MSTAS Conference Proceedings*. Research Gate.

Uraz, T. U. (1993). *Tasarlama, Düşünme, Biçimlendirme*. İTÜ Mimarlık Fakültesi.

Vural-Cutts, A. (2018). *Teknoloji Etkisi*. XXI Dergisi. http://www.doganhasol.net/mimarlik-ve-teknoloji.html

Williamson, T., Radford, A., & Bennetts, H. (2003). *Understanding Sustainable Architecture*. Spon Press.

Zenter, Ö. (2018). *Kinetik Biyomimetik Yaklaşımların Mimari Tasarımda İşlevsel Esneklik Amaçlı Kullanılması*. Yüksek Lisans Tezi, Gazi Üniversitesi Fen Bilimleri Enstitüsü.

Zenter, Ö., Özmen, F., & Yıldırım, T. (2024). Deprem Sonrası Çocuk Özel Eğitim Yerleşkesi Mimari Tasarım Deneyimi. *Journal of Architectural Sciences and Applications*, 9(Special Issue), 270–292. 10.30785/mbud.1334865

Zuk, W., & Clark, R. H. (1970). *Kinetic Architecture*. Van Nostrand Reinhold Company.

Chapter 10
Creative Experimental Architectural Design Teaching

Bartosz Sliwecki
https://orcid.org/0000-0002-6231-967X
Bialystok University of Technology, Poland

Adam Jakimowicz
Bialystok University of Technology, Poland

Szymon Andrejczuk
https://orcid.org/0009-0004-1054-7955
Bialystok University of Technology, Poland

Maciej Poplawski
Bialystok University of Technology, Poland

ABSTRACT

This chapter explores computer-aided architectural design (CAAD) in architectural education, focusing on innovative tools in design studios. A collaboration between AAAA University of Technology's Architecture Faculty and AuReLa Laboratory, it investigates form-finding through emotions, particularly fear's impact on design. The chapter demonstrates 3D tools' versatility for various design aspects, from abstract to more technically feasible. Additionally, it presents an approach integrating AI-generated images into architectural design, highlighting AI's potential in creating almost real time concept designs. Findings show a dichotomy in architectural education: students using abstract tools in their third semester struggle technically later, while those focusing on technical skills initially limit their creative expression. This emphasises the need for balance in architectural curricula between abstract and technical skills, but also challenges the academic community into using novel tools to constantly modernise their design teaching methods.

DOI: doi

EARLY STUDIO CONTENT

The specificity of the works conducted at the Faculty of Architecture of "XXX" University of Technology revolves around the freedom to adapt and experiment with teaching methods, and be able to modify our approach based on each semester outcomes and the relationship of the student - study course in the short (up to two semesters after the initial class) and long term (up until the end of the full study course). Students attend a mandatory class called Computer Aided Architectural Design during their third semester of classes, in which they pick up the basics of the use of diverse softwares suites as an assisting tool in the earliest stages of architectural design. Softwares vary from year to year, starting from the use of Cinema4D in the years 2010-2018, to the introduction of Blender in 2018 (is currently in constant teaching curriculum), as well as basics of Lumion, Twinmotion and Unreal Engine in 2020.

Class topics, however, have been proven to be the most influential part of the design studio (Achten, 2003), like in the case of our experimental process, as their orchestration and implementation brought the most vivid results in the students' performance and overall graduate quality (Asanowicz, 1996). Early stage design tasks have always been one of the most important moments in the development of architecture students' creative process and skills (Lizondo-Sevilla et al., 2019), (Saghafi et al., 2015), as their strategic moment in time allows for the introduction of a design school narrative to begin to make sense, but at the same time enough time to explore and evolve their skills in the later parts of the course. At times, the topics' atypical and seemingly contingent nature may seem odd to the student, as topics range from anything like the task of designing a solitary miniature home to the design of one's fear as a three dimensional model. These topics are constructed based on the results of verbal interviews and informal talks with mentors and previous semesters' class teachers regarding the collective skills and difficulties, which greatly influence the upcoming topic and focus points. Talks are also being constantly held with the class teachers who follow up after CAAD class to gather short term results of past groups, as a follow up measure to ensure appropriate balance and quality of technical to creative freedom.

The teaching staff of Computer Aided Architectural Design class of the third semester of first degree studies were allowed to freely modify and redesign the class curriculum based on their experiences and feelings regarding the needs and expectations of the students. Teachers could conduct class without the need to integrate their content with other teachers of the same class but at different times with different groups of students. Around half of the CAAD third semester teaching staff decided to autonomously conduct and design class materials in a modified manner, while the remaining half continued working as they had in the previous years. The following is a brief representation of selected works which, in the authors' perspective, appropriately portrays the style and environment of the Faculty of Architecture at "XXX" University of Technology. Mentioned project results are in chronological order, starting from 2017/2018 up until the work in progress of 2022/2023.

Facade, Form, Space

One of the most visual differences in the change of student's project outcomes was noticed when more expressive forms began appearing as a result of inquiries such as "Can I?", "Should I?", "Would it be acceptable?". Certain individuals started to show interest in experimental methods of form finding and form presentation, such as the use of tessellation mesh modifiers. These created extremely heavy and cumbersome models that, when textured and lit properly, resulted in interesting forms for possible further development. While not suitable to be called a technically well made 3D model, their expressive forms were regarded as an intriguing approach to the creation of space and form as a result of a learning process in conceptual architectural design (Attoe & Mugerauer, 1996).

Figure 1. Selected works from the early stages of experimental form finding. On the left is a corridor-like space designed by Agnieszka Skorulska, on the right is an open-functioned architectural form made by Aida Katarzyna Jastrzebska.

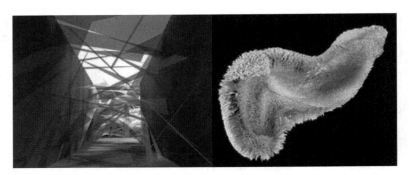

This particular group of around 32 students was subjected to a transitional phase, as their design tasks were to design, model and render a facade, form and space in the span of one semester. Previous years of CAAD class were based on this three step subject, which is why students were expecting the same of the class even before attending third semester, as the results from past years were displayed on the walls outside the classroom. Much of the previous works were of constructive nature, which meant that they could possibly be built in real world scale using known construction methods. Forms generated after this class were beginning to no longer take the shape of buildable objects and possible buildings, due to their uncommon nature and lack of adhesion to the ground. This however, also carried a problem of finding a suitable end point of a given design, as the freeform approach lacked a clear definition, thus proving to hinder a disproportionate focus on one of the three design tasks that were to be finalised by the end of the semester. Reflecting on those challenges, the course design had to be modified as to allow the students to have more control on the time spent on a given design and to allow them to be graded by a chosen set of outputs, rather than to expect all of the designs to be finished, regardless of the quality and effort put into the latter ones (Figure 1).

Simulation as a Medium for Experimental Forms

The following year, the subject was further altered, by removing the first and second task and focusing on the personal development of students in the three dimensional world by learning more experimental methods of creating 3D models such as particle physics, fluid simulations, parametric modifiers. A greater focus was made present on the importance of the method of achieving the form, as well as presenting it as a final image. This, in the end, provided the teachers with an assortment of much higher quality images of more expressive and experimental forms that deviated from traditional concepts of architectural design. From the received almost 50 designs, not one presented the virtual form as the prevalent barnhouse (Kalakoski & Thorgrimsdottir, 2022) depiction of modern architecture that we, as part of the design community, are seeing all too commonly used today. A possible downside of was noted at the start of the given semester, that the projects the students would work on would not be considered as architectural content, and such experiments would risk being disapproved by more experienced and of more traditional approach professors at the faculty.

By using simulation as a means to "generate" work, students focused their creativity on simulation environment settings, quality of simulations and the final presentation. Most of the semester was spent on tweaking particle settings in fluid simulations, arranging attractor fields and managing boundaries while maintaining a general idea of what the final output may look like. This, for the most part, proved very time consuming, as most of the authors never had prior experience with physics simulations and expected quality results with mediocre settings in record times, which in the end proved otherwise. For the teaching staff, this approach meant diving much deeper than anticipated into miniscule modifications that would sometimes save a given simulation setting from being scrapped and forced to drastically over simplify the form and reduce the possible quality of the final outcome.

As a result, most of the designs turned out rather odd and underwhelming, as the final renderings exceeded the time frames of the design studio and had to be drastically modified, mainly by downsampling and reduction of mesh density. The teaching staff came to a unanimous decision to withdraw from this approach for future cases, as the topic not only proved too difficult for most students, but also resulted in fairly low satisfaction of learned skills in general architectural design.

Emotional Sculptures in the Process of Form Finding

With the ability to continue modifying the virtue of the class, the next year of students was given the chance to further rethink the way we design architecture and consider what is and is not architectural form. Focusing on unorthodox architectural forms, students received a task to define and depict their greatest fear, and present it in a way that is both terrifying for the author, and interesting to look at by others. It should be noted that this proved to be one of the most challenging tasks yet, as it required more time than anticipated working individually with the students to verify their understanding of the topic. Early stages of this design task brought concepts of trivial haunting nature; the use of skeletons, dark spaces, foggy dead forests displayed in unexciting scenery. When inquired again about their greatest fear, the authors of the banal designs gave intriguing and personal answers that were later transformed into much more compelling designs compared to the primary concepts (Figure 2).

In the realm of architectural education, the exploration of emotions, particularly complex ones such as fear, presents a unique and potentially transformative avenue for enhancing creativity among architecture students. This concept, while somewhat unconventional within the traditional architectural curriculum, offers a rich tapestry of creative possibilities that can significantly augment the pedagogical process (Varinlioğlu et al., 2018). This exploration can be particularly impactful in a design studio setting, where the tangible translation of abstract emotions into physical spaces can challenge and expand the creative boundaries of students.

The incorporation of emotional dimensions into architectural design is not entirely new. Theories of architecture have long acknowledged the emotional impact of built spaces on individuals. However, the deliberate use of complex emotions like fear as a conceptual tool in the design process represents a more novel approach. Fear, in this context, is not merely about creating spaces that evoke a sense of dread or anxiety but rather about using the multifaceted aspects of this emotion to inspire innovative design thinking (Nanda et al., 2014). Fear can be interpreted in numerous ways – from the fear of environmental degradation to anxieties about social disconnection – each offering a unique lens through which students can conceptualise and approach architectural design.

In a design studio setting, this approach would involve guiding students through a process of identifying, understanding, and translating fear into architectural forms. This process begins with a phase of introspection and discussion, where students are encouraged to explore and articulate their interpretations of fear. This exploration can be facilitated through various means, including literature, film, art, and personal experiences, providing a rich source of inspiration (Asanowicz, 2004).

Following this, students would engage in the conceptualization phase, where these emotional interpretations are transformed into tangible design ideas. This phase challenges students to think beyond conventional architectural paradigms, considering how abstract emotional concepts can be manifested in spatial design, materials, and form. For instance, the design of a building that embodies the fear of environmental decay might incorporate sustainable materials and organic forms, reflecting a harmonious yet uneasy relationship with nature.

Figure 2. The fear of losing a sibling. Student Maria Jablonska designed and modelled this visual depiction of her greatest fear. Her inspirations were the disembodiment of skin from muscle tissue during the process of cooking meat.

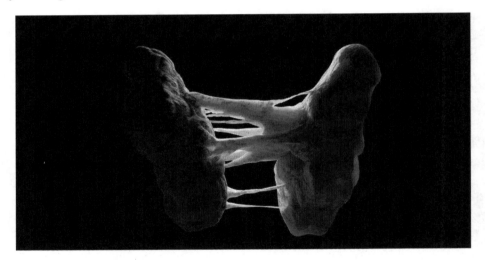

The integration of fear as a conceptual tool in architectural design has profound implications for creativity. It compels students to engage with architecture at a deeper, more introspective level, pushing them to create designs that are not just aesthetically pleasing but also emotionally resonant. This approach can lead to the creation of spaces that are not only functional but also rich in narrative and symbolic meaning, offering a more immersive and thought-provoking experience to the inhabitants. Moreover, this method fosters a higher level of critical thinking and problem-solving skills. Students are required to grapple with complex emotional concepts and translate them into practical design solutions, a process that enhances their cognitive flexibility and creative problem-solving abilities.

Creative Experimental Architectural Design Teaching

Home Office Technical Limitations

Upon receiving urgent feedback from the staff of urban design and large area architectural design that students are struggling with producing of quality 3D models of simple geometric shaped buildings, the design studio had to shift the focus from very organic and expressive forms to more traditional and physically realistic designs in order to tilt the balance from the experimental to the technical aspects of architectural design. The next group of students was tasked with designing a secluded, single dweller home with a view. This time, the experimental aspect of class revolved around the freedom to choose sites and not limit themselves to most modern physical constraints, but to maintain a feeling of verisimilitude in the construction sense.

The span of the semester was held mostly online due to the COVID-19 outbreak, and had many difficulties of the mentoring, focus and willpower nature, as some designs experienced numerous, full-scale transformations. The ability to use computer heavy simulations and experimental functions was very limited, as the undergrads still worked on low capability home office hardware, most of whom were only finding out that it would be near impossible to render on their private computer a month before the deadline. Hand-in proved to be both interesting and slightly disappointing, as the majority of designs consisted of ever present gable roofs, but at the same time showed an increased interest in quality visual presentation of the designs (Figure 3).

Figure 3. A home with a view by Jakub Trusiewicz (left) who excelled in the visual aspects of his design, and wanted to create something realistic, while Patrycja Dyra (right) primarily focused on thinking outside the box in regards to concept design, all the while keeping the presentation quality at an appropriate level.

The consequent CAAD class was also held in a similar fashion, but with the increased popularity and use of Unreal Engine as a tool for presenting results in a static fashion. Unfortunately, the sheer complexity and steep learning curve of the software proved to be too time consuming for the students and many of them resolved back to using tools like Lumion and Twinmotion, which has a more relaxed user interface and workflow. As a result, feedback from other teachers of the faculty was mainly about the increased technical abilities of the general public of the given year, with higher awareness of rapid presentation methods. On the other hand, however, visually the designs began to return to monotonous and oversimplified forms, especially that of the latter residential design classes. In contrast to the exploration of complex emotions like fear in conceptual design (Shearcroft & Geoff 2021), the implementation of more pragmatic, "down-to-earth" approaches in computer-aided architectural design (CAAD) courses, such as designing homes in realistic settings, has yielded a different set of outcomes. This approach, while aligning closely with the practical aspects of architectural education and meeting the expectations of subsequent course modules taught by other faculty members, has been observed to result in a relatively uniform and less adventurous spectrum of student designs.

In our design studio, the shift towards a more "down to earth" approach, focusing on the practical aspects of residential design in realistic settings, was initially implemented to bridge the gap between theoretical concepts and real-world applications. This method emphasises the practicalities of architectural design, including adherence to building codes, structural feasibility, and functional layouts, which are undoubtedly crucial skills for budding architects.

However, an unintended consequence of this pragmatic approach has been a noticeable homogenization of student designs. The designs, while proficient in meeting practical requirements and realistic constraints, often lacked the innovative and experimental qualities that are typically encouraged in early design education. The projects tended to converge towards safe, conventional solutions, reflecting a certain reticence to venture beyond established architectural norms. The trend towards more conventional designs raises questions about the balance between creativity and practicality in architectural education. While it is essential for students to develop skills that are directly applicable to professional practice, it is equally important to foster an environment where creative exploration is encouraged. The challenge, therefore, lies in finding a middle ground where students can experiment and innovate while also developing a sound understanding of practical design considerations.

In response to the observations of a trend towards more conventional designs within our studio, we initiated a process of reevaluating our pedagogical strategies. This reevaluation led us to explore ways to reintegrate elements of creative exploration into the more pragmatic design tasks that had become a staple of our curriculum (Billings & Akkach, 1992). Our approach involved revising the design briefs to ensure that, while they remained grounded in reality, they also included elements or challenges that would encourage students to think more creatively. For instance, we had students engage in projects that required designing a conventional residential home, but with a specific focus on sustainable living or integrating unique cultural elements.

AI IN CAAD TEACHING

Recognizing the need to invigorate the creative process, we began exploring more novel tools to incorporate artificial intelligence in concept design. This exploration was aimed at harnessing the potential of AI to expand the boundaries of traditional design methodologies, offering students a new dimension of creative possibilities. The integration of AI tools was seen as a means to stimulate innovative thinking, allowing students to generate and explore a wider array of design concepts more rapidly than conventional methods would permit (Figure 4).

Creative Experimental Architectural Design Teaching

Figure 4. Cabin in the woods concept designs. Tasked with creating early stage concepts of a temporary settlement / cabin in the woods, students began experimenting with different materials, methods of placement, forms, all through the communication with the neural network of Stable Diffusion. Designs and prompts were created by Marcin Ciulkin (left) and Szymon Siwicki (right).

In the contemporary realm of architectural design, the integration of Artificial Intelligence (AI) marks a paradigmatic shift, heralding a new era of creativity and efficiency. Today's architects harness AI not only as a tool for simplification but as a collaborative partner in the design process (Nagakura 2017). The advent of AI in architecture is exemplified by sophisticated software such as Rhino with its Grasshopper plugin, and Autodesk's suite of generative design tools, which have revolutionised the way architects conceptualise and execute their visions. These platforms employ algorithms that can analyse complex datasets, allowing for the optimization of design elements based on specific criteria such as material usage, energy efficiency, and spatial dynamics. This AI-augmented approach enables a form of generative design where myriad possibilities are explored in a fraction of the time traditionally required, pushing the boundaries of architectural innovation (Lukovich & Tamas, 2023).

A key aspect of this evolution is the emergence of generative models as a potent tool in the architect's arsenal. Unlike traditional design methodologies that often progress linearly, image generation models facilitate a non-linear, iterative process. It allows architects to input design parameters and receive a plethora of generated design options, each uniquely calibrated to the input criteria (Harapan et al., 2021). This process not only accelerates the ideation phase but also introduces a level of design variation and creativity previously unattainable (Figure 5). The AI-generated designs often reveal unconventional and innovative solutions, challenging architects to think beyond their standard design lexicon. This is particularly pivotal in early-stage conceptualization, where the rapid generation of diverse design alternatives can significantly enrich the creative dialogue.

Figure 5. Another example of an Early (December 2022) generation by Michał Breczko from "AI.rchitecture Workshops" with the use of the early Stable Diffusion models available in 2022

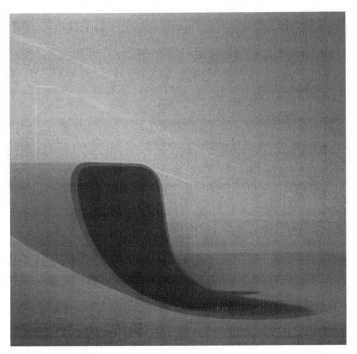

However, the integration of AI in architectural design is not without its challenges. The reliance on algorithm-driven solutions risks diminishing the architect's direct creative input, potentially leading to a skills gap in traditional design methods. Moreover, the ethical implications, particularly concerning data privacy and the homogenization of design, warrant cautious consideration (As et al., 2018). As we stand at the cusp of this technological revolution in architecture (Steenson, 2022), it is imperative to strike a balance between embracing AI's potential and preserving the indispensable human elements of creativity and intuition that have long been the bedrock of architectural design.

Building upon the aforementioned advancements in the field of AI in architectural design, the design studio at the Faculty of Architecture of "XXX" University of Technology stands as a pioneering example of how these innovative technologies can be assimilated into the educational sphere. This venture, particularly aimed at first and second-year students, is an exploratory journey into the integration of Stable Diffusion models, leveraging Discord as a collaborative and communicative platform, and intertwining these with traditional CAD/CAAD practices.

This initiative represents a novel approach in architectural education. By introducing Stable Diffusion models into the curriculum, the studio is not only keeping pace with the rapid advancements in architectural technology but also propelling students to the forefront of design innovation. These AI models serve as a digital muse, offering students a plethora of design possibilities that transcend the conventional boundaries of early architectural education. The use of Stable Diffusion allows students to experiment with complex design ideas, which, in the traditional pedagogical approach, might have been deemed too advanced for their level. This exposure to advanced AI tools at such an early stage in

Creative Experimental Architectural Design Teaching

their architectural journey is instrumental in shaping a new generation of architects who are adept at harmonising technology with creativity (Debrah et al., 2022).

The studio's utilisation of Discord as a medium for interaction and exchange further exemplifies the innovative spirit of this program. Discord, primarily known for its prevalence in gaming communities, is repurposed as a dynamic, real-time platform for students to share ideas, receive feedback, and collaboratively refine their designs. This digital forum fosters a sense of community and ongoing dialogue, essential in the creative process, allowing students to engage with their peers and instructors in an interactive and accessible environment. The blend of synchronous and asynchronous communication on Discord ensures that learning and collaboration are not confined to the physical studio space, thus extending the boundaries of architectural education beyond traditional limits.

Balancing Creativity and Engineering Skills

In juxtaposing AI-driven design processes with CAD/CAAD drawings, the studio strikes a crucial balance. While the AI models offer a new lens through which to view architectural and urban design (Czarnecki & Chodorowski, 2021), the importance of foundational skills in CAD/CAAD is not undermined. Students are encouraged to translate the AI-generated concepts into precise architectural drawings, a process that not only grounds the AI concepts in the realities of architectural design but also reinforces their technical skills. This dual approach ensures that while the students are propelled into the future of design with AI, they remain firmly rooted in the essential skills that form the backbone of architectural practice.

In the context of the architectural design studio at the Faculty of Architecture of "XXX" University of Technology, the integration of artificial intelligence, particularly through the use of Stable Diffusion models, represents a significant pedagogical advancement. This technological integration, primarily aimed at enriching the educational experience of first and second-year students, brings forth the challenge of balancing the expansive creative potential afforded by AI with the stringent technical and engineering requirements intrinsic to realistic architectural design (Turrin et al., 2011).

The introduction of AI into the curriculum fundamentally alters the traditional paradigm of architectural education. It provides students with the unprecedented ability to generate a wide array of design concepts at an accelerated pace. The Stable Diffusion models serve as a catalyst for creativity (Po et al., 2023), enabling students to explore a multitude of architectural possibilities. However, this surge in creative freedom necessitates a corresponding emphasis on the practical aspects of architecture. The primary educational objective thus becomes guiding students in the critical evaluation and refinement of AI-generated concepts (Figure 6), ensuring that these designs are not only innovative but also viable within the constraints of real-world architectural practice (Abioye et al., 2021).

Figure 6. Student Patrycja Grochowska's design which was remade several times to incorporate a believable physical constraint of the floating capsule, as to increase the realism factor of the generated image

A crucial aspect of our pedagogical approach involves the transition from the ideation phase, heavily reliant on AI-generated designs, to the precise drafting phase utilising AutoCAD. This transition is a critical educational juncture, as it compels students to apply their foundational knowledge of architectural principles and engineering constraints to the AI-generated concepts. The process of translating these concepts into detailed architectural plans in AutoCAD is not merely a technical exercise; it represents a complex synthesis of creativity and feasibility. Students are required to critically assess each design, considering factors such as structural integrity, material viability, and functional practicality, thereby bridging the gap between imaginative design and practical application (Dash & Sharma, 2022).

In our role as educators, we place significant emphasis on mentorship and the development of critical thinking skills. We continuously engage with students to cultivate an understanding of the importance of balancing innovative design with technical pragmatism (Duniewicz & Magdziak, 2022). This involves rigorous discussions and critiques (Lu et al., 2023), focusing on the viability of AI-generated designs in terms of architectural engineering principles. Such an approach is instrumental in developing a comprehensive skill set in our students, enabling them to navigate the multifaceted challenges of modern architectural design.

Therefore, our studio's endeavour is not just to introduce students to the latest advancements in AI but to instil a deep understanding of the complexities involved in transforming AI-generated concepts into feasible architectural solutions (Rabbani et al., 2021). This focus is crucial in preparing our students for the demands of the architectural profession, where the successful integration of creative and technical competencies is essential for the conception and realisation of sustainable and impactful architectural projects.

Creating the Toolset

In implementing the integration of AI into our architectural curriculum at the Faculty of Architecture of "XXX" University of Technology, a significant preparatory phase was undertaken by both the teaching and technical staff. This phase was crucial in ensuring that the Stable Diffusion models were not only appropriately tailored for educational purposes but also accessible and user-friendly for our students. The preparation involved the customization of Stable Diffusion models for integration into Discord bots (Kruglyk et al., 2020), as well as the careful selection of the most current, creative, and safe models available from sources like CivitAI and HuggingFace.

The initial focus of our technical team was on adapting Stable Diffusion models to function efficiently within Discord. This adaptation required the development of custom bots capable of interfacing with the Stable Diffusion API, enabling students to generate architectural designs directly through Discord. The design of these bots emphasised user-friendliness and intuitive interaction, considering the diverse technical backgrounds of our student body. Moreover, these bots were engineered to handle a high volume of design requests simultaneously (Xie et al., 2022), ensuring a smooth and efficient user experience (Figure 7) and (Figure 8).

Concurrently, a thorough evaluation of available models on platforms such as CivitAI and HuggingFace was conducted. This evaluation aimed to identify models that exemplified the latest advancements in AI-generated creativity while adhering to strict ethical standards and safety in content generation. The selection criteria focused on the models' ability to produce a wide range of architectural styles and contexts, aligning with the diverse educational goals of our studio. Moreover, ensuring the ethical compliance of these models was paramount, necessitating a rigorous vetting process to avoid any generation of biassed or inappropriate content.

Figure 7. Statistical use of the available Discord image generation bots in the course of the summer semester of 2023. The most frequent time of use was in the hours of class time, on Wednesday between 10:15 and 15:10. The second grouping of most frequent use is the day before class between 19:00 and 01:00.

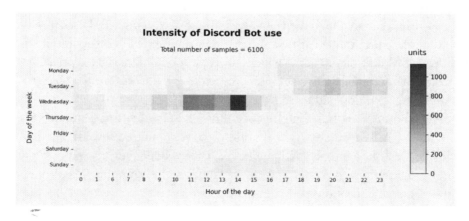

Figure 8. Statistical use of the available Discord image generation bots in the course of the summer semester of 2023. Additional times of use remained semi-active after class time, especially between 18:00 and 21:00 as well as between 22:00 and 01:00 of the next day.

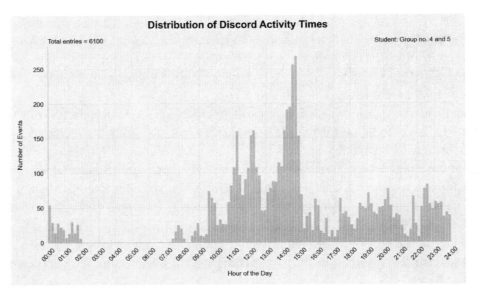

An integral component of this preparatory phase was the training and familiarisation of our faculty with these new technological tools. Comprehensive workshops and training sessions were organised, equipping the faculty with the necessary skills and knowledge to effectively guide students in using the AI tools and integrating them into their design projects. This training was essential not only for the effective use of the tools but also to enable faculty members to provide technical support and troubleshoot potential issues.

To further assist students in their design endeavours, the team developed detailed guidelines and resources. These resources included step-by-step tutorials for using the Discord bots, best practices for design generation using Stable Diffusion, and important ethical considerations in the context of AI-generated designs. Additionally, a repository of inspirational materials, case studies, and examples of AI-generated architectural designs was made accessible to students through Discord, providing them with a rich source of inspiration and learning.

In the implementation of artificial intelligence through Stable Diffusion models within the Faculty of Architecture at "XXX" University of Technology, we encountered several practical challenges that significantly influenced our approach and outcomes. These challenges, rooted in technological limitations and systemic disruptions, provided critical insights into the complexities of integrating advanced computational tools in an educational environment.

One of the primary issues faced was related to the functional limitations of the Discord bots, which were employed as intermediaries for students to interact with the Stable Diffusion models. The bots, while designed to facilitate an intuitive and seamless interface, experienced inconsistencies in performance. This was particularly evident in their processing capabilities (He & Kaiming, 2016), where some bots failed to efficiently handle the volume or complexity of requests. These inadequacies led to delays and, in some instances, a complete inability to generate the requested architectural designs. This issue was not merely a technical hurdle but a pedagogical one (Wahyuningsih & Baidi, 2021), as it disrupted the flow of the learning process and hindered the students' ability to engage effectively with the AI tools.

Compounding these technical difficulties was the challenge of limited computational resources, a direct consequence of constrained financial allocations to our department. The deployment of AI, particularly models as advanced as Stable Diffusion, requires substantial computational power, typically necessitating high-end hardware specifications. The infrastructure available within our studio, limited by budgetary constraints, struggled to meet these demands, resulting in slower processing times and a reduction in the overall efficiency of the design generation process. This resource limitation presented a significant obstacle in fully realising the potential of AI integration in our architectural curriculum.

Additionally, the integration process was further complicated by disruptions caused by routine updates to the Windows operating system. These updates, integral to maintaining system security and performance, occasionally resulted in compatibility issues with the AI tools and the Discord bots. The aftermath of these updates often entailed software malfunctions or necessitated reconfigurations, leading to interruptions and delays in the educational activities. The unpredictability and frequency of these updates added a layer of complexity to managing the AI tools, requiring constant vigilance and adaptability from our technical support team.

In response to these challenges, our team undertook a multi-faceted approach to mitigate their impact. For the Discord bots, this involved extensive code revisions and improved integration with the Stable Diffusion API. To address the limitations posed by inadequate computational resources, we explored various optimization strategies and actively sought additional funding for hardware upgrades. Furthermore, we adopted a more strategic approach to managing system updates, aligning them with periods of reduced academic activity to minimise their disruptive impact.

These challenges, encountered during the initial phases of AI tool integration, provided valuable lessons in the practical aspects of deploying advanced technologies within an educational setting. They underscored the necessity for ongoing technical support, resource optimization, and adaptability in curriculum design. These experiences have been instrumental in refining our approach, enabling us to more effectively harness the potential of AI in enhancing architectural education.

The final aspect of this preparation involved establishing a protocol for ongoing monitoring and updating of the AI models and Discord bots, with the help of ChatGPT among others (Rane & Nitin, 2023). This protocol ensured that the tools remained current with the latest developments in AI technology and were continuously improved based on the feedback received from students and faculty. This iterative approach to tool refinement has been instrumental in maintaining the relevance and efficacy of the AI integration in our architectural curriculum.

The AI Design Process

In the design studio at the Faculty of Architecture of "XXX" University of Technology, the pedagogical approach to integrating artificial intelligence in architectural design follows a structured, multi-step process (Soliman, 2017). This process is meticulously designed to guide students through the various stages of architectural design, from conceptualization to finalisation, leveraging the capabilities of Stable Diffusion and AutoCAD. The following outlines the sequential steps undertaken in this innovative educational approach:

Step 1: Generation of Architectural Concepts using Stable Diffusion

The first step involves the utilisation of Stable Diffusion, an AI-powered generative model, to create numerous architectural designs. Students are tasked with generating varied images of a house set in a unique environment. This step encourages creative exploration, allowing students to experiment with different architectural styles, settings, and compositions. The AI model's ability to rapidly produce diverse designs provides students with a broad spectrum of conceptual possibilities, fostering creativity and innovation in the initial design phase (Abdelhameed, 2017).

Step 2: Selection of the Optimal Design

Following the generation of multiple designs, students engage in the critical process of selecting the most promising architectural concept for further development. This cherry-picking stage is crucial as it requires students to evaluate the designs based on aesthetics, originality, and potential for practical realisation (Fross et al., 2015). The chosen design serves as the foundation for subsequent stages, marking the transition from abstract AI-generated concepts to concrete architectural planning.

Step 3: Dimensional Quantification and Drafting in AutoCAD

The third step involves translating the selected AI-generated design into a quantifiable architectural plan. Students meticulously analyse the chosen design to ascertain its dimensions and spatial layout. Utilising AutoCAD, these dimensions are then accurately drafted, transforming the conceptual AI-generated image into a detailed and technically sound architectural drawing. This phase bridges the gap between AI-driven creativity and the precision required in architectural drafting.

Step 4: Generation of Interior Renders using Stable Diffusion

With the exterior architectural plan drafted, the focus shifts to the interior. Students return to Stable Diffusion to generate interior renders, applying the same creative process used in the initial stage. This step allows students to conceptualise interior spaces that are in harmony with the external architecture, ensuring a cohesive design narrative.

Step 5: Refinement of Drawings and Integration of Interior Designs

Once the interior renders are generated, students work on integrating these designs with the existing architectural plans. This involves modifying and refining the original AutoCAD drawings to accommodate the interior concepts. The process is iterative, requiring continuous adaptation and adjustment to ensure that the interior designs are feasible within the established architectural framework.

Step 6: Finalisation of the Design Poster

The final step in the process is the creation of a comprehensive design poster. This poster encompasses both the exterior and interior designs, along with detailed architectural drawings. It serves as a visual and technical summary of the students' work, showcasing their ability to seamlessly integrate AI-generated concepts with traditional architectural drafting. The design poster is not only a culmination of the students' creative and technical efforts (Figure 9) but also a tangible representation of their learning journey through the integration of AI in architectural design.

Creative Experimental Architectural Design Teaching

Figure 9. Final hand-in by Mateusz Suszko. The poster represents the compilation of the initial generated designs, the technical drawings, interior renders and extra interior items.

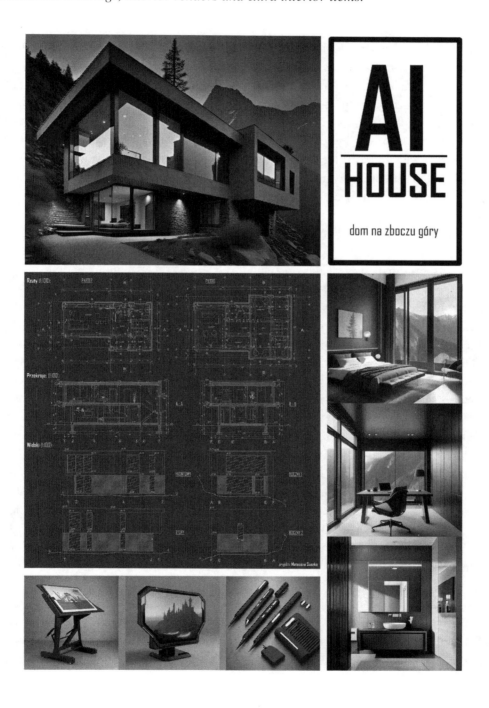

Impacts and Insights

The integration of artificial intelligence, particularly through the use of Stable Diffusion models in the architectural curriculum at "XXX" University of Technology, presents an opportune moment to reflect on its impact on student skills and creativity, the balance between traditional and AI-assisted design methods, and considerations for future curriculum development. These aspects are critical in understanding the broader implications of such technological integrations in architectural education.

The introduction of AI into the design process has significantly influenced the skill set and creative capabilities of our students. On one hand, AI tools have empowered students to explore a wider range of design possibilities than would be feasible with traditional methods alone (Stouffs, 2015). The ability of AI models to generate diverse and complex designs rapidly has expanded the students' creative horizons, encouraging innovation and experimentation. This exposure to AI-assisted creativity has also necessitated the development of new skills, including the ability to effectively interact with AI tools, interpret AI-generated outputs, and integrate these outputs into a coherent design process.

However, there is a concern that over-reliance on AI could potentially impact the development of foundational architectural skills. The ease and speed with which design options can be generated by AI might lead to a diminished emphasis on manual sketching and conceptualization skills, traditionally considered essential in architectural training (Alexander, 1977). Therefore, it is imperative to strike a balance, ensuring that while students are adept at using AI tools, they also continue to develop and refine their fundamental design skills. The challenge of integrating AI into the architectural curriculum is not just about incorporating new technologies but also about maintaining a synergy with traditional design methods. This balance is crucial for several reasons. First, it ensures that students are well-rounded in their skill set, capable of engaging with both traditional and contemporary design practices. Second, it acknowledges that while AI can significantly enhance the design process, the creative intuition and critical thinking inherent in traditional methods remain irreplaceable.

In our curriculum, we have endeavoured to maintain this balance by using AI as a complementary tool rather than a replacement for traditional design methods. For instance, while initial concepts are generated using AI, students are still required to engage in manual drafting and model-making to refine these concepts. This approach ensures that students appreciate and understand the value of both methodologies, recognizing that each has its unique strengths and applications in the architectural design process.

Looking ahead, there are several considerations for future curriculum development. Firstly, as AI technology continues to evolve, it is vital to continuously update the curriculum to incorporate the latest advancements and ensure that students are exposed to the most current tools (Figure 10) and methods (Ruiz-Montiel & Manuela, 2013). Secondly, there needs to be an ongoing evaluation of how well the balance between traditional and AI-assisted methods is being maintained, making adjustments as necessary to ensure that both are given adequate emphasis. Additionally, ethical considerations related to the use of AI in design must be integrated into the curriculum. As students become more reliant on AI tools, it is important to educate them about issues such as data privacy, bias in AI algorithms, and the environmental impact of high-powered computing used in AI processes (Epstein et al., 2023). Finally, fostering a collaborative environment where students can critically discuss and reflect on their experiences with AI tools is essential. This not only aids in the learning process but also prepares them for professional practice, where collaboration and critical evaluation are key components of successful architectural projects.

Figure 10. One of the more up to date generations from Magdalena Essel, a first time user of AI tools for architectural image generation, with the use of Stable Diffusion XL. This new generative model allows for much more photo realistic and believable designs.

DISCUSSION

As researchers and teachers, we found out about the importance of balancing the right proportions of the types of experimental design methods that we introduce to our students at the early stages in the architectural design course. Having students perform more technically focused tasks during the second and third semester of studies results in a greater percentage of individuals who excel in the technical stages of the architectural design process, but at the same time generates a similar proportion of students who display a lack of enthusiasm and freedom of expression when faced with more open tasks (Billings & Akkach, 1996). Similarly, an equal but opposite result was noticed in the final year of studies of the students, where their course of studies had more instances of technical issues and problems of the engineering aspect of the design process, but at the same time generated some of the more eye pleasing thesis dissertations.

While the above mentioned may seem like a result to be expected of, the observations of the staff at the Faculty of Architecture had in fact favoured the collection of two consecutive groups of students who were less technical in their approach to studies, but had more abilities to express their design preferences with the use of experimental form finding tools and methods (Asanowicz, 2008). In the words of some of the staff, students "suggested more radical and surprisingly odd designs" at the early stages of class topics, which were later rationalised and coherent with modern design trends. The downside of this approach is the increased amount of negative comments from partnering professional design studios and architectural companies that directly display their slight disapproval for preparing students with a lower technical focus and higher design frivolity (Kılıçaslan & Kalaycı, 2021). In the eyes of the faculty, it is much more important and difficult to teach students to be more creative than it is to understand technicalities of the tools and methods in the design process, into which the professional architecture employer can make adjustments and improvements after taking in new staff.

Graduates that finished their course within the past 4 years expressed their thoughts regarding our methods, as appropriately vectored but with need of further development. Some atelier owners and our graduates' employers mentioned that while students had basic understandings of a wide variety of technical aspects in architectural design, many of them lacked the ability to provide fair solutions to design problems. Fairly simple problems proved very difficult for most students, as they had trouble with finding creative ways to look for solutions, while merely proposing forms that lacked creativity and deeper thought.

In the design studio's evolving pedagogical approach, we are now focusing on achieving a balance between various technological tools, including artificial intelligence, Computer-Aided Design (CAD), Building Information Modeling (BIM), and 3D printing, especially in the initial stages of architectural design. The current curriculum tasks students with utilising AI platforms such as Stable Diffusion, MidJourney, and DreamStudio, not only to conceptualise designs but also to engage in a nuanced interaction with these advanced tools. This approach is designed to broaden the students' understanding and proficiency in a diverse set of design tools, fostering a comprehensive skill set that encompasses both traditional and innovative methodologies.

The objective of this integrated approach is twofold. Firstly, it aims to introduce students to a range of modern tools in architectural design, ensuring they are well-equipped for the evolving demands of the profession. Secondly, it seeks to encourage unconventional approaches to conceptual design by leveraging the unique capabilities of community-driven, open-source tools. By engaging with AI in the design process, students are exposed to new ways of thinking and designing, which can significantly enhance their creative abilities.

This blend of AI, CAD, BIM, and 3D printing is expected to yield significant educational outcomes. It may produce individuals who not only excel in utilising alternative tools in the design process but also contribute to the further development of these technologies (Stouffs, 2018), tailoring them more specifically to the needs of architects. This holistic approach to integrating technology in architectural education is instrumental in preparing students to be versatile, innovative, and forward-thinking in their future architectural endeavours.

REFERENCES

Abdelhameed, W. A. (2017). Creativity in the initial phases of architectural design. *Open House International*, 42(1), 29–34. 10.1108/OHI-01-2017-B0005

Abioye, S. O., Oyedele, L. O., Akanbi, L., Ajayi, A., Delgado, J. M. D., Bilal, M., & Ahmed, A. (2021). Artificial intelligence in the construction industry: A review of present status, opportunities and future challenges. *Journal of Building Engineering*, 44, 103299. 10.1016/j.jobe.2021.103299

Achten, H. H. (2003). New design methods for computer aided architectural design methodology teaching. *International Journal of Architectural Computing*, 1(1), 72–91. 10.1260/147807703322467441

Alexander, C. (2018). *A pattern language: towns, buildings, construction*. Oxford university press.

As, I., Pal, S., & Basu, P. (2018). Artificial intelligence in architecture: Generating conceptual design via deep learning. *International Journal of Architectural Computing*, 16(4), 306–327. 10.1177/1478077118800982

Asanowicz, A. (1996). Teaching and learning-full brainwash. In *Education for Practice-14th Conference on Education in Computer Aided Architectural Design in Europe (eCAADe)* (pp. 51-54). Lund: eCAADe. 10.52842/conf.ecaade.1996.051

. Asanowicz, A. (2004). Computer, Creativity and Unpredictability. *Digital Design Methods*, 350-354.

Asanowicz, A. (2008). How to Find an Idea?-Computer Aided Creativity. In *Architecture in Computro [26th ECAADe Conference Proceedings]* (pp. 735-742). Research Gate.

Attoe, W., & Mugerauer, R. (1991). Excellent studio teaching in architecture. *Studies in Higher Education*, 16(1), 41–50. 10.1080/03075079112331383081

Billings, K., & Akkach, S. (1992). A study of ideologies and methods in contemporary architectural design teaching: Part 1: Ideology. *Design Studies*, 13(4), 431–450. 10.1016/0142-694X(92)90171-6

Czarnecki, B., & Chodorowski, M. P. (2021). Urban Environment during Post-War Reconstruction: Architectural Dominants and Nodal Points as Measures of Changes in an Urban Landscape. *Land (Basel)*, 10(10), 1083. 10.3390/land10101083

Dash, B., & Sharma, P. (2022). Role of artificial intelligence in smart cities for information gathering and dissemination (a review). *Academic Journal of Research and Scientific Publishing*, 4(39).

Debrah, C., Chan, A. P., & Darko, A. (2022). Artificial intelligence in green building. *Automation in Construction*, 137, 104192. 10.1016/j.autcon.2022.104192

Duniewicz, A., & Magdziak, M. (2022). Typology of Tactile Architectural Drawings Accessible for Blind and Partially Sighted People. *Sustainability (Basel)*, 14(13), 7847. 10.3390/su14137847

Epstein, D. C., Jain, I., Wang, O., & Zhang, R. (2023). Online detection of ai-generated images. In *Proceedings of the IEEE/CVF International Conference on Computer Vision* (pp. 382-392). IEEE.

Fross, K., Winnicka-Jasłowska, D., Gumińska, A., Masły, D., & Sitek, M. (2015). Use of qualitative research in architectural design and evaluation of the built environment. *Procedia Manufacturing*, 3, 1625–1632. 10.1016/j.promfg.2015.07.453

Harapan, A., Indriani, D., Rizkiya, N. F., & Azbi, R. M. (2021). Artificial Intelligence in Architectural Design. [INJUDES]. *International Journal of Design*, 1(1), 1–6. 10.34010/injudes.v1i1.4824

He, K., Zhang, X., Ren, S., & Sun, J. (2016). Deep residual learning for image recognition. In *Proceedings of the IEEE conference on computer vision and pattern recognition* (pp. 770-778). IEEE.

Kalakoski, I., & Thorgrimsdottir, S. (2023). Learning from the secondary: Rethinking architectural conservation through 'barn architecture'. *Journal of Material Culture*, 28(2), 199–220. 10.1177/13591835221123953

Kılıçaslan, H., & Kalaycı, P. D. (2021). A Joint Manifesto for Design Studios based on Residuals and Experiences. *Periodica Polytechnica Architecture*, 52(1), 66–74. 10.3311/PPar.16758

Kruglyk, V., Bukreiev, D., Chornyi, P., Kupchak, E., & Sender, A. (2020). Discord platform as an online learning environment for emergencies. *Ukrainian Journal of Educational Studies and Information Technology*, 8(2), 13–28. 10.32919/uesit.2020.02.02

Lizondo Sevilla, L., Bosch Roig, L., Ferrer Ribera, M. C., & Alapont-Ramón, J. L. (2019). Teaching architectural design through creative practices. *Journal of the Faculty of Architecture*, 36(1), 41–59.

. Lu, H., Yang, G., Fei, N., Huo, Y., Lu, Z., Luo, P., & Ding, M. (2023). *VDT: General-purpose Video Diffusion Transformers via Mask Modeling*.

Lukovich, T. (2023). Artificial Intelligence and Architecture Towards a New Paradigm. *YBL Journal of Built Environment*, 8(1), 30–45. 10.2478/jbe-2023-0003

Nagakura, T. (2017). Acadia 2017 Disciplines & Disruption. *Proceedings of the 37th Annual Conference of the Association for Computer Aided Design in Architecture*. Acadia Publishing Company.

Nanda, U., Pati, D., Ghamari, H., & Bajema, R. (2013). Lessons from neuroscience: Form follows function, emotions follow form. *Intelligent Buildings International*, 5(sup1), 61–78. 10.1080/17508975.2013.807767

Po, R., Yifan, W., Golyanik, V., Aberman, K., Barron, J. T., Bermano, A. H., & Wetzstein, G. (2023). *State of the art on diffusion models for visual computing*. arXiv preprint arXiv:2310.07204.

Rabbani, M., Bashar, A., Atif, M., Jreisat, A., Zulfikar, Z., & Naseem, Y. (2021). Text mining and visual analytics in research: Exploring the innovative tools. In *2021 International Conference on Decision Aid Sciences and Application (DASA)* (pp. 1087-1091). IEEE. 10.1109/DASA53625.2021.9682360

Rane, N. (2023). Role of ChatGPT and Similar Generative Artificial Intelligence (AI) in Construction Industry. *SSRN* 4598258. 10.2139/ssrn.4598258

Ruiz-Montiel, M., Boned, J., Gavilanes, J., Jiménez, E., Mandow, L., & Pérez-de-la-Cruz, J.-L. (2013). Design with shape grammars and reinforcement learning. *Advanced Engineering Informatics*, 27(2), 230–245. 10.1016/j.aei.2012.12.004

Saghafi, M. R., Mozaffar, F., Moosavi, S. M., & Fathi, N. (2015). Teaching methods in architectural design basics. *Ciência e Natura*, 37, 379–387. 10.5902/2179460X20868

Shearcroft, G. (2021). The joy of architecture: Evoking emotions through building. *Architectural Design*, 91(1), 108–117. 10.1002/ad.2660

Soliman, A. M. (2017). Appropriate teaching and learning strategies for the architectural design process in pedagogic design studios. *Frontiers of Architectural Research*, 6(2), 204–217. 10.1016/j.foar.2017.03.002

Steenson, M. W. (2022). Architectural intelligence: How designers and architects created the digital landscape. *MIT Press*.

Stouffs, R. (2018). Implementation issues of parallel shape grammars. *Artificial Intelligence for Engineering Design, Analysis and Manufacturing*, 32(2), 162–176. 10.1017/S0890060417000270

Stouffs, R., & Rafiq, Y. (2015). Generative and evolutionary design exploration. *Artificial Intelligence for Engineering Design, Analysis and Manufacturing*, 29(4), 329–331. 10.1017/S0890060415000360

Turrin, M., Von Buelow, P., & Stouffs, R. (2011). Design explorations of performance driven geometry in architectural design using parametric modeling and genetic algorithms. *Advanced Engineering Informatics*, 25(4), 656–675. 10.1016/j.aei.2011.07.009

Varinlioğlu, G., Pasin, B., & Clarke, H. D. (2018). Unconventional formulations in architectural curricula: An atelier on design for outer space architecture. In *Proceedings of the 15th International Conference on Engineering and Product Design Education (E&PDE)* (*Vol. 15*, pp. 93-105). Research Gate.

Wahyuningsih, E., & Baidi, B. (2021). Scrutinizing the potential use of Discord application as a digital platform amidst emergency remote learning. [JEMIN]. *Journal of Educational Management and Instruction*, 1(1), 9–18. 10.22515/jemin.v1i1.3448

Xie, C., Wang, Y., & Cheng, Y. (2022). Does artificial intelligence satisfy you? A meta-analysis of user gratification and user satisfaction with AI-powered chatbots. *International Journal of Human-Computer Interaction*, 1–11.

Chapter 11
Excessively Undisciplined Works:
On Situating the Architectural Design Studio Off-Centre

İrem Küçük
https://orcid.org/0000-0002-5725-6002
Gazi University, Turkey

ABSTRACT

This study deals with the pedagogy of architectural design studios. By analyzing atelierz as a case study, it builds a discussion on situating the architectural design studio off-center, implementing experimental pedagogy, and producing excessively undisciplined work. Dealing with such a subject is crucial in exploring and discussing how architectural knowledge and skills, which cannot be fully accommodated within the scope of architectural education, are made accessible, used, and produced in the studio. The first part of the study, divided into three parts, explains what is off-center in architecture. The second part discusses the need to adopt an experimental pedagogic approach to situate the studio off-center and explains the experimental fiction of atelierz. The third part exemplifies the fictions and works of atelierz, discussing the excessively undisciplined nature of the knowledge and skills they lead to. Considering the conceptualizations, pedagogic fiction descriptions, and experiences presented, the opportunities and risks of situating the studio off-center are discussed.

INTRODUCTION

Architecture covers a wide range of knowledge as the art of creating space. While shaping various and unique spaces, it operates with a wide range of spatial-temporal knowledge that affects every aspect of life (Yılmaz and Aksu, 2019). Like many other fields of knowledge, architecture consists of both well-established and accepted information at its center and less accepted or scattered information on its periphery. Knowledge at the center is based on tried and tested methods and findings with an established, sustainable, static structure. Knowledge at the periphery, on the other hand, is based on intuitive, fictional, and experimental methods, with its unestablished, scattered, dynamic structure (Aksu, et al., 2011). The center and the periphery, through their constant interaction, construct architecture and form

DOI: doi

an ever-expanding field of knowledge. However, due to its expansiveness, architecture cannot have sharp boundaries. This situation is also decisive in the shaping of architectural education. Accordingly, the knowledge that architecture covers can only partially fit within the duration and scope of an architectural education. (Salama 2015) Given this vastness, while educational programs may include courses that extend to the unaccepted or scattered information of the periphery, the primary focus is on ensuring the transmission and continuity of central knowledge. On the other hand, the architectural design studio, the integrative mechanism of architectural education, has a suitable structure for using and synthesizing all kinds of information that education provides or cannot provide and has a suitable structure for expansion (Aksu et al., 2011). Its creative and investigative potential, providing an integrative field for iterative practice, can offer a dynamic space for addressing the unique needs and processes of architectural research (Hawkes 1995) Moreover, the flexible structure of the studio, which can vary according to different pedagogical approaches, is noteworthy because it allows for the development of fictions that can host a vast educational content extending beyond the center.

Depending on the pedagogical approach adopted, the educational content of the architectural design studio can be situated at the center to transfer, and process established knowledge. It can equally be situated off-center by shifting towards the periphery to process less accepted or yet-to-be-accepted scattered knowledge and produce new data-driven connections. The concept of "off-center" can be understood in the context of broad spatial-temporal data, where different disciplines can interact through the extension provided by their peripheries. With this understanding, situating the studio off-center means designing within ambiguity and fluidity, allowing for interaction and free connection with different fields and unprocessed, raw information. This kind of situatedness calls for an experimental pedagogy. Moreover, the existence of an experimental design practice in the studio, because it extends the space-time data dealt with, realizes a different production from the works that can be situated directly at the center. It organizes scattered information into an established form that cannot be situated within the boundaries of a specific discipline and does not belong directly to any discipline. Therefore, it is possible to define the design works produced in this field as excessively undisciplined works.

With this understanding, this study proposes shifting the architectural design studio towards the periphery to situate it off-center, aiming to equip architecture students with an understanding of the expanding field of architectural knowledge. It seeks to provide them with fundamental skills and comprehension to continuously develop, re-construct, and expand their knowledge and abilities in this field. Accordingly, the study highlights the necessity of rethinking the studio's ways of operating at off-center and introduces an experimental pedagogical approach. Discussing this experimental approach in relation to the work produced in the studio, it showcases the productive discussions and research-based dynamic educational content that arise from producing excessively undisciplined work, both within studio processes and during presentation and communication stages.

This study deals with the experimental pedagogical approach, fiction, and works of an architectural design studio, namely atelierz. It is one of the vertical design studios in Gazi University, Faculty of Architecture, Department of Architecture, where undergraduate second-, third-, and fourth-year students work together. Atelierz defines an original and autonomous workspace that integrates design education with research, working as a design laboratory creating experimental studio fictions shaped in thematic series. By analyzing atelierz as a case study, this study builds a discussion on situating the architectural design studio off-center, implementing experimental pedagogies, and producing undisciplined works in the studio. Dealing with such a subject is crucial in exploring and discussing how architectural knowledge and skills, which cannot be fully accommodated within the scope of architectural education, is made accessible, used, and produced in the studio.

With this approach, the first part of the study, divided into three parts, explains what is off-center in architectural design and deals with it through its experimental nature in the context of the excessively undisciplinary relational opportunities it inhabits. The second part discusses the need to adopt an experimental pedagogic approach to situate the studio off-center and explains the experimental pedagogy and training fiction of atelierz. The third part exemplifies the studio fictions and works of atelierz, discussing the excessively undisciplined nature of the knowledge and skills they lead to. Considering the conceptualizations, pedagogic fiction descriptions, and experiences presented, the opportunities and risks of situating the studio off-center, constructing experimental studio fictions, and producing excessively undisciplined works are discussed. The pedagogical approach of atelierz is reflected upon, and the future of architectural education, particularly architectural design studios, is discussed in terms of the extensions it creates within architectural education.

RETHINKING OFF-CENTRE IN ARCHITECTURE

> From the moment of my birth, I lived with pain at the center of my life. My only purpose in life was to find a way to coexist with intense pain. (Haruki Murakami, The Wind-Up Bird Chronicle)
> I was a black center in the middle of all the nature. I was nothing, but I could do anything. (James Franco)

In discussing the off-center in architectural design, the relationship between the center and the periphery and the conceptual extensions developed in the context of this relationship provides a tool for addressing the issue. In the discussions produced in the context of architecture, the center and the periphery are explained as two different states of being, distinct from each other but also related. One is associated with centripetal orientations, the other with centrifugal orientations. The center is discussed in the context of wisdom, which forms an integrated knowledge structure, while the periphery is discussed in the context of information, which represents raw data structures. Whereas its inclusiveness, integration and continuity characterize the one, the other is described by its tendency to diffuse, productivity and capacity for change. (Hancock, 1987) While the center is discussed in the context of the field of continuity it creates, it is associated with the concepts of stability, continuity, permanence, unity, and similarity. On the other hand, while the periphery is discussed in the context of the dynamism it creates, it is associated with the concepts of change, evolution, becoming, temporality, plurality, and difference. (Khansari, 2015) The one is distinguished by its tendency to perpetuate and the other by its tendency to trigger change. However, despite their differences on an almost polarizing level, the center and the periphery are conceived beyond being sharply separated and conflicting structures. They are discussed as integrated structures that complement and create each other. Although the center tends to maintain itself, it has the potential to change by incorporating changes from the periphery. Divergently, the periphery has the impulse to resist disintegration by holding on to the established structures provided by the center, although it tends to change them. In this regard, it is mentioned that if both the center and the periphery operate independently, there is a risk of either solidification in the center or dispersion in the periphery. It is emphasized that the problematic relationship and interoperability between these

Excessively Undisciplined Works

two structures should be studied rather than making one superior to the other. (Hancock, 1987) From this perspective, the center and the periphery can be seen as stable and increasingly unstable extensions of the same whole, as structures in dialogue. While the center creates a gravitational pull that gathers knowledge structures around itself and holds them together, the information structures freed from the influence of the center's gravitational pull towards the periphery become dispersed and tend to spread outwards and become more open to interaction. On the other hand, the off-center shows an existence from which possible information can be produced by enveloping all this unity and leaking it through its gaps.

Although the center-periphery integrity can be seen and described, the off-center cannot be described because it contains inertia that has not taken shape. In this sense, the off-center can be conceptualized as a kind of dark matter that penetrates and surrounds the center-periphery assemblages and allows for the interaction of different centers. The off-center settles between the destabilizing extensions of the center that spread out towards the periphery, creating a completely unstable, multidimensional fluidity.

Figure 1. Center-Periphery and off-center relations of a discipline and interaction of disciplines at the off-center

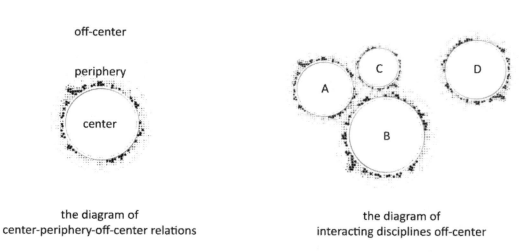

the diagram of
center-periphery-off-center relations

the diagram of
interacting disciplines off-center

Therefore, because of its instability, the periphery shows an inevitable inability to fully grasp what lies within and beyond itself, as Hancock points out. (Hancock, 1987) On the other hand, thanks to the extension of the centers of different formations in the periphery, there is the possibility of meeting outside the center and the spontaneous formation of fields of interaction within the fluidity of the off-center. (Figure 1) There is always the danger of getting lost in the ambiguity of decentralized interaction. However, the existence of things is as much about the influence of what is outside of them as it is about themselves. Extending to the outside opens space for thought and action, for things to emerge from their existence and reconstruct themselves. Acting outside the center can be transformed into a creative process in which the risks are reduced to a tolerable level, depending on the relationship between the center and the periphery. The distance from the existing allows one to recognize its hiddenness, to create new understandings and to reconstruct it. Off-center has the potential to become a medium for creating such a distance, thanks to its otherness, which penetrates almost to the center.

The off-center situation makes it possible to intervene freely in things, placing them in a deferred interval. Constructing a deferred interval is about opening a fictional experimental space that can potentially contain all kinds of data apart from the usual existence of space and time systems. It offers a view from the outside (Yılmaz, 2018). Through constructing an interval of delay, it becomes possible to realize a state of dissolution that allows one to reconstruct things. This kind of dissolution brings things back to their state of being, detaches them from their references and allows for spontaneous associations that allow for chance and arbitrariness. (Deleuze, 2001) (Deleuze and Parnet, 2008, pp.177-185) When things are put together through connections, there is a juxtaposition of unusual things or things put together in unusual ways. Although sometimes random gatherings lead to chaotic situations that make no sense, sometimes they lead to the emergence of original formations through creative connections. In this field, where it is not possible to definitively verify the functioning of a particular route, experimental processes take place that cannot be replicated in the same way. Thus, situating the studio off-center requires a dexterity that allows it to exist in its momentary, fluid state of being.

The experimental nature of being "off" is discussed in the context of challenging conventional practices and encouraging thought-provoking perspectives in architecture. As stated, the experimental imaginative power in this field becomes active and triggers creative formations. It is asserted that experimentalism is waiting to be discovered beyond the center, within the possibilities beyond boundaries. Accordingly, going on adventures and exploring unconventional ideas is highlighted as the fundamental condition for engaging with this field (Boym, 2017). By discovering hidden potentials and grasping momentary interactions, off-center offers a deep exploration field of joyful play. In this sense, off-center can be defined as a playful space characterized by spontaneous interactions that are instantaneous and unrepeatable. It is a space of improvisational action that evolves with unconditional intention and without predetermined conditions. In this sense, it provides a favorable context for conducting architectural design and architectural research practices together in an interactive manner. Taking up the transformation of the architectural design studio into a research laboratory, Atelierz explores ways of situating the studio's context in the off-center. The fictions developed by the studio with this understanding are designed on the basis of creating multiplicity in the studio, triggering experimental processes and improvisational actions, and forming the integration of research and design.

Situating the Architectural Design Studio at the Off-Centre and Experimental Studio Fiction

> I would like to swim against the stream of time: I would like to erase the consequences of certain events and restore an initial condition. (Italo Calvino, If on a Winter's Night a Traveler)

Situating the architectural design studio at the off-center is about moving it away from the center, towards the periphery, with the will to swim against the current, defying the intense gravity of the center. The studio unfolds into a fluid and interactive space where the field of architectural design expands, and data interacts in unstable multiplicities without being suppressed, separated, or marginalized. However, such a situation poses challenges in managing the flow of design processes and fictionalizing the studio

Excessively Undisciplined Works

in a way that allows flexibility and fluidity. atelierz fictionalizes studio series to rethink studio fiction in the context of design themes and design processes. It focuses on exploring and experiencing experimental processes where unpredictable leaps or simultaneous processes can occur beyond defined, predictable processing cycles to activate the experimental nature of the design. It explores ways of using the act of design as a discovery tool to understand the nature of things. In this sense, the pedagogical approach of the studio is designed to provide a ground for each designer to discover themselves by reconstructing themselves as they construct the design. Beyond specific spatial solutions based on formal creations, programmatic arrangements and structural formations, the training given in the studio is fictionalized to create an entity of reflection and construction on both architecture and the architect himself, which the architect can continue to create afterwards.

While atelierz creates experimental training fictions to situate the studio at the off-center, loose structures are assembled that allow for change by considering the actors in the studio and their relational situations, thematic frameworks, and simultaneous, differentiating flows in the processes.

As a vertical design studio where second, third and fourth-year students work together, atelierz works with students with different levels of knowledge and experience. In each training period, the studio work is carried out with a group of about 60-70 people, including the studio coordinators and the students. Working with a large group of students is advantageous for organizing studio training, individually and collectively in smaller groups, and for building multi-layered networks of interaction in the studio. However, the actors who effectively shape the studio training are not limited to the coordinators and students. Organizing events such as trips, lectures, workshops, juries, exhibitions, panels, and competitions to open the studio to the outside world increases the number of actors contributing to the process and enriches the studio. The relationships between all the actors involved in the process, continuously or for short periods, can be diversified and reconstructed at different stages. Students can experience working in large and small groups as well as individually. The coordinators can also develop different forms of interaction among themselves and the students through individual encounters, pairings, and collective encounters. The external actors involved in the process can also be articulated in the relational networks of the studio, depending on how they are involved.

In creating the studio fiction, atelierz fictionalizes extensive thematic frameworks that allow interaction with different disciplines and arranges these frameworks as intricate schemes. Since its establishment, atelierz has shaped all its working periods in thematic series formed by sub-themes shaped around specific main themes. The first of these series is "The Figure of the Architect", which spans six periods. It was designed to question the architecture's definition and the architect's identity. It is structured with the sub-themes of "1 Rebellion Architecture/Rebel Architect", "2 Anywhere Out of the Space", "3 Digital Craft/Digital Craftsman", "4 Chaos", "5 Architecture on the Threshold/ Architect on the Threshold", "6 Architecture of Playing/Player Architect". Simultaneous with the "The Figure of the Architect" series, another series specially designed for the Graduation Project is Back to the Future/the Slum. It problematizes the design of future urban settlements in the context of the formation and construction of slums. Another series, "The Becomings of House," covers two study periods. It questions the potential of creating urban structures with the evolution of the house as a basic spatial structure by transforming it into different spatial structures such as teahouses, madhouses, jailhouses, bookhouses. The last thematic series, which is the subject of this study and has continued throughout eight study periods and continues, is "The Codes of Contemporary Architecture",. "1 Puzzle Architecture/ Memory of Space", "2 Porsuk River Forced to Flow Still", "3 2020+20", "4 Becomings of Earth", "5 Becomings of City", "6 Becomings of Body and Space", "7 Contemplation Spaces I/ Educational Spaces", "8 Contemplation Spaces II/Living Capsules", "9 Contemplation Spaces III/ Urban Collages at the Intersection of Remembering, Forgetting and Dreaming""Cetennial Architecture (1923-2023)", "Cetennial Architecture (2023-20123)"and "Topiagram I" are structured as sub-themes. A series of sub-themes are constructed around the central theme to create the thematic series. The sub-themes, each of which forms the framework of a training period, create the content of the central theme by being articulated with each other and interrelated from different aspects. In this sense, the thematic series created are not closed wholes with a defined beginning or end. On the contrary, each thematic series is an open structure that allows new sub-themes to be articulated or reconsidered. This form of thematic framework allows the studio to exist not only as a training medium but also as a field of research that functions like a design laboratory. In this way, the studio functions as a framework for design experimentation shaped by the research, and the discussions in the thematic context reconstruct the studio theme. Thus, the training content given in the studio is constantly shaped by the integrity of the design and research activities, which, thanks to the openness of the thematic series, produce fringes in various aspects.

Figure 2. Atelierz's studio timeline program

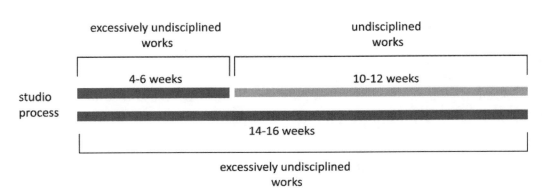

Atelierz's studio process is shaped by the integrity of the design activities that extend into architecture and outside. While this integrity is divided into "excessively undisciplined works" and "undisciplined works" in some training periods, in others, they are intertwined as only "excessively undisciplined works". The part called "excessively undisciplined works" refers to design activities within broad design contexts and creating architectural extensions through the production of artistic works without the studio theme being limited to a specific design discipline. These activities are carried out to enable students to become familiar with the use of different disciplinary methods/tools to structure their thinking, to develop their skills in using these tools and to gain different perspectives in approaching a design problem. During the design activities, where all kinds of digital or analogue tools/devices are allowed to interact with different disciplines, installations will be produced and placed in the spaces of the school or in the designated exhibition spaces. "Undisciplined works", on the other hand, refers to design activities that focus on spatial design studies. These activities are carried out by students who shape the context of their design problem within the studio theme, design the program and create a structural entity. During the production of undisciplined works, it is essential to internalize the learned ways of doing and the skills acquired during the production of excessively undisciplined works and to use them to shape the expression of space. In this direction, the formation of hybrid forms is supported by the interactive use of all kinds of methods/tools. The aim is for students to produce architectural works as designers who instrumentalize technology and produce with artistic sensitivity and craftsmanship. When excessively undisciplined and undisciplined works are handled as two separate parts, the excessively undisciplined works, which form the first part of the 14–16 weeks studio process, are spread over a 4-6 weeks period. Students carry out their design work in groups of 6-10 people. Artists (painters, sculptors, musicians) and designers from different professions are invited to evaluate the works produced, and a public event is organized to exhibit the work according to the content of the first part. The undisciplined works that make up the second part are produced over 10-12 weeks. It is carried out collectively or individually, in groups of 2-4 people, depending on the number and interaction of the students in the studio. The works produced in this part are also presented to the jury for evaluation and to the public at events held in architectural environments. When excessively undisciplined and undisciplined works are considered interrelatedly, the whole studio process is intertwined with different interrelated design activities. A broad assessment group of architects and artists is formed to evaluate the works produced (Figure 2).

Excessively Undisciplined Works

> Blind and unwavering undisciplined at all times constitutes the real strength of all free man. (Alfred Jarry)

Two sub-themes from the series Codes of Contemporary Architecture are discussed to illustrate the experimental educational fictions of the atelierz and the works produced in the context of these fictions. These themes are 'Becomings of Body and Space', which occurred during the pandemic, and Contemplation Spaces I / Educational Spaces', which occurred in the post-pandemic period. It shows the working of atelierz in different design environments, one of which allows the studio to be fictionalized, executed, and produced in a virtual environment and the other in a physical environment.

The Becomings of Body and Space

The theme of 'The Becomings of Body and Space' considers the body as a spatially constitutive structural element on the one hand and problematizes space as a mechanism that reconstructs the body on the other. It explores the body and space as two manifestations of a single state of being. With an approach that questions both the body and space as design objects, it is a theme that explores the immanent relationship between them as calm/tense, conflicting/reconciling and integrating/separating. As the studio takes place in a virtual environment, an experimental space has been opened to use media and tools for designing, expressing, and exhibiting work in a virtual environment.

The process was divided into two parts. The 'excessively undisciplined work' part lasted five weeks and was devoted to understanding the body in operational continuities and discussing its spatial extensions. The students, divided into eight design teams of 9-10 people, studied the body's movement in the context of different action themes, researching the body, the poses of the body's movement, the transitions between different poses and the body elements that create the poses. They expressed the spatial patterns created by the body using various topological mapping methods that make the movement forms of the action visible. Meanwhile, each student created analogue and digital models with their body measurements according to their body characteristics. They then designed teamwork by interacting and associating these models through the virtual environment. Each design team produced body movement diagrams that discussed the action theme, individually and collectively, using specific methods of analysis and association (Figure 3).

Figure 3. Excessively undisciplined works of "The Becomings of Body and Space"

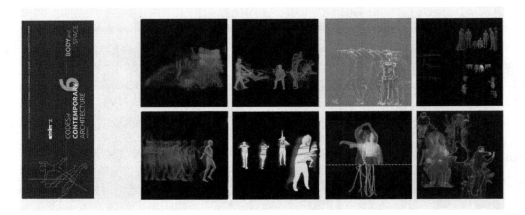

Figure 4. Undisciplined works of "The Becomings of Body and Space"

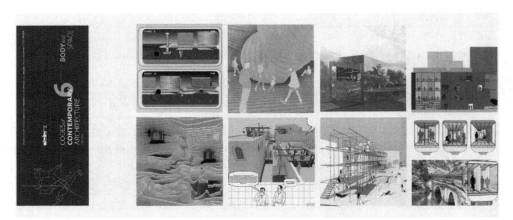

Excessively Undisciplined Works

The "undisciplined works" part of the studio, which spanned ten weeks, focused on designing a performance space tailored to a specific theatrical text in a city of the students' choice within Turkey. Additionally, the project involved creating a digital animation of the theatrical performance within the designed spaces. The students, divided into twenty-three design teams of 2-4 members each, tackled the challenge of designing a performance space specific to their chosen theatrical text. Simultaneously, they were required to develop a spatial organization that would serve as a public space unique to the selected city (Figure 4).

Working on the design of space in the context of the body encouraged students to explore anatomy, choreography, and performance art, fostering off-center relationships. The inclusion of different cities in Turkey and various theatrical texts as contexts created multiplicity, expanding the scope of research. The presence, movement, and spatiality generated by the body as the most fundamental space were investigated. Accordingly, the relationships established by the body at its own, architectural, and urban scales were examined and reimagined. Performing bodily research in both segments allowed for improvisation, triggering and supporting experimental processes. Transforming these performances into spatial expressions and constructs using digital analysis, drawing, and animation tools made the discoveries and research conducted beyond architecture visible and facilitated their transfer into the field of architecture. The proliferation of the produced works across multiple digital platforms, and their experimental nature allowed them to exist as open works, providing an inspiring force.

Contemplation Spaces I/Education Spaces

The theme of "Contemplation Spaces" explores playful architectural productions and discusses the potential of "carnivalesque" formations for architecture. "Contemplation Spaces", a sub-thematic series under the central theme of the Codes of Contemporary Architecture, was discussed through different spatial contexts and contents.

Figure 5. Excessively undisciplined works of "Contemplation Spaces I/ Education Spaces"

Figure 6. Undisciplined works of "Contemplation Spaces I/ Education Spaces

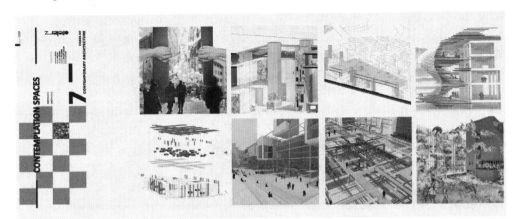

The first one focuses on educational environments in architecture. The design problem was constructing the educational environment as a carnival that enables people to reconstruct themselves and objects. Conducting the studio in a physical environment has created an experimental and experiential space, enabling students to directly transform their educational surroundings.

As with the previous theme, the studio process was divided into two parts. The "excessively undisciplined works" part, which lasted six weeks, was dedicated to discussing and experiencing carnivalesque spatial arrangements in the context of different conceptual contents. Divided into nine design teams of 6-7 people, the students transformed the spaces of the Architecture Department into a playground by producing installation works. Using materials like cloth, masks, cardboard boxes, plastic tubes, balls, balloons, tin foil, newspaper, printing materials, paint, and methods like sewing, hanging, glueing, and attaching, the installations have been designed on a performance basis. The designed group works were placed concerning each other in the common spaces, where the classrooms of the architecture department were opened, and a carnival was constructed in which the space was reconstructed in a playful way (Figure 5).

The "undisciplined works" part, which lasted ten weeks, was dedicated to redesigning the Maltepe campus in Ankara in Turkey, where the students are educated. The students, divided into twenty-four design teams of 2-3 people, considered the site on which the campus is located as volumetric integrity and worked on the spatial, programmatic and structural restructuring of the volume outside the existing buildings on the site. Students were encouraged to develop unusual perspectives on the spatial arrangement in which they live and to produce experimental spatial constructs. In the production of the works, digital design tools were used in intensive interaction with analogue design tools, taking advantage of the physical studio environment (Figure 6).

Working on space design within the context of carnivalesque structures has created a broad context for expanding into different fields of knowledge and thought, thanks to the diverse nature of the carnivalesque. This approach allowed for an off-center exploration. Having students address their own educational environments supported by inventive research inspired by the creative nature of architectural education. The nature of spaces where architectural education is delivered was questioned regarding the content and activities involved. In the first part, the focus was on the interior setups of the architecture department, while the second part explored how an architecture school could be designed with dialogic, carnivalesque content in an urban context. The production of performance-based installations throughout the process allowed for improvisation in both constructing and experiencing, fostering an experimental workflow. The experiences gained from building installations were then transferred to designing an architecture school in an urban context, creating a channel for transferring research beyond architecture into the field of architecture. Additionally, working in a spatial context that the students directly experienced and lived in helped them internalize and experientially reflect on the subject matter. Throughout the term, all research on architectural education and its spaces was discussed through architectural project productions, utilizing analogue or digital drawing, modelling, and animation tools. This approach provided a practical perspective on the subject. The simultaneous or sequential repeated construction of the works developed during the studio process, in various forms such as installations, performances, drawings, models, and animations, enabled multiple productions of content and expression. This, in turn, has encouraged the creation of more interrelated and experimental works.

CONCLUSION

Atelierz aims to construct the studio as a design laboratory where design and research are integrated, considering that architectural knowledge extends beyond the boundaries of disciplines. In this direction, it proposes situating the studio off-centre to interactively conduct research and design activities. By situating off-center, atelierz critically examines the pedagogical content and processing of the studio, incorporating experimental content and processes into its agenda. It explores ways of establishing integrity of researching, thinking and building within experimental processes. In this sense, the practice maintained by the studio creates a intertwined way of exploring, understanding and doing to access, use, and reproduce architectural knowledge and skills.

This study discusses architectural design studio education with an experimental pedagogical approach regarding context-scope, methods and productions. The fictions developed by the studio are designed on the basis of creating multiplicity in the studio, triggering experimental processes and improvisational actions, and forming the integration of research and design. The study structures research on the studio's situating off-centre, its experimental processing and its production of excessively undisciplined works. In the context of the explanations on the situating, fictions and works of the studio, by exemplifying two periods of the studio, what is researched, how it is researched and what is produced through design in the studio is revealed. As the findings show, in the studio:

- Within the framework of open-structured fictions suitable for developing different research and design topics, research and design works that diversify both in terms of the subject they deal with and the production media they use are produced.
- Through the encouragement of experimental processing based on improvisation, original ways of researching, thinking and doing develop
- Through the orientation of the production of open-structured undisciplinary works, it has been revealed that inspiring and questioning works are produced through the interactive use of different production media.

The studio constructions and studio works created in line with the experimental pedagogical approach of Atelierz contribute to both the theoretical and practical fields of architecture with the transdisciplinary connections they establish, the research and discussion areas they open, and the innovative and experimental methods they develop. The studio's off-center situating and experimental working create the potential for developing original theoretical and practical architectural content and structures. Spreading across a broad field that encourages creativity and exploration enables the production of unique, interdisciplinary, and open-structured experimental works. Additionally, it fosters the construction of distinctive architectural identities that are specialized with versatile knowledge and skills.

By its very nature, designing in the chaotic field of off-centre, capable of unlimited expansion, runs the risk of becoming entrenched by adhering to accepted trends or being lost in uncertainty where all references are lost. Nevertheless, atelierz's construction of an experimental field that can be extended to anything related, even the existing or the non-existing, opens a space for discovering the intuitive and performative design skills necessary to design in a flow that reveals the original. In this sense, the studio keeps on its agenda the construction of research-based training structures that question the knowledge and skills acquired in the design studio where the architects of the future are trained in the face of the problem of dreaming and realizing the architecture of the future.

ACKNOWLEDGMENT

Thanks to Adnan Aksu, who is the founder of atelierz and we work together to develop experimental training fiction, to Tuğba Ersen, Ezgi Başar, Sinem Yıldırım and Deniz Uygur, who are the studio coordinators, to Sefa Ercan, Sinem Görücü, Aysu Kuştaş who supported the studio for the theme of "Contemplation Spaces I" and to all the students of atelierz who contributed to the research and design studies carried out during all these studio periods, for making possible this paper to be written.

REFERENCES

Aksu, A. (2016). "Dur Bir Mola Ver": Dünyayı Değiştirmeye İhtiyacın Var. In *Mimarlık Eğitiminde Pedagoji ve Pratik Arasında Var Olmak Symposium Book* (pp. 1-10). İstanbul Kemerburgaz University, İstanbul.

Aksu, A., Küçük, İ., & Çağlar, N. (2011). *Mimari Tasarım Eğitimi Söylemleri 2: Bütünleşme*. In YTU 2th National Symposium, İstanbul.

Aksu, A., & Yılmaz, İ. (2019). *Mimarlığın İcadı Mimarın İnşası, Mimarlık Okullarında Tasarım Stüdyoları: Farklı Denemeler*. Yem Yayın.

Atölye Z ile 'Beden ve Mekan Halleri'. (2021, May 21). Arkitera. https://www.arkitera.com/haber/atolye-z-ile-beden-ve-mekan-halleri/

Atölye Z ile 'Çağdaş Mimarinin Kodları' Dizisi. (2020, June 20). Arkitera. https://www.arkitera.com/haber/atolye-z-ile-cagdas-mimarinin-kodlari-dizisi/

Boym, S. (2017). *The Off-Modern*. Bloomsbury Publishing. 10.5040/9781501328961

Çağlar, N., & Aksu, A. (2017). *Tenekeden Mimarlık*. Şevki Vanlı Yayınları.

Çağlar, N., & Aksu, A. (2021). *Mimarlığı Öğrenmek, Yapmak, Yazmak Üzerine Spekülasyonlar, 1919-2019 Samsun Yüzüncü Yıl Mimarlık Konuşmaları*. TMMOB Mimarlar Odası Samsun Şubesi Yayınları.

Deleuze, G. (2001). *Empiricism and Subjectivity*. Columbia University Press.

Deleuze, G., & Parnet, C. (2008). The Actual and the Virtual. In *Dialogues* (pp. 177–185). Flammarion.

Hancock, J. E. (1987). Continuity, Change and the "Edges" of Architecture. *Journal of Architectural Education*, 40(2), 26–28.

Hawkes, D. (1995). The Centre and the Periphery: Some reflections on the nature and conduct of architectural research. Arq-architectural. *Research Quarterly*, 1(01), 8–11. 10.1017/S1359135500000051

Khansari, M. G. (2015). Defining "Center and Edge" Concepts and Their Relationship with Durability and Dynamism in Architecture. *Armanshahr Architecture & Urban Development*, 8(14), 13–22.

Küçük, İ., & Aksu, A. (2023). Rethinking the Pedagogical Fiction of the Architectural Design Studio. Periodica Polytechnica. *Architecture (Washington, D.C.)*, 1–10.

Salama, A. M. (2015). *Spatial Design Education: New Directions for Pedagogy in Architecture and Beyond*. Routledge.

Salama, A. M., & Osbourne, L. (2009). Unveiling the experiential dimension of field/work in architectural pedagogy.

Yılmaz, İ. (2018). *Rethinking Design Space in Architecture*. [Doctoral dissertation, Gazi University.

Chapter 12
Active Learning Strategy for First-Year Design Studio:
The ÖzU Case

Derya Yorgancıoğlu
https://orcid.org/0000-0002-5583-3515
Özyeğin University, Turkey

Semra Aydınlı
https://orcid.org/0009-0001-7573-0919
Özyeğin Univrsity, Turkey

Beyza Şat
Özyeğin University, Turkey

Doğa Dinemis Aman
https://orcid.org/0000-0002-9076-3401
Özyeğin University, Turkey

Burçin Mızrak Bilen
Özyeğin University, Turkey

Gizem Efendioğlu
Özyeğin University, Turkey

Zümrüt Şahin
Özyeğin University, Turkey

Mert Zafer Kara
https://orcid.org/0000-0002-1864-2541
Özyeğin University, Turkey

ABSTRACT

This study aims to examine the active learning strategy applied in the first-semester design studio, the 2023-2024 fall semester, in the Department of Architecture at Özyeğin University in Türkiye. The ÖzU Case differed from traditional basic design pedagogy, where the design problem is divided into its components and the basic elements and principles of design are discussed through a part-to-whole approach. Methodologically based on a case study analysis, the examination dwells on the following themes: (1) Student engagement in learning process, (2) cooperative learning, (3) role of the tutor, (4) multiplicity of teaching and learning activities, and (5) flexibility and adaptability of space. The study revealed that the active learning strategy enabled ARCH 101 Design students to grasp a holistic approach to design and develop ways of seeing with the mind's eyes, through the integration of the learning by experiencing and learning by doing activities.

DOI: doi

THE IMPORTANCE OF ACTIVE LEARNING IN DESIGN EDUCATION

In the 21st century a paradigm shift from teacher-centred to student-centred pedagogy, informed by the constructivist learning approach, manifested itself in the field of design education. According to this paradigm shift, people construct their knowledge and worlds of meaning through their own experiences and reflections based on these experiences.

Design education requires an active learning environment based on a dialogue between tutor and student, encouraging different learning styles and students' authorship in their learning processes (Abdelmonem, 2014; Coorey, 2016). Active learning strategy is essential for the first-semester design studio that is expected to enable a critical and constructive learning environment for students who encounter design studio pedagogy for the first time (Boucharenc, 2006; Yorgancıoğlu, et al., 2023). First-year design students are introduced to new ways learning informed by an experimental, iterative, and experiential approach dwelled in thinking-doing unity and a new type of knowledge that is "conceptually learned and experientially grasped" (Erkök, et al., 2005: 63).

Active learning strategy focuses on learning how to learn to attain life-long learning ability. Different than passive learning approaches that dwell on the transfer of knowledge from teacher as an authority, to student as a recipient of knowledge, active learning approaches supports direct involvement of students to their own learning processes which aims to help them learn how to learn through a dialogue that involves asking and answering questions to discover new ways of thinking, understanding, interpreting, and transforming knowledge (Biggs, 1999; Enomoto et al., 2022). In design education, the tutor moderates this dialogue by constructing an intellectual atmosphere in which students discover new ways of thinking, understanding, and interpreting architecture, design elements and principles (Aydınlı & Kürtüncü, 2018). Within this atmosphere design knowledge is contextually transformed, created, and constructed by students' curiosity, motivation, and awareness on sense of place, opening the doors into design through discovery. Active learning strategy gives way to critical thinking within this intellectual atmosphere and enhances creative thinking, while also motivating students to open their mental locks through curiosity. It initiates a mental process that addresses cognitive and affective dimensions of the learning process. The student is seen as an active learner who tries to create meaning and make interpretations based on existing mental modes and new experiences (Köseoğlu & Tümay, 2013). This approach is also based on learning by doing theory, developed by John Dewey, which encourages confronting reality and questioning and expressing oneself. For Dewey (1963), a creative mind that can establish a network of relationships makes learning easier. Dewey's theory of learning by doing has some parallels with the active learning strategy in the design studio that encourages the formation of transformative knowledge in a constructivist learning environment. According to a constructivist approach, learning occurs as a process of knowledge formation in different contexts (Özden, 2013). Thus, the determining factor of the quality of education is not storing knowledge but using it contextually and creating new knowledge from it.

THE STRUCTURE OF ARCH 101 DESIGN COURSE

ARCH 101 Design course covered the modules of "Project 1: Conceptualization and Visualization", "Project 2: Multidimensional Spatial Experiences," and "Project 3: Human-Space Relationship." It consisted of 5 sections and 140 students in total and was conducted twice a week in a large joint studio environment in which all the tutors, research assistants and students interact with each other. A design brief given for each project was supported by theoretical presentations and discussions. Students worked both individually and as groups to develop their designs. In each section, tutors gave both one-on-one feedback to student projects, but also initiated group discussions and peer reviews. Additionally, joint pin-ups and juries were convened, in which students received feedback from other sections' tutors and learned from other students' projects. This multiple feedback model allowed knowledge transfer and co-creation both in sections and in the whole ARCH 101 studio, which in turn enhanced the formation of a critical and creative design culture.

The AAAA case differed from traditional basic design pedagogy, where the design problem is divided into its components and the basic elements and principles of design are discussed with a part-to-whole approach. To divide the whole problem into separate components to make it easier to address, and to address each portion separately has been one of the characteristic features of twentieth century intellectual life. As a result, many architects have lost the "big picture" that might give rise to associations and connotations of different knowledge types (Kurokawa, 1998). In response to the loss of the big picture in AAAA case, a shift from the conventional model of teaching to an active learning strategy is adopted. The problem with this mainstream approach was that the students could hardly internalize and transfer this basic knowledge and skills to their following design projects. A holistic approach to active learning strategy gives rise to possibilities of seeing with the mind's eyes and grasping the big picture of design elements and principles. The discourse on "the whole is more than sum of its parts" helps students to understand and interpret these design elements and principles in relation to each other and within a web of relations. Active learning begins with the whole and expands to include the parts, emphasizing the pursuit of student's questions, curiosity, and interest in architecture (Aydınlı & Kürtüncü, 2018). Students' own questions and curiosity are also used to promote "learning how to learn" strategy. The outcome-oriented past study experiences of students based on rote learning at the upper secondary education and before, are quite unserviceable and create a challenge for the design education. Diverse ways of thinking, problem solving, researching, creative knowledge usage and production are fostered among the students. Giving room for plurality in approaching design problems is prioritized. Although first-year design students need guidance, the old behaviour patterns of formula or prescription seeking as passive learners are transformed. The group work abilities are encouraged and supported.

ARCH101 Design course offered at AAAA is based on the active learning strategy that has two tactics: (1) learning by experience and (2) learning by doing. Learning by experience takes place through "seeing with the mind's eye" where all design elements and principles are in relation to each other to generate an awareness and sensibility on the built and natural environments. Learning by doing approach supports students in transferring the awareness and knowledge they develop through theoretical and conceptual discussions and the sensory experience they gain by interacting with the environment, into the design production processes. By drawing sketches, designing composition and collage studies, generating physical models, and testing the material potentials/limitations they learn designing by through making. Design knowledge is contextual and variable; thus, the strategy to learn design knowledge is more important than the method to teach design knowledge (Goldschmidt, et al., 2010). A teaching and learning dialogue that fosters a learning atmosphere dwelling on the discovery -rather than transmission- of knowledge should be created. Discovering knowledge through intuition is becoming indispensable in contemporary education systems and it encourages learning by experience and learning by doing through which students internalize design knowledge for themselves according to their own requirements (Aydınlı & Kürtüncü, 2018). Accordingly, the active learning strategy applied for ARCH 101 Design studio is examined under

5 themes: (1) student engagement in learning process, (2) cooperative learning, (3) role of the tutor, (4) multiplicity of teaching and learning activities and (5) flexibility and adaptability of space.

Figure 1. Multi-layered structure of ARCH 101 design studio

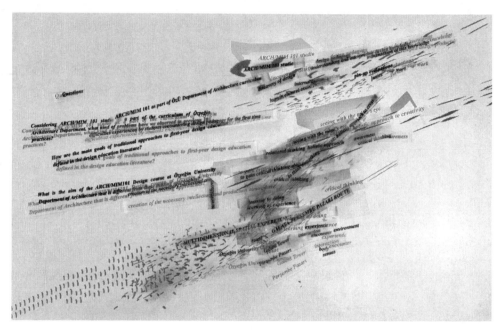

Student Engagement in Learning Process

A design studio structured as an active learning environment should encourage the students to freely share their ideas, participate in feedback processes, and discuss each other's works to develop critical and creative insights about design and architecture. In this way, the design studio transforms into a "self-motivated learning environment" and enhances students' self-development, confidence, and interpersonal skills (Abdelmonem, 2014). Active learning strategy foremost orients design student to be actively engaged in and to take more responsibility for their learning. ARCH 101 Design projects triggered the students to experience their environment on their own and represent their experiences through design via different techniques. The studio covered tutor seminars, working in studio together, and student pin-up presentations. The seminars were mainly held by tutors while the pin-ups were presented by students, both enabling a critical discussion and an exchange of knowledge. In the pin-up sessions, students acted as tutors while explaining their work, and the design elements and principles they used. In studio hours, students practiced learning by doing exercises. Rather than giving specific directives for specific design problems, tutors emphasized individuality and one's unique way of seeing.

Figure 2. Students taking active roles in their learning processes

In Project 1, ARCH 101 students discovered (instead of research) design elements and principles in relation to the first day presentation entitled "seeing with the mind's eye", by drawing sketches and taking photos at AAAA Campus. Their active role is seeing with the mind's eye through a coordination between hand-mind-eye. Pin-up discussions helped them to conceptualize and visualize their experience (instead of observation) at AAAA Campus. Thus, they practiced both learning by experience and learning by doing strategies. In Project 2, the students walked along and experienced Galata- Perşembe Pazarı axes through multi-dimensional parameters such as culture, social life, tangible and intangible assets of history. They transformed their experiential records such as sketches, photographs and short video shoots into collage works, mental maps and montage studies. Students learned to integrate knowledge of design elements and principles by experiencing and doing. In Project 3, the students discovered new ways of thinking, understanding, and interpreting design elements and principles by doing compositions through cut and fold technique. Body extension exercises created by cut and fold technique pointed to learning how to design an extension that acts together with existing structures. Installation project, as a group work, reflected this idea through strategies of "acting together" and "site specific structures" through which students inquired how to design a new building as an extension of the existing environment. They focused on how to touch / intervene in the existing environment through a human-environment relationship awareness.

Cooperative Learning

According to Johnson and Johnson (2018), cooperative learning is the foundation of active learning. A characteristic feature of active learning environments is the inclusion of collaborative learning activities that encourage learning from each other and learning together. As much as the student transforms and constructs knowledge through his/her own experiences, co-construction of knowledge is achieved through working together, engaging in different learning styles and understanding group dynamics. Collaborative working and learning experiences support understanding and respecting different ideas, which in turn enhances the development of students' critical and creative thinking skills. This is based on the consideration that humans are social beings and learning occurs as a social phenomenon. In ARCH 101 Design studio cooperative learning was employed in pin-ups, juries, and group work studies. Students are confronted with common problems and experiences as a group. While designing an installation as part of Project 3, they learned how to discuss their ideas, through brainstorming, for producing design

Active Learning Strategy for First-Year Design Studio

alternatives for installation. Group projects helped them to learn how to work with others, how to deal with paradoxes and challenges, and they become aware of the crucial role of listening to other ideas and rethinking them to reach out the best solution.

Figure 3. Groupwork projects enhancing collaborative learning

Role of the Tutor

To encourage the students to take more active roles in their learning processes, the role of tutor should shift from an authority or a source of knowledge to a facilitator who search for a balance between "informing", "directing" and "encouraging" students in the design studio (McDonnell, 2016). The tutor facilitates students' participation in design feedback processes by empowering them "to talk and communicate about buildings, feelings, ideas, perceptions and experiences" (Abdelmonem, 2014, p. 42). The tutor orients the students to wonder, think, ask questions, and inquire what, why and how they are doing. In other words, the students are encouraged to reflect on their own learning processes.

Top-down instructions or a hierarchy between students and tutors are avoided in ARCH 101 Design studio. The tutors gave seminars, initiated discussions with students, and formed an atmosphere to hear students' ideas. Tutors acted as a guide, taking the lead, and sometimes preferred to step back for observation. They also assisted peer-to-peer learning and collective brainstorming in pin-ups. In Project 1, the tutors tried to activate curiosity and motivation for the students to discover design elements and principles. Rather than teaching or transferring design knowledge, they tried to prepare an environment that would allow students to explore design knowledge on their own. In Project 2, the tutors started discussions about design elements and principles during the site-excursion and underscored the reciprocal relationship between the tangible and intangible assets of built environment. They asked questions such as "what makes Perşembe Bazaar different?" that gives rise to thinking in a different way. In Project 3, the tutors motivated the students to initiate brainstorming sessions as groups, to decide the final structure / installation for the place they chose in the faculty building. Discussions on site specific constitutions helped students learn how to design an intervention, which material to use and how to design material joint details without using glue for free standing structures about 2.00 meters high. The students were motivated to design a detail for repeating modules to create unity in variety.

Figure 4. Tutors initiate the discussion in feedback processes

Multiplicity of Teaching and Learning Activities

Giving room for diverse and multiple teaching and learning activities is a prerequisite for creating a learning environment in which the students take more active roles in their own learning processes. Design studio tutors structure the learning process in a way that encourages student engagement and transformative learning. Problem-solving, group working, peer review, class discussions, writing, and fieldwork are among the methods that can be applied together in a design studio based on active learning strategy. Hands-on activities that support learning by doing are of great importance. In the design studio the students experience hands-on activities not only to transform a design idea into a tangible phenomenon through 2D and 3D representation techniques, but also to generate new ideas by using the act of making as a tool for thinking. Consequently, hands-on activities pave the way for students to initiate a reflective dialogue with the subjects and the processes of design.

The learning by experience and learning by doing as two main approaches of active learning strategy of ARCH101 were made manifest in multiple individual and groupwork activities: these activities covered presentations by the instructors, site excursion, students work in different formats– from sketch to 2D work, from montage to 3D work, etc. Students experienced methods of listening, watching, experiencing, doing, presenting, discussing, evaluating, criticizing. In Project 1 and Project 2 experience and thought were interrelated nourishing each other. Project 1 covered studies of seeing with mind's eye, free hand drawings, collage works, pin-up discussions, dialogues within the group, spatial experience, in which the students conceptualized and visualized their experiences by 2D and 3D compositions. In Project 2, multidimensional spatial experience was based on understanding and interpreting the social, psychological, spatial, cultural potentials of the environment. Students developed mental maps, collage and montage works and 3D models as their interpretations and reflections of their spatial experiences. In Project 3, students worked on understanding the potential of contrast in light and shadow effects using cut and fold techniques. They designed a structure for the body and represented body-extension works moving in accordance with their bodies. In this way, the experience and thought are constructed through the physiology of the body. During the installation project the collaboration within the group became crucial for intermediate decisions during the design process.

Active Learning Strategy for First-Year Design Studio

Figure 5. Presentations, hands-on practices, digital tools, and site excursions

Flexibility and Adaptability of Space

A learning environment where actors play active roles in the learning process and multiple learning approaches are used is expected to be flexible and adaptable as a physical space. In other words, designing spaces to enable more diverse, inclusive, and flexible teaching and learning processes is essential for an active learning strategy. The spatial, technical and furniture organization in a studio should allow the use of different parts of the studio space for different learning activities or bringing tables together for group discussions or pin-up evaluations. These organizations would support tutor-student dialogue and a sense of freedom, which in turn would enhance the formation of a culture of critical and creative thinking and production in the studio. ARCH 101 Design was conducted in one big studio space having a projector and a screen for seminars, allowed joint feedback sessions in which all students worked and presented collectively. Movable furnishing enabled the adaptation of studio environment according to different learning strategies. Walls and windows were also used as panels in the pin-up sessions. Alongside the studio, site visit walking acted as a studio benefiting from site seeing, discussion on site and data gathering (sketch, sound/visual recording). As part of Project 1, lectures were given both in the auditorium and the studio as learning environments/spaces of design principles and elements. Students discovered design knowledge through experiencing AAAA Campus. Pin-up sessions enabled them to express themselves through collage works and 3D compositions. In Project 2, students explored the design principles and elements of space as an integrated whole via site excursion to Perşembe Bazaar. They interpret these design principles and elements in the studio through collage and montage studies and pinup sessions. For the installation design, as part of Project 3, the whole faculty building became a learning space as the students figured out the importance of place / sense of place in the design process. Accordingly, throughout the semester the scale of learning space for ARCH 101 studio shifted from urban space to a small-scale space such as under-stair area in the faculty building.

Figure 6. Using space/learning from space in multiple ways

CONCLUSION

In all three interrelated modules of ARCH 101 Design studio, students took active roles in discovering new knowledge through spatial experiences ranging from micro to macro scale (the city, campus, faculty building and their own body), and transforming and reconstructing this knowledge through intuitive, critical, and creative thinking filters. Unlike their previous learning experiences, active learning processes generated by curiosity and discovery about design helped the students explore their own potentials and constraints by developing new thinking and production skills. They became active participants of a more effective learning process in the studio environment by asking questions, discussing, and discovering that a question may have more than one different answer. The fact that all sections carried out both conceptual discussions and learning by doing experiences together increased the students' possibilities of learning from each other and together. Discovering the ways to convey their design ideas, and thus opening their ideas to evaluation by others was a challenging experience for the students. The formation of a cooperative learning environment made them realize that multiplicity of ideas potentially enriches design learning. Tutors' role in arousing curiosity about design, triggering but not controlling the design discovery and learning processes, enabled the 'learning by experience' and 'learning by doing' components of the ARCH 101 design studio to be realized. Tutors fulfilled this role by guiding the students to ask questions and to reflect on their own learning experiences. Keeping this curiosity and interest alive for students who were encountering design pedagogy for the first time and who had different learning tendencies was a challenge for the studio tutors. To achieve this, tutors researched and/or produced different content, delivered this content through different tools, and used different methods in which the students could experience generating ideas, discussing them, putting them into practice, and generating new ideas through practice. While the students expressed themselves better with the methods they were more prone to, methods that challenged them more (such as group work) became the driving force for them to develop better skills in this direction. The flexible structure of the studio space created an active environment that allowed for varied production and feedback experiences, and also helped students establish a more engaged relationship with the space, own the space, and feel like members of a learning community. Consequently, ARCH 101 Design studio enabled students to experience curiosity and discovery about design with a holistic approach from whole to part and in an active learning environment, unlike the common design studio approaches in the first year, where design principles and elements are discussed separately through part-to-whole processes.

REFERENCES

Abdelmonem, M. G. (2014). Transcending boundaries of creativity: Active learning in the design studio. *International Journal of Architectural Engineering Technology*, 1(1), 38–49. 10.15377/2409-9821.2014.01.01.5

Aydınlı, S. & Kürtüncü, B. (2018). Paradigm shift in studio culture. *ITU A/Z, 15*(3), 91-108.

Biggs, J. (1999). What the student does: Teaching for enhanced learning. *Higher Education Research & Development*, 18(2), 57–75. 10.1080/0729436990180105

Boucharenc, C. G. (2006). Research on basic design education: An international survey. *International Journal of Technology and Design Education*, 16(1), 1–30. 10.1007/s10798-005-2110-8

Coorey, J. (2016). Active learning methods and technology: Strategies for design education. *International Journal of Art & Design Education*, 35(3), 337–347. 10.1111/jade.12112

Dewey, J. (1963). *Experience and education*. Collier Books.

Enomoto, K., Warner, R., & Claus Nygaard, C. (2022). *Active learning in higher education: Student engagement and deeper learning outcomes*. Libri Publishing Ltd.

Erkök, F., Eren, C., Uz Sönmez, F., & Aydınlı, S. (2005). A paradigm shift in the first-year design education. *ITU A|Z, 2*(1/2), 62-78.

Goldschmidt, G., Hochman, H., & Dafni, I. (2010). The design studio "crit" teacher-student communication. *Artificial Intelligence for Engineering Design, Analysis and Manufacturing*, 24(3), 285–302. 10.1017/S089006041000020X

Johnson, D. W., & Johnson, T. R. (2018). Cooperative learning: The foundation for active learning. In Brito, S. M. (Ed.), *Active learning - beyond the future*. IntechOpen.

Köseoğlu, F., & Tümay, H. (2013). *Bilimde yapılandırıcı paradigma: Teoriden öğretim uygulamalarına*. Pegem Akademi Yayınları.

Kurokawa, K. (1998). *From machine age to the age of life*. Book Art Ltd.

McDonnell, J. (2016). Scaffolding practices: A study of design practitioner engagement in design Education. *Design Studies, 45*(Part A), 9-29.

Özden, Y. (2013). *Eğitimde yeni değerler*. Pegem Akademi Yayınları.

Yorgancıoğlu, D., Aman, D. D., & Şat, B. (2023). Inquiring the generative capacity of urban abstraction and mapping for first-semester basic design studio. *IDA: International Design and Art Journal*, 5(1), 42–56.

Chapter 13
Cultivating Sensibility:
A Semester's Journey Through an Introductory Design Course

Ece K. Açıkgöz
https://orcid.org/0000-0002-2780-1911
Ankara Bilim University, Turkey

Mehmet İlhan Kesmez
Ankara Bilim University, Turkey

ABSTRACT

This chapter explores an introductory design course for architectural education, emphasizing the importance of transcending conventional standards and embracing uncertainty. Rooted in objectivism and existentialism, it encourages students to question assumptions and explore beyond the visible. Through a semester's experience of carefully curated assignments and iterative processes, it showcases how design principles are culminated in the synthesis of accumulated knowledge into visionary design solutions. It highlights the transformative journey of preparing students to navigate the complexities of creative challenges and contribute meaningfully to the design profession. Through comprehensive exploration of curriculum development and student learning experiences, it offers insights into the interplay between theoretical principles and practical application in design education, providing practical implications for educators, curriculum developers, and policymakers aiming to foster the next generation of creative thinkers and innovative problem solvers in design and architecture.

INTRODUCTION

In today's evolving world, traditional professional boundaries are fading, opening new opportunities for individuals to explore their creative potential in an era increasingly reliant on intelligent automation for productivity. As we confront the imminent future where understanding humanity is essential for

DOI: doi

survival, nations are prioritizing support for creative industries, echoing Bertrand Russell's vision in 'In Praise of Idleness' (2020) of redirecting surplus labor towards cultural enrichment.

This chapter outlines a two-decade effort to introduce students to design, which is an essential mission for today's increasing demand for creativity, initiated at XXXX University's Department of Architecture, and continued at YYYY University's Department of Interior Architecture and Environmental Design. Drawing from extensive hands-on experience, it discusses the foundational principles of the course, which primarily focuses on the students' unique identities as designers and highlights the 2023-2024 fall semester's Introduction to Design Course at YYYY University as a case study. Through this example, it is explored how student design projects contribute to the curriculum and encourage students to embrace uncertainty as a catalyst for growth.

The semester's example showcases how the course process is designed around the objective to provide a framework for students to develop their own design approaches by pushing them beyond their comfort zones. Selected design works of students demonstrate outcomes of exploring the unknown. Ultimately, the chapter emphasizes the course's ethos: the belief that embracing uncertainty is not only vital but essential for personal and professional development.

The Motives Behind Forming and Developing an Introductory Design Course for Architectural Education

Modern educational practices suffer from fragmented knowledge, which Santos et. al. (2017) argue fails to meet societal needs and hinders pedagogical innovation. Similarly, Pasha et. al. (2020) note that in architecture education, a focus on technical skills over core principles leads to a disjointed curriculum. This gap often leaves out the integration of visual arts and architectural history, which is crucial for fostering intrinsic motivation in design learning. Throughout the formation and development of the course, a holistic philosophical stance is adopted to address the contemporary educational challenge of compartmentalized information (Peikoff, 2018) within architecture. Rooted in objectivism and existentialism, the course fosters an insightful understanding of design by emphasizing "sensibility in design thinking," echoing Ayn Rand's (1943) objectivist perspective in "The Fountainhead." The objectivist thought argues that in essence, assuming personal responsibility means maintaining artistic integrity and not succumbing to external pressures or popular trends in design, and stiving to elevate and idealize the human spirit (Rand, 1971). Assuming this responsibility aligns with embracing existentialist ideas (Kierkegaard and Marino, 2013). Accordingly, the course encourages students to interrogate the given information, assume personal responsibility, and explore themes like alienation and universality, thus breaking barriers to holistic design comprehension.

The pedagogical approach, guided by Mr. Ziya Tanalı in XXX University years, arose from the need to communicate that art extends beyond thematic art (Tanalı, 2020) as program music (Kregor, 2015). The course's evolution, including the establishment of two separate courses at XXX University – focusing on the analysis of artistic expression and cognitive processes in design thinking, introduces the transformative concept of "sensibility." These courses have aimed to ignite students' interest in the sensory content of artworks, unraveling the pleasure found in understanding deeper layers of life and systematically delving into the nature of thought within architectural design.

Thus, the central theme of the course is formed to emphasize the importance for design students, to surpass conventional standards, welcome the unfamiliar, and develop an awareness that extends beyond overt communications. This journey from analysis to sensibility represents a transformative endeavor in architectural education, breaking down barriers and fostering a comprehensive understanding of design that goes beyond traditional paradigms, emphasizing the pragmatist (Rylander Eklund, 2022) and existential (Sartre, 2007) dimensions.

The course's foundation emphasizes transcending cognitive constraints by moving beyond didactic techniques, embracing practical demonstrations and active student participation. Critiquing the hierarchical prioritization of form in current pedagogical practices, it challenges the application of design principles without substantive understanding (Lerner, 2005), bridging the gap between self-expression and guiding frameworks, and emphasizing sensibility and the expansive nature of artistic cultivation. An example for this attitude is by Kim (2006), who discusses the potential downfalls of reducing design education to solely teaching design principles, as it can neglect the experiential and relational qualities of design.

Adopting a student-centered mindset, the course explores both student and educator perspectives, focusing on understanding present spaces and fostering positive educational journeys. The inaugural assignment directs students to question their existing conceptions and observe behavioral responses, emphasizing effective communication through inner motivation, curiosity, humor, and respecting personal identity. Belluigi (2011) holds an example argument that goes parallel to the assumption of this approach, where students are given the freedom to pursue their personal visions. The evaluative methodology centers around the concept of "delta," signifying the disparity between a student's initial position and the culmination of their experiential journey, emphasizing the infusion of a "personal motive" into the design process.

As a method to serve for the integration of knowledge, lectures on art form a fundamental aspect of the formation of the course. These lectures delve into the evolution of painting to inspire self-motivation and illustrate the link between art's content and form. Comparing different historical periods, like medieval versus post-Renaissance art, reflects changing aesthetics and values (Figure 1). Pre-lecture assignments and discussions on various artists, alongside readings like Gombrich's "Story of Art," encourage open-mindedness and recognition of art's cultural and historical tapestry.

Figure 1. Giotto's "Virgin and Child Enthroned, Surrounded by Angels and Saints (Ognissanti Maestà)" reflects medieval religious symbolism, while Leonardo da Vinci's "The Virgin and Child with St Anne and a Lamb" from c. 1508 showcases post-Renaissance realism. The contrast highlights the evolution of aesthetic approaches in art.

Sources:
Giotto's "Virgin and Child enthroned": (https://www.uffizi.it/en/artworks/virgin-and-child-enthroned-surrounded-by-angels-and-saints-ognissanti-maesta)
Leonardo da Vinci's "The Virgin and Child with St Anne and a Lamb":(https://www.italian-renaissance-art.com/Virgin-and-Child.html)]

The curriculum's music lectures highlight the parallels between music and architecture, exploring how performance variations and musicians' perspectives reveal personal sensibilities. Art's content versus sensibility is distinguished, with content being structured and sensibility going beyond it, as seen in Jimmy Hendrix's improvisations or Impressionist art's intuition (Sawyer, 2000).

Similarly, lectures on world history guide students to comprehend art within dynamic historical contexts, emphasizing the course's purpose—an encounter with art for personal development and as a thinking instrument, advocating for a balanced approach between self-expression and guiding frameworks. This perspective aligns with thinkers like Benedetto Croce (2017) and John Dewey (1958), viewing aesthetics as a form of communication that conveys personal expressions. Literature has examples of this approach specifically for the role of art in enhancing creativity in design students (ie. Kinsella, 2018; Silva Pacheco, 2020).

The course systematically guides students through a transformative journey, challenging traditional educational practices, and encouraging meaningful connections and personal sensibilities. It critiques practices like rote memorization, restricting expressions deemed proscribed to prompt diverse thought patterns, fostering simplicity and plainness in design work, integrating cultural content seamlessly with assignments. Deliberately structured exercises progress from 2D to 3D thinking, enriched by encounters with art, research, and expression of impressions. Juries cultivate a culture of self-criticism, enabling learning from errors and offering opportunities for correction, with the final assignment serving as a showcase of genuine design motives.

The following part of the chapter demonstrates a semester's example of student works and how they evolved not only in complexity but also in an understanding of an integrated body of knowledge that serves as a foundation for learning to design architecturally.

Implementing Insights: A Semester's Journey Through Design Briefs and Student Works

Since this will be a single-term case study, the basic framework used in each application of the course will be expressed. As a 1st semester design course for architectural education, it is composed of three major parts. The first part is called "commencing with the design act". The second part is composed of more determinate design questions to guide the students with certain limitations like permissible materials, joints, or color scales regarding the design act. In this part, the program is designed around a structural problem to be solved solely with the given materials' capacities, and several design questions that requires a connection among a spatial solution and a theme without any concrete contextual input. In the third part, the essential elements of the design problem—its structure, spatial aspects, and themes—are incorporated into the expected design work as the final assignment. Additionally, it is explored how the design solution fits within a specific context.

In the context of the Fall 2023-2024 Introduction to Design course at YYYYY University, Department of Interior Architecture and Environmental Design, the forthcoming section of this paper aims to elucidate the assigned tasks and pivotal junctures that have informed the instructors' approach to selecting assignment sets. This selection process is informed by feedback garnered from students' submissions in preceding assignments, and their verbal expressions in the assessment sessions as juries (Rutherford, 2020) on how they handled their design processes, providing valuable insights for curriculum refinement and instructional enhancement.

The First Part: Commencing Assignments

This part of the semester program is a recurring feature for all students and involves assignments carefully chosen from a pool created by instructors (Table 1). The primary focus is on nurturing design thinking skills, including problem definition and idea generation, essential for a comprehensive understanding of design work. Central to this process is cultivating students' inner sensibility, fostering unique and authentic creative expression. Through engagement with assignments, students gradually challenge preconceived notions about architecture and design, learning to question assumptions and approach problems with courage and creativity. This iterative process, often termed as 'transition', prepares students to develop a deeper understanding of design thinking and embrace the complexity of creative challenges.

Cultivating Sensibility

Table 1. Assignments of the first (Commencing) part of the 2023-2024 fall semester design studio

Date	Assignment Name	Brief Description
6 Oct. 2023	Name	Express your opinion about yourself on an A4 size sheet of paper.
9 Oct. 2023	King's Speech	Reflect on the movie "King's Speech" and translate its impact into a creative response as a 2D composition.
12 Oct. 2023	The Little Prince	Conduct research on "The Little Prince" and Antoine de Saint Exupery.
16 Oct. 2023	Take Five	Listen to "Take Five" and translate its essence into a 3D representation.
19 Oct. 2023	Shampolion's Stone and Near East History	Research the Shampolion's Stone and the history of 2000 BC - 400 BC in the Near East. Submit you research summary.
26 Oct. 2023	Start - Journey - End (or, Entrance - Passage – Arrival)	Design a scaled model that uses flow of space with a special emphasis on the human scale that you are expected to use in your design work.
2 Nov. 2023	Column – Wall – Love	Create a 3D spatial composition based on the given concepts. Pay attention to structural, textural, colour, lighting, and transparency potentials of the materials used.

Each time a course is offered, the beginning of each term includes an evaluation phase in which instructors observe and reflect to plan future instructional strategies. The first mid-term jury (Figure 2) where the students display their commencing assignments' design works, allows them to articulate how their understanding of design thinking is becoming. This process also helps identify latent designer attributes in students, fostering authentic dialogues between students and educators to nurture their design and artistic abilities.

Figure 2. Example presentation of the first mid-term jury of the 2023-2024 fall semester design studio

At the beginning of the semester, students engaged in exercising design work with the "Name" assignment where they were expected to creatively delineate their identities without using traditional naming conventions. This is an example how the existing information for a given input is expected to be questioned. This task encourages students to explore new conceptual territories and break away from conventional thinking paradigms. This goes parallel with what Akoury (2020) argues about the function of drawing, which bears witness to internal mental percepts, concepts, feelings, and images as a design thinking instrument. By challenging what identity is, students are prompted to cultivate intrinsic motivation and envision transformative possibilities, enhancing the depth and quality of their creations (Figure 3).

Figure 3. Example student works of the "Name" assignment of the 2023-2024 fall semester design studio

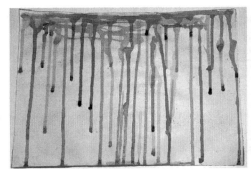

Another commencing assignment, the analysis of the film "King's Speech", focusing on its personal significance for students, is used as a method aimed at fostering meaningful viewing experiences. Through collaborative evaluations, students were asked to deconstruct the structure of the film, examining its narrative arcs and cinematographic techniques for their applicability to design. This is an art-based collaborative methodology (Paez & Valtchanova, 2022) and the process highlights the challenges of translating cinematic tools to a two-dimensional design, offering insight into the complexities of cross-medium interpretation and individual spectatorship subjectivity (Figure 4).

Cultivating Sensibility

Figure 4. Example student works of the "King's Speech" assignment of the 2023-2024 fall semester design studio

The assignment involving "The Little Prince" was designed to prompt students to critically assess their reading habits and comprehension levels by delving into de Saint Exupery's background and motivations. This task challenges surface interpretations, urging students to discern deeper meanings and validate their personal emotional responses to the text. Despite initial tendencies towards superficial regurgitation, students are encouraged to engage in introspective analysis, emphasizing subjective engagement over rote academic interpretation.

The "Take Five" Assignment functioned as a rhythmic exercise in the curriculum of commencing assignments, challenging students to translate the essence of the music piece into a 3D design experiment. This task introduces three-dimensional thinking, highlighting the complexities of translating elements between divergent mediums. As Rand (1971) posits, both music and architecture share a commonality: neither relies on symbols to convey meaning. Students grapple with representing abstract musical motifs visually, necessitating a deep understanding of musical meaning making to achieve a cohesive design solution (Figure 5). Through analysis of student works, instructors illustrate the principles of rhythmic design, offering valuable insights into the significance of rhythm within design thinking.

Figure 5. Example student works produced for the "Take-Five" assignment of the 2023-2024 fall semester design studio

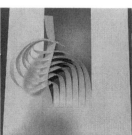

The exercises associated with the assignments titled 'Start-Journey-End' (Figure 6) and 'Column-Wall-Love' (Figure 7) constitute essential elements of the course curriculum, designed to engage students in the practical application of spatial components, while also emphasizing fundamental design principles. These assignments provide students with a critical opportunity to explore design principles within the context of spatial concepts. By working with scaled miniatures of envisioned spaces, students confront the tangible manifestations of abstract design principles, bridging the realms of abstract ideation and tangible spatial definition. This distinctive pedagogical approach enables students to integrate concrete spatial elements into their abstract 3D design thought processes, marking a pivotal juncture in their design education.

Figure 6. Example works of students produced for the "Start-Journey-End" assignment of the 2023-2024 fall semester design studio

Cultivating Sensibility

Figure 7. Example presentation of the Column-Wall-Love assignment of the first semester design studio

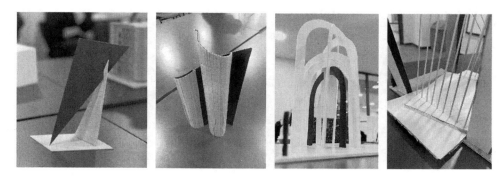

Conclusively, the commencing assignments serve as the foundation of the semester, laying the groundwork for students' journey through the course. Carefully curated to cultivate design thinking, these initial exercises foster an evolution in students' understanding and application of design principles. As students transition from familiar concepts to unexplored territory, they learn to question assumptions and tackle challenges with courage. This phase prepares them for deeper exploration in traversing assignments which are going to be given in the following part of the chapter. They guide students through structural, thematic, and functional challenges. Drawing upon foundational skills, students refine their ability to integrate theoretical principles with practical application, marking a natural progression in their design journey characterized by growth, reflection, and creative exploration.

The Second Part: Traversing Assignments

This part of the course delves into the intricacies of space definition, introducing concepts like structure, narrative, and theme. Students transition from abstract questions to concrete requirements, navigating increasingly complex spatial problems while maintaining sensibility within the design process. Emphasis is placed on understanding scale within 3D compositions and developing artistic appreciation. The objective is to merge structural integrity and thematic conceptualization into a cohesive design process, reaching a higher level of complexity (Table 2).

Table 2. Assignments of the second (traversing) part of the 2023-2024 fall semester design studio

Date	Assignment Name	Brief Description
16 Nov. 2023 20 Nov. 2023	Structural Bridge Design with Hinged Joints	Design a bridge that can span 100cm length with an additional 0,5 kg weight on it. Only materials shorter than 20 cm will be accepted. Use of glue or any king of rigid joint is prohibited.
30 Nov. 2023	Book Nook Design	Design a book nook inspired by the play "Cyrano de Bergerac" of Edmond Rostand (1942). Capture the feeling of a scene and display photographs on the shelves with other books. Shoot the photo from an angle and in the light that best presents your design.
4 Dec. 2023	Stand Design for Book Nooks	Design a fair stand for a book fair, specifically showcasing book nooks, in a 1/10 scale corresponding to a cube with dimensions of 270 cm x 270 cm. The design principle emphasizes creating voids within the solid cube, which are represented by smaller cubes obtained by dividing 270 by 3 (resulting in 90 cm, 30 cm, and 10 cm). Students must adhere to a monochromatic colour scheme, selecting a hue and adjusting saturation to be less than 50% using black and white paint.

The Structural Bridge Design with Hinged Joints Assignment emphasized structural integrity solved with geometric links and balanced aesthetics achieved through minimal material use and smart joint techniques. Students were tasked with designing joints independent of adhesives or excessive rigidity, considering factors like stability and load-bearing capacity. This problem encouraged systematic geometric solutions to balance the bridge's overall load. Class discussions during critiques highlighted the direct relationship between structural and aesthetic integrity (Figure 8).

Figure 8. Examples of structural bridge design with hinged joints assignment produced for the 2023-2024 fall semester design studio

Holding the thematic focus as primary in design, the "Book Nook" Design Assignment challenged the students to embody the essence of a story's ambiance within their designs. They were tasked with translating the romanticism, wit, and drama of the narrative into a tangible space that captures the spirit of the tale. By shooting a photo from a specified angle and in optimal lighting, students added a layer of visual storytelling, highlighting the significance of presentation and atmosphere in conveying their design's inspiration. This assignment required students to creatively interpret the literary elements of "Cyrano de Bergerac," or any literary artwork that they choose resulting in cohesive and visually compelling book nook designs (Figure 9).

Figure 9. Book nook design examples of student works produced for the 2023-2024 fall semester design studio

The Book Nook Stand Design assignment integrates previous assignments from the traversing stage, challenging students to balance form, function, aesthetics, circulation, and thematic cohesion within specific constraints. This encourages creativity, problem-solving skills, and attention to detail in their design process. In addition to given constraints, students addressed circulation challenges, ensuring smooth movement within the stand. They selected themes to enhance the visitor experience, tying together aesthetics, book nook arrangement, and color scheme to invite exploration (Figure 10).

Figure 10. Stand design for book nooks assignment examples of student works produced for the 2023-2024 fall semester design studio

As students navigate through the intricacies of spatial definition and thematic cohesion in this part of the course, they transition from abstract conceptualizations to concrete design requirements, enriching their understanding of scale, structure, and narrative. Through assignments like the "bridge structure" and "book nook" designs, students are challenged to merge structural integrity with thematic conceptualization, fostering a deeper appreciation for the interplay between form and function. The integration of these assignments culminates in the Book Nook Stand Design, where students harmonize various design elements to create immersive and inviting spaces. This progression underscores the transformative journey of design education, preparing students for the culminating challenge of the final project, where they will synthesize their accumulated knowledge and skills into a cohesive and visionary design solution.

The Final Part: An Integrating Assignment

In the final part of the semester, students faced the challenge of integrating their individual design themes with construction limitations, environmental factors, and functional complexities. The design problem of a weekend house for gardening by a lakeside was chosen to encompass these challenges (Table 3). Harmonizing the house with the natural surroundings and carefully planning interior spaces within a compact area were key objectives. Additionally, selecting precast reinforced concrete elements required considerations of weight, connections, and structural safety. Students utilized temporary joints in model

Cultivating Sensibility

creation to experiment with spatial configurations, while optimizing interior space quality with proposed furnishings. The design presentations aimed to capture students' personal visions for living in the space.

Table 3. Assignment for the final (integrating) part of the semester

Date	Assignment Name	Brief Description
5 Dec. 2023 28 Dec. 2023 8 Jan. 2024	Final Studies	Design a weekend house for gardening by a lakeside for two people. The enclosed area must be 50 to 70 square meters. Use the provided precast reinforced concrete building elements to be assembled on site. Produce each element in advance before creating the 3D model. Include topography and interior furnishings. Produce enough elements to experiment with space configurations, ensure your model defines functional interior spaces for a weekend house dedicated to gardening.
11 Jan. 2024	Pre-Jury Submissions	Bring your model and drawings including plans and sections, perspectives.
15 Jan. 2024	Final Jury Submissions	The final jury assignment requires a 1/20 scale model, a plan, a section, and an elevation for a weekend house by a lakeside. Express your true self through this design, capturing the essence of how you envision living in that space.

Figure 11. Final project announcement leaflet and examples of students' works produced for the 2023-2024 fall semester design studio

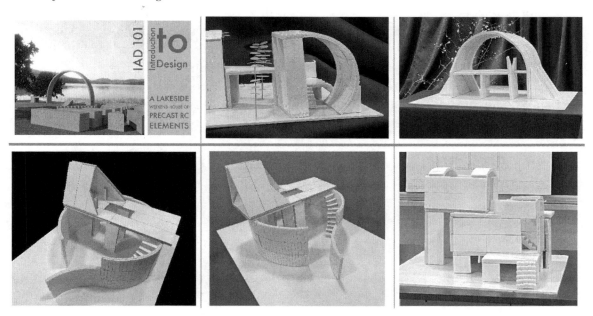

The culmination of the semester's coursework presented the students with an academically demanding assignment, representing the apex of complexity encountered thus far. This marked the first instance wherein students were confronted with a multifaceted challenge characterized by inherent constraints and limitations, which is a common approach in the design pedagogy (Iavarone & Birer, 2020). The resultant outputs of this assignment served as a testament to the intricate interplay between dimensional and technical constraints within a design problem. Several solutions proposed by the students underscored the successful integration of design principles, sensibility, and structural integrity, exemplifying a commendable level of proficiency and technical expertise (Figure 5).

CONCLUSION

In navigating the realms of art, architecture, and design, this comprehensive course serves as a transformative conduit, imparting a holistic understanding of the design process. From cultural integration to jury presentations, the collaborative journey dynamically shapes the curriculum, addressing the imperative for humanity to find meaning in creativity for a meaningful life. Distinguishing between content and sensibility in art, the course empowers students to transcend limitations, fostering simplicity in design work. Assignments exemplify the transformative nature of student endeavors, instilling a deep appreciation for the interconnectedness of art, history, and architecture—a foundation for cultivating sensible design and embracing the inherent unpredictability of the creative process.

In the example of one semester's experience, by tracing the evolution of curriculum development and exploring students' learning experiences, this research offers a nuanced understanding of the complex interplay between theoretical principles and practical application in design education. Future studies can build upon the insights provided here to further investigate the efficacy of different pedagogical approaches, the role of sensibility-oriented experiences in design thinking, and the impact of holistic curriculum development on students' creative growth and professional development. Additionally, longitudinal studies tracking students' progress over time could provide valuable data on the long-term effects of introductory design courses on students' career trajectories and contributions to the design profession. With this study it is expected to introduce an understanding of design education and offer practical implications for educators, curriculum developers, and policymakers seeking to cultivate the next generation of creative thinkers and innovative problem solvers in the ever-evolving landscape of design and architecture.

REFERENCES

Akoury, C. (2020). Apprehending the creative process through drawing in the foundation design studio. *International Journal of Art & Design Education*, 39(1), 113–125. 10.1111/jade.12223

Belluigi, D. Z. (2011). Intentionality in a creative art curriculum. *Journal of Aesthetic Education*, 45(1), 18–36. 10.5406/jaesteduc.45.1.0018

Croce, B. (2017). *Aesthetic: As science of expression and general linguistic*. Routledge.

Dewey, J. (1958). *Art As Experience*. Capricorn Books, G. P. Putnam's Sons.

Iavarone, A. H., & Birer, E. (2020). The concept of limits in architecture as an instructional tool for design education. *Journal of Design Studio*, 2(2), 111–130. 10.46474/jds.814390

Kierkegaard, S., & Marino, G. (2013). *Fear and trembling and the sickness unto death*. Princeton University Press.

Kim, N. (2006). A history of design theory in art education. *Journal of Aesthetic Education*, 40(2), 12–28. 10.2307/4140227

Kinsella, V. (2018). The use of activity theory as a methodology for developing creativity within the art and design classroom. *International Journal of Art & Design Education*, 37(3), 493–506. 10.1111/jade.12147

Kregor, J. (2015). *Program music*. Cambridge University Press. 10.1017/CBO9781139506397

Lerner, F. (2005). Foundations for design education: Continuing the Bauhaus Vorkurs vision. *Studies in Art Education*, 46(3), 211–226. 10.1080/00393541.2005.11650075

Paez, R., & Valtchanova, M. (2022). Art and Design: How Artistic Practices Enrich Design Education. In Cunha, M. F., & Franco, J. R. G. (Eds.), *Handbook of Research on Active Learning and Computational Thinking in Engineering Education* (pp. 38–55). IGI Global., 10.4018/978-1-7998-7865-0.ch001

Pasha, Y. N., Adnan, S., & Ahmed, N. (2020). Positioning historical evidences in architectural education: Review of methods and contents. *Open House International*, 45(4), 481–507. 10.1108/OHI-05-2020-0032

Peikoff, L. (2018). *Teaching Johnny to Think: A Philosophy of Education Based on the Principles of Ayn Rand's Objectivism*. Blackstone Publishing.

Rand, A. (1971). *The Romantic Manifesto*. Penguin.

Rand, A. (2005a). *[1943]. The Fountainhead*. Plume.

Rostand, E. (1942). *Cyrano de Bergerac* (Siyavuşgil, S. E., Trans.). Maarif Matbaası.

Russell, B. (2020). *In praise of idleness: And other essays*. Routledge. 10.4324/9781003059493

Rutherford, S. (2020). Engaging students in curriculum development through design thinking: A course design case. *International Journal of Designs for Learning*, 11(3), 107–125. 10.14434/ijdl.v11i3.25359

Rylander Eklund, A., Navarro Aguiar, U., & Amacker, A. (2022). Design thinking as sensemaking: Developing a pragmatist theory of practice to (re) introduce sensibility. *Journal of Product Innovation Management*, 39(1), 24–43. 10.1111/jpim.12604

Saint-Exupéry, A. (1943). *Le petit prince [The little prince]*. Verenigde State van Amerika: Reynal & Hitchkock (US), Gallimard (FR).

Santos, C. M., Franco, R. A., Leon, D., Ovigli, D. B., & Colombo, D. (2017). Interdisciplinarity in Education: Overcoming Fragmentation in the Teaching-Learning Process. *International Education Studies*, 10(10), 71–77. 10.5539/ies.v10n10p71

Sartre, J. P. (2007). *[1948]. Existentialism is a Humanism*. Yale University Press.

Silva Pacheco, C. (2020). Art education for the development of complex thinking metacompetence: A theoretical approach. *International Journal of Art & Design Education*, 39(1), 242–254. 10.1111/jade.12261

Tanalı, Z. (2000). Sadeleştirmeler. *Ankara: Alp*.

Chapter 14
Digital Explorers/ Digitalized Explorations:
A First-Year Architectural Design Studio Experiment on Distant Urban Interventions

Senem Yildirim
Gazi University, Turkey

Arzu Özen Yavuz
https://orcid.org/0000-0002-7197-289X
Gazi University, Turkey

ABSTRACT

First year design education is one of the most challenging stages of architectural education. Although first-year architectural design studio mainly follows the footsteps of Bauhaus Ecole in many institutions focusing on establishing an abstract way of thinking while preparing students for upcoming architectural design studios, some institutions design their curriculum to address the fundamentals of architectural design in the first year. Gazi University's Department of Architecture follows this path where first year education is treated as a stage where abstract thinking is introduced, while also acting as an intermediary step to use basic design thinking to design habitable units. Focusing on Architectural Project II, the chapter explores the teaching methodologies of first-year design studio taught at Gazi University and aims to present the specific pedagogies, design strategies, and students' approaches to first-year education on the project conducted during Spring semester of 2021 titled Digital Explorers/Digitalized Explorations: Distant Urban Interventions to Istanbul's Kadikoy.

INTRODUCTION

Traditionally the practice of architectural design is learned through a project-based "studio" approach. Design studio is a fundamental part of the architectural education. It is, as Lee Shulman defines, architecture's "signature pedagogy". (Shulman, 2005) Gross and Do (1997) described the architectural design studio as follows:

DOI: 10.4018/979-8-3693-2329-8.ch014

> In studio, designers express and explore ideas, generate and evaluate alternatives, and ultimately make decisions and take action. They make external representations (drawings and three-dimensional models) and reason with these representations to inquire, analyze, and test hypotheses about the designs they represent. Through the linked acts of drawing, looking, and inferring, designers propose alternatives and interpret and explore their consequences. (Gross et.al, 1997)

The design studio is a complex and multi-dimensional environment. It is the site of both innovation and uncritical replication. Globally, the culture of architectural education revolves around the design studio, and the methodologies of teaching in design studios fundamentally share the common aim to produce critical pedagogies that liberate students from uncritical teaching methods which demand their submission to old fashioned ways. However, the pedagogical approaches to teaching in design studios vary not only between different institutions but also among studios at various levels of architectural education within the same institution.

First-year studio is a prime example to observe this shift in pedagogies of teaching architectural design as it is the prime year the students are introduced to the basic concepts of design. As a result, the teaching methods, concepts and tools used in a first-year design studio is -and should be- fundamentally different than that of later years in architectural education. Akdeniz and Aksel states that during the first-year education, "students should be encouraged to cultivate the liberty of subjective thinking, which involves taking intellectual risks, making seemingly disjointed cognitive leaps, and developing multiple ideas concurrently. They should remain receptive to novel interpretations and creative perspectives." (Akdeniz & Aksel, 1989) Therefore, fostering an environment where creative problem-solving is embraced is essential.

Although in many institutions first-year architectural education follows the footsteps of Bauhaus Ecole and focuses on establishing an abstract way of thinking with the aim of preparing students for the upcoming years where architectural design is taught, some institutions design their curriculum to address the fundamentals of space and architectural design in the first year. Gazi University's Department of Architecture stands out where the first-year curriculum is not only a platform for fostering abstract thinking but also a crucial phase for the introduction of basics of architectural design. This foundational stage enables students to apply their understanding of basic design principles to an experimental project, culminating in the creation of habitable units. The focal point of this discussion is the studio course, Architectural Project II, which encapsulates this pedagogical approach.

This paper explores the teaching methodologies of first-year design studio taught at Gazi University, Department of Architecture, and aims to present the main characteristics, specific pedagogies, and students' approaches to first-year education in Gazi University on the project conducted during Spring semester of 2021 in the studio of Architectural Project II titled "Digital Explorers / Digitalized Explorations: Distant Urban Interventions to Istanbul's Kadikoy."

FIRST YEAR STUDIO EDUCATION: PEDAGOGIES, METHODOLOGY, CHALLENGES

The aim of first year design education is to facilitate an abstract way of thinking for students while initiating a spatial thinking where they were introduced the basics of designing architecturally. The curriculum of the first-year design studio varies from institution to institution. In some cases, the first-year architectural education is treated as a way of solely introducing the principles of abstract thinking, what commonly referred to as basic design, while introduction to architectural design is left to the second-year design studios, examples of which in some variation include RIBA associated schools of architecture (RIBA, 2014), programs in United States that follows the principles established in K-12 process which was initially a brainchild of New-Bauhaus school (Lerner, 2005), and universities in Turkey including Middle East Technical University of Ankara. (Komez-Daglioglu et.al, 2020)

Our take in first-year architectural education in the Department of Architecture at Gazi University is to surpass the teachings of basic design to give it an architectural take. Designed as two courses taught each semester that are complementing each other, the main aim of the first-year architectural education at Gazi University is for students to have an architectural understanding on the issues of not only form, material and structure which are fundamental outputs of Basic Design education, but also of site, context and architectural program.

First year design education in Department of Architecture at Gazi University includes two modules. First module taught on the first semester of first year is Basic Design and is followed by Architectural Project II in the second semester of the first year, a course we referred to as Introduction to Architectural Design. Although this paper mainly focuses on the studio of Architectural Project II at Gazi University's Department of Architecture, it is important to discuss the first-year design education as a whole and a continuing segment, as these two modules court one another. Therefore, throughout this study, the main aim is to unfold the relationship between the two studios taught at first year, the pedagogies used in the first-year design education, and learning outcomes of these studios together with changing teaching techniques dictated by the Covid 19 pandemic of 2020 while focusing on a specific project conducted in the Architectural Project II studio during semester of Spring 2021 titled "Digital Explorers / Digitalized Explorations: Distant Urban Interventions to Istanbul's Kadikoy."

Basic Design

The basic design education, which is implemented as a freshmen year studio training at Design Schools across various creative disciplines—including architecture—holds paramount importance in shaping students' intellectual frameworks. Despite its practical and contextual differences among the institutions worldwide, the basic design studio commonly aims to facilitate the students constituting a design language and a way of abstract thinking while introducing skills such as communication, visualization, and representation leading to architectural design thought process. Today, the curricular and procedural distinctions of most basic design studios are set as bare adaptations of Bauhaus origin in which various fields of art and design were associated in an interdisciplinary manner.

Our take in the teaching methodology for Basic Design is similar to the Bauhaus Ecole in its interdisciplinarity. The Bauhaus Vorkurs (the Foundation Course) was as a versatile, enduring prototype for combining art, design, and architectural studio education and formed the foundation of Basic Design courses taught at architecture schools globally. (Kaufman, 1965) Designed by the artist Jonathan Itten in 1919, "Vorkurs" was a proposal about a trial semester where students would experiment on a universal abstracted visual language deriving ideas from adjacent disciplines of architecture that are also design-based. (Itten, 1965) This very idea of teaching an abstract way of thinking formed the basis of the first-year architectural education in many institutions worldwide. (Ozkar, 2017)

The basic design studio at Gazi University follows a similar teaching methodology. The main aim is to establish an abstract way of thinking by introducing basic principles of design, while encouraging learning/deriving from design-adjacent fields and tools of visual communication. However, teaching first year studio is universally challenging as it is the stage where the students are introduced to the basic principles of design which usually are alien concepts for them. This task is especially proven to be challenging for the case of Gazi University, an institution who welcomes students from all over the country and has a diverse student profile who come to architectural schools with no previous education on design, art, or architecture. (Salem, et.al., 2019)

Therefore, the first step towards establishing an abstract thinking is to reconstruct the students' existing norms on "aesthetics" to leave them enough space to find their own unique ways of design. While the motive of the Basic Design studio is clear, the teaching pedagogy was proven to be difficult to establish. In this regard, the main pedagogy used throughout the first-year design education in Gazi University is inspired by Jean Piaget's Constructivist Approach.

When it comes to Constructivist Pedagogy, the first name that comes to mind is Jean Piaget. Piaget emphasized that active participation in any student's learning process plays an important role, his theories on "learning through exploration" has become the basis for student-centered teaching practices. (Jonassen, 1991) Shaped on the idea of reconsidering the learner as an active individual seeking meaning, "the constructivist stance maintains that learning is a process of constructing one's own meaning as it is how people make sense of their experience." (Merriam & Caffarella, 1999) The notion of "exploring" in this sense is central to the constructivist pedagogy, as Piaget claims that unlike traditional teaching methods where the learners passively acquire knowledge through direct instruction, leaving the students to construct an understanding through exploring in the process of learning helps create an environment that supports a sustainable learning experience. In this case, constructivist pedagogy claims that it is important to create a learning environment that "restructures knowledge" where "learning motivations such as curiosity and discovery are balanced." (Piaget, 1972) Assimilating Constructivist pedagogy to architectural education, however, is not a new concept. Many first-year architectural design studios have been structured around John Dewey's "learning by doing" theory. (Dewey, 1986) Dewey's claim that a creative mind facilitates learning through understanding, internalization and interpretation that could be possible with a "learn by doing" approach has seen suitable for studio environment, where students' learning skills are traditionally improved by assigning design problems for them to develop creative solutions.

Basic Design Studio in Gazi University is inspired by Dewey's "learning by doing" theory, while combining this paradigm with Piaget's theory on "learning by exploring" and is structured around a curriculum strictly designed for diverse student profile of Gazi University's Department of Architecture to encourage as Aydinli calls is "learning to learn," which in the case of Gazi University requires an unlearning of existing norms to reconstruct new and personalized norms on design and aesthetics for students. (Aydinli, 2015) The curriculum of Basic Design is structured around three stages, each serving as a preparation for the next. These steps are designed to ensure that by the end of the term, students grasp the fundamental concepts of basic design from two-dimensional to three-dimensional composition. At the same time, through weekly exercises, students are encouraged to internalize abstract thinking methods by exploring ways of deconstructing their existing norms of aesthetics and constructing their own design styles. As foreseen by the constructivist approach, the outcomes of the basic design course are not uniform but personalized for each student representing their individual journeys of finding meaning

Digital Explorers/Digitalized Explorations

through exploring. Thus, the main goal of the course is to facilitate students in discovering their own basic design discourses.

Starting with working on two dimensional compositions, the curriculum is then followed by an assignment given to encourage the students to design compositions that are in-between two- and three-dimensions; and final project of the semester is to design three dimensional compositions. The main goal for the end of the course is that the students would have a grasp on three dimensional compositions, and the formal relationships of solids and voids which would help them develop necessary skills for the next step when they start to design habitable places and the relationships of one spatial void to another while developing and intellectual sensitivity on art, design, and architecture.

The main objective of assignments to design two-dimensional compositions is to encourage students to play with different geometrical forms and colors, while reconstructing their individualized aesthetic norms. In that regard, incorporating interdisciplinary case studies into weekly assignments, as learning and researching from other disciplines are proven to be helpful. The assignments borrow cases from other design-adjacent fields as design problems to work for them on their abstraction and compositions. Whether it be literature, cinema and even fashion, we choose case studies to inspire the students in their projects, while widening their perspectives to deconstruct their existing norms of aesthetics **(Figure 1)**.

Figure 1. Two-dimensional project examples from basic design studio

The transition from a two-dimensional composition to a three-dimensional one was proven to be very difficult for students however it is both a crucial step to prepare them for Architectural Project II where students were introduced to the concept of habitable space, also act as an intermediate challenge for students to explore new compositional relationships to grasp a better understanding of Basic Design. Various methods were adopted during this stage to help the students to develop a better understanding for transformation from a two-dimensional composition to a three-dimensional one. One particular example is from an assignment where the students were given a single cardboard to fold it into a structure to better understand the transition from a surface to a solid and void **(Figure 2)**.

Figure 2. "Fold" project examples from basic design studio

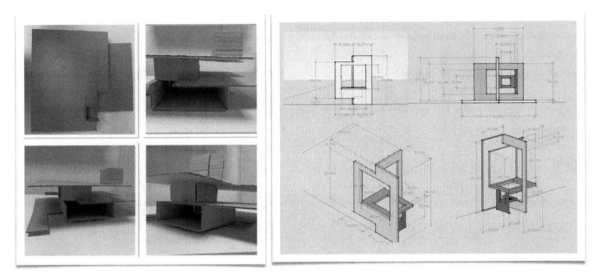

For their final project, the students build three-dimensional compositions to grasp the uses of form and texture, together with structure on assignments designed to have intersections with other artistic fields. Working in groups for the final project, the students are usually assigned a problem that would require them to research and learn from a design-adjacent discipline. The final project of 2022 Fall semester is a good example to demonstrate the methodological approach that searches for intersections between design-based disciplines for teaching Basic Design as the main subject of the final project was choreography, body, and space, and the students ended up researching different categories of dance and appropriating and abstracting bodily moves into three-dimensional compositions **(Figure 3).**

Figure 3. Three-dimensional project examples from basic design studio

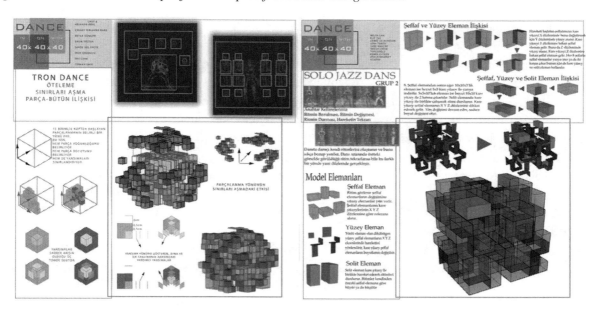

By the end of Basic Design studio, the students are expected to have a fair understanding of the relationship of solids and voids. In the second semester of the first year, the education methods shift to use that understanding as a base to develop a sensitivity towards designing architecturally.

Architectural Project Two

Although, as mentioned before, the first-year education is generally and globally formed around Basic Design education, Architectural Project II differentiate itself by acting like an introductory course for designing architecturally. The main aim of Architectural Project II is to expand the experience the students have on formal relationship of solids and voids to give equal attention to topics of program, the context and the site. The main concern for the course is to introduce context as an input for design to give the relationship of solids and voids an architectural turn/touch. The studio is designed to encourage students to discover the importance of context in designing habitable spaces, while being introduced to proposing and designing a program which is as important as the formal relations themselves.

In terms of pedagogy, Architectural Project II builds on the Constructivist approach introduced during the first semester, however, while maintaining "learning by exploring" as the central method, in the second term, the studio slowly transitions to a Constructivist learning principle referred to as "Situated Learning" to introduce the concept of context to the students. Situated Learning principal initially developed by Lave and Wenger states that learning is an inherently social process and that it cannot be separated from the social context in which it happens. (Lave & Wenger, 1991) This principal focuses on creating challenges in which the real-world scenarios or problems can be recreated or simulated. (Seels, 1995). Transferring this technique to the design studio, Architectural Project II pedagogy accepts that knowledge is actively constructed by individuals through their interactions with objects, space, and the city, hence, the creative learning in the studio should be enforced in relation to the context, in the studio's case: the site. The design problem in Architectural Project II takes place in the real-world context, and the learning objective of the studio is first to transfer the prior knowledge on the act of learning through exploring into the ability to synthesize and organize actual, habitable spaces.

The curriculum for Architectural Project II has three stages: analyzing the site, restructuring the site and finally designing a habitable space. Understanding and designing relevant to the context is the main concern of this studio, as so the site analysis is a significant stage of the course. We believe that establishing a conscious design approach that is sensitive of place and context is the first step towards gaining a sense of responsibility towards not only the physical surroundings, but also social and cultural aspects of the context is the fundamental of an architect's practice. Therefore, Architectural Project II is designed to establish the foundations of such sensitivity for students.

For this studio, context is the key of designing a project and the first stage of the curriculum focuses on a given site. The students are assigned a specific site in the beginning of the semester, and following the principles of Situated Learning, site visits become a central step towards creative learning. Understanding the context is pivotal for Architectural Project II, as the teaching technique heavily relies on students' understanding and internalizing not only the physical aspects of the site but its lived experiences: the cultural, social, and even economical aspects of its surroundings. After site visits, the students are expected to conduct research and develop analysis of the physical, social, and cultural aspects of the given site to have a better understanding of the general context that they will solve the design problem for.

The design problem in Architectural Project II usually focuses on reconstructing an urban space where students can analyze and understand the dynamics of urban texture together with its social and cultural relationships. The curriculum of the studio consists of two stages. Since it is the first time the students are introduced to the notion of site and context, the first stage of the course focuses on the reconstruction of the site in an abstract way to encourage students to dwell on the knowledge they gained during Basic Design studio in terms of abstract thinking, and transform that knowledge into a more architectural setting, incorporating the abstract language with the newly-introduced concept of the site and context to reconstruct the site. Until the second stage, the students work in groups. Working in groups was proven to be more efficient for students as the sites given are relatively large in scale and working in groups is proven to be useful, while group work provides a peer-to-peer learning environment which is essential for developing their creative mindsets.

After reconstructing the sites during a given project, during the second stage of the projects, the students start designing their own individual projects on the reconstructed sites where they propose their individual programs which the site analysis that they have conducted give valuable insight for. The expected individual projects are usually small in scale, varying from a single shed to a housing block, from an art hub to a group of interrelated units. As small as the scale of the proposed project is, the students are given flexibility and are encouraged not to limit their creativity when proposing the program as designing a program itself is an important skill to learn. By the end of the semester, the main goal for them is to gain knowledge on designing a habitable space while paying attention to human scale, the surroundings and the context.

The main focus of Architectural Project II studio is context, and the site visits form a fundamental part of the course. The case study selected for this paper is a significant case to re-evaluate the methods for understanding, observing, and analyzing the site without physically visiting it, as the case study here is a project conducted during the heydays of pandemic where the site visits were not possible.

DIGITAL EXPLORERS/DIGITALIZED EXPLORATIONS: AN EXPERIMENT ON DISTANT URBAN INTERVENTIONS

The case study of this paper is a project conducted in Spring 2021 semester titled "Digital Explorers / Digitalized Explorations: Distant Urban Interventions to Istanbul's Kadikoy." As mentioned before, the notion of contexts and site visits are the central concern and the backbone of this course. In this sense, the Spring 2021 project poses a significant case since studio had to be conducted remotely as it was a time in the midst of the global pandemic.

The case study discussed in this article was the project conducted during a period just after a national lockdown in Turkey. Gazi University's Department of Architecture conducted all courses remotely including the studios, just like many higher education institutions all over the world. By Spring 2021, Turkey just got out of a national lockdown however the pandemic measures were still in action. Higher education had to continue remotely, and we had to conduct the studio from afar with students residing all over Turkey, therefore, the possibility of travel was out of question.

The lockdown conditions not only forced the studio to change teaching techniques in order to acclimate to a new studio environment, a virtual one. It also drastically affected the pedagogy of the studio whose central theme revolves around site visits. As the Architectural Project II studio depends heavily on face-to-face interactions of teacher and the learner, as well as the social interactions of students as peers to fuel each other's creativity, we have shifted our teaching methodology to imitate a social process of collaborative dialogue in the virtual space. The main problem for the lockdown period for the studio is to recreate the environment of where learning is "co-constructed through interaction, negotiation and collaboration between students and tutors and between students and their peers." (Smith, 2022) Although, the virtual studio environment proved to be challenging to structure because of the apparent risks of students' possible lack of social interaction with their instructors as well as their peers because of its intrinsic socio-spatial character of the virtual platforms, Iranmanesh and Onur claims that students reported an increase in conducting self-directed research and acquiring new skills during virtual studio sessions. (Iranmanesh & Onur, 2021) While the virtual studio strengthen the individual journeys of exploration, in Architectural Project II, we shifted our teaching techniques to create a virtual learning community to help students develop "an awareness built within the virtual environment and in the appreciation, generation and exchange of knowledge in collaborative ways."(Rodríguez-Ardura & Meseguer-Artola, 2016) Instead of individual table critics, we transformed the virtual studio where students actively listen and participate each other's design critics, while conducting informal critique sessions in the waiting rooms of the digital platforms used for virtual learning.

Moreover, without the traditional means of site visits, we started circling around the idea to build the semester's project to be inspired by this very impossibility of physically visiting a place. In this case, the principal of Situated Learning that inspired the design of Architectural Project II studio was transformed to focus less on the ways the students physical interact with the space and more on finding new ways of social interaction with a context. This approach together with the co-construction of studio environment into a virtual social circle helped shifting the studio pedagogy towards a more inclusive version of social constructivism pedagogy which supports a learning model through social interaction (Powers, 2001).

In this regard, going back to Piaget's assessment of constructivist approach which states, "learning is a series of internalized actions" and realizing a real-life situation is crucial for the students to make the mental connection with the initial design problem, we reconstructed the real-life scenario to acclimate and imitate the new normal in the studio: understanding, analyzing and learning from a social distance

(Piaget, 1972). While the studio still centered around the theme of exploring, the methods of exploring had to be changed. Instead of using a method to experience through physical interaction with the site, the studio methodology in this semester evolved to encourage the students to empathize with the users and actors of a given context, a key method of social-constructivism method developed by Lev Vygotsky on Paiget's original theory. According to Vygotsky, social interactions is the key to learning and the students of the studio had to reconstruct their traditional experience of social interaction into a digitalized interaction with the context: the site and its users (Vygotsky, 1978).

The theme of the project "Digital Explorations/Digital Explorers" were chosen exactly for this reason. The title of the project both reflects the main theme of the studio: "learning by exploring," while also assimilating to the social environment of the new normal. Therefore, for the semester under lockdown, the studio shifted its pedagogy to "learning by digitally exploring," and the title digital explorations, while referring to "exploring, discovering" also denoted to a new way of social-constructivism: interacting with the site and the user digitally.

This very notion of digitally accessible sites gave us the idea of the project: "digital explorers and digitalized explorations". The idea was finding means to virtually visit the site and gather as much information as students can. It started as an experiment, and upon discussing the most likely accessible cities around Turkey, Istanbul was the first choice for the project. Besides Istanbul being a metropolis, which makes the city more easily and digitally accessible in the digital age, Kadikoy, located on the "Anatolian part" of Istanbul is one of the trendier areas of the city for the last few years, which makes it very attractive to visitors and tourists, while this popularity opened channels for Kadikoy to be more digitally explorable.

After assigning the project to the students, their first assignment was to find creative ways to digitally explore the site. Although, we anticipated the students would gravitate towards more traditionally known and easily accessible methods to digitally explore the site, including using Google Street view, visiting digital archives, or finding documentaries and video logs on Kadikoy. However, the students transcended our expectations by coming up with a more diverse way of exploring the site.

On top of using the more traditional ways of digital explorations they have also discovered that Istanbul municipality has established a website named "Digital Observation Deck" that visitors can log in and watch the landmarked spots in Istanbul from real-time cameras. They even accessed traffic cams (Mobese in Turkish) to access popular traffic routes while they also investigated street cams. The students also used social media, the digital depository of our time, in a very significant way and by tracing accounts on Instagram, they managed to form an aerial view of Kadikoy by collaging posts shared on the platform.

Before they started their site analysis, since Kadikoy holds a very dense and large portion of the city, we divided Kadikoy into smaller portions and we divided the students to work in groups. We approximately had 120 students for this course, and they are grouped in 16, to hold 6 to 8 students for each group **(Figure 4)**.

Digital Explorers/Digitalized Explorations

Figure 4. Kadikoy: Divided zones

Although every zone had a slightly different characteristic and its own unique texture and demographic, it was interesting to see commonalities between them in the students' analysis, while also observing how different groups approach to the same zones of the city with different attitudes. Some groups were interested in the history, historical layers, changing texture of the city over years, the effects of urbanization and overall pattern of Kadikoy. They had dived into digital archives and followed interviews, data, and documentaries developed on the site. They treated the problem as if the site is physically accessible and preferred to approach to the site by not focusing on the pandemic conditions or the explorer's perspective, but rather learnt about the site through documents collected on the site. It was significant to observe how much they could trace on the site through archives and how much collected data would give clues about the context. Meanwhile, there are couple of themes in terms of explorers of and exploring Kadikoy that seemed to excite the student groups. First was, expectedly, the voyeur eye, the explorer's experience in Kadikoy. Their curiosity about the voyeur eye eventually evolved into deeper discussions in studio meetings on notion of Flaneur. Some groups dwelled on the concept of Benjaminian flaneur as a modern urban spectator, an amateur detective and investigator of the city. (Benjamin, 1983) and started circling around the idea of how we can reinterpret the Flaneur in 21st century especially in the pandemic conditions which brought up many other subjects including digital nomads, distant visits, and even distant interventions to the site that was never physically visited. Picking up from that point, the tourist's perspective became a topic of interest. The groups started developing analysis on tourist routes, popular routes and zones of interests from the visitors' perspective. While some groups focused more on the voyeur eye, the eye of the visitor, the flaneur; some groups focused on the effects of the presence of these voyeurs/flaneurs/tourists for the local community and how the presence of tourism effects the neighborhood in terms of privacy as Kadikoy is mostly composed of residential settlements. The themes such as private zones, residential and commercial areas, the user profiles of locals/residents, as well as workers' communities in the area came to focus **(Figure 5)**.

Figure 5. Group site analysis for the project "Digital Explorers / Digitalized Explorations: Distant Urban Interventions to Istanbul's Kadikoy"

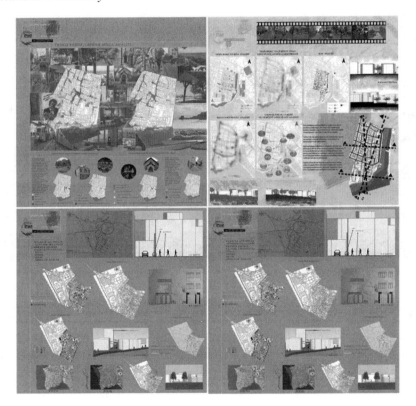

On top of that, the aspects that are indigenous to Kadikoy, as the center of youth as well as elderly, a central zone for art and music, a zone of many landmarks with a loaded history were discovered by students which were helpful for them for reconstructing the site and proposing a program later. It was interesting to see how two different groups used same theme to analyze the site like mapping through sound and noise, and one focused on it to trace the flaneurs' footsteps while the other used it to trace the areas of privacy, or the effects of visitors' presence on changing texture of commercial zones of the site. After they have conducted the site analysis, the students move onto restructure the site. Whether the focus is the physical forms and relations derived from the site: such as the organization of streets and buildings, the texture of the site, and even slopes and plains of topography; or immaterial and non-physical relationships/characteristic of the site: such as the users and user profiles (pedestrian routes, dense zones, accessible and inaccessible areas, thresholds and even user patterns and demographics); the students

Digital Explorers/Digitalized Explorations

started abstracting the relations they found within the site into a series of solids and voids to design a context-inspired three-dimensional composition with an architectural twist.

The examples of restructured sites from the Kadikoy project presented a variety of approaches. Working on the data gathered through social media, some groups were inspired by the vistas through Kadikoy. Using different Instagram accounts, and pictures from Google Street view to scan which areas are photographed the most while interpreting the rest as black zones, they abstracted the site as two clashing clusters of orthogonal and oblique shapes to design their composition. Another group worked on the travels of sounds and used the noise as a determining factor to trace the areas that are more accessible or popular, contrasting it with the zones that are "noise cancelling" as areas that are more private. They used the noise as an input to trace continuity and flow in the site. One group worked on themes of obstacles, borders, and thresholds of the site that effects the pedestrian movement and accessibility while providing possible privacy in a densely visited yet residential area. They used folding as a method to represent these borders, obstacles and thresholds between physical structures as well as to present a better pedestrian perspective to the site. Similar to this approach, some groups focused on the duality of the site that holds a dense visitor population on the one hand, while also hosting a large residential area. Representing that duality in two different forms, one flowing in and out of site, while the other more rigid and static; the group designed overlapping and intermingling layers to represent two clashing population in the site. While aforementioned groups focused on tracing the pedestrian movement, some groups focused more on the physical texture and formal relations within the site. Approaching to the topography as a one big filter, allowing flow and continuity on one side, and forming physical obstacles and creating isolated fields on the other, the students created filters on different layers: the topography, the building facades, the streets and cul-de-sacs, even trees, each create obstacles or allowed flow within the site, which the group abstracted their forms into **(Figure 6)**.

Figure 6. Reconstructed sites for the project "Digital Explorers / Digitalized Explorations: Distant Urban Interventions to Istanbul's Kadikoy"

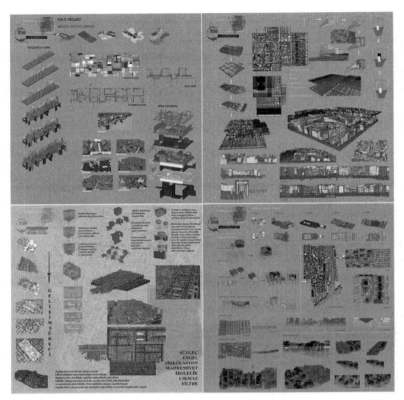

Restructuring of the site was the preliminary stage to introduce the basics of architectural sensitivity, while also giving the students the opportunity to use the knowledge they accumulated in Basic design. This particular stage is the distinguishing characteristic of the studio we teach at Gazi University that combines the abstract thinking of Basic Design with the fundamental notion of contextual sensitivity. As can be seen in the project examples, as an intermediary stage between Basic design and architectural design, the exercise of restructuring the site contributes vastly to first-year architectural education. After restructuring the site, the project moved onto the next stage that is to propose an architectural program and designing a small-scale space. Before diving into their individual projects, the students are given three keywords to reflect on which would help them to propose their programs. They were asked to choose an actor, **"who are they designing for"**, an action, **"what are they designing"** or **"serving to which function?"**, and finally, if necessary to choose a medium that would help them to narrow down the action: "the actor is doing the action via what?" The actors that students have chosen for their projects varied from designing for different age groups, for different communities, to designing for wanderers and even for animals. The actions they came up with was parallel with the project theme of exploring and experiencing: walking, driving, running, and observing. As an example, the medium, in this case would be the vehicle the actor is driving, which would shape the program more towards to have a function that is experienced by driving-through. Following the keywords given to them, the students proposed their programs.

There were a variety of stimulating program topics they came up with, however they can be summarized in common sub-themes as: places embracing the subculture of Kadikoy, or indigenous to Kadikoy; places for the pandemic, the new normal; places that are inclusive as well as spaces specifically designed for wanderers. The individual projects, then were developed over these programs. In the final stage, the main aim for the students is to design spaces that are habitable, designed with the consideration of a human scale and a function. The main expectation from the students at this stage is to have a sensitivity towards and having a grasp on skills such as attaining functions for each space, considering circulation and accessibility through spaces, and a basic understanding on the scale and use of the spaces **(Figure 7)**.

Figure 7. Program proposals for the project "Digital Explorers / Digitalized Explorations: Distant Urban Interventions to Istanbul's Kadikoy"

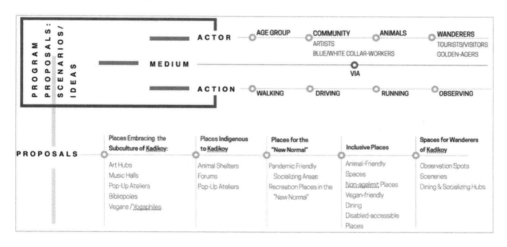

The final project examples demonstrate that, while the students still work with geometrical forms and their relations with each other, they developed the awareness that those forms now hold functions, and we can observe how each stage in our curriculum contributed to achieving a sensitivity to design architecturally **(Figure 8)**.

We believe that Architectural Project 2 acts as a necessary intermediary between Basic Design, and other studios where the problems of design get more complicated and more intricate. The main contribution of the studio to the architectural education is that it acts as an intersection of Basic Design and architectural design, and the exercise making this possible is the stage where students reconstruct the site. In this sense, the educational methods used in Architectural Project II of Gazi University Department of Architecture not only differentiates itself from other equivalent institutions as the first-year design education strategies in other faculties commonly focus on introducing the form in an abstract way, as our studio focuses on the form with a function, and for the first-year design education, we observe that this methodology vastly help them to solve more complicated architectural problems in the following years. As a unique exercise, restructuring the site provides a unique opportunity for students to use basic design knowledge in an architectural setting. Moreover, with the introduction of the concept of site as an early stage in the course, the students develop a contextual sensitivity while still experimenting with forms as they are taught in basic design.

The main principle here is to provide them with the knowledge that: firstly, the base of architectural design is form as well as function; and secondly, the context affects and shapes the form, as it affects the program of any architectural entity that is built. While the program that the students proposed are inspired by the context itself, it is also important to note that the individual functions of each volume they design works in harmony with the other volumes as our main aim for this studio is to guide the students to design their projects as a coherent whole, with the context, and in itself. Our studio's main principle is to introduce a context-aware sensitivity for students in the earliest stage possible in their education, and for this particular project, we believe that we encouraged them to find alternative methods for understanding the site, not only in its physicality but also through its social and cultural aspect which is a crucial lesson to learn to practice architecture in our century. Moreover, as they were introduced to the digital tools for not only designing but also investigating, we believe our studio acts as an important step of an architect's education, as for an architect to thrive in 21st century practice of architecture, digital investigation becomes as important as the design itself as the world is gradually being digitalized.

Figure 8. Final projects for "Digital Explorers / Digitalized Explorations: Distant Urban Interventions to Istanbul's Kadikoy"

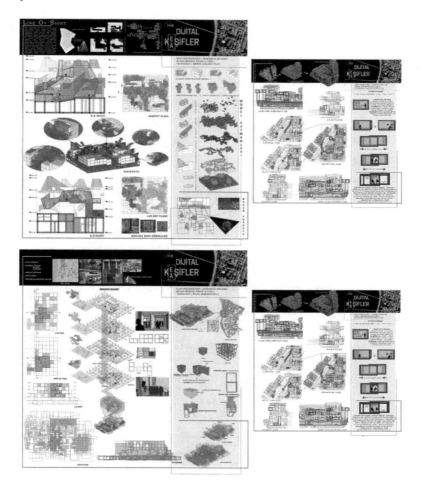

While keeping in mind that this is the first time the students face such a challenge for designing a space with a function, and the fact that the projects are expected to have raw edges, it is important in this stage to build an awareness on the site, the surrounding, the function and formal relationships of not one solid to another void, but of a habitable space to another. The main challenge in the studio is drawing parallels between Basic Design and Architectural Project II, so that students can put their newly gained abstract thinking in use in the latter course, while reminding the students architectural design feeds from basic design however is not limited by it. It is a delicate balance to encourage students to experiment with forms while reminding them the constraints of site, and structure. In this sense, we evaluate the studio of Architectural Design II as an introductory course to architectural design where introducing the site, the context, the program, the function, and the scale helps the students to get ready for their later years in the architectural education in our institution, when their knowledge on designing architecturally refines and finesse.

CONCLUSION

Design studio, although a fundamental part of architectural education, is taught with varying methodologies at institutions all around the world. Since there is no fixed methodology for teaching design studio, and the design studio experience itself is intended to perform outside of any established/traditional norm, the radical differences in pedagogies between architectural schools are only expected. However, in terms of first-year architectural education, there is a commonality between architectural schools where the curriculum is designed around teaching abstract thinking while leaving addressing the issues of context, function and even structure to the later years of education. In Gazi University's Department of Architecture, we designed an alternative curriculum where the introduction of context sensitivity is a vital part of first-year education. Taught in the second semester of first year, the studio of Architectural Project II is designed to combine the students' knowledge on abstract thinking with a context-sensitive approach where they design small scale, habitable projects for an actual site, while as an intermediary stage they exercise abstracting the site with the data they gathered as a result of conducting site visits and site analysis and from the influences they get from the physical, cultural and social aspects of a given site.

This paper aims to present the pedagogies involved in teaching the studio of Architectural Project II, a studio whose methods are designed around the subject of context. For a studio that is heavily dependent on the concept of site visits and site analysis, the pandemic context had been a challenging time as physically visiting a site was out of question. As the pandemic forced us to re-adjust the methods we have used before the pandemic, we had to replace physical site visits with more creative methods while maintaining the main focus of the studio which is the context. The case study this paper discusses is the outcomes of that experiment: a project we have conducted during spring semester of 2021 titled "Digital Explorers / Digitalized Explorations: Distant Urban Interventions to Istanbul's Kadikoy." This project became a prime example for presenting the challenges the students and the instructors are facing during the semester not only before but also during the pandemic. It was also crucial in proving the importance of developing context-sensitivity in first-year architecture students and there can be found methods to creatively address the issues of context, function, and structure together with abstract way of thinking which we believe is important for the first-year architectural education.

ACKNOWLEDGMENT

All authors contributed equally to the writing of the manuscript.

We are grateful for the efforts and contribution of research assistants Elif Tektas, Sena Gulbahar-Tuncel, Gulce Sozen, Gizem Ozerol, Saliha Erdurmus, Abdullah Eren Demirel, Metin Kurumak and Elif Cam to our studio and to the project "Digital Explorers / Digitalized Explorations: Distant Urban Interventions to Istanbul's Kadikoy."

REFERENCES

Akdeniz, H., & Aksel, E. (1989). Güzel Sanatlar Fakültelerinde Temel Sanat Eğitimi Üzerine Düşünceler Ve Bir Bakış Açısı [Reflections on Basic Art Education in Fine Arts Faculties: A Perspective], *Güzel Sanatlar Fakültelerinde Temel Sanat Eğitimi Semineri*. Hacettepe Üniversitesi Güzel Sanatlar Fakültesi Yayınları. Ankara.

Aydınlı, S. (2016). Tasarım Eğitiminde Yapılandırıcı Paradigma: 'Öğrenmeyi Öğrenme'. [Constructivist Paradigm in Design Education: 'Learning to Learn']. *Tasarım + Kuram, 11*(20), 1-18.

Benjamin, W. (1983). *Charles Baudelaire: A Lyric Poet in the Era of High Capitalism* (Zohn, H., Trans.). Routledge.

Dewey, J. (1986). Experience and Education. *The Educational Forum*, 50(3), 241–252. 10.1080/00131728609335764

Gross, M. D., & Do, E. Y. (1997). The design studio approach: Learning design in architecture education. In J. Kolodner & M. Guzdial. (Eds.), *Design Education Workshop: EduTech/NSF, College of Computing* (pp. 208-221). London: Brill.

Iranmanesh, A., & Onur, Z. (2021). Mandatory virtual design studio for all: Exploring the transformations of architectural education amidst the global pandemic. *International Journal of Art & Design Education*, 40(1), 1–17. 10.1111/jade.12350

Itten, J. (1965). The foundation course at the Bauhaus. In Kepes, G. (Ed.), *Education of vision* (pp. 104–121). George Braziller, Inc.

Jonassen, D. H. (1991). Objectivism Versus Constructivism: Do We Need a New Philosphical Paradigm? *Educational Technology Research and Development*, 39(3), 11–12. 10.1007/BF02296434

Kaufman. (1965). The visual world today. In J. J. Hausman (Ed.), *Report of the commission on art education* (pp. 13-34). Washinigton, DC.: National Art Education Association.

Komez-Daglioglu, E., Pinar, E., Gursel-Dino, I., Yoncaci-Arslan, P., & Bas-Butuner, F. (2020). Teaching Architectural Design Studio Remotely: The Introduction to Architectural Design Course at METU. *Journal of Design Studio*, 2(2), 143–147. 10.46474/jds.820352

Lave, J., & Wenger, E. (1991). *Situated Learning: Legitimate Peripheral Participation*. Cambridge University Press. 10.1017/CBO9780511815355

Lerner, F. (2005). Foundations for Design Education: Continuing the Buhaus Vorkurs Vision. *Studies in Art Education*, 46(3), 211–226. 10.1080/00393541.2005.11650075

Merriam, S., & Cafferella, R. (1999). *Key theories of learning. Learning in adulthood: A comprehensive guide* (2nd ed.). Jossey Bass.

Özkar, M. (2017). *Rethinking Basic Design in Architectural Education: foundations past and future*. Routledge. 10.4324/9781315740003

RIBA. (2014). *RIBA procedures for validation and validation criteria for UK and international courses and examinations in architecture.* RIBA. <https://www.architecture.com/-/media/GatherContent/Validation-Procedures-and-Criteria/Additional-Documents/ValidationProcedures2011SECONDREVISION2MAY2014pdf.pdf>

Rodríguez-Ardura, I., & Meseguer-Artola, A. (2016). What leads people to keep on e-learning? An empirical analysis of users' experiences and their effects on continuance intention. *Interactive Learning Environments*, 24(6), 1030–1053. 10.1080/10494820.2014.926275

Salem-Gur, O., & Dundar, M. (2019). Re-thinking Basic Design Course in Architectural Education in Turkey. *Intercultural Understanding*, 9, 7–14.

Seels, B. (1995). *Instructional Design Fundamentals: A Reconsideration.* Educational Technology Publications.

Shulman, L. S. (1987). Knowledge and learning: Foundations of the new reform. *Harvard Educational Review*, 57(1), 1–22. 10.17763/haer.57.1.j463w79r56455411

Smith, C. (2022). Socio-constructivist pedagogy in physical and virtual spaces: the impacts and opportunities on dialogic learning in creative disciplines'. *Architecture_MPS 22*, 1.

Vygotsky, L. S. (1978). *Mind in Society: Development of Higher Psychological Processes.* Harvard University Press.

Chapter 15
On the Threshold:
A Transitionary Architectural Design Studio

Esin Boyacıoğlu
Gazi University, Turkey

Hilal Aycı
Gazi University, Turkey

Bengi Su Erürkmen Aksoy
https://orcid.org/0000-0002-2745-5772
Gazi University, Turkey

Bilge Beril Kapusuz Balcı
Gazi University, Turkey

ABSTRACT

Architectural education, rooted in historical models like Beaux-Arts and Bauhaus, has long shaped pedagogical practices focusing on formalism and functionality. However, contemporary discourse suggests a need for a paradigm shift towards addressing social and cultural dimensions in architectural education. This chapter explores the evolution of architectural pedagogy through the lens of Studio 201 (atölyeikiyüzbir), a design studio experience spanning over two decades at the Gazi University Department of Architecture.

INTRODUCTION

Formal architectural education, which started with Beaux-Arts in France in the 17th century, continued on this single model for a long time until the Bauhaus model was established in Germany in the aftermath of World War I as a reflection of the developing technology and new understanding of architecture and its education. Bauhaus's teaching experimentation, which has a long-run presence in architectural education in many countries, including Turkey, promotes critical, creative, and pragmatic thinking. However, it emphasizes the architectural form concerning the concepts of function, hygiene, and economy and less

DOI: 10.4018/979-8-3693-2329-8.ch015

on the social and cultural issues in daily life. Salama (2007) argues that despite immense changes in architecture and urban life, today's architectural education is still influenced by or based on these two models' rules and principles (Salama & Wilkinson, 2007). He expresses his concerns about academia's stance on ignoring everyday life's real problems and emphasizes the potential or opportunities of the multilayered human experience. Design studio pedagogy 1, or 'the education of designing the built environments,' deals with the social dimension since the built environment is grounded in human tradition (Salama, 2017). At the same time, the studio as "a model for design education" (Wang, 2010: 173) and as an "active site where students are engaged intellectually and socially" (Dutton, 1987: 16) should be enhanced with similar concerns.

This paper presents a design studio experience that has expanded over 20 years. Studio 201 (*atölyei-kiyüzbir*) was established to counteract the difficulties of the 3rd-semester students who completed their first-year architectural education. The initial aim of Studio 201 is to translate the students' conception of abstract space and its modes of representation (compositional and graphical skills) into a process that deals with the physical space through its material and social dimensions while preparing the students for the following vertical design studio. In that sense, the third semester of the design studios was designed as a 'threshold studio' that occupies a transitionary space between basic design studios and vertical design studios. To better explain the studio's concept of "threshold," it is necessary to briefly explain the distinctive education model in the Gazi University Department of Architecture. First, an overview of the educational framework of the department within which Studio 201 operates will be presented, contextualizing its role within the broader architectural curriculum. Secondly, a detailed exploration of Studio 201's structure, objectives, and pedagogical approach, highlighting its unique position as a 'threshold studio' in architectural education. Then, Studio 201's objectives and the main steps involved in the studio process will be analyzed, elucidating its overarching goals and guiding principles. Finally, the methodology will be examined by revisiting the design problems assigned to students in different and particular semesters, before and after the COVID-19 pandemic, to point out the -obligatory- changes and investigate its probable effects on the transformation of the method. A showcase of projects undertaken by Studio 201 students provides insights into applying the studio's principles and methodologies practically.

THE STRUCTURE OF THE DEPARTMENT OF ARCHITECTURE

The Department of Architecture at Gazi University has an eight-semester curriculum. Initially, the curriculum design module's structure comprised vertically structured architectural design studios, which followed the first two basic design studios. In these vertical design studios, all the students from the third to seventh semesters worked in a structure that enabled them to communicate intensely, regardless of the differences in the design problems they were assigned. The department launched a 'threshold studio' coded M201 in 2000. It was structured as an introductory studio for the following vertical design studios. Thus, Studio 201 aimed to equip the students with the necessary basic architectural knowledge, encourage them to be innovative, help them translate their intuitional sense of design into conscious design processes, and achieve a critical way of thinking.

THE STRUCTURE OF THE STUDIO 201

The teaching staff of Studio 201 consists of full-time academics specialized in various fields of architecture and practitioners with outstanding architectural experience in professional life who contribute to the department as part-time instructors. This composition is essential to provide an eligible and experienced team with theoretical and practical knowledge in an extended field of architecture, enabling full coverage of theoretical and practical essentials for the students.

WHAT ARE THE MAIN STEPS? THE OBJECTIVES OF STUDIO 201

Studio 201 mainly aims to focus on three significant processes as

- Understanding / Research and Analysis
- Designing / Creativeness, Experiencing and Innovation
- Presenting / Representation and Experimentation

These three processes are to be run either consequent or parallel to each other and structured in their evolution to cope with the students' different approaches and individual capacities.

The process of understanding is structured in the perception of the design problem with one's recognition, analyzing the site and environmental factors, contextual thinking within the perspectives of culture, history, and society, functional analysis, and the fractions of the program (size and the proportion of spaces and interspaces relations; relations between serving and served spaces, vertical and horizontal circulations), activities and events, and the way of life which should take place.

Designing is the most challenging process since it enhances the students' scenario, clarifying and classifying the obtained data from the conceptualization process to be involved in the design process. The students are expected to deal with the concepts of complexity, uncertainty, uniqueness, and identity; they are also likely to correlate the architectural theory and design experience, the intuitions and realities, technology, and the use of materials. Diagramming, sketching, drawing, and 3-D modeling are design tools.

The presentation process includes working with the conventional modes of architectural representation, such as orthographic drawings, sketching, and modeling, while encouraging the students to experiment with different media, including artistic tools such as moving images. Since representation is a process of creation and production, the methods of design and presentation are juxtaposed through experimental acts of the students through representational tools.

HOW ARE WE DOING? THE METHOD OF STUDIO 201

Starting the design process in the first years of architectural education can be considered the most challenging phase in adapting the architectural language and translating abstract conceptions of space into a physical architectural one. The studio, as a model for architectural design pedagogy, commonly addressing 'problem-based' or 'project-based' learning, becomes a space for this transition where the studio instructors guide the students in their search for producing solutions through bilateral critical reviews

(Bridges, 2007 cited in Rodriguez et al., 2018: 341). To cope smoothly with this transition, Studio 201 assigns two architectural design problems: the first is a subsidiary with a simple, functional problem. In contrast, the second and the main ones regarding the architectural program are relatively complex. The syllabus clarifying both design problems is handed out at the beginning of the semester, with a complementary reading list and numerous excursions to the given site. The reading list provides clues for the students to form their conceptual framework for the problem. At the same time, the site excursions involve their subjective observations and participation in the site to encourage them to introduce their first critical approach to the context they would engage with.

The first design problem, to be completed in about three or four weeks, is relevant and subsidiary to the main design task of the semester. The architectural program assigned is at most 50 square meters and is tied to everyday activities such as dwelling, working, and walking activities, which are engaged in everyday life. Thus, the task is to transfer a well-known activity into an architectural body/form within a brief period. This first task is given on the same site as the second one to accelerate and ease the process of critically analyzing the physical and social context. This very first problem-solving task is extended and enhanced through "a reflective conversation with the materials of the situation" in Schön's terms (1988: 4 cited in Wang, 2010: 175) and presents the reflective character of the studio as a conversation between the participants; instructors and the students. So, starting a "conversation" in the studio that requires students' participation also contributes to Studio 201 in providing a 'threshold' between the basic design studio and the following architectural design studios. In this sense, the fragmentation of the design problem and process of the first problem-solving process addresses Studio 201's transitionary character. It could be defined as the studio's 'hidden curriculum' in Dutton's (1987: 16) conceptual terms. At the end of the first phase, all projects are evaluated in a colloquium-like jury regarding their conceptual, spatial, and formal approaches.

The semester's main design problem, which is at most 1500 square meters, begins right after the first evaluation. The students are asked to re-read the theme, program, and urban context and represent the problem through their own interpretation and conceptual framework referring to the readings they pursued. Specialists and researchers are invited to give lectures to the studio to share their expertise on the context and the architectural program with the students. At the same time, the studio's teaching staff provides theoretical and practical knowledge throughout the semester.

After two weeks of research and one-to-one critiques, minor juries are held in cooperation with the two tutors and their groups of students every week. Minor juries revolve weekly through rotations and alterations in the combination of instructors. This method allows the students to discuss their design proposals with each staff member, distinguish subjective inclinations, and experience critical thought in creating a shared and open ground for discussions. Thus, the students are urged to gain the ability to express themselves not only through architectural representation but also by verbally engaging with the vocabulary and concepts of architecture. At the end of the semester, each design proposal is discussed and evaluated by a final jury, which is held again as a 'forum' open to all, like a colloquium. All the projects are exhibited at the studio or as a part of an intervention in the common spaces of the department following the final jury. As another significant component of the studio method, the exhibition calls for further conversations that transcend the studio and expand the learning environment.

WHAT HAVE WE DONE? PROJECTS FOR 2019-20 AND 2020-21 FALL SEMESTERS

In this section, to see how Studio 201's long-standing methodology operates and which mandatory changes needed to be realized in the method -due to the Covid-19 outbreak, the project topics and student projects for the pre-pandemic 2019-2020 fall semester and the pandemic 2020-2021 fall semester will be examined.

Design Problem One: Pedestrian Bridge and Information Center in Maltepe, Ankara

During the 2019-2020 fall semester, the studio focused on Ankara's historic core. The site chosen for the semester was near the new High-Speed Train Station (HSTS), on the opposite side of the main boulevard, where our university campus in Maltepe, Ankara, is also located.

The central (and historical) train station of Ankara, which was designed by Turkish architect Şekip Akalın in 1937 as a new modern architectural typology of the rising new capital of Turkey, stands behind the recently constructed new train station, yet almost invisible in the shadow of the 'spectacular' scale of the new one. The intention behind the focus on a location next to the central train station is related to introducing students to a project site that is a portal in character since the train stations are the buildings that act as gateways for cities to circulate people and goods (Bozdoğan, 2008). In this regard, the assigned project site and the historical train station are of great importance in the context of the historical part of Ankara.

The functional change and the over-dimensional scale of the new HSTS transformed the overall context in that particular place. In assigning the project, a vacant space just opposite the HSTS building -and near our Faculty building- was seen as a potential area for discussing new problems. Due to the new building's location, being at the edge of a boulevard with very fast-flowing vehicle traffic that divides the city, the need for a pedestrian bridge emerged to connect the project area to the station and the historical site of Ankara. In addition, claiming to be a gateway to the city, the new station needed support with a space that could function as an information center that could give information on the historically multilayered context of Ankara. Therefore, a pedestrian bridge that was expected to connect the HSTS building with the Information Center was assigned as the first project. The Information Center was given as the main architectural design problem.

The first assignment was an important exercise and a tool for understanding and analyzing the project site and searching for the potential approaches to the site, including the possible placement decisions for the Information Center. It should be noted that the main project was expected to be produced differently than the first. The first (Figure 1) project was intended to be considered a means to understand the area, and the main project could have been designed differently from the first one. However, even though it was not obligatory, some students used their pedestrian bridge as a starting point. They mediated its potential for the Information Center and benefited from the subsidiary design task.

Figure 1. The first project/pedestrian bridge

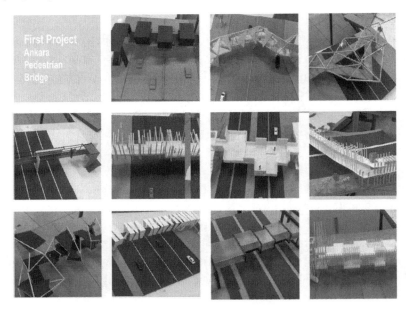

By mediating architectural elements and forms in both design problems, students dealt with the actions of 'welcoming' and 'connecting' in terms of greeting people who are new or already familiar with the city (Figure 2, 3, 4, 5). Throughout the semester, mediating the students' scenarios and projects, notions like publicity and public spaces, and actions like connecting, meeting, and encountering were discussed, and spatial equivalents of these concepts and actions were investigated. In their projects, students designed open/semi-open/closed spaces/green spaces and did research into their relations.

Figure 2. Ankara Information Center/ Selver Kurt-İlknur Özkılıç

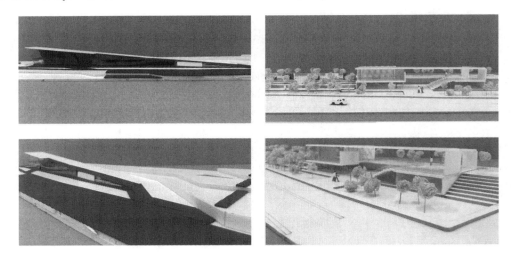

Figure 3. Ankara Information Center/ Kübra Canbaz-Tuğçe Sevinç

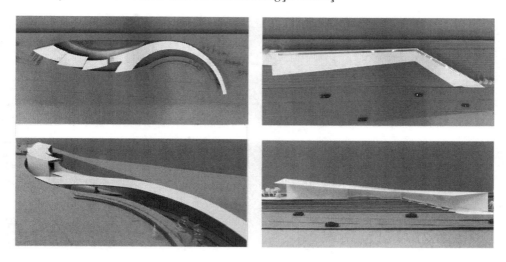

Figure 4. Ankara Information Center/ Sevde Nur Erdem-Beyza Demircan

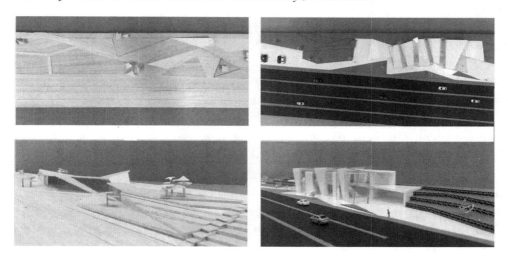

Figure 5. Ankara Information Center/ Şevval Güner-Buse Cini

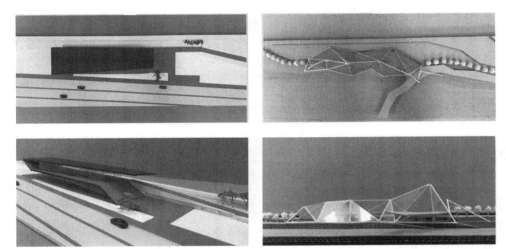

Design Problem Two: Neighborhood Health, Support and Solidarity Center (NHSSC) in Maltepe, Ankara

The 2020-2021 fall semester had to be practiced entirely online due to the measures taken during the pandemic. In that semester, when distance learning was obligatory, the necessity of making some changes in Studio 201's methodology emerged in line with the experiences gained in the previous semester (Boyacıoğlu, 2021), and since students were living in and attending the classes from their hometowns all over Turkey and even the world.

While discussing the project topic, it was essential to understand better the new situations and experiences caused by the COVID-19 pandemic, which is still ongoing globally. Therefore, it was decided that the design problem needed to focus on the new spaces that the new daily lives have reproduced, reconsider the new normal, and change perceptions of the emerging spatial organizations of the new daily routines. So, in the process, the aim was to rethink and reproduce the spaces in which people come together, the possibilities of encounters, and the inside-outside relations within the limitations of the new normal that provide and answer the needs and expectations on different scales.

The design problem for that semester was defined as a space that functions as a healing center on the "scale of a neighborhood." It was regarded as an environment that was accessible from the houses where the citizens had to spend most of their daily lives. With the COVID-19 pandemic, the importance of Family Health Centers was on the agenda regarding citizens having direct and rapid access to health services on a neighborhood scale. However, as spaces for health, family health centers need to be improved in terms of functional and spatial needs. Therefore, in the Neighborhood Health, Support and Solidarity Center (NHSSC) (Figure 6, 7, 8, 9, 10), as named in the syllabus, the aim was to provide access to health and support services simultaneously. It is important to note that the NHSSC was thought to propose diversified uses, such as seminars and meetings in crises such as pandemics, so citizens living in the same neighborhood can unite for solidarity. Therefore, students were expected to propose a project to rethink the given architectural program around the citizens' new social and physical needs and health services.

The design problem of this peculiar semester expanded the given 'site' of the project to the cultural and social dimension of the built environment, encouraging the students to deal with the design problem through a multiscalar (from building scale to neighborhood scale) and multilayered (formal concerns as well as social and psychological concerns) approach.

One difficulty was determining this center's 'project site,' which, as mentioned above, aimed to function on a neighborhood scale. This was caused by the fact that the students had gone to their hometowns when distance learning started. For this reason, the students could not physically experience any site to be given. So, the decision was to choose a site that the students were familiar with, which was a part of their daily experience before the pandemic. Therefore, the land next to the large green public park, Fatih Park, on the edge of which one of Maltepe metro station's exits was assigned as the project site. This metro stop is of great importance since it is a part of the route used by most students accessing the campus via the subway.

As the site was well-known and experienced by the students, it was decided not to practice the first project, a long-standing phase in Studio 201's methodology, as a transitory process in preparing for the architectural design and a better understanding of the site. In contrast, the critical review of the architectural program and the site was already evident in the given problem. So, this was the first change that had to be made during the online distance-learning semester—focusing on a single project aimed at rethinking and working on the program for longer.

Figure 6. Neighborhood Health, Support, and Solidarity Center/ Elif Erkol (left)

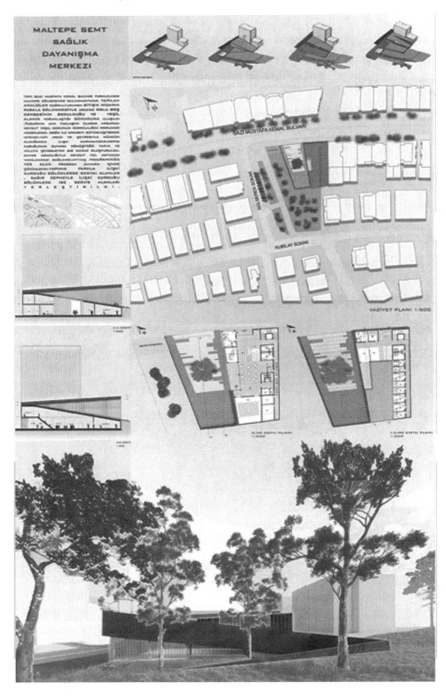

On the Threshold

Figure 7. Neighborhood Health, Support and Solidarity Center/ Oğuzhan Cesur (right)

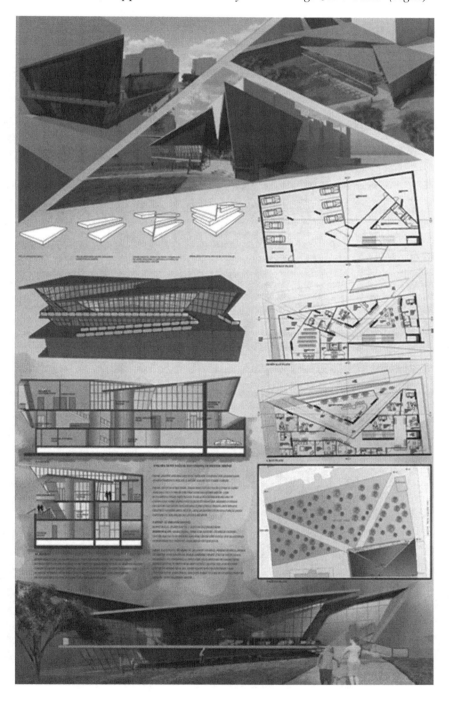

Another change was to give up making physical models, one of the essential tools students use when they start doing their first architectural project. This decision, which was made unwillingly by the instructors, was also caused by difficulties arising from the students' inaccessibility to materials -because of lockdowns- and challenges in sharing the physical 3D model on the 2D computer screen. However, as seen from the projects referred to here, it can be claimed that the students quickly learned the 3-D modeling programs and handled the situation very well.

Figure 8. Neighborhood Health, Support and Solidarity Center/ Sümeyye Özelçi (left)

Figure 9. Neighborhood Health, Support and Solidarity Center/ Sedanur Çakmak (right)

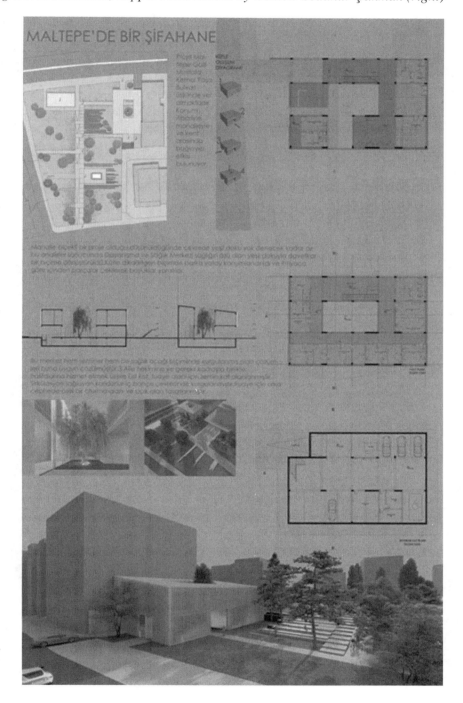

Figure 10. Neighborhood Health, Support and Solidarity Center/ Ceyda Ece Kıymaz

CONCLUSION

Established as a 'threshold studio' in the 1999 - 2000 academic year, Studio 201 has successfully fulfilled its mission of fostering critical thinking and multidisciplinary problem-solving skills among students. This transitionary position could be observed in the student's final products at the end of the semester and via feedback from the subsequent design studios. For Studio 201, the spatial qualities and urban context must be evaluated with the quality of the project in its material sense, such as drawings and models. Additionally, the attempt to encourage the students to put their design concepts into appropriate language within the architecture discipline terminology and the ability to conceptualize and theorize their work is one of the most critical tasks Studio 201 is trying to achieve. By integrating abstract design concepts with material and social considerations, Studio 201 has transcended traditional pedagogical models, preparing students for the complexities of contemporary architectural practice. Different design approaches are developed due to the intellectual backgrounds of students, mentors from both academia and professional practice, and studio composition. The students are encouraged to solve design problems by representing them with different tools and within the interdisciplinary field of architecture. Despite challenges posed by the COVID-19 pandemic, Studio 201 has adapted to new hybrid learning environments, further enriching the studio experience and expanding its impact within architectural education. The conventional and virtual design studio engagement created different forms and vocabularies of communication and interaction through a flattened hierarchy of the studio composition on the virtual flat screen of a video-oriented environment. Looking ahead, Studio 201 remains committed to nurturing the next generation of innovative architects capable of responding to societal changes and contributing to adaptive and resilient forms of architecture in uncertain times.

REFERENCES

Boyacıoğlu, E. (2021). THEME: 'Distance' Learning: Online Possibilities, Limits, Challenges [1] Interviews. *Arredamento Mmarlık*, 346, 57–59.

Bozdoğan, S. (2008). *Architecture Profession in Pre-Modern/Pioneer Chicago: 1871-1909, Vienna-Chicago: Metropolis and Architecture*. Bilgi University Press.

Dutton, T. A. (1987). Design and Studio Pedagogy. *Journal of Architectural Education*, 41(1), 16–25. 10.1080/10464883.1987.10758461

Öztürk, M. N., & Türkkan, E. E. (2006). The Design Studio as Teaching/Learning Medium—A Process-Based Approach. *International Journal of Art & Design Education*, 25(1), 96–104. 10.1111/j.1476-8070.2006.00472.x

Rodriguez, C., Hudson, R., & Niblock, C. (2018). Collaborative Learning in Architectural Education: Benefits of Combining Conventional Studio, Virtual Design Studio and Live Projects. *British Journal of Educational Technology*, 49(3), 337–353. 10.1111/bjet.12535

Salama, A. M. (2007). Introduction: Legacies for the Future of Design Studio Pedagogy. In Salama, A. M., & Wilkinson, N. (Eds.), *Design Studio Pedagogy: Horizons for the Future* (pp. 2–8).

Wang, T. (2010). A New Paradigm for Design Studio Education. *International Journal of Art & Design Education*, 29(2), 173–183. 10.1111/j.1476-8070.2010.01647.x

Chapter 16
Teaching Design Studios Face to Face and Online:
Perspectives and Recommendations

Abdullah Al Mahmud
https://orcid.org/0000-0002-2801-723X
Swinburne University of Technology, Australia

ABSTRACT

This chapter presents reflections on teaching an introductory design studio to first-year industrial design and architecture students. The unit was taught online in 2020 and face-to-face in 2021. To improve online delivery, student feedback was gathered and analyzed thematically. Along with personal teaching reflections, the feedback was used to identify challenges and facilitating factors in online delivery. Findings showed that students appreciated having live support from the lecturer throughout the online class, rather than relying on recorded lectures, and benefitted from seeing each other's finished work. However, students expressed dissatisfaction with the limited options for developing the course's required prototypes. The experience suggests that design studios can be partially offered online successfully. However, students must have access to design workshops for specific weeks. This chapter documents the challenges of adapting a design subject for online delivery, with recommendations for academics who intend to develop engaging online design courses.

INTRODUCTION

Student engagement is critical to student retention in higher education. Students are more likely to continue their studies if they have clear goals, an active learning environment, and opportunities to participate in learning activities (Gray & DiLoreto, 2016). It has been found that active learning (i.e., a situation where students spend 18% of their time in discussion groups, 27% of their time practicing their skills by doing, and 31% of their time teaching others) is most effective. Active learning has significant impacts on retention rate (up to 76%) (Barkley & Major, 2020). Generally, students learn better when engaged with their peers through group work, peer review, and a hands-on approach (Kinzie, 2005). In addition, learning outcomes must be connected to real-world issues so that students are aware of the implications of their learning.

Many teaching approaches, such as blended learning, flipped classrooms, and studio-based practices, have been used to enhance students' learning and engagement in higher education. In studio-based teaching practice, students learn in a physical space and work on problem-based learning. Student retention improves when students are exposed to social connections and group activities throughout their studies (Crowther, 2013). Such active engagement helps build relationships with peers and makes learning enjoyable. Studio-based teaching is a way to engage students while they solve design problems iteratively (Cennamo, 2016).

Other approaches, such as the flipped classroom, also engage students in creative practices. In the flipped classroom method, students are given access to lecture materials before class, usually via a video reading of the lecture (Alvarez, 2012; Berrett, 2012; Gren, 2020). As a result, class time can be used to engage the students in group work, discussion, or providing formative feedback. To achieve the best learning outcomes, it is essential to build an environment that promotes active learning (Barkley & Major, 2020). Therefore, teaching methods such as the flipped classroom have drawn the attention of academics in recent years (Akçayır & Akçayır, 2018). The flipped classroom has both advantages and disadvantages. Advantages identified by researchers include improved learning performance (Bhagat et al., 2016), increased learner satisfaction (Bösner et al., 2015), increased engagement (Khanova et al., 2015), higher levels of motivation (Huang & Hong, 2016), and increased knowledge (Galway et al., 2014). In addition, this approach supports flexible (Nguyen et al., 2016) and individualized learning (González-Gómez et al., 2016). The approach also has limitations, such as increased student workload (Smith, 2013) and teachers (Wanner & Palmer, 2015). Also, students might have limited time to prepare before the class (Al-Zahrani, 2015). Despite these limitations, the flipped classroom seems a worthwhile model to apply in higher education, especially in design and architecture. It is student-centered and supports active learning (Lai & Hwang, 2016), as students engage in activities rather than passively listening to lectures. Furthermore, the flipped classroom environment supports collaborative learning since students can spend class time involved in collaborative activities with their peers. Such collaboration is visible in studio-based design education (Rich et al., 2015). Therefore, flipping the learning content seems ideal for design education, where it enhances collaboration and student engagement in a studio-based teaching approach.

FLIPPED CLASSROOM APPROACH IN DESIGN AND ARCHITECTURE EDUCATION

Several researchers have applied the flipped classroom model in design and architecture education. The following section summarizes those studies while comparing and contrasting the approaches.

Costa and Sánchez (2022) conducted a bibliographical analysis of engineering courses to understand how the flipped classroom approach has been applied to teach structure to architecture students. They determined that the traditional teaching model may not be appropriate for teaching architectural structure, and the flipped classroom is the approach that best supports pre-class, in-class, and post-class activities. The authors reviewed engineering courses because they found that the application of flipped classrooms to teach structure in architecture is limited; however, they noted that the flipped classroom model can be applied in teaching architecture, and that it supports personal learning.

Coyne et al. (2017) adopted a flipped classroom approach in a study of a postgraduate-level architecture class of more than 100 students at the Edinburgh School of Architecture and Landscape Architecture. The lecturers were architects. Pre-recorded lecture content, including PowerPoint slides, supported the flipped classroom approach. In addition, the university's learning management system provided relevant resources such as reading lists and quiz items. Coyne et al. (2017) evaluated their flipped classroom approach based on lecturers' and students' perspectives. Lecturers found that students were more engaged, and classroom attendance was high. Students' feedback showed that they were satisfied with the quality of the course.

Another study conducted by Elrayies (2017) proposed applying the flipped learning model to a 'lighting and acoustic' course as part of problem-based learning pedagogy. The author proposed a 4-week course delivery plan, outlining the pre-class assignment and in-class activities to provide problem-based learning in a flipped classroom model. Though the outcome of the offering was that the course was not formally evaluated, it was important to bring attention to the flipped classroom approach in architectural design education. Similarly, Galiana and Seguí (2016) used a flipped classroom approach to teach Structural Mechanics at the School of Architecture of the European University of Valencia. Students had to prepare materials that dealt with the course and were not explained in the class. Teachers provided supportive learning materials such as a bibliography, internet resources on the subject, and videos to be viewed beforehand. Students worked on the task individually for two weeks, after which each student was required to play the role of the teacher and explain a concept to the rest of the group. Students were required to give 20-minute oral presentations and pose questions to generate debate and discussion. Finally, each student had to answer some questions asked by the tutor. Student feedback revealed that students found the teaching method interesting, and 50% of the participants believed that the flipped classroom positively impacted their learning. The authors stated that a flipped classroom is valuable to student engagement because of the way it fosters active participation in the learning process.

A recent study involving fourth-year interior architecture students assessed how the traditional and flipped classroom models are perceived by students (Ozenen, 2023). The study results show that students who attended a flipped classroom had higher grade point averages than those in a traditional classroom. The study confirmed previous findings that flipped classrooms enhance the student learning experience.

These examples show how various flipped classroom models have been applied in design and architecture education. When using a flipped classroom approach, certain adaptations may further enhance learner engagement. Liu (2019) used the flipped classroom approach in an Architectural Design of Housing course. In the study, Liu practiced face-to-face teaching in the flipped classroom supported by visualization tools to help students visualize the teaching content and related activities. 90% of students were satisfied with the teaching model and were willing to pursue the course using the flipped classroom approach.

Although lecturers and students typically interact face to face in a flipped classroom approach, virtual or online teaching with this approach is also possible. For example, Peng et al. (2022) combined a flipped classroom with online learning to introduce the virtual flipped classroom, which they implemented in three postgraduate design programs across three Australian universities. The authors reflected that their virtual flipped classroom approach is potentially more valuable than traditional face-to-face learning and teaching. Also of potential value is the hybrid method, which offers some of the ease of online courses without dropping all face-to-face contact (Triyason et al., 2020; Young, 2002). A mixed teaching style involves recording traditional lectures and providing online access to both lectures and evaluations, ultimately making the teaching productive. While each of the above approaches would be suitable for teaching design students, the hybrid approach might be ideal given that it maintains authentic teaching and assessment approaches.

Face-to-Face vs. Online Delivery of Design Studios

Traditionally, design studios are offered face to face in physical spaces. Delivering them online creates specific challenges for students, thus making it more difficult to engage learners (Simamora, 2020). However, teaching design studios online can become necessary, as it was during the COVID-19 pandemic. Students of traditional design studios where face-to-face teaching is provided may be reluctant to have such units delivered online. Students may not be comfortable learning online since they would miss their physical studio, drawing boards, in-class interaction and, above all, the design workshops (Alnusairat et al., 2021). Researchers have identified various factors that may hamper students' progress in online learning; for example, a lack of face-to-face interaction and difficulty critiquing student work (George & Walker, 2017).

During the COVID-19 pandemic, several design schools worldwide adopted online studios (Abu Alatta et al., 2023; Al Maani et al., 2021; Ceylan et al., 2021; Jones & Lotz, 2021; Khogali, 2020; Komarzyńska-Świeściak et al., 2021). Based on course content and required deliverables, there were variations in how those online classes were offered. Although offering design studios online may not be an ideal scenario, it might be the only way to maintain the continuity of students' learning during emergency restrictions such as those experienced during the COVID-19 pandemic. Moving a design studio online is a significant task, and much can be learned from each online studio offered during the pandemic. However, existing studies did not compare the experience of offering a design studio face-to-face with that of offering it online. Therefore, this chapter reports how a face-to-face design studio was delivered online and provides reflections on students' learning experiences, including feedback from students.

The remainder of this chapter is organized as follows: The next section describes the teaching approach, studio projects, and assessment procedure used. Following that will be a section explaining the methods used for data collection and analysis. Next, the results will be presented, followed by discussion and conclusion.

TEACHING APPROACH

Unit Overview and Teaching Methods: Adaptations for Online Delivery

At our university, we provide an Introductory Design Studio. This is a compulsory unit for undergraduate first-year students in the Product Design Engineering, Industrial Design, and Bachelor of Interior Architecture programs. The unit can be taken as an elective or as part of a minor area of study by students studying communication design, digital media design, and other engineering disciplines. This is a 12.5-credit unit involving two two-hour classes (face-to-face) per week. The unit is offered twice a year. The first component is a two-hour studio, which runs for 12 weeks, in which students design a bus shelter. The second component involves a design workshop for two hours per week, running from weeks one to five. In this component, students receive training to create physical models. The final component is a seven-week studio component (two hours per week), in which students work on sustainable lighting design. A significant part of this component is tearing down a lighting product and conducting a life cycle analysis.

The unit as a whole aims to provide an introduction to design and development processes, exploring aspects of research, concept/idea generation, concept development, and the communication of design outcomes. Students investigate design methodology. Design briefs are used as parameters for projects. In this way, project-based learning occurs, relevant to the design and engineering principles of interior-built environments and products. Emphasis is given to idea development and creativity. Three-dimensional forms are developed to assist the design process. This aspect requires an introduction to occupational health and safety protocols for the workshop. The unit also enhances students' understanding of sustainability, including the environmental impacts of products, methods of mapping these impacts to create new designs, life cycle analysis, and life cycle thinking. Students are given feedback on their progress in attaining several skills, such as creative thinking, problem-solving, communication, organizational skills, working independently, and working in multidisciplinary teams.

Due to COVID-19, the studio was delivered online. Several changes were made to make it suitable for online delivery. For example, the critical instructions of the class were recorded and posted on the Canvas learning management system one week before the class. Zoom was used to run the online studios. Instead of accessing the design workshop and having hands-on training, students were given online model-making tutorials. In addition, students were instructed to make their models from paper or cardboard, which are easily available at home. Zoom breakout rooms were created to enable group work and project meetings. In addition, we used discussion boards and weekly quizzes to engage students in learning and check their learning progress.

Summary of the Studio Projects

In the face-to-face studio, students completed two projects over twelve weeks and were given hands-on training on physical model making. The first of the two projects required them to design a bus shelter. Their design was to be inspired by the style of an influential designer assigned to each group. The main intention of this project is to have students experience the world of design, not just design in Australia. The challenge is to be inspired by the philosophy of a given designer and contextualize that philosophy in a local environment. Students need to observe current bus stops or shelters in their local environment and pay close attention to how people use and interact with these. Bus shelters are present in all cities worldwide and are easily accessible; however, they are used purely for waiting, which is never a desirable activity.

Students are to design a bus shelter suitable for their local context. (See Figure 1 for some example designs.) They need to obtain photographic documentation of bus shelters and stops in their area and understand how people interact with them. This starts as an individual activity, from which students then develop concepts with their group members. To relate their local area to their final design, they need to investigate the following questions: How can the experience of waiting for a bus be changed? Is the bus shelter interactive? Will the space be desirable? Students must understand the characteristics of the town they visit, observe how locals use and interact with bus shelters, take note of the materials that current shelters are made of, and consider how those materials withstand different climatic conditions.

Figure 1. Physical models developed by students with the assistance of our design workshop staff as outcomes of the face-to-face design studio

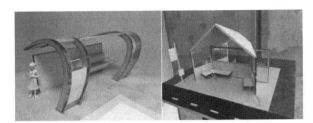

Image source: Author

Design Workshop

The 5-week component was run from our design workshop. Model making is an essential skill for all design students. (See Figure 2 for some example models.) It teaches fundamental skills and vital occupational health and safety (OH&S) requirements to ensure that students can work independently and creatively in the workshop. Initial OH&S induction is essential. We provide a quick introduction, an eye safety video, a tour of the workshop facilities, and a test. We split the students (24 students per class) into three groups, giving each a training session on hot wire instruction, disk and bobbin sander instruction, and drill press. Later, over four weeks, students execute two projects using blue foam for model making. Both projects aim to familiarize students with the use of expanded foam and other soft materials as a foundation for physical prototyping. Foam, a quick prototyping material, is used with sketching to help visualize size, proportion, and ergonomic features.

Figure 2. Example of a foam car model and a guitar model developed by design workshop staff at the end of workshop training

Image source: Author

The final component of the workshop was the sustainable lighting studio. A wide variety of portable lighting products are available as consumer goods, and these are typically treated as short-life disposable items. Such products can be seen in most homes and offices. These products have high environmental impacts. The sustainable lighting studio project asks students to research existing portable lighting products and redesign them, with a focus on significantly improving environmental impacts. Looking to the future, 'revisioning' enables the designer to imagine new forms, functions, and technologies that push the boundaries of what might currently exist. This project develops students' understanding of the environmental impacts of products, teaches them to map these impacts, and introduces them to Life Cycle Analysis (LCA), Life Cycle Thinking, and DFE (Design for Environment) strategies. The course then aims to teach students how to use this understanding to design new products with improved LCA characteristics.

During the COVID-19 pandemic, students of the online course completed the same assignments as they would have completed in the face-to-face class. However, the models were developed based on the materials available to the students. To support students' model-making work, instead of basing models on the bus shelter project, we added a project that facilitated model-making with available materials at home, such as paper, cardboard, or cereal boxes. The new project asked students to experiment with 'expressive cubes' and transform the cube into an object and space. Some students were able to visit local stores and buy plywood or transparent plastics for their models. Because the university campus was closed due to COVID-19, it was not feasible to use our design workshop. However, we sent some basic model-making kits, such as sanding sticks and cardboard, to the students based on their requests.

Teaching and Assessment Procedure

On average, the unit has 150 students spread over several studio classes, with a maximum of 24 in each class. The unit is coordinated by one academic and taught by several. The Canvas system is the central access point for all of the unit's teaching resources. The unit has no traditional final examination; instead, students are assessed based on their accomplishments in several individual and group projects. In the first studio component, students are assessed on their research report, two in-class presentations, one design portfolio, and a physical model. In the workshop-training component, they are evaluated based on the quality of the two models submitted for review. Finally, in the second studio component, students are assessed on their sustainable design portfolio, return brief, and presentation of the final concepts. All assessments are based on rubrics specially designed for each component. When the course was delivered online, all assignments except for physical models were submitted to Canvas. Weekly studio lectures were posted on Canvas before each class for students to review. The actual studio time could be used for individual or group activities. In the studio sessions, the students were given formative feedback on their progress. Two days before each studio class, students were reminded via Canvas of the upcoming studio class and its associated activities.

In the first studio component, students are assisted in building their personal development plan (PDP). This is typically an A4 document in which students set individual learning goals for each week and write any concerns related to their study. These concerns are then discussed with their tutors. Students review it each week, and at the end of the semester, they reflect on it and submit it to their tutor for final feedback. This method helps students to focus on learning activities.

Table 1. Overview of the activities, deliverables, and assessment procedure

Activities	Teaching strategy	Duration	Major activities and submission	Assessment procedure
Studio 1: Designing a bus shelter	Studio-based and flipped classroom	Week 1-12	-Research report (Individual) -In-class presentation -Design folio (group) -Physical model (group)	-Turn-it-in (plagiarism check) -Assessment rubric
Workshop safety training: Training Brief	Face-to-face hands-on training/Online via Zoom	Week 1-5	-Creating 3D object (i.e., Guitar and car) using blue foam (individual)	-Assessment rubric
Studio2: Sustainable design	Studio-based and flipped classroom	Week 6-12	-Design folio (group)	- Product teardown -In-class/Zoom presentation -Assessment rubric

METHODS FOR EVALUATING THE UNIT'S DELIVERY

We have taken reflective practice as an approach to evaluating the teaching and learning experience in this unit. We have offered the face-to-face version of the unit for the last ten years, during which we continually improved its delivery based on students' feedback. In 2020, due to the COVID-19 pandemic, the unit was delivered online for the first time, for two semesters. Offering the unit online was not our preferred method. However, the university's physical buildings were closed, and the city was under strict lockdown. Given these circumstances, running the unit online was deemed necessary, and it needed to be done with very short notice. The unit had a component that involved developing models in the design workshop, but providing students access to the workshop was impossible. To address this, we changed the requirements for model-making materials and gave students the flexibility to use materials found at home (such as paper) or available from a local store. Nonetheless, students might have preferred to access the design workshop. To gain an understanding of students' satisfaction with our teaching methods, an anonymous survey was conducted after 12 weeks, so that delivery of the unit might be improved. Participation in the survey was voluntary. Students provided ratings expressing their level of satisfaction with the unit (e.g., "overall, I am satisfied with the unit") using a Likert scale (1 = strongly disagree to 10 = strongly agree). In addition, the students provided comments on the strengths and weaknesses of the teaching approach, teaching materials, and support from the lecturer. The unit was delivered online twice during the year (i.e., one offering each semester), and informal feedback about the unit was gathered after every class. We calculated mean satisfaction on the unit from the Likert-scale data, and qualitative comments were analyzed deductively under the categories 'likes', 'dislikes' and 'recommendations.' To evaluate the face-to-face delivery of the unit, we used our reflections and student feedback on the way the unit was delivered in 2021.

RESULTS

Students' Deliverables and Feedback on the Face-to-Face Studio Class

Student feedback on the satisfaction survey (Likert scale 1-10) shows that overall, students were satisfied with the unit. The mean satisfaction rating in Semester one was 7.56 (SD=2.01; response rate 44.81%), and the mean in Semester two was 8.28 (SD=1.72; response rate 23.36%). Students indicated that they appreciated the unit, and that the most enjoyable part was access to the design workshop with hands-on training provided by the workshop staff. The student feedback shows that the top five things that students liked were: 1) access to the design workshop and model making, 2) the bus shelter project, 3) support from the teacher, 4) timely communication, and 5) combining the theory and practical components.

Students' enjoyment of the unit was indicated in their comments during the content analysis. For example, one student said, "This unit can teach me a lot of design skills and knowledge." The best component of the unit, as identified by the students, was the workshop training provided. In survey comments, students described their favorite aspect as "bringing our design into life in the workshop and the opportunity to learn how to use the equipment," or, "the workshop component as I enjoyed learning how to use all the different tools and create the blue foam models." Other students stated: "The workshop component provided valuable model-making techniques and methods for future use," "The workshop was a lot of fun and beneficial for me," and "The building of the bus shelter was great."

Students did a substantial amount of group work in both studios. Students worked in groups to generate design concepts, select concepts, and make detailed designs and models. (See Figures 3 to 6 for an example project.) Although they were working within a group, students were required to show individual contributions. To provide the best possible group experience, we tried to place one industrial design or interior architecture student in each group. We observed that students appreciated the interdisciplinary collaboration. For example, one student said, "Working with others from different design disciplines was very rewarding for me." In addition to group work, students did several individual activities such as report writing and presenting their research findings in the class. We used the "turn-it-in" function of Canvas to check for plagiarism. This was beneficial for students in improving their reports. Students were allowed to check the similarity of their reports to other writings and submit an improved version to Canvas. We found this to be very helpful for the first-year students unfamiliar with the plagiarism checking process.

As we revealed lecture content before the studio class, students could spend additional time on activities in the studio class. Students also received emails via Canvas every week informing them of upcoming studio activities and deadlines. The students appreciated this approach, and consequently, their attendance was almost 100% every week. Another aspect appreciated by the students was the formative feedback provided to each group every week. Each group of students had a weekly five-to-ten-minute feedback session with their tutor, where they discussed the project's progress, followed by an individual discussion on their personal development plan (PDP). Students indicated that this teaching strategy provided a friendly environment and enhanced their confidence in accomplishing the assignments. Furthermore, as significant work was achieved weekly, students felt that they had accomplished major milestones.

Figure 3. The initial mock-up ("quick and dirty") design of the bus shelter. The materials used were cardboard and blue foam.

Image source: Lucy Callahan and Jack Brown

Teaching Design Studios Face to Face and Online

Figure 4. The model-making process (Part 1). Here, the bus shelter model was designed using plywood and acrylic.

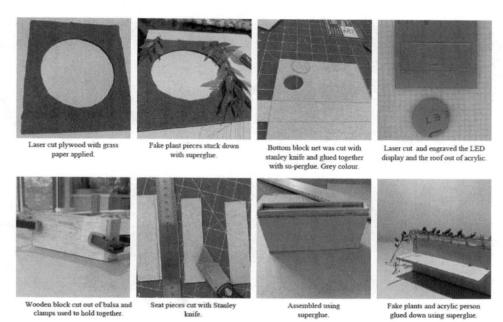

Image source: Lucy Callahan and Jack Brown

Figure 5. The model-making process (Part 2). Images show how acrylic sheets were painted and other model components were decorated.

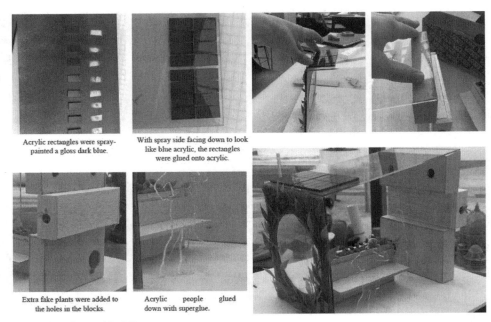

Image source: Lucy Callahan and Jack Brown

Figure 6. A model developed during a 12-week face-to-face class. Final model photos of a bus shelter.

Image source: Lucy Callahan and Jack Brown

Students' Deliverables and Feedback on the Online Studio Class

Students' mean satisfaction with the unit was 7.18 (SD=2.14; response rate 36.36%) in Semester one and 7.24 (SD=2.39; response rate 38.82%) in Semester two. Students could see each other's design work online. However, they wished to see the physical models in person, which was impossible during the online class. Overall, the students were happy that they could view each other's work and provide feedback on it. One student expressed this by noting that "being able to view each other's work in further depth and provide each other with feedback" was an important aspect of the course.

The interactivity that occurred despite the class being online was a new experience for the students. Most students enjoyed collaborating and receiving feedback online. Students mentioned that the model-making task was enjoyable. (See Figures 7 to 9 for an example of a model developed during the online delivery of the studio.) They also indicated that they liked the way the project briefs allowed extensive thinking and concept generation.

Figure 7. An example of model making during the online studio. The models were made from photocopy papers.

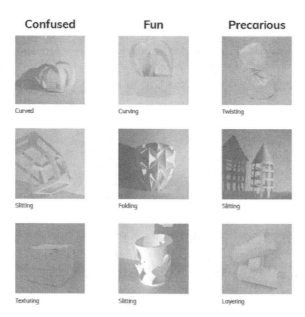

Image source: Tulip Vy

Figure 8. Two cubes were chosen to be transformed into a space called "Lungo," a Latin word meaning "connect."

Image source: Tulip Vy

Figure 9. The final design of Lungo

Image source: Tulip Vy

Students appreciated how quickly the course was adapted for online delivery; however, most believed that this unit was better suited to in-person teaching. In the survey, one student commented: "I think it would be nice to learn in person, but obviously that isn't an option. However, they've done really good work to help us learn and study this unit." Another stated: "There are no aspects of this unit that could be improved on. It was a great subject, and I think it would have been better if we had been in an on-campus class."

Since this is a studio-based, hands-on unit, students found it challenging to deliver the assignments without having access to the usual tools or labs required for these briefs. This was noted in survey comments such as: "This unit is only difficult because it is online; it is a very hands-on subject and, therefore, would be better on campus, but given the circumstances, it is understandable that it can't be."

While students bought the model-making materials themselves, they sometimes could not find suitable materials in local stores or experienced postal delays. Therefore, limited model-making resources were a significant concern for most students. Some students suggested the idea of providing model-making kits as an alternative. One student wrote: "I think if we were provided kits, it would be a lot easier than sourcing materials ourselves during the pandemic."

Some students, especially those in rural areas, reported technical issues while submitting assignments to Canvas due to slow internet connections. One student commented:

> It can be hard submitting assignments because it takes a while to go through and then can show that it was late submitted; my submission for the last task took 15 minutes to go through (not only me ... it's happened to other students too).

Another wrote:

> I have been happy with how this subject has transitioned over to online subjects, and I particularly enjoy the Zoom meetings, but sometimes, due to how far I live out, I get very bad reception, more so now than ever. It has, therefore, been helpful to have that rundown of what was said in each [tutorial]/workshop in the case I drop out of range for 20 minutes or so.

Students preferred to have shorter videos to watch before and during the class. They also suggested providing more time for class discussions. However, they requested more videos on model making, as well as more guidance on different model-making techniques. Student comments noted their desire for "Shorter videos and more class discussions," and, "Maybe providing more details on recommended materials for making models, and more videos on making models."

DISCUSSION

This chapter documents our experience delivering a design studio both face to face and online and compares the two methods of delivering the unit. Based on our experience and student feedback, face-to-face delivery offered a much-appreciated opportunity to work at the design workshop, which has a great facility for model making. However, our experience suggests that students prefer to have essential lecture materials and related resources posted to the learning management system before the class. This practice is in line with the flipped classroom model (Akçayır & Akçayır, 2018). Overall, higher satisfaction ratings were observed in the face-to-face design studio sessions where students could use the wide range of model-making materials available in our design workshop. Similar findings were observed in a study conducted during the COVID-19 pandemic, where students pursuing urban design expressed a preference for face-to-face studio-based learning (Peimani & Kamalipour, 2022).

Because the response rate was low, it is not possible to generalize the feedback survey findings. In addition, because the course contents were continually improved, and because of the difference in requirements for model-making, a direct comparison between the face-to-face delivery and online delivery of the unit is not possible. However, students' comments on improving the unit suggest that their dissatisfaction with the online delivery was largely related to the inaccessibility of the design workshop facilities during the pandemic. This suggests that if a unit has significant model-making activities, running the class for the whole semester as a flipped classroom may not be ideal. It is recommended that a design studio like ours allow some weeks (e.g., four weeks) on campus so that students can access workshop facilities to develop the required models. For instance, in future online iterations of our course, the first eight weeks could be run virtually using a flipped classroom model, and the remaining four weeks could be devoted to face-to-face contact at the design workshop. Overall, it can be concluded from the teaching experience that a hybrid delivery of the design unit is acceptable. This resonates with the findings of an existing study where a hybrid model was applied to teach basic design to architecture students (Abu Alatta et al., 2023).

During the face-to-face delivery, we found that student engagement was high while they worked on model-making activities in the design workshop. By contrast, in the online studio, it was not possible to observe their levels of engagement when making models, as they developed those models outside of their online studio time. However, the delivered models were of high quality in both cases. The only difference was that in the face-to-face delivery, the models were built using a range of materials such as plywood and acrylic. Since students had to hand in those models physically, they were very keen for any last-minute fixes to deliver the best possible outcome. In the online delivery of the unit, due to COVID-19, students were not required to provide the physical models. Instead, they were required to show them to the lecturer in the online class and create a video presentation of each model. This meant that it was not feasible for lecturers to see the nitty-gritty details of how the models were made. Nonetheless, the overall construction of the models in the online studios was deemed sufficient, and the quality of some was excellent, as vetted by fellow students. Thus, in a unit where model-making is paramount, the flipped classroom approach may not allow those teaching to grasp the full learning journey of the students. One recommendation to overcome this issue would be to run the last four weeks of the 12-week semester in a face-to-face setting in the design workshop. Doing so would allow lecturers to see the learning journey and provide the required hands-on support to students.

From weeks six to eleven, students' attendance in the online classes was relatively low compared to their attendance in face-to-face classes. However, in week 12, when students had to present their work, attendance was above 95%. Therefore, we cannot conclude that there were any differences in the attendance patterns between online and face-to-face delivery. When presenting their project work and providing feedback on each other's design outcomes in week 12, students in the online and face-to-face classes were equally engaged. Because the week 12 presentation was assessed, students were motivated to attend and show their engagement. Therefore, it is recommended that a virtual design studio should have several checkpoints where students receive feedback from tutors and peers so that they are encouraged to engage in learning activities and provide positive learning experiences.

The online learning experience was entirely novel for the students. They had not expected this mode of learning for this unit but had to accept it due to the pandemic. Other factors, such as state-wide lockdown, also impacted students' learning experience, as did technical challenges, such as the poor internet connection experienced by some students. Similar challenges were reported in a study where researchers measured Architecture students' satisfaction with online learning during COVID-19 (Alnusairat et al., 2021). Despite these challenges, lecturers and unit convenors in our unit taught using a virtual flipped classroom model similar to that used by Peng et al. (2022). However, our approach has some key differences. For instance, unlike Peng's (2022) course, our unit placed a great deal of focus on developing a series of models. Making these models required materials, training, and specialized facilities. Therefore, it was wise to change the requirements for materials, including part of the design brief. We observed that students enjoyed making a range of models during the course's online delivery.

Limitations and Future Work

There are several limitations of this study. The study is primarily reflection-based and exploratory. The online delivery of the unit was offered twice in 2020, while face-to-face delivery of the unit has been offered for ten years. Therefore, a direct comparison of our experiences in each format would not be balanced. Also, a better analysis would require obtaining richer insights from the tutors who taught the course during the pandemic. In addition, it would be helpful to gather student feedback from semi-structured interviews to understand their experience with the online delivery of the course. However, when offering the course, time constraints prevented us from formally gathering the views of the tutors and students. This is also a limitation of our study. Although the COVID-19 pandemic has ended, it would be useful to run the online delivery of the unit again and more thoroughly measure students' and teachers' perspectives to develop further recommendations and guidelines.

CONCLUSION

We adopted a blended teaching approach, a flipped classroom, and a studio-based teaching method to teach first-year students. Over time, we updated the unit content and applied a hybrid approach during the COVID-19 pandemic. Through our teaching of this unit, it can be seen that the mixture of a studio-based and flipped classroom approach, in combination with a personal development plan for each student, provides an engaging learning environment. Through feedback, we improved the students' overall satisfaction with the unit and increased their engagement, which contributed to a positive learning outcome. Some aspects of online delivery were appreciated by students, such as real-time feedback and viewing their peers' design outcomes. However, students were dissatisfied with the model-making task as they could not access the design workshop and were unable to use the materials usually required for model-making. In addition, they faced internet issues submitting design folios to Canvas due to the size of the scanned folios. Our analysis suggests that design studios can be partially offered online; however, students need to be able to access design workshops for specific weeks. For example, in our 12-week course, we could run the online studio for four to six weeks, then follow it with a face-to-face model-making studio that gives access to a design workshop for the remaining six weeks. This would better satisfy the needs of students. We hope that our experience can be helpful to other educators who would like to enhance student engagement in online studio teaching.

ACKNOWLEDGMENT

We acknowledge the contributions of the design workshop personnel who provided training to the students and assisted in supporting the model-making activities. Thanks also to the students who agreed to include their works in this chapter. We also thank the unit convenors who continually improved the unit contents, including the design briefs, from the time that the unit was first introduced.

REFERENCES

Abu Alatta, R. T., Momani, H. M., & Bataineh, A. M. (2023). The effect of online teaching on basic design studio during COVID-19: An application of the technology acceptance model. *Architectural Science Review*, 66(6), 417–432. 10.1080/00038628.2022.2153791

Akçayır, G., & Akçayır, M. (2018). The flipped classroom: A review of its advantages and challenges. *Computers & Education*, 126, 334–345. 10.1016/j.compedu.2018.07.021

Al Maani, D., Alnusairat, S., & Al-Jokhadar, A. (2021). Transforming learning for architecture: Online design studio as the new norm for crisis adaptation under COVID-19. *Open House International*, 46(3), 348–358. 10.1108/OHI-01-2021-0016

Al-Zahrani, A. M. (2015). From passive to active: The impact of the flipped classroom through social learning platforms on higher education students' creative thinking. *British Journal of Educational Technology*, 46(6), 1133–1148. 10.1111/bjet.12353

Alnusairat, S., Al Maani, D., & Al-Jokhadar, A. (2021). Architecture students' satisfaction with and perceptions of online design studios during COVID-19 lockdown: The case of Jordan universities. *Archnet-IJAR: International Journal of Architectural Research*, 15(1), 219–236. 10.1108/ARCH-09-2020-0195

Alvarez, B. (2012). Flipping the classroom: Homework in class, lessons at home. *Education Digest*, 77(8), 18.

Barkley, E. F., & Major, C. H. (2020). *Student engagement techniques: A handbook for college faculty*. John Wiley & Sons.

Berrett, D. (2012). How 'flipping the classroom can improve the traditional lecture. *The Chronicle of Higher Education*, 12(19), 1–3.

Bhagat, K. K., Chang, C.-N., & Chang, C.-Y. (2016). The impact of the flipped classroom on mathematics concept learning in high school. *Journal of Educational Technology & Society*, 19(3), 134–142.

Bösner, S., Pickert, J., & Stibane, T. (2015). Teaching differential diagnosis in primary care using an inverted classroom approach: Student satisfaction and gain in skills and knowledge. *BMC Medical Education*, 15(1), 1–7. 10.1186/s12909-015-0346-x25879809

Cennamo, K. S. (2016). What is studio? In *Studio Teaching in Higher Education* (pp. 260–271). Routledge.

Ceylan, S., Şahin, P., Seçmen, S., Somer, M. E., & Süher, K. H. (2021). An evaluation of online architectural design studios during COVID-19 outbreak. *Archnet-IJAR: International Journal of Architectural Research*, 15(1), 203–218. 10.1108/ARCH-10-2020-0230

Costa, E. N. P., & Sánchez, J. (2022). Flipped classroom for teaching structures in architecture courses. In *Structures and Architecture A Viable Urban Perspective?* (pp. 1011–1017). CRC Press. 10.1201/9781003023555-121

Coyne, R., Lee, J., & Petrova, D. (2017). Re-visiting the flipped classroom in a design context. *Journal of Learning Design*, 10(2), 1. 10.5204/jld.v10i2.281

Crowther, P. (2013). Understanding the signature pedagogy of the design studio and the opportunities for its technological enhancement. *Journal of Learning Design*, 6(3), 18–28. 10.5204/jld.v6i3.155

Elrayies, G. M. (2017). Flipped Learning as a Paradigm Shift in Architectural Education. *International Education Studies*, 10(1), 93–108. 10.5539/ies.v10n1p93

Galiana, M., & Seguí, L. (2016). Implementing flipped classroom in the School of Architecture. ICERI2016 Proceedings, Galway, L. P., Corbett, K. K., Takaro, T. K., Tairyan, K., & Frank, E. (2014). A novel integration of online and flipped classroom instructional models in public health higher education. *BMC Medical Education*, 14, 1–9.

George, B. H., & Walker, A. (2017). Social learning in a distributed environment: Lessons learned from online design education. *Educational Media and Technology Yearbook*, 40, 53–66. 10.1007/978-3-319-45001-8_4

González-Gómez, D., Jeong, J. S., Airado Rodríguez, D., & Cañada-Cañada, F. (2016). Performance and perception in the flipped learning model: An initial approach to evaluate the effectiveness of a new teaching methodology in a general science classroom. *Journal of Science Education and Technology*, 25(3), 450–459. 10.1007/s10956-016-9605-9

Gray, J. A., & DiLoreto, M. (2016). The effects of student engagement, student satisfaction, and perceived learning in online learning environments. *The International Journal of Educational Leadership Preparation*, 11(1), n1.

Gren, L. (2020). A flipped classroom approach to teaching empirical software engineering. *IEEE Transactions on Education*, 63(3), 155–163. 10.1109/TE.2019.2960264

Huang, Y.-N., & Hong, Z.-R. (2016). The effects of a flipped English classroom intervention on students' information and communication technology and English reading comprehension. *Educational Technology Research and Development*, 64(2), 175–193. 10.1007/s11423-015-9412-7

Jones, D., & Lotz, N. (2021). Design education: Teaching in crisis. *Design and Technology Education: An International Journal*, 26(4), 4–9.

Khanova, J., Roth, M. T., Rodgers, J. E., & McLaughlin, J. E. (2015). Student experiences across multiple flipped courses in a single curriculum. *Medical Education*, 49(10), 1038–1048. 10.1111/medu.1280726383075

Khogali, H. (2020). The effect of COVID-19 corona virus on sustainable teaching and learning in architecture engineering. *Modern Applied Science*, 14(8), 44–58. 10.5539/mas.v14n8p44

Kinzie, J. (2005). *Promoting Student Success: What Faculty Members Can Do*. (Occasional Paper No. 6). National Survey of Student Engagement.

Komarzyńska-Świeściak, E., Adams, B., & Thomas, L. (2021). Transition from physical design studio to emergency virtual design studio. Available teaching and learning methods and tools—A case study. *Buildings*, 11(7), 312. 10.3390/buildings11070312

Lai, C.-L., & Hwang, G.-J. (2016). A self-regulated flipped classroom approach to improving students' learning performance in a mathematics course. *Computers & Education*, 100, 126–140. 10.1016/j.compedu.2016.05.006

Liu, L. (2019). Face-to-face teaching in the flipped classroom supported by visualisation tools–Taking the course of "Architectural Design of Housing" as an example. *International Journal of Emerging Technologies in Learning*, 14(3), 220. 10.3991/ijet.v14i03.10106

Nguyen, B., Yu, X., Japutra, A., & Chen, C.-H. S. (2016). Reverse teaching: Exploring student perceptions of "flip teaching". *Active Learning in Higher Education*, 17(1), 51–61. 10.1177/1469787415616727

Ozenen, G. (2023). Self-Assessment and Learning Outcome Evaluation of Interior Architecture Students Using Flipped Versus Traditional Classroom Education Models. *SAGE Open*, 13(4), 21582440231209891. 10.1177/21582440231209891

Peimani, N., & Kamalipour, H. (2022). The future of design studio education: Student experience and perception of blended learning and teaching during the global pandemic. *Education Sciences*, 12(2), 140. 10.3390/educsci12020140

Peng, F., Kueh, C., & Cetinkaya Sendas, M. (2022). Design pedagogy in a time of change: Applying virtual flipped classroom in design higher education. *Journal of Design. Business & Society*, 9(1), 41–56.

Rich, P. J., West, R. E., & Warr, M. (2015). Innovating how we teach collaborative design through studio-based pedagogy. *Educational Media and Technology Yearbook*, 39, 147–163. 10.1007/978-3-319-14188-6_11

Simamora, R. M. (2020). The Challenges of online learning during the COVID-19 pandemic: An essay analysis of performing arts education students. *Studies in Learning and Teaching*, 1(2), 86–103. 10.46627/silet.v1i2.38

Smith, J. D. (2013). Student attitudes toward flipping the general chemistry classroom. *Chemistry Education Research and Practice*, 14(4), 607–614. 10.1039/C3RP00083D

Triyason, T., Tassanaviboon, A., & Kanthamanon, P. (2020). Hybrid classroom: Designing for the new normal after COVID-19 pandemic. Proceedings of the 11th international conference on advances in information technology, Wanner, T., & Palmer, E. (2015). Personalising learning: Exploring student and teacher perceptions about flexible learning and assessment in a flipped university course. *Computers & Education*, 88, 354–369.

Young, G. (2002). 'Hybrid' Teaching Seeks to End the Drive Between Traditional and Online Instruction. *The Chronicle of Higher Education*.

Chapter 17
The Relationship Between Professional Practice and Architectural Education in Turkey

Mehmet Emre Arslan
Istanbul Kultur University, Turkey

Salih Ceylan
Bahcesehir University, Turkey

ABSTRACT

One of the biggest challenges in architectural education is its necessity to adapt to a continuously evolving professional environment. In many countries, professional organizations such as chambers of architects and educational institutions work together to come up with various strategies and formulae that strengthen the bond between the two. However, the rigid system imposed to the higher education institutions in Turkey hinders architecture schools to propose effective strategies for creating such bonds. Historical research on the topic indicates that this bond has become weaker in time. Currently, concerns reflect on the opinions of various stakeholders. As a result, there are various comments on architectural education to become more sufficient for the professional environment. This chapter aims to draw a framework for the relationship between education and practice in Turkey. It elaborates on the past, present and the future of the relationship from local and global perspectives.

INTRODUCTION

It is widely acknowledged that architectural education, with its vocational structure, is expected to prepare students for the challenging environment of architecture and construction. Therefore, the contents of the education curriculum and the design studios must be arranged according to the emerging needs and requirements of the professional world. However, in the current stance of the practice, there is an

DOI: 10.4018/979-8-3693-2329-8.ch017

Copyright ©2024, IGI Global. Copying or distributing in print or electronic forms without written permission of IGI Global is prohibited.

ongoing debate on the lack of professional preparedness level of young architects when they graduate from the university to start their careers.

The theoretical framework of the study consists of an overview on the recent history of architectural education in the World and in Turkey, current attempts to create relations between education and practice, and the emerging theories for the constitution of stronger connections on the course from education to profession. Research shows that until the 1970's, professional life and academic education were in the same line. However, this situation changed in the last decades due to various reasons, such as the overall reduction in the education quality in the universities, and the rapid evolution in the architecture practice under the influence of information and communication technologies. There have been recent attempts by the Chamber of Architects in Turkey to strengthen the link between professional practice and architecture education, as well as other attempts by different organizations to create or strengthen the link between these two.

In recent years, institutions from around the globe have been engaged in research examining the relationships between education and professional practice, with the aim of strengthening them for the benefit of future generations. For instance, Turkish Chamber of Architects' report in 2017 contains significant information about architectural education in Turkey (Aycı&İlerisoy, 2018). A questionnaire conducted among 2220 young architects who recently registered in the chamber reveals that 56% of the attendants had a negative opinion on having been informed well about the environment of architectural practice (TMMOB Chamber of Architects Ankara, 2017).

Additionally, academic studies on the subject also contribute to the attempts for the solutions about the lack of communication between education and profession. This chapter presents a study with this purpose, offering a multifaceted view of the subject from various vantage points. In the scope of the study, the topic is going to be observed from the perspectives of different personas such as students, academics and professionals. The paper has the following research questions on the relationship between professional practice and education in architecture:

1. What is the historical background of the relationship between architectural education and the profession? How does it affect today's architecture environment?
2. To what extent are architecture students ready to start their professional career? Are they getting enough knowledge, skills, competencies for competing in the architectural market?
3. How is the academy's perspective for meeting the requirements of the profession in the education curriculum? How does it support students and academics to get ready for architecture practice?

This study suggests that the absence of professional architects in architecture schools may result in a lack of practical knowledge. In the scope of this study, suggestions will be made on how to fill the gap in practical knowledge in the academic field of architecture. However, firstly it is necessary to examine the historical background of practicing architects in the academy.

HISTORICAL FLOW

The history of architectural education in Turkey is marked by westernization and modernization efforts. For that reason, following European educational trends is the major policy while modernizing the education. It can be stated that there are four thresholds in the history of architectural education in Turkey. One of them is the westernization effort during late Ottoman period while Beaux Art style and education is effective. The second threshold is the proclamation of the Turkish Republic and the modernization of education by German architects and engineers until the 1950s. The third period is the influence of American education systems in relation to the American version of the Bauhaus. The fourth period is the period after the 1980s when the military coup led to the destruction of existing institutions and the creation of a new high education system. Within the scope of this chapter, the development of the architecture education in Turkey will be summarized in parallel with the history of architecture education in the West.

Academic architectural education started with the inauguration of the Académie d'Architecture on 3 December 1671 in France. It was the first institution to be devoted solely to the study of architecture, and its school was the first dedicated to the explicit training of architectural students. The Académie was abolished in 1793, during the revolutionary turmoil that besieged France at the end of the eighteenth century, although the architectural educational tradition that arose from it was resurrected with the formation of the École des Beaux- Arts and prevails in the ideologies and activities of schools of architecture throughout the world today (Griffin, 2020).

Perhaps the most fruitful way to assess the relationship between the Académie and French architecture is to examine the built work undertaken by the members of the Académie who had the most sway over its ideological trajectory, namely the *professeurs* (Griffin, 2020). At the early years of the academy, it cannot be said that there is a strong connection between the academy and professional works. However, in the following years, it is seen that the influence of educators working in the academy has increased in the professional architectural environment.

The Académie d'Architecture was subjected to a series of changes in parallel with the political and cultural transformation of France during 19th century. Following a series of name and structure changes, Ecole des Beaux Arts was established to provide a workshop centered education in art and architecture. The Beaux Art school of architecture is the first example in the history of architecture in that it created a mainstream architectural language. Although its predecessor, the Académie d'Architecture, often evokes neoclassical architecture, most of the architects who practiced architecture in Europe in the 17th century were not school graduates, and architectural knowledge appeared to be inherited from the family. Therefore, it is unknown whether the resulting architecture was under the influence of the school. In the Beaux Art school, we are faced with a specific architectural language developed and taught in architecture school. This language, called Beaux Art Architecture, was effective from the mid-18th century to the late 19th century, and continued to be effective in some places in the first half of the 20th century.

Beaux Art architecture appears as an architectural movement spread all over the world. This architectural movement, whose stylistic language was formed by neoclassical elements, was also influenced by the technological developments of the age and used architectural technologies such as iron and concrete. Vedat Tek, who worked as an architect in the second half of the 19th century in Turkey and was one of the architects of important buildings such as the Sirkeci Post Office, also found his way to the Ecole de Beaux Art. We can say that the classical architectural language seen in Turkey in the 19th century was brought to Turkey by architects who were trained in the Beaux Art approach in Europe. Alexandre Vallaury is one of them. Born in Istanbul as the child of a Levantine family, Vallaury received his architectural education at Ecole des Beaux Art and realized many buildings in 19th century Istanbul. Vallaury is also one of the founders of Sanayi-i Nefis Mektebi, which was established to provide education within the structure of Ecole des BeuaxArt. It is believed that Vallaury played a role in the design of the school's educational program from its founding years to the periods when national trends were strengthened and local architectural approaches, which some have called the first national architectural period, were particularly prevalent. As will be mentioned later, as nationalist movements increased their effectiveness, Beaux Art aesthetics gave way to national tendencies.

The institutionalization of architectural education in Turkey begins with the organization of Hassa Architects. As a result of the research, according to the sources, the names of the Hassa Architects Organization and its employees are encountered towards the end of the 15th century, and it is possible that the Hassa architects may have been organized to form an organization within the palace, especially during the period of Fatih Sultan Mehmet (Taş, 2003). After the Hassa Architects Association, the Turkish Architects and Engineers Association was established and the first steps of professional organization were taken. Architects trained here are specialized and assigned according to the building types needed by the empire. In civil architecture works, an educated architect character cannot be mentioned. These structures are built by masters and journeymen, with building knowledge passed down from generation to generation.

Bozdoğan (2012) claims that the radical modernization of architectural and engineering education in the Ottoman Empire in a European direction began in the first half of the nineteenth century, when the Hassa Mimarları Ocağı, the traditional institution where Ottoman architects were trained in the classical period, was abolished. However, efforts to modernize the architectural profession began at the end of the 18th century. In 1795, Mühendislikhane-i Berri Hümayun was established. Its main purpose was to teach the military techniques needed by the army. The architecture of some military structures such as military camps, barracks, bridges and fortifications was also the responsibility of the engineering school from Hassa architects. Thus, the foundation of an architectural organization different from the Hassa quarry was laid on the engineering axis. Muhendishane-I Berri Hümayun continued to provide architectural education until 1833.

Westernization efforts in the field of construction activities continued with the Tanzimat Edict in 1839. With the Tanzimat, the Ministry of Public Works was established to manage the construction activities in the Ottoman Empire and major construction activities were carried out through this ministry. However, the real change in terms of architectural organization took place with the establishment of the General Directorate of Foundations Construction and Repair Committee within the Ministry of Foundations and the appointment of Architect Kemalettin as its head. While Architect Kemalettin was initially interested in the renovations of some properties belonging to the Foundations, after the appointment of Ürgüplü Hayri Efendi to the Ministry in 1910, the staff of the Technical Construction and Repair Committee was expanded, with the intention of increasing the production of new buildings in order to provide income for the Foundations. It is ensured that it operates as a central architecture and construction organization. This organization, which can be called the Kemalettin School, allows the training of a number of architects, engineers and builders who apply the national architectural approach in all regions of the country. In this way, the Construction and Repair Committee of the Ministry of Foundations becomes the focal point of the First National Architecture movement. Among the architects and engineers who worked with Mr. Kemalettin, most of whom were his students; People who will continue the national architectural principles even after the death of the architect, such as Alaaddin, Ali Talat, Mehmet Nihat (Nigizberk), Hüsnü (Tümer) and Cemal Bey, are appointed (Dedekargınoğlu et al., 2023).

The effort to provide architectural education in accordance with Western norms in Turkey began in the late 19th century. The two schools established during this period, Sanayi-i Nefise Mektebi and Hendese-i Mülkiye Mektebi, are symbols of the first engineering and architecture schools.

Professional Practice and Architectural Education in Turkey

The main purpose of the establishment of Hendese-I Mülkiye, which was established in 1884, was to train new bureaucratic staff to work in the Ministry of Public Works, which had a staff of unqualified non-Muslims educated in Ottoman and European schools (as cited in Baydar, 2012). In 1909, the school was placed under the management of the Ministry of Public Works, a final separation from its previous military past. Although the name Hendese-I Mülkiye does not give much clue about the architecture-related content of the curriculum, the scope of the program was wide enough to allow graduates to choose architecture as an area of specialization (Baydar, 2012). In 1890, German architect Auguste Jahmund was appointed head of the school. Although there is no definitive information about the purpose of Jachmund's coming to Istanbul, who was also the architect of the Sirkeci Train Station, which was built in the Orientalist style in Istanbul, the most probable reason is that the German companies and the German Government responsible for the railway construction in Turkey at that time. It can be assumed that he came to Istanbul as a result of his assignment. Kemalettin Bey, Jahmun's student, states that the education program at Hendese-I Mülkiye is based on a structure focused on drawing and design, mostly done at a desk, rather than the construction site-oriented, on-site and leaf-weaving model of previous years. According to Baydar (2012), this indicated a historical transformation. The basis of architectural knowledge was no longer geometry knowledge and construction site experience, but design capacity. This transformation was clearly visible when the curriculum of military and civilian schools were compared. The emphasis given to geometry and mathematics in military schools was replaced by drawing and design courses in civilian schools. Less importance was given to the construction site and the focus shifted to the drawing table (Baydar, 2012).

Although courses on architecture were also given at Hendese-I Mülkiye, there was a need to establish a school to specialize in art and architecture education. For this purpose, Sanayi-i Nefise Mektebi was founded in 1882. It was founded during the reign of Abdühamid. The first director of the school was Osman Hamdi Bey, who received his art education at Ecole des Beax-Art. Painting, sculpture, architecture, art and calligraphy courses are given together at the Sanayi-i Nefise School, whose educational curriculum is derived from the Ecole des Beaux Art. The school structure of Sanayi-i Nefise Mektebi, the forerunner of today's Mimar Sinan University, was designed by Alexandre Vallaury, who would later run the school's architecture program. Alexandre Vallaury carried out the architectural program of the school between 1883 and 1908 at Sanayi-i Nefise School, and many important structures such as the Ottoman Bank General Directorate, Public Debt Building and Pera Palace were built during his teaching at Sanayi-i Nefise School. These buildings, where local elements and neoclassical elements are used eclectically together with a typical orientalist perspective, bear the influence of Beax Art.

Sanayi-i Nefise Mektebi was the school of many of the pioneers of Turkish architecture in the Republican period. Among these, there are pioneer architects of Turkish architecture in the Republican period, such as Sedat Hakkı Eldem and Seyfi Arkan.

Figure 1. Sanayi-i Nefise Mektebi - Fine Arts Academy, SALT Research, Tlabar Family Donation, 1927

The management of the architecture departments of Hendese-I Mülkiye and Sanayi-I Nefise Schools, which were managed by foreign architects until the end of the 19th century, changed hands with the increase in national tendencies and the reaction to architectural styles representing European-based movements. With the national movements coming forward at the end of the century, the management of these two schools passed to Turkish architects, and Architect Vedat Tek and Kemalettin Bey became active in the academy as students of the first teachers. Both Vedat Tek and Kemalettin Bey are active practicians as the architects of important buildings. It is known that the students of Vedat Tek has internship opportunities as well in the construction of his buildings. This expresses that theory and practice closely linked with each other within the scope of the educational system at these two schools.

At every point where Turkish architecture transformed by being influenced by the political environment, the management of these two schools also transformed. As a result of the Republican elite's demand for a new architecture under the influence of Bauhaus, the influence of Vedat Tek and Kemalettin Bey ended, and the era of foreign educators and architects Bruna Taut and Ernst Egli began. With the death of Atatürk, the re-strengthening of nationalist tendencies and the beginning of the period defined as the second national architectural period, the management power in these two schools passed to Turkish architects again. Both schools, which were restructured in the 1940s, transformed from schools into universities. Sanayi-I Nefise Mektebi turned into Istanbul State University of Fine Arts, the predecessor of today's Mimar Sinan University, and Hendese-I Mülkiye Mektebir turned into the Graduate School of Engineering and later into Istanbul Technical University.

Istanbul Technical University was founded in 1944 and the faculty of architecture has existed since its founding. It is seen that the Bauhaus influence was widespread in the early periods at ITU, which continued to be nourished by architects from Germany, like its predecessor Hendese-I Mülkiye Mektebi.

While examining the educational structure of the ITU Faculty of Architecture in the founding years and the relationship of individuals with the Bauhaus, Belkıs Uluoğlu states that it is known that many of the faculty members who managed project studios at the school in those years did not coincide with the dominant modernism discourse of the day in terms of approach and were not in close relations with transnationalism. On the other hand, there are enough clues to make us think that the program of the school in its first years of establishment (1940s) was influenced by the Bauhaus and the environment it created, with the emphasis on Basic Design courses, modeling workshops and technique - and therefore the knowledge of making - (Uluoğlu, 2009). Clemens Holzmeister taught at ITU between 1940-1949 and Paul Bonatz between 1946-1955. The German (central European) influence, which started with August Jachmund, one of the Hendese-I Mülkiye teachers, continued for many years.

The name of Sanayi-I Nefise school, which was established as an educational institution under the influence of Beauax Art, was changed to the Academy of Fine Arts in 1928. In 1930, Swiss architect Ernst Egli was appointed head of the architecture department, modernizing architectural education. After Egli's resignation in 1936, Bruno Taut organized his architectural education for a short time until his death in 1938. The following years in the academy were organized around the identity of Sedat Hakkı Eldem. The school changed its name to Istanbul State Academy of Fine Arts in 1969 and was renamed Mimar Sinan University in 1981. The architectural education approach at Mimar Sinan University has always focused on drawing and building knowledge, and has carried its founding philosophy to the present day. (Here it is not intended to say that the school continues its education in a neo-classical structure, far from today's technologies. It is just that attention is drawn to the school's emphasis on building knowledge and drawing techniques, unlike other architecture schools.)

The 1950s are a period in which international relations began to develop in Turkey, shaped by dynamics such as the transition from a single-party political system to a multi-party system and the development of the market economy. The 50s, when American hegemony began to be felt in every field, also point to internationalization in architectural education. Bauhaus collapsed as a result of Nazi pressure, and Bauhaus architects spread all over the world, but mostly in America. Between 1950 and 1980, architectural education in Turkey was influenced by the Bauhaus approaches established in America.

Figure 2. A project critic in Istanbul Technical University Gümüşsuyu Campus (Around the table from left to right: Emin Onat, Clemens Holzmeister, Friedrich Hess ve Paul Bonatz, Salt Research, Harika-Kemali Söylemezoğlu Archive)

The establishment of the Middle East Technical University and the opening of METU Faculty of Architecture, Turkey's relations with the American governments improved after 1950, American capital entered the country with Marshall aid, modernization in agriculture increased, agricultural vehicles such as tractors affected the workforce structure in rural areas, rural-to-urban migration increased and It corresponds to a period when the slum problem emerged. Middle East Technical University was established in 1955 with the support of the University of Pennsylvania and the United Nations, and the faculty of architecture was opened in 1956. It is stated that the architectural education system implemented at METU is shaped according to the model that emerged in America after World War II and is a continuation of the Bauhaus education system. As a matter of fact, American experts took part in the establishment of the school and cooperation was made with American Universities influenced by the Bauhaus education model (Uysal, 2009). Although it underwent various revisions until 1968, it can be said that an education program in which the Bauhaus influence was felt was basically followed.

The political environment that developed in the partial freedom provided by the 1961 constitution also affected universities, and especially since the end of the 1960s, the political economy of the formation of the built environment began to be discussed in academic environments in the context of Marxist criticism. With the military coup in 1980, a higher institution to regulate universities was established, the uniformization of universities was aimed, and all kinds of political approaches were blocked.

It can be said that architectural education in Turkey and the world after 1980 includes plural approaches. In particular, the introduction of computer technologies into education life, the appearance of complex geometries in the architectural field and school projects, the influence of postmodernism and globalization concepts have affected architectural education both in the world and in Turkey.

Since the second half of the 1980s, the unbridled growth of cities and the problems it created, the level of the slum problem and the uneven geographical development created by the liberal economy have become increasingly controversial in academic circles. In addition, small-scale construction activities are concentrated in the urban environment. For example, constructions carried out by small-scale contractors on a single-apartment scale with the build-sell system have begun to play an important role in the formation of the urban environment. The gap between the architectural thought produced in the academy and the architecture practiced in practice has begun to widen.

The dominance of practicing architects in the academy began in the late 19th century and continued until the 1980s. in Turkey. According to Tanyeli (2007), until these years, 'teachers' defined the center of the architectural design world. The most important architects are the teachers of certain schools. Kemalettin Bey at the Engineering School, Sedad Hakkı Eldem at the Academy, and Emin Onat at Istanbul Technical University are some of the examples. Back then, the architecture schools often acted as their office. This group of practitioner-academics was influenced by the experimental and positivist architectural approaches developed in British and American universities. Starting from 1960s, universities started to shift the profile of architecture professors from practitioners to academics (Tanyeli, 2007). Emin Onat at Istanbul Technical University is one of the examples for this shift.

The paradigm shifts in the academy in Turkey went hand-in-hand with the evolution of the chamber of architects. Their perspective on the architectural profession had a direct impact on the formation of architectural education back then. From its establishment in 1954 until the mid-1960s, the main agenda of the chamber of architects was to protect the professional rights of its members and increase their share in the construction industry. During this period, with the increase in population in cities due to migration from rural to urban areas, the need for architectural services increased, and new architecture schools were opened for this purpose. Their curricula were influenced by the chamber of architects, as same people were in the management of the chamber and the architecture schools. Although there was an increase in the number of architects throughout the 1960s, it can be said that the professional conditions of architects were comfortable due to the increasing work volume. However, in the 1970s, due to the increasing number of architects and the shrinking economy, unemployment began to occur in the field of architecture. As a result, architects formed a radical opposition group supported by their own professional organizations. The economic recession, high inflation and the collapse of investment programs, parallel to the rapid proletarianization of architects, created a major crisis in the construction industry (Yücel, 2007). This opposition is based on a Marxist perspective and points to economic disorders, which also carry the dynamics of the architectural profession, as the main source of the disorder in the urban environment. In this context, a group has formed in the academic environment that is critical of the dynamics of urban development. In this sense, the chamber of architects tries to intervene in urban-related processes and has shifted its priority to the protection of the right to the city rather than the protection of the professional rights of its members. This situation also changed the priorities of the chamber of architects and educational issues became less important for them.

CURRENT SITUTAION

According to Aydemir and Jacoby (2020), professional practice and research and learning in architecture have become integrated over the last decade. However, strengthening the bond between the academy and practice in architecture is still an important concern for the discipline globally and locally. It is also important for the society to have a strong bond between education and practice to sustain itself. Bergström (2014), structuring his study on the work of Dana Cuff's book: *Architecture: The Story of Practice*, evaluates the role of practice in architecture education, and the role of education in architecture practice. Noel (2020), suggests the reimagination of design education and puts a finger on the role of practice therein. In parallel, University of Hartford Department of Architecture, a NAAB accredited program, conducted a practice-oriented education curriculum by actively involving practicing architects in the studio and the classroom, creating strong relations with industry through office and construction site visits, and providing strategic guidance in matters of fund-raising, accreditation, and management (Petry, 2002).

Currently, there are more attempts to provide the connection using different methods, most of them focusing on the design studio and opportunities provided for students by professional architects in the design studio. Therefore, next chapter elaborates the nature of the design studio, followed by the attempts in Turkey and rest of the world to maintain the consistency between architectural education and practice.

Nature of the Design Studio

Architectural education is the process that prepares students for the professional environment and its challenges. Its curriculum generally consists of 6, 8, or 10 semester continuum, depending on the country and the level of education. Each semester consists of some theoretical, technical, and practical courses, with the design studio in the focal point. Theoretical courses are mostly lectured by academics, as the practical and technical courses are undertaken by academics and practitioners together. Especially, design studio courses, that are considered the core of architectural education (Schön, 1987; Salama, 1995), are the ones where practitioners are employed most frequently, for they hold first-hand experience about emerging market conditions and developments in the industry. Design studios are the courses with the most credits in the curriculum, and the place where the students spend most of their time at an architecture school (Hettithanthri and Hansen, 2022). Therefore, they have a significant role in this process. In the design studio, students have the opportunity to express their architectural ideas and creativity through a variety of communication techniques and methods, including drawings, physical models, computer models, photography, video clips, and more. Additionally, it is the most suitable place for students to experience possible scenarios they will face in their professional career, in addition to meet practicing architects and learn from their experience in the field. In the studio, students typically follow a methodical approach to developing their designs, with the aim of expressing their ideas primarily through physical models and sketches, but there are also different methods to make the design studio a more effective environment for education, as well as practicing the profession (Ibrahim and Utaberta, 2012). The relationship between the student and the instructor in the design studio is more like a master-apprentice relationship. Projects are advanced through discussions with the instructors at desk critiques, which provide a supportive and collaborative environment for learning. This methodology in the design studio, accepted by most of the architectural schools in the world, necessitates the involvement of professional architectural practitioners in the design studio for a more reliable and applicable architectural education. It also strengthens the bond between education and practice in architecture.

Current Situation in the Globe

The main initiatives that act for strengthening the bonds between education and practice are mostly architectural associations, and public or private organizations for architecture, in addition to educational institutions. The concerns about the role of practice in architectural education are reflected on various documents and studies. UIA (2017) states that continuous interaction between the practice and teaching of architecture must be encouraged and protected. RIBA (Royal Institute of British Architects) states that it is vital to obtain input from a diverse range of practices in order to fully understand how best to implement them into architectural education (RIBA, 2016). With this aim, different committees such as Architects Registration Board (ARB), Quality Assurance Agency (QAA), RIBA Validation Criteria & Procedures; and applications like Professional Practice Experience (PPE), sandwich course, integrated course, and work based learning are developed for the training of architects. In the white paper it published, RIBA points out to the unprecedented societal, environmental and economic challenges that are faced by the profession and it states that it is only possible to overcome those challenges through dialogue across the architecture sector between academia and practice (RIBA, 2023). ACSA (The Association of Collegiate Schools of Architecture), in its white paper for architectural education, defines architectural education programs as instructional programs that prepare individuals for professional practice in the various architecture-related fields and focus on the study of related aesthetic and socioeconomic aspects of the built environment (ACSA, 2018). Accordingly, the emphasis on the practical issues in architectural education shall not be ignored.

National Architectural Accrediting Board (NAAB) in the U.S. calls attention to lifelong learning, which is crucial for the training of an architect. In the *Conditions for Accreditation* document it is stated that the practice of architecture demands lifelong learning, which is a shared responsibility between academic and practice settings (NAAB, 2020). Likewise, RIBA (2020) worked on a framework for education and professional development, based on 6 education themes and values such as; Health and Life Safety; Ethical and Professional Practice; Structure, Construction and Resources; History, Theories and

Methodologies; Design Processes and Communication; and Business Skills. The framework also includes 4 mandatory competences and 10 Continuing Professional Development (CPD) Core Curriculum titles. The figure below shows the general outline of the proposed framework.

Figure 3. RIBA education and professional development framework

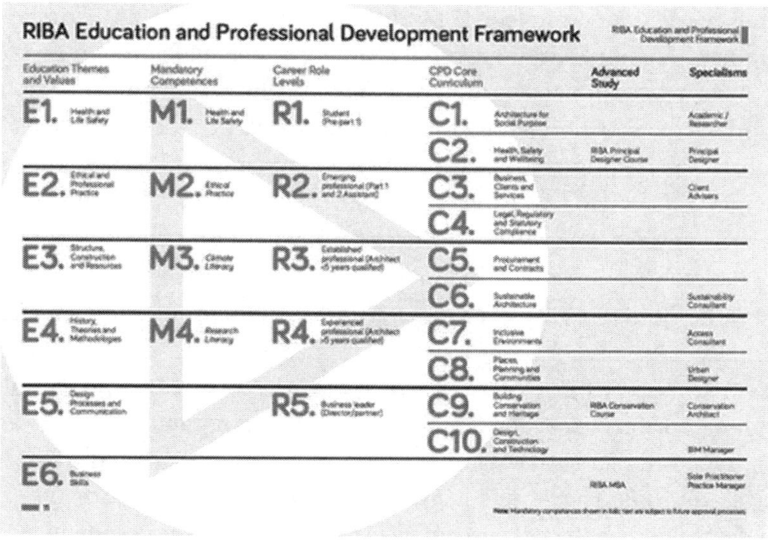

(RIBA, 2020)

In this framework, a flexible and variable career path for architects are presented. At this point, RIBA emphasizes the importance of diversity and specialization in the profession throughout the carrer of archtiects, providing a mutual relationship between education and practice.

Current Situation in Turkey

It can be asserted that the chamber of architects' current perspective on architectural education is similar to their perspective in the past. However, the free flow of architects and academics observed especially in Anglo-Saxon countries rarely works successfully within the inflexible structure of the university system in Turkey. It should be mentioned that there is a gradual erosion of the identity of the teacher architect. Teacher architects, the attractive role models of the past, are replaced by architect architects (Tanyeli, 2007). The segregation between the academy and the profession has become deeper from past to present. After the dominance of architecture educators in the academy has disappeared, the need for practical knowledge in the academy is being met by professional architects teaching part-time in the academy. Many architects who is at the top of their profession or newly emerging successful architects contribute to the architectural education in this sense. However, its effects are limited and have less influence on the nature of architecture education than expected.

On an institutional level, the endeavour to create strong relations between education and practice in architecture becomes visible from time to time. Attempts by the chamber of architects, architectural education accreditation board, as well as by educational institutions come into prominence, mostly aiming for a more efficient and productive professional environment.

In 2007, a group of academic pioneered by Prof. Dr. İhsan Bilgin has formed a graduation school in under the umbrella of Istanbul Bilgi University, proposing an education model to strengthen the link between academia and professional world. Their model relied on 3 folds: Design studio, theoretical courses, and site trips (trips to different cities). According to this model, design studio courses would be held by practicioners. The theoric courses given by academics would be supporting the design studios. They were proposing a designated workplace for students with a designated worktable and computer, assuming that the student will be using that space as his/her own office. Even though this model filled an important place in the architecture education for some years, the effect of it to the quality of architecture education became quite limited because of having limited number of students and unstable university management in Turkey.

In 2020, Turkish Chamber of Architects published the Turkey Architectural Education Policies document, mentioning various aspects of architectural education and their effects on the professional environment of architecture (Turkish Chamber of Architects, 2020). The document mentions the term "professional ethics" multiple times, featuring it as an important aspect of the profession. Likewise, the concept of professional practice is also given importance in the document. The report states that strengthening the relationship between architectural education and practice is one of the main concerns of architectural environment in Turkey, and mentions the *contradictions in the field of practice with the knowledge of in-school education* and *problems about lifelong learning in practice* as problems of architectural education in the country.

MiAK is the National Architectural Accreditation Board in Turkey, established in 2006 with the purpose of improving architectural education through evaluation and competency studies and thus contributing to social welfare by training better educated and higher quality architects (miak.org). In their accreditation conditions document, the importance of strong bonds between education and practice in architecture is emphasized clearly. Section 2.4 in this document is about the knowledge, skills and competencies that the graduate must gain, and one of the five subsections is about professional environment. At that point it is mentioned that Architectural education should aim at students who can be enterprising and take risks; who are able to develop ethical responsibility and a critical attitude towards employers, society, public interest and legal limitations; and who can work in cooperatively in teams and have leadership skills (http://miak.org/?p=sayfalar&sayfa_id=84).

Another attempt for strengthening the link between education and practice is the establishment of foundations or non-profit organizations in architecture field. Such foundations or organizations are established by volunteer architect groups or architecture offices. The main purpose of such organizations is not to educate the young graduates in a structured undergraduate education, instead they are proposing some programs in different periods focusing on current discussions and challenges in architecture and cities.

Architectural educational institutions in Turkey are also concerned about training competitive and adequate young architects for the professional environment. As the educational system in Turkish universities is not flexible, they need to come up with new ways to achieve this goal. For instance, some universities work towards providing more effective opportunities for professional practice for their students, as some of them try to create relationships between the industries and students through cooperative offices. Additional elective courses about professional practice, ethics, project and construction management, in addition to extracurricular activities such as workshops, seminars, or conferences are methods used by architectural schools to help their students for having a head start in their professional career.

SUGGESTIONS FOR THE FUTURE

Despite the endeavour of different mechanisms to create better relationships between education and practice in architecture in Turkey, the educational system and its applications, along with the current professional environment enclose flaws for their integration. Additional minor or major actions need to be taken for a better relationship. Given all concerns, to propose useful solutions to close the gap between professional career and architecture education is not easy. There is no *one-size fits all* comprehensive solution but to create some usefull models that is usefull in its own context may be possible. Suggested strategies for stronger relationships between architectural education and practice in the scope of this chapter are as follows:

Architectural educators must be in close relationship with the practice to keep themselves updated about the developments in the market and industry. UIA (2017) mentions that research and publication should be regarded as an inherent activity of architectural educators and may encompass applied methods and experiences in architectural practice, project work and construction methods. Accordingly, academics working at architectural educational institutions must be encouraged and supported towards practicing in the industry. Current law in Turkey does not allow architects working in the academie to work in the market. Changing this and academics starting to work in the market would not only increase the quality of education, but also increase the overall quality of architectural practice.

Hosting practicing architects has various advantages for architectural education, especially the design studio. According to Legeny et al. (2018), the fundamental pier of today's architectural education is mostly the practicing architect teaching a small group of students in a studio. However, it is also a challenge and sacrifice for the practicing architects to dedicate some of their times for this educational activity that does not offer a direct benefit for them. Therefore, working at an educational institution must be made more favourable for practicing architects who are eligible for that job. On the other hand, the process of selecting the practitioner to work at the architecture school is another challenge. Principles and criteria for the position of lecturer or studio instructor at the architecture schools need to be defined clearly, and only the eligible people with the right educational formation need to be appointed for these positions. Moreover, considering the number of architecture faculties, it seems quite difficult to employ a sufficient number of experienced architects in architecture education.

The professional practice is an integral element of the educational curriculum in architecture schools and must be organized better to be more effective for the professional development of the students. With this aim, architectural offices and construction companies should be educated and become more aware of the importance of the professional practice. The idea of creating an accreditation system for professional practice in architecture would be also possible.

Another strategy to increase the effectiveness and importance of the professional practice in the curriculum is to make it a full year or full semester mandatory that supports the students to spend longer and more effective time in an architectural office or construction site. This one year mandatory practice could be executed after the graduation and only after successful completion of this process the architect would be accepted to be a member of the chamber. Thus, the practicing students would be considered more like a junior architect in offices which would also positively change the attitude towards them.

There are other problems in the education system that are obstructing the connections between education and the practice. In overall, the architectural education system needs more flexibility and freedom, allowing more instant changes and interventions in the curriculum. More courses about project management, construction management, microeconomics, negotiation skills, etc. could help students to start their career with more confidence. Additionally, international and intercultural relations would also support the training of well equipped young architects.

Last but not least, and probably as a prerequisite for all the aforementioned strategies, the amount of architects, architecture students, academics, and architecture schools must be kept under control. Currently, these amounts are too high in Turkey and they keep going high every year. If the presented amount is higher than the needs of the industry, there would be no chance to achieve any goals of architects or architectural institutions due to economic reasons.

CONCLUSION

When the thoughts on the incompatibility between architectural education and the professional field are examined, it is seen that mostly all stakeholders of education and professional architecture sector are responsible for this. These stakeholders are the structure and curriculum of architectural education, academicians, higher education institutions, chambers of architects and architectural offices. Considering the structure and curriculum of architectural education, it is thought that the courses containing more practical knowledge will generally enable the training of young architects who are more compatible with practical life. Internship obligations are created for this purpose and the student is expected to experience a real architectural action in a limited time. When viewed from the perspective of higher education institutions, we see that architectural education and all other forms of education are put on the same level. Objections to this are frequently voiced in the academy's management apparatus, and comparisons are made with education periods in different countries and complaints are made about the inadequacy of the 4-year architectural education. It can be seen that the chamber of architects also focuses on similar points. There is a reluctance in architectural offices to employ a young architect who has just graduated from the architecture department. For example, when looking at job postings in the field of architecture, it is seen that a professional career of at least two years is mandatory. Office owners' or managers' complaints about the competence of graduated architects mostly focus on the limited drawing competence and inadequacy of technical knowledge. As a result, it is thought that the competence level of an architect who has just graduated from university is not sufficient for architectural practice.

However, it would be too harsh to expect that architecture students are fully competent in all fields of practice on the first day of graduation. However, it is a decent expectation that graduates are in a certain level of knowledge and experience, and able to adapt and respond to new challenges and environments. Therefore, the mission of architectural education is not to train students towards every possible challenge they will possibly face, but to teach them the ways of flexible learning and adapting themselves to such situations. Additionally, the role of ongoing professional education in architecture needs to be acknowledged by the industry and its stakeholders. Moreover, the practice also needs to accept the role of education in the formation of the profession in the future. The relationship between education and practice is mutual and the nature of the practice, especially its future, gets shaped by the education as well. Therefore, the developments and trends in architecture education needs to be followed and initialized by the stakeholders in the architecture and construction industry.

It may be considered to support organizations that aim to improve the skill sets of young graduates through various fondations and architectural offices. Inadequacy of 4-year architecture education may unofficially be eliminated by such organizations by proposing additional design studio practice.

To conclude, it shall be stated that the practice of architecture as a whole with its educational and professional environments is a very dynamic and evolving concept. Therefore, both environments need to be continuously updated to stay eligible. Especially, the developments in technology like artificial intelligence or virtual reality, together with the needs and requirements of the industry such as sustainability and energy efficiency must be followed and implemented into educational curricula by the policymakers of architectural education and institutions. Additionally, educational or practical developments in various parts of the world shall be followed and adapted into the relevant divisions of the profession. All in all, it is crucial for the practice of architecture that educational and professional environments are in close relationship and collaboration.

REFERENCES

ACSA. (2018). *ACSA White Paper on Architectural Education Research and STEM*. Association Of Collegiate Schools Of Architecture, Washington, D.C.

Aycı, H. & İlerisoy, Z.Y. (2018). Mimarlık Eğitimi Meslek Pratiğinin Simulasyonu Olmalı mı?: Akademi, Büro ve Şantiye Alanlarında Yarı Yapılandırılmış Mülakat Yöntemi ile Bir Değerlendirme. *Online Journal of Art and Design, 6*(5).

Aydemir, Z. A., & Jacoby, S. (2020). *Design research and a shift in architectural education and practice.* EAAE-ARCC International Conference & 2nd VIBRArch: The architect and the city, Valencia, Spain.

Baydar, G. (2012). *Osmanlı-Türk Mimarlarında Meslekleşme*. Mimarlar Odası Yayınları.

Bergström, A. (2014). Architecture and the rise of practice in education. *Architectural Theory Review*, 19(1), 10–21. 10.1080/13264826.2014.894604

Dedekargınoğlu, C., Kutluoğlu, O., & Şumnu, U. (2023). *Ankara Palas'ın Merdivenleri*. Çizgilerle Modern Türkiye Mimarlığı Serisi, Karakarga Yayınları.

Griffin, A. (2020). *The Rise of Academic Architectural Education: The Origins and Enduring Influence of the Académie d'Architecture*. Routledge, Newyork.

Hettithanthri, U., & Hansen, P. (2022). Design studio practice in the context of architectural education: A narrative literature review. *International Journal of Technology and Design Education*, 32(4), 2343–2364. 10.1007/s10798-021-09694-2

Ibrahim, N. L. N., & Utaberta, N. (2012). Learning in architecture design studio. *Procedia: Social and Behavioral Sciences*, 60, 30–35. 10.1016/j.sbspro.2012.09.342

Legeny, J., Spacek, R., & Morgenstein, P. (2018). Binding architectural practice with education. *Global Journal of Engineering Education*, 20(1), 6–14.

NAAB. (2020). *Conditions for Accreditation* (202nd ed.). National Architectural Accrediting Board.

Noel, L. A. (2020). "A Time for Change: Reimagining Design Education", Dialogues. *The Intersection of Emerging Research and Design for Learning*, (04), 14–15.

Petry, E. (2002). *Architectural Education: Evaluation and Assessment*. 32nd ASEE/IEEE Frontiers in Education Conference, Boston, MA. 10.1109/FIE.2002.1158116

RIBA. (2015). *RIBA Education Review May 2016 Update*. Royal Institute of British Architects.

RIBA. (2020). *The Way Ahead: An introduction to the new RIBA Education and Professional Development Framework and an overview of its key components*. Royal Institute of British Architects.

Schön. (1987). *Educating the Reflective Practitioner: Toward a New Design for Teaching and Learning in the Professions*. Jossey-Bass.

Tanyeli, U. (2007). *Mimarlığın Aktörleri, Türkiye 1900-2000*. Garanti Galeri.

Taş, M. (2003). *Osmanlı'dan Günümüze Yapı Üretiminde Mimarlık Meslek Örgütlenmesinin Gelişimi*. Uludağ Üniversitesi Mühendislik-Mimarlık Fakültesi Dergisi.

Turkish Chamber of Architects. (2020). *Turkey Architectural Education Policies (Türkiye Mimarlık Eğitimi Politikası)*. TMMOB Mimarlar Odası.

Türkiye Mimarlık ve Eğitim Ortamıyla İlgili Bilgiler. (2017). *TMMOB Mimarlar Odası*.

UIA. (2017). Charter for Architectural Education: Revised 2017 Edition. UNESCO-UIA Validation Council For Architectural Education, International union of architects.

Uluoğlu, B. (2011). *İTÜ Mimarlık Fakültesi'nin Kuruluş Yılları: Holzmeister, Bonatz, Diğerleri ve Mimarlık Eğitiminin Örgütlenmesinde Orta Avrupalı İzler, Bauhaus: Modernleşmenin Tasarımı, Türkiye'de Mimarlık, Sanat, Tasarım Eğitimi ve Bauhaus içimde*. İletişim Yayınları.

Uysal, Y. Y. (2011). *ODTÜ Mimarlık Fakültesi Mimarlık Bölümü'nde 1956-1980 Yılları Arası Eğitim Sistemi, Bauhaus: Modernleşmenin Tasarımı, Türkiye'de Mimarlık, Sanat, Tasarım Eğitimi ve Bauhaus içimde*. İletişim Yayınları.

Yücel, A. (2007). *Çoğulculuk İş Başında: Türkiye'nin Bugünkü Mimarlık Manzarası. Modern Türk Mimarlığı 1900-1980 içinde* (Holod, R., Evin, A., & Özkan, S., Eds.). TMMOB Mimarlar Odası.

Chapter 18
Green Studio With Different Education Methodologies Based on Sustainability

Figen Beyhan
Gazi University, Turkey

Merve Ertosun Yildiz
Gazi University, Turkey

ABSTRACT

Design studios have great importance for architecture education because they consist of an interactive process carrying out theory and practice together. In design studios, many discussions about design processes focus on different approaches, and many alternative design methods are produced. Studio V, one of the architectural design studios at AAA University, offers students design practice both inside the school and on out-of-school technical trips. Studio V determines sustainability as the basic concept and experiences the spirit of the place with knowledge from the past. It aims to develop the student's ability to analyze, perceive, construct, criticize, question, and design. This chapter explains the concept and execution style of Studio V and illustrates the end-of-term products through a few student projects. It ends with an evaluation of the scope of the studio and its teaching methods.

INTRODUCTION

It is a proven fact by scientific studies that climate change and environmental problems, which have become common problems in all countries, are closely related to the design, construction, and usage processes of built environments. The concerns about the right to live in a green world for future generations have brought all the countries of the world to the point of joint action, and solutions have started to be produced with the agreements made, the regulations arranged, and the various incentive models promised by determining the targets within the scope of sustainability.

Architecture is a crucial discipline that has the potential to be the leading representative and implementer of a fight for environment and climate change by a leading role in the design and construction of built environments. Architects, with the decisions they make in the design and construction processes

DOI: doi

and the application methods, carry out highly effective tasks in issues that have turned into today's main problems, such as land use, resource conservation, energy consumption, rate of carbon emissions, waste management, environmental pollution. The theoretical, technical, and ethical vocational education process of architecture, which the European Union accepts as one of the three basic human-oriented disciplines, significantly affects the task processes of architects. So, raising awareness of architects within the scope of their responsibilities regarding the natural environment, built environment, and ongoing lives that they intervene while they are still in their vocational training processes, raising awareness about sustainable architectural design for combating environment and climate change, developing their skills and competencies, teaching strategies and methods in producing approaches related to sustainability is notably essential.

On the other hand, architectural education, unlike other disciplines, is built on learning due to doing and experiencing (Taber, 2011). Architectural design studios, which enable these environments of making and experience, are the most significant part of architectural education. In the architectural education process, the design studios that allow students to show, make, break, and experience their creativity constitute the focal point of education (Pasin, 2017). Koester defines the studio as an active learning environment and an inspiring experience students love (Koester, 2003). Design studios develop the creative potential and creative thinking of architect candidates. These studios aim to teach knowledge and gain experience to the candidate architect. Actors in the role of lecturer and student, physical environments, subjects with different content, design problems, and processes are the elements of design studios. In addition, physical environmental requirements such as studio environment and layout are among the factors that affect students' productivity and learning activities in the studio (Abdelbaky et al., 2022). Architectural design studios enable students to develop their analysis, perception, constructing, criticizing, questioning, and designing skills by providing students with design experiences under the leadership of the executive. Evaluating and utilizing much knowledge from other disciplines like philosophy, sustainability, history, building technologies, engineering, economy, etc., design studios allow architect candidates to turn theory courses into practice with these principles.

Studio V, also known as Green Studio at the Architecture Department of the Gazi University, is one of eight architectural education studios. The main approaches of Studio V are based on a sustainable architectural design together with many principles and techniques relating to building design and construction. Studio V tries to bring its students to see, listen, and understand design areas with all contexts and reinterpret according to today's requirements of the spirit of the place.

The studio carries out the vertical system in which the students have different levels from second to fourth grade in the education process in the same semester. Implementing the vertical studio in architectural design programs' curricula aligns with the need to introduce novice students to holistic and contextual thinking approaches inherent in education in these fields (Liem, 2012). Vertical studios are considered micro-information communities (Youssef, 2016). The key feature of the vertical studio model is that students from different years collaborate to address specific themes. Vertical studio environments produce better learning outcomes because they facilitate collaboration among students from various educational levels. It provides an environment where students can convey their knowledge/ knowledge more effectively, and those who do not know can learn more easily from those who know. This creates more opportunities for educators to implement curriculums (Peterson, Tober, 2014). The vertical studio model aims to add to and strengthen design skills in this context. Thus, it seeks to create student-to-student learning opportunities linked to assignments to transform visual observations and perceptions of the built environment into two- and three-dimensional representations using manual and digital drawing techniques. Also, the vertical studio system allows students to see different potentials by offering multiple solution perspectives on a problem (Smatanová et al., 2020).

THE STUDIO V CONTENT

For the architects, who have a significant role in the design and construction of the built environments that cause environmental problems and climate change, it is an important issue to raise awareness of architects about their responsibilities for threatening the future of the world and future generations' rights for living due to their works in the professional education processes. So, sustainable architecture's definition, scope, strategies, and design approaches must be included in the architectural education processes, and future architects must have business capabilities with sufficient technical knowledge and experience. Because of that, this studio aims to enhance architecture students' awareness about their significant role in the design and construction of built environments that cause climate change and environmental problems and develop their competence to produce solutions.

In its emergence, the concept of sustainability has included the interest and knowledge of many disciplines based on understanding environmental, social, and economic development. Due to the problems caused by the built environment, such as global warming, climate change, and the depletion of natural resources, it has imposed many responsibilities on the discipline of architecture. In this context, two different design approaches could be mentioned at the intersection of sustainability and architecture. The first is architecture, which reconstructs traditional architectural methods that are in harmony with nature, and the other is architecture, which benefits from the contributions of technology to sustainability with designs that can cause the least harm to the environment by using the potential of existing technology. The important thing is that architecture also protects nature, and sustainable architecture is considered a way of thinking. With this in mind, Studio V aims to present its students with a design philosophy that focuses on people and nature and develops approaches to sustainability philosophy based on knowledge and experience (Figure 1).

Figure 1. The optimum design process with a philosophy based on knowledge and experience

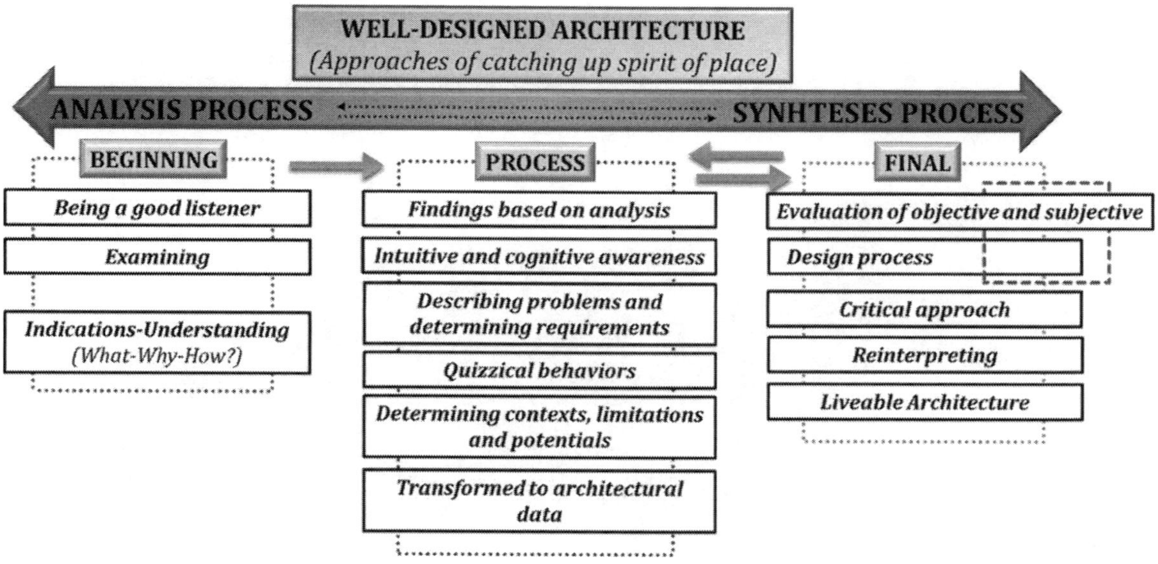

WELL-DESIGNED ARCHITECTURE
(Approaches of catching up spirit of place)

ANALYSIS PROCESS ←·········→ SYNHTESES PROCESS

BEGINNING
- Being a good listener
- Examining
- Indications-Understanding (What-Why-How?)

PROCESS
- Findings based on analysis
- Intuitive and cognitive awareness
- Describing problems and determining requirements
- Quizzical behaviors
- Determining contexts, limitations and potentials
- Transformed to architectural data

FINAL
- Evaluation of objective and subjective
- Design process
- Critical approach
- Reinterpreting
- Liveable Architecture

According to this philosophy, paying attention to the rhythmic relationship between architecture, life, and nature, which constantly changes, transforms, and develops, is essential. In that context, architecture, defined in terms of basic concepts of Vitruvius and improved by sub-concepts coming from changing life conditions due to time, must be reconsidered as focused on design, technique, and practice utilizing quite different missions and responsibilities today (Figure 2).

Figure 2. Interaction between architecture, life, and nature

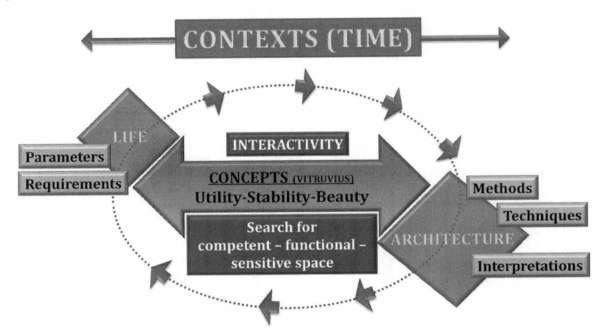

All these concepts in Table 1 are among the most important parameters considered and evaluated in the design processes. It is emphasized that the built environment, which is the product of architecture run as an action against nature, especially within the natural environment, needs to be rethought. In this context, the concept of sustainability, which has become the agenda of all countries of the world since the 20th century, is highlighted. The basic philosophy and execution process of the studio is sustainability. Thus, studio students are encouraged to rethink architecture in the context of sustainable architecture.

Table 1. The main concepts of architectural studio

UTILITY	STABILITY	BEAUTY
Functionalism	Structure	Esthetic
Technology	Technology	Technology
Memory	Construction	Form
Context	Context	Context
Psychology	Material	Art
Sociology	Detail	Proportion
Ideology	Safety	Scale
Identity	Durability…	Balance
Protection		Color
Cultural heritage		Harmony

continued on following page

Table 1. Continued

UTILITY	STABILITY	BEAUTY
Sustainability		Contrast
Philosophy		Repetition
Acceptability		Authenticity...
Privacy...		

From this point of view, the concept of place is brought to the fore. Because every new architectural design is realized in a "place" that expresses more with its unique geographical, socio-cultural, economic, and architectural components. With its physical qualities, life-related actions, economic activities, historical and cultural values, and users, the place is considered the most important context that directs the design. At this point, competent solutions compatible with the ground are developed with the GENIUS LOCI approach. The Genius-Loci is of Latin origin and associated with the protective spirit of places in Roman mythology, could be described with the concept of "spirit of the place", which represents the distinctive features of a place (URL 1). In other words, Genius-Loci expresses how the contexts of the place affect the built environment and how they bring different textures, forms, and meanings to the place. Genius-Loci foresees the analysis of the existing built environment and the structural culture formed by the effects, events, and experiences of the past with holistic approaches, understanding its philosophy and using it as a reference for the new built environment (Figure 3).

Figure 3. Place, built environment, holistic architectural design approach relations

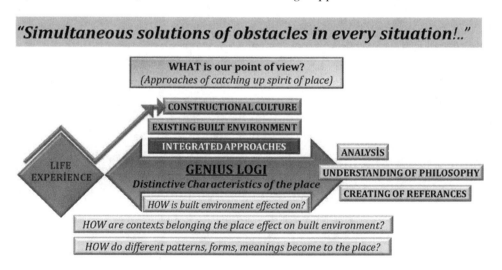

Incompatible or inadequate design decisions, exempting from the characteristic structure of the place, degrade the quality of the lives it will serve. Having well-designed projects based on knowledge and experience, it is necessary to know everything that affects the design, it is necessary to be aware of everything that affects the design. An orderly and systematic process of intuitive awareness and discovery brings questioning. It is the crucial beginning point of designing that the objective and subjective evaluations of contexts, limitations, and potentials within the scope of the final design. Meanwhile, unplanned, unqualified, and valueless, wrong architectural decisions are discussed and sought a solution in the studio by the students and academicians. The main issues in that process are the following: lost identity, lost culture, lost history, lost sense of belonging, disrupted aesthetic values, transformation to the concrete environment, lost green, changed macro and microclimate, increasing carbon emission, increasing energy dependence, consumed resources, etc. Understanding and interpreting design philosophies existing in traditional or vernacular architecture are significant in that solution process. The parameters from these philosophies should be evaluated together with today's building technologies.

Design Process at the Studio V

There are too many great examples of vernacular architecture originating from the practical needs of different topographical, geographical, and climatic conditions, cultures, building materials, or techniques in all regions of Anatolia. These are significant information sources from the settlement scale to the building. On the other hand, experiential learning is a process in which the learner is active and places information in the mind at the end of different cognitive stages according to their characteristics (Kolb, 1984). Observations and reflections consisting of tangible experiences in the learning process lead to the creation of abstractions and generalizations (Smith and Kolb, 1996). Because of that, Studio V looks out for choosing different project sites in other cities for all semesters. A technical visit is organized in a town in various regions to analyze project sites every semester. The visits are natural, cultural, and social learning laboratories for the studio members. These technical visits increase the interest and responsibility for the environment, the student's awareness about how contexts of the place affect the built environment, and how they bring different patterns, forms, typologies, and meanings to the site. In addition, the visits significantly develop the spirit of the students of the studios relating to sharing information, producing something together, and having a good time. All studio members share many things for days and learn the value and power of cooperation. Also, technical visits provide the opportunity to practice many tasks in a limited time. So, it contributes to raising individuals to be socially and environmentally conscious, manage time effectively, and develop views and behaviors according to the place. Studio V has organized eighteen technical visits except for the two pandemic semesters.

The studio team briefs the students on the project topic and concept at the beginning of the semester and builds the project process in two phases. The scheme of the first phase is given in Figure 4.

Figure 4. The scheme of phase one

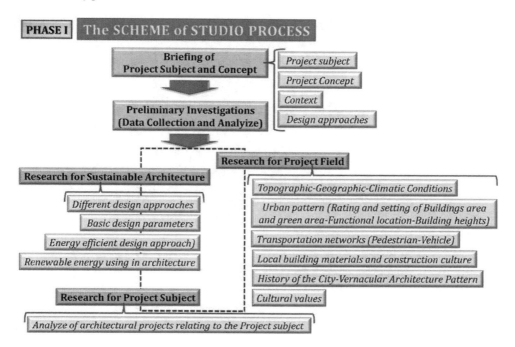

Firstly, a preliminary research process starts in three weeks. Students are expected to work in groups during the research process, which begins by searching for a solution to a given problem. Group work is based on collaborative teamwork in problem-solving processes, which aligns with constructivist education theory's ideals (Edelson, Pea, & Gomez, 1996). Associating individual differences and skill diversity in group work is advantageous in terms of consistency in departmental programs (Kember, 2009), which can potentially increase the quality of learning. Before the technical visit, every group studies their research subject, including existing situations in the project site, what sustainable architecture is content, and the scope of the project topic. They systematically collect theoretical information from literature and project sites and analyze all information using different methods such as swot analysis or Lynch analysis for transforming architectural data. Then, they present their works to other friends and discuss the potential and limitations of the site, as well as the project topic and aims. Finally, the analysis sheets with information about the project subject and place are prepared and presented to each other. Thus, the first phase is completed. Figure 5 presents sample analyses from the first phase.

Figure 5. Final products of phase one

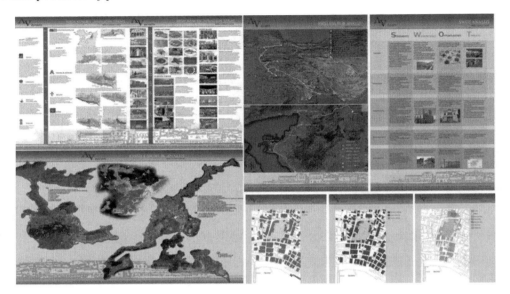

After finishing phase I, the students are ready for the technical visit, approximately three or four days at the project site. On the project site, the studio students examine on-site, analyze the abovementioned issues, take photos, and draw sketches. On the last day of the visit, the students present the final sheets, including the site analysis. The instructors of the studio criticize the sheets. That is the last step of technical visiting. Analyze sheets as primary references are redesigned according to the last critics and hung in the studio during the semester for use in all design processes.

Studio V is one of the vertical studios in the department hosting students from different years in the same context. All students continue to design the process using the same project concept and on the same site. However, architectural programs and scale are different. Thus, students are encouraged to follow their teachers' criticisms during class hours.

This process provides the opportunity to witness different approaches to similar questions and problems, learn from other's results, and make connections (White, 2000).

Phase II is a criticizing period that starts after the technical visit. The studio lecturers criticize the students' projects throughout the semester. Students reconsider their decisions in line with the criticisms. That cycle continues until the end of the semester (Figure 6).

Figure 6. The critics in the studio: Phase two

After the technical visit, the students lay out concept sheets and project scenarios describing their design decisions. At this stage, the students evaluate the information obtained in Phase 1 and determine individual approaches belonging to their projects considering the principles of Studio V. Afterward, they study the concept of their projects and decide their contexts. Students develop an architectural program with project topics according to their scenarios. Then, they start designing the process according to their architectural approaches. The design process is continued as panel critiques with students individually throughout the semester. The critique method is panel criticism, meaning that each student appears before a jury, and the others follow other's critical processes. All students from different levels keep up with all presentations in the panel and know different approaches. At the end of the semester, the projects of all students evaluated during the whole semester are presented to the final jury.

Firstly, concepts and scenarios described as their projects are wanted from every student when they return from the technical visit. At this stage, the students evaluate the information obtained in Phase 1 and determine individual approaches considering the principles of Studio V. Afterward, they study the concept of their projects and decide their contexts. Students develop an architectural program with project topics according to their scenarios. Then, they start designing the process according to their architectural approaches. The design process is continued as panel critiques with students one by one throughout the semester. Each student appears before the jury all semester. All students from different levels keep up with all presentations in the panel and know different approaches. At the end of the semester, the projects of all students evaluated during the whole semester are presented to the final jury.

Student Projects in Normal Semesters

Studio V has run the studio studies according to the abovementioned concept since 2012. There are several student projects belonging to Studio V are presented below:

One of the project sites of Studio V was Datça in the spring semester of 2016-2017. Datça was chosen for the project because of its protected areas, historical settlement, and geographical location. The project concept was defined "Eco Balance: DATÇA from yesterday to tomorrow". The project topic was to design a social settlement consisting of a center of local art education, art galleries, housing buildings, and social spaces. The studio team was concerned about how a new settlement should be designed to protect historical and environmental values.

A student from the studio, Aykut Bulut, who is in the last classroom, designed a project for that subject. He tried to use the prevailing wind to reduce the cooling loads (energy consumption) in a hot, dried climate zone. According to his concept, he brought together the prevailing wind with the streets at the project site to ensure that the wind passed around the building envelope and went inside spaces. So, energy consumption for comfort conditions was minimized in outdoor and indoor spaces. All design decisions about orientation, building shape, façade design, and space organization were determined according to this aim. This project was successful in designing passive cooling methods.

Figure 7. The final sheets of the project in Datça/ Muğla

In the spring semester of 2017-2018, the project site was determined in Kaş. Kaş is a small touristic city with excellent natural features, including green areas and a sea. At the same time, there are successful examples of traditional architecture according to its climate and topographic conditions. The project concept was ''Touch to Kaş by Biophilic Design Approach.'' The project topic was designing a

Spiritual Therapy Centre as a hotel complex that had a biophilic design approach. Biophilic design in architecture is expressed as a design that allows the continuation of human-nature interaction and the beneficial effects of nature in built environments. In addition to modern buildings with biophilic approaches, it is possible to see biophilic elements in historical buildings. In that context, Studio V aimed to find biophilic parameters referencing new designs in vernacular architecture.

The concept of one of the studio students, Feyza Halı, was to learn from Nature. She presented her project topic, "Kaş is in the footsteps of the Stones." She had kept up with stone patterns in the city and its environment. She interpreted the pattern of stone in nature and designed a settlement to accommodate geography by being parallel to the coast. It is seen that the design focused on using green, water, and local building materials, which becomes prominent in settlement patterns following stone marks in the project. Other biophilic criteria in the project are visual connection with nature, non-visual connection with nature, non-rhythmic sensory stimuli, thermal land airflow variability, presence of water, connection with natural system, biomorphic patterns, materials connection with nature, complexity, and order (Figure 8).

Figure 8. The final sheets of the project in Kaş/ Antalya

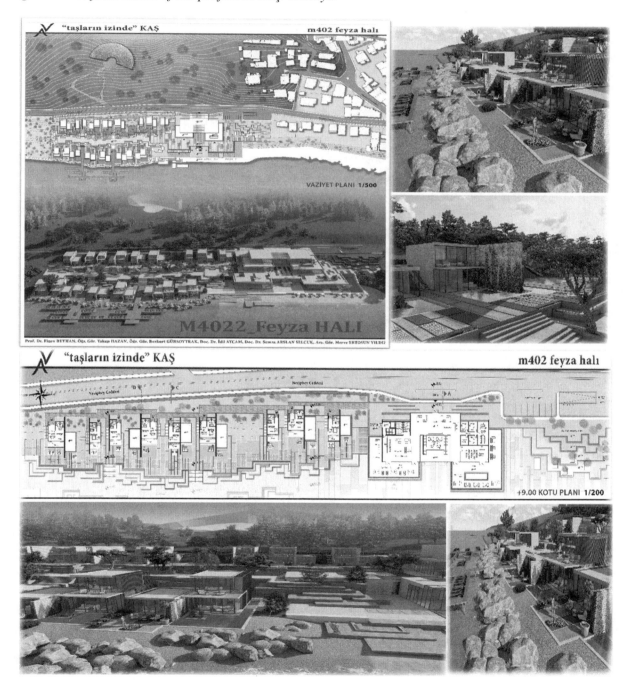

Pandemic Semester

The negative impacts have been seen in education because of the COVID-19 epidemic and many dynamics of daily life. As a result of the measures taken, universities have switched from face-to-face to online education. All education units, especially art and design faculties, where practice and workshops are at the forefront, were greatly affected. The pandemic affected the teaching method, project subject, project site, etc., of Studio V. There were some difficulties in the first weeks of the process. Then, everyone adapted to the conditions quickly and learned many things relating not only to new education techniques but especially to the value of being face-to-face.

The technical visit has been impossible Compared to other semesters because of conditions. So, the project site was determined as Ankara, where the students were educated, and the project subject was rethinking sheltering culture due to today's new dynamics. The analysis sheets, including the site, new conditions, changed expectations, and sustainable design, were studied in digital literature. The potential of new digital technologies benefitted all steps. Lecturers frequently ask students who are candidates for architecture what the best solutions for a better life might be and how a livable environment in the city center could be another argument all semester.

A third-class student, Emre Aşağıdere, designs an example project in that semester. The main goal of the design is to produce a potential place with green areas that work like lungs in the dense texture of the city in the living areas. More green areas have been created in social areas without disturbing the topography. The site in the green axis extending to Kızılay Square was designed as a starting point of the green axis, and this green axis is supported by green roofs in places in vertical lines. A third-class student, Emre Aşağıdere, designs an example project that semester. The main goal of the design is to produce a potential place with green areas that work like lungs in the dense texture of the city in the living areas. Social areas having more green areas have been created without disturbing the topography. The site in the green axis extending to Kızılay Square was designed as a starting point of the green axis, and this green axis is supported by green roofs in places in vertical lines. These green roofs allowed people to meet with nature from their homes. Besides, each facade is designed to meet performance requirements according to orientation. It paid attention to the wall and window ratios in the design phases and used shading elements to provide comfortable spaces for continental climate conditions in Ankara (Figure 9).

Green Studio With Different Education Methods Based on Sustainability

Figure 9. The final sheet of the project in Maltepe/ Ankara

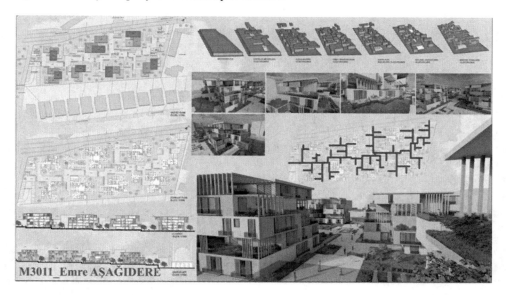

Another project semester during the pandemic was to design an ecovillage within the scope of a new formation for a livable environment in Gölbaşı. This project was run within the framework of the corporation with Gölbaşı Municipality. Principles of Studio V, like sustainable design, energy efficiency, water harvesting, and paying attention to local characteristics, were significant parameters for the project design. It was important that the settlement could be self-supporting without outside support. At the same time, it was essential to protect the eco-balancing of the project site because it was on the coast of Mogan Lake, an important natural area. So, the balance between the natural and built environments was paid attention. Low-rise buildings were designed to utilize the sun as a renewable energy source to produce energy. The balance between open, semi-open, and indoor spaces was observed for microclimate. According to performance requirements, all facades were designed in different types. Some areas were thought of as organic agriculture areas (Figure 10).

Figure 10. The final sheets of the project in Gölbaşı/Ankara

DISCUSSION

With the potential of increasing industrialization and developing technology, the built environment is held responsible for the emergence of climate change and environmental problems. Reaching higher levels of livability in the design of built environments brings difficult and complex design processes. Architecture is the leading actor in developing built environments and should be a part of the solution by developing methods. Each building to be designed should not be considered independent of the site where it will be. All decisions affecting the design should be determined as human and environmentally sensitive.

In this respect, studio lessons are the basis of architectural education and are extremely important. Because theoretical and practical knowledge are learned together, student-lecturer interaction is at the forefront in the studios. Besides, studios are educational spaces with a multi-layered and holistic structure that accommodates different thinking and learning methods. In addition to the known techniques, technical visits, which are multidimensional educational activities run outside the school, are another teaching method that allows students to learn by experiencing, living, and balancing the relations between people and the natural environment. Students develop practices of reading, understanding, and interpreting the architectural environment and ways of seeing and thinking. In addition, through environmental awareness and awareness, students develop a different way of thinking about knowledge production and structuring.

The concept of place is the determinant of the original value in traditional architecture and has brought intense experiences to the design. The identity of the place is its hidden value in the visibility and legibility of life traces with unique qualities. The design philosophies that form the essence of the building culture that develops with the local contexts existing in traditional architecture can be a reference for today's and future architecture. In addition, the basic approaches of sustainable architecture, such as land use, energy conservation, material selection, water conservation, waste management, and providing comfortable conditions, overlap with the design philosophies of traditional architecture. Integrating these teachings from the past with the possibilities offered by construction technologies can be a way of thinking correctly in architectural education. The proper design of this road is so important because it brings the sustainability approach to life.

ACKNOWLEDGMENT

Thanks to Yakup HAZAN, the part-time lecturer of Studio V, for his contributions.
Thanks to all students of Studio V, especially Aykut Bulut, Feyza Halı, Emre Aşağıdere, Şeyda Babayiğit, for their projects.

REFERENCES

Abdelbaky, L., Elfiki, S., & Barakat, H. (2022). The Impact of Furniture Arrangement upon Experiential Learning in Architectural Design Studios, with Reference to Cairo, Egypt. *Civil Engineering and Architecture*, 10(7), 3028–3045. 10.13189/cea.2022.100718

Bashier, F. (2014). Reflections on architectural design education: The return of rationalism in the studio. *Frontiers of Architectural Research*, 3(4), 424–430. 10.1016/j.foar.2014.08.004

Edelson, D. C., Pea, R. D., & Gomez, L. (1996). Constructivism in the Collaboratory. In *Constructivist Learning Environments: Case Studies in Instructional Design* (pp. 151–164). Educational Technology Publications Inc.

Kember, D. (2009). Nurturing Generic Capabilities Through a Teaching and Learning Environment Which Provides Practise in Their Use. *Higher Education*, 57(1), 37–55. 10.1007/s10734-008-9131-7

Koester, R. J. (2006). Centers for regenerative studies: Graduate studio experiences in education for sustainable design. *Proceedings of PLEA2006 - The 23rd Conference on Passive and Low Energy Architecture*, (pp. 659-664). Research Gate.

Kolb, D. A. (1984). *Experiential Learning: Experience as the Source of Learning and Development*. Prentice-Hall.

Leim, A. (2012). Teaching Strategic and Systems Design to Facilitate Collaboration and Learning. *Formakademisk*, 5(1), 29–48. 10.7577/formakademisk.374

Pasin, B. (2017). Rethinking the design studio-centered architectural education. A case study at schools of architecture in Turkey. *The Design Journal*, 20(sup1), S1270-S1284.

Peterson, M., & Tober, B. (2014). Institutionalising the Vertical Studio: Curriculum, Pedagogy, and the Logistics of Core Classes with Mixed-Level Students. *Proceedings of AIGA Connecting Dots Conference*. AIGA.

Schön, D. A. (1984). The architectural studio as an exemplar of education for reflection-in-action. *Journal of Architectural Education*, 38(1), 2–9. 10.1080/10464883.1984.10758345

Smatanová, K., Gregor, P., & Šeligová, A. (2020). Pros and cons of the vertical and horizontal design studios in architects' education. *Global Journal of Engineering Education*, 22(3).

Smith, D., & Kolb, D. (1996). User Guide for the Learning Style Inventory: A Manual for Teachers and Trainers. Boston: MA McBer(Mc Berand Company).

Taber, K. S. (2011). Constructivism as Educational Theory: Contingency in Learning, and Optimally Guided Instruction. *Educational Theory*. Nova. https://www.merriam-webster.com/dictionary/genius%20loci#h1

Wang, T. (2010). A New Paradigm for Design Studio Education. *International Journal of Art & Design Education*, 29(2), 173–183. 10.1111/j.1476-8070.2010.01647.x

White, R. (2000). *The Student-Led 'Crit' as a Learning Device, Changing Architectural Education: Towards a New Professionalism*. London: E and fN Spon.

Youssef, K. A. (2014). Horizontal Design Studio versus Vertical Design Studio: A Tale of Two Architecture Schools. *7th International Conference of Education, Research and Innovation (ICERI2014),* Seville, Spain.

Chapter 19
The Multi Project as the First Encounter With the World of Integrated Design

Tom Veeger
University of Technology, Eindhoven, The Netherlands

ABSTRACT

The Multi is a project in the third year of the bachelor of the department of Built Environment (AAAA) and the first encounter with the world of integrated design. Today's building demands have become increasingly complex which necessitates the preparation of students for a practice in which they are ready to cooperate in design teams in close interaction with all disciplines. The multidisciplinary assignment is a practical assignment designed to train students in solving problems with a high level of complexity. An additional goal is teaching students how to cooperate in a team in which every student takes responsibility for a specific domain.

EDUCATION

Education in the Department of the Built Environment (Eindhoven University of Technology) aims to prepare students for multidisciplinary design teams (Graaff & Kolmos, 2003) (Kolodner et al, 2003). The Bachelor program offers a broad range incorporating essentials of urbanism, architecture, structure, building physics, real estate, construction, services et cetera. This broad BSc program lays a foundation for students and is followed by a Master program that focuses on specialization. There are five specializations: Architecture, Urban Design & Planning, Structural Design, Building Physics & Services, Real Estate Management & Development. As an educational project, the Multi has a long history of more like 15 years and is developed from the diversity that the faculty holds. While the first year of the bachelor's program is designed as an orientation to the various disciplines within the faculty, the second year aims to give the student a further deepening in one of the chosen disciplines. For many students, the first two years in terms of design work are highly individualistic in focus with little to no experience of collaboration outside their own discipline. The third year which is divided into two semesters where the

DOI: doi

The Multi Project as the First Encounter With the World of Integrated Design

Multi is the first semester, all students are required to work together on this design task (Wijnen, 2000) (Swagten et al, 2010) (Goldschmidt et al, 2010) (Gómez Puente et al, 2013).

MULTI CHAIN

Building up our built environment is rarely a 'stand-alone' activity. Generally, there will be many stakeholders and participants who all have their own desires, expectations, wishes, knowledge, and experience. In order to arrive at a successful result all participants will need to supply their own specialisms and cooperate in accommodating demands and specialisms of others. If for example, we were designing a car and for some private reason the wheel designer specialist decided it would be best to use square instead of round wheels, the whole car-design would fail. We all depend on creativity and cooperation of each other (Moonen & Veeger, 2014).

For this project we have grouped participating specialisms in two chains which link up at both ends:

- System Physics - Urban - Real Estate – Architecture
- Architecture – Structural Design – Building Physics

These two 'chains' form the basis of the tutoring groups which are available during the whole semester.

Iterative Design Cycle

Development of all designs starts with an analysis of the brief and the context. A huge amount of information needs to be gathered and structured. It is essential to respond to this mass of information by formulating a first review which addresses all aspects of the brief: an integrated preliminary proposal. Inevitably this will be a rough assumption.

By attempting to draw and specify all aspects of this proposal, many imperfections and mistakes will become evident. This will lead to a new round of formulating an integral proposal for solving the problems posed by the brief. This further elaboration must again be worked through to accommodate all aspects of the design team's expertise.

By repeating this cycle of formulating proposals, finding flaws, updating requirements, and reformulating a sharper proposal the project with each iteration.

In the fields of system engineering, design-research and many others, this iterative cycle is referred to in many types of diagrams and names, but the basis for all is similar. Acronyms such as ICCI, MYP, DOCA and many others are used to describe this process.

Whatever the name or the diagram attached to the description of this design-process, the basis lies in the execution of a number of cycles (try Googling on 'design cycle steps'). Each cycle in the process demands a lot of work and all participants are required to contribute their share every time. Designs must be developed and specified as far as possible and everyone should be prepared to re-do their work after the evaluation, which ends a cycle and forms the start of a new one.

Figure 1. Integral design in two chains

The structure we follow in most projects consists of a sequence of phases and runs from a Conceptual Proposal – Preliminary Design – Final Design – and further towards Specifications and Working Design whereby each phase is presented in an increasingly accurate and detailed plan: **Each phase-presentation is the outcome of one cycle**. (Graham, 2003) (Salama, 1995) (Proveniers & Westra, 2009) (Moonen & Veeger, 2016). Also, in for example Naval Architecture, design processes follow a similar iterative process. The Design Spiral, shown by Prof. Hans Hopman during his inaugural address at TU Delft in 2007 illustrates this clearly.

During the MULTI we aim to take you through **three cycles** of this iterative process in developing your Group Final design (Mid-term – Carrousel and Group Final). The student will finish MULTI individually by doing an individual elaboration on a carefully focused Disciplinary subject.

Working in Teams

The MULTI is conducted in multidisciplinary teams of 6 to 7 students. These groups are defined beforehand, and we aim to have all essential disciplines represented in each group. The composition of the team remains unchanged throughout the project. The team as a whole is responsible for the final product. If there are more team members with the same discipline they will agree beforehand on how and on which discipline they will work. This should be done in consultation with the team and the Monitor at the beginning of the project. If there is a discipline which is not represented in the team, two team members should take the responsibility together.

To be able to work in smaller groups and have more focused guidance of several tutors we have arranged tutoring in two 'Chains' For each of those domains, requirements are defined in the design Project Brief. The entire team is responsible for the realization of these requirements.

The Multi Project as the First Encounter With the World of Integrated Design

The 'MULTI-chain diagram' shown above, presents an overview of related subjects and important disciplines for each of those areas. But never forget that all disciplines are interrelated: Structural Design and Building Physics for example are essential for reaching goals in the Urban field and System Physics and Building Typology relate directly to Real Estate and

Figure 2. Hans Hopman, design spiral in naval design

(van Bruinessen et al, 2013)

STRUCTURAL DESIGN CONSIDERATIONS

ESA: Training

Part of the learning goals in this project is to understand the way teams cooperate. The fact that different disciplines are dependent on each other can create tensions in the group. When cooperation is not smooth, this will show in the final result. On the other hand, by making use of each other's qualities, group members can improve the process as a whole.

When clear agreements and assignments are formulated up front so expectations are clear, individual members can be explicitly addressed when others feel cooperation could be improved.

During the ESA training following themes will be addressed:

- Decision making in a professional team. Reflection on Belbin-roles and feedback to team members on a number of specific issues;
- Dealing with feedback from group members – peers;
- Self-reflection and mutual reflection between team members;

During the MULTI semester each group will have three meetings. They serve to support the group process and there will be no grading from these meetings. Proceedings are off-the-record and strictly confidential. These meetings are mandatory.

ESA* = team of student psychologists, part of the office of education support service of the TU/e. Assessment requirements

Monitor

The Monitor will have a weekly meeting of 30 minutes per group. Participation is mandatory for all students. The Secretary of each group will prepare meetings (together with Chairperson) by setting an agenda and keeping minutes. A standard meeting agenda will be supplied and can be used as a guide to structure the process. If there are any issues which concern group performance, they should be addressed and discussed during these meetings. Specific agreements and decisions resulting from these discussions will be noted by Monitor-team (Moonen & Veeger, 2013).

The Monitor(team) tracks and guides group dynamics and has a mandate to act in extreme and group-threatening situations. In these exceptional circumstances the Monitor:

- Can intervene in a team and even dismiss a student from a team or the MULTI
- Can influence the individual grading of the Carrousel and/or Group Final group-results.

The Multi Project as the First Encounter With the World of Integrated Design

The Assignment 2022: Breda Achter de Stallen

The MULTI project of 2022 is focused on an area in the Breda city centre, known as 'Achter de Lange Stallen (Behind the Long Stables) or more prosaically as 'Mols parking'. It has for decades had a practical use as a parking area, furnishing its owners with a decent revenue although there have been numerous attempts to develop it into a more attractive part of town which also earns a higher revenue than the parking fees (interests of respectively the municipality and owners), the last attempt having been aborted in 2013. And now we, as the MULTI team are involved in the latest attempts to generate a new vision and realize new ideas on how this area can be regenerated successfully.

Figure 3. Breda, Achter de Lange Stallen

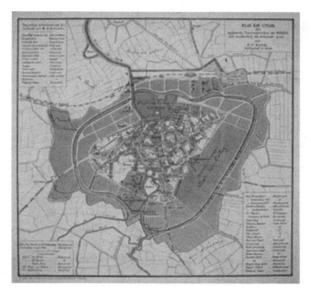

Historic Outline Achter de Stallen

Breda is an old, fortified city in the south-west of our country and is well known for the presence of the KMA, the Royal Military Academy. The city has, during the last millennium been the focus of numerous sieges and battles, aiming to exploit its strategic location. Like many other old cities in the Netherlands it has grown from a clustering of dwellings and traders houses, around the main church, expanding with abbeys and monasteries and later manufacturing facilities to become a serious town. Increasing military and economic value of this town led to it being protected by consecutive series of moatings and fortifications, finally resulting in the spectacular fortifications in the 17th century system of a Vauban-like fortress.

As military firepower increased during the late 18th and 19th century, city fortifications began losing their importance and fortifications began to be dismantled. It is a process that can be seen in cities all over the Netherlands and the rest of Europe (think of the Vienna Ringstrasse for example). For Breda this occurred between 1869 and 1881. The fact that all these grounds were owned by a single owner, usually the Ministery of Defence, who preferred to do business with a limited number of project developers (yes, even in those days!) made large scale and uniform city expansions possible. It meant that many cities were suddenly surrounded by a quite uniform ring of housing blocks for new businesses, new public buildings such as schools, tax offices, post offices and theatres, new railway lines and stations, new harbour facilities, new public parks etc. This structure can be seen in many Dutch towns.

Figure 4. 1861 restructuring of Breda fortifications

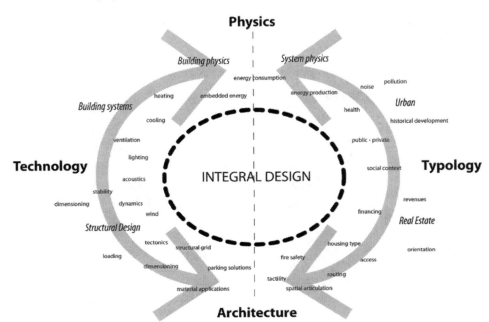

This map clearly shows the restructuring of land for new street plans (yellow), private developments (pink) and military grounds for KMA and barracks (orange) the largest orange surface later became the Chassée terrain which served as a military exercise domain until the late 20th century. The 'Lange Stallen', the stables building, can be seen as a long strip along the eastern edge of this area.

The Green Campus-plan by OMA (1994-2000) outlined a new anti-traditionalist restructuring of these grounds as a collection of autonomous, high-quality, iconic buildings, scattered over a green carpet. The Lange Stallen, uncomfortably found themselves at the edge of this development and the Chassée grounds are still present in the city-scape as an area that wants to become integrated. This is one of the aims of this MULTI project.

The Multi Project as the First Encounter With the World of Integrated Design

PROGRAM OF REQUIREMENTS

Three Colours

The site encompasses around 14.700 m2 and has, besides accommodating social housing units in the linear monumental 'Lange Stallen' building, been a public parking space for many decades. The owners, Dura Vermeer and BPD are now making a sum annually on parking fees and would, if possible, want to contribute to developing an attractive, lively and comfortable new building development as part of the urban realm of Breda.

The municipality wants a more attractive solution than the barren open-air parking for the currently available 300 parking places (roughly). We are going to help them.

For this MULTI we have defined three zones:

- The construction area, the RED-zone (owned by BPD and municipality, approx. 14.700 m2)
- The urban context, the YELLOW-zone (formulate proposals for integration and improvement)
- Existing monument, the Lange Stallen, in GREEN (consider this a <u>to be renovated</u> monument so feel free to adapt or alter the building)

Specifics

There is room for exciting new ideas for this part of town. Please carefully read and follow the latest documents we supplied in Canvas and consider the minimum program of requirements for designing and calculating **inside the RED-ZONE** for all disciplines (!) as consisting of:

- **Housing** in a mix of 2 or 3 price and financing categories (i.e. collective, private, social, mid-price and luxury) for to be specified target groups. Consider all types of single and multiple persons and/or households (experimental housing projects with communal facilities, single space studio, two-room, three-room or larger apartment or terrace house / patio-dwelling).
- **Other functions**, such as retail, café, hotel, cultural etc. are to be considered in small scale units but regarding market developments (think of current developments towards web shops and decreasing purchasing power) the spaces need to be adaptable. So, no Primarks, H&M or AH, but rather street level parts of the plan are to be designed as flexible functions (i.e. shop, office of workshop lining streets).
- **Mobility:** A mobility plan for all users is to be developed and should include strategies for minimising private car use, parking, and ownership such as car sharing, public transport etc. as means of meeting environmental aims. Starting point is the desire for parking at least 300 visitor cars + 1 per dwelling (average) and 500 bicycles but reduction of car number is the aim.
- **Urban culture and finances:** count on a FSI of around 2 for the RED-zone for the site to contribute sufficiently to both the urban cultural atmosphere and the financial goals. The RED-zone measures 14.700 m2 so count on 2 x 14.700 = 29.400 m2 gross area building.
- **Environment**: calculate how much m2 can be constructed, within climate budgets (CO_2), and try to increase that to make a solid business case:

- ○ **Existing** constructions in this area to be climate neutral by 2050
- ○ **New** constructions to be climate neutral by 2030

- **New** public spaces need to support or improve the climate change adaptation strategy of the city (heat-island, wind, water retention and management etc.)

Compensation measures outside the RED-ZONE must be within the boundaries of municipality Breda. IMPORTANT NOTICE: The interests of respective stakeholders are clearly not aligned so you will need to come with well argumented proposals to solve issues. The RED-ZONE is the hard demarcation of the site, and all calculations must relate to this area. It means, for instance that if your calculated CO2 compensation requires measures outside the RED-ZONE, such as a couple of 4 MW wind-turbines, or hectares of PV panels, they will need to be financed by revenues within the RED-ZONE in your project. You will then draw them to scale in plan and elevation, calculate the farmland that needs to be acquired, the investment costs of constructing wind-turbines and their infrastructure.

CONCLUSION

As an educational project, the Multi brings together learning objectives as learning to collaborate and to clarify the role of the various disciplines for the student and to visualize the strong dependencies within teamwork. For the first time, the student thereby comes close to a complex task that will be common later in his professional career. What we experienced as teachers is that after going through the Multi, the choice of a discipline in the undergraduate final project became clear to the student. What makes it extra interesting is that the Multi often involves working together with municipalities and real estate developers on an actual task in which these external parties appreciate the designs of the student teams and make them part of the process to arrive at a real project, check the website https://www.multi-tue.info (The mix of a real task and its complexity makes it a challenge that is experienced by the students as very intensive but afterwards is seen as an important step in their education.

REFERENCES

Clough, G. (2004). *The Engineer of 2020: Visions of Engineering in the New Century. National Academy of Engineering Washington*. The National Academies Press.

de Graaff, E., & Kolmos, A. (2003). Characteristics of problem-based learning. *International Journal of Engineering Education*, 19(5), 657–662.

Goldschmidt, G., Hochman, H., & Dafni, I. (2010). The design studio 'crit': Teacher-student communication. *Artificial Intelligence for Engineering Design, Analysis and Manufacturing*, 24(03), 285–302. 10.1017/S089006041000020X

Gómez Puente, S. M., Eijck, M. v., & Jochems, W. (2013). Empirical Validation of Characteristics of Design-Based Learning in Higher Education. *International Journal of Engineering Education*, 29(2), 491–503.

Graham, E. M. (2003). *Studio Design Critique: Student and Faculty Expectations and Reality*. [Doctoral dissertation. Louisiana State University]. Electronic Thesis & Dissertation collection.

Kolodner, J. L., Camp, P. J., Crismond, D., Fasse, B., Gray, J., Holbrook, J., Puntambekar, S., & Ryan, M. (2003). Problem- based learning meets case-based reasoning in the middle-school science classroom: Putting Learning by DesignTM into practice. *Journal of the Learning Sciences*, 12(4), 495–547. 10.1207/S15327809JLS1204_2

Moonen. S.P.G., & Veeger, T.T. (2013a). *Organization and assessment of a multidisciplinary project*. Proceedings, Project Approaches in Engineering Education: Closing the gap between university and industry, Eindhoven, the Netherlands. https://research.tue.nl/nl/publications/organization-and-assessment-of-a-multidisciplinairy-project

Moonen. S.P.G., & Veeger, T.T. (2013b). *Evaluation assessment carrousel for multidisciplinary design projects*. Proceedings, 11th International Detail Design in Architecture (DDiA), Kaohsiung, Taiwan. https://adk.elsevierpure.com/ws/portalfiles/portal/59224404/OHI_Vol.40_No.2.pdf

Moonen, S. P. G., & Veeger, T. T. (2014). Preparing students towards the complexity of today's practice: startup in a multidisciplinary assignment. In Ö. Dincyürek, S. Hoskara, & S. M. Vural (Eds.), *International conference unspoken issues in architectural education*(UIAE'14), (pp. 299-319). Eastern Mediterranean University Press. https://research.tue.nl/nl/publications/preparing-students-towards-the-complexity-of-todays-practice-star

Moonen, S. P. G., & Veeger, T. T. (2016). Evaluation assessment carrousel: providing feedback in different stages of a problem-based learning-assigment. In S. Emmitt (editor), *Building our Future: Proceedings of the Integrated Design Conference*. University of Bath https://research.tue.nl/nl/publications/evaluation-assessment-carrousel-providing-feedback-in-different-s

Proveniers, A., & Westra, J. (2009). The Evaluation Carrousel: an Assessment Tool for Interdisciplinary Science Innovation Education. in Education. in Kouwenhoven. W. (Ed.) *Advances in Technology, Education and Development*. Springer.

Salama, A. (1995). *New trends in architectural education: Designing the design studio*. [Doctoral dissertation]. Raleigh NC: Tailored Text & Unlimited Potential Publishing.

Swagten, J. P. M., Moonen, S. P. G., & Wennekes, I. (2010). *The proof of the pudding is in the eating. Engineering Education 2010: Inspiring the next generation of engineers.* Birmingham UK Higher Education Academy Engineering Subject Centre, Loughborough University.

van Bruinessen, T., Hopman, J. J., & Smulders, F. E. H. M. (2013). *Towards a different view on ship design the development of ships observed through a social-technological perspective*. Proceedings, ASME 2013 32nd International Conference on Ocean, Offshore and Arctic Engineering, Nantes, France 10.1115/OMAE2013-11585

Wijnen, W. H. F. W. (2000). *Towards Design-Based Learning*. Eindhoven University of Technology Educational Service Centre.

Chapter 20
Beyond the Planetary Architecture

Lucija Ažman Momirski
University of Ljubljana, Slovenia

ABSTRACT

The design studio is an enjoyable experience and a creative atmosphere in a community of young students and their supervisors, where new ideas and imaginative design proposals emerge. The design studio can be complemented by workshops in the form of short-term courses, which are a dynamic component bringing students and practice together. In general, workshops are a quality-control tool to evaluate the themes and processes of a design studio. The design studio topics are very diverse, and the students had to discover all the fundamental questions of dwelling from scratch; they had to question every detail of the starting point of the design. Working beyond planetary architecture offered students the opportunity not only to develop innovative designs, but also to address the essential reasons for habitation. A critical review of the projects was offered to the students at the end of the design studio course by external students and supervisors, and some projects were refined by more precisely defining the values they represent or carry.

INTRODUCTION

The design studio unites students and professors in new design work. It is at the heart of the study of architecture, urban design, and landscape architecture. However, just as it is an opportunity for the production of innovative ideas, each studio is also an innovation in its own right.

My studio teaching experience started through design workshops in 1994 and 1995. Andrew Herscher and I prepared and carried out two summer schools in Izola and Ljubljana: 1) Found Places: Archaeological Sites and Marginal City Spaces, and 2) Interpreting the Site: Archaeology, Architecture, City. The topics and methods of the workshops ranged from learning archaeological methods as an eye-opener, followed by archaeological deciphering of neglected and degraded urban areas in Ljubljana, the capital of Slovenia (which later developed into more thorough research on degraded urban areas), to proposals for representations of archaeological "found places" (which also further contributed to my doctoral studies in archaeology and architecture).

DOI: 10.4018/979-8-3693-2329-8.ch020

A year later, the workshop became a planning tool acknowledged by the Ministry of the Environment and Physical Planning of Republic of Slovenia, which has prepared a public invitation for co-financing Slovenian municipalities in carrying out urban design workshops and tenders (Ažman Momirski & Dimitrovska Andrews, 1997). Through this activity, the Physical Planning Office wished to facilitate solutions to important urban issues in Slovenian towns. The workshop, as a period of discussion and practical work in which participants share their knowledge and experience, also involved teachers and students at the University of Ljubljana's Faculty of Architecture. The scope of the design work expanded as the workshops established themselves as an opportunity for scholars and experts from Slovenia and abroad to work together on critical and multifaceted issues in contemporary architecture and urban planning. This has grown to provide an opportunity for active participation and involvement of the general public and the business community in the design process. The workshop did not involve citizens and residents on a large scale at the outset; the response of the business community has also been slow and cautious, but it was a new and challenging issue to add to the design teaching process. The workshop also offers completely new and unexpected ideas, and here the role of young people is irreplaceable: it is above all a program of continuous learning and an ideal combination of practice and research, based on relaxed, unencumbered vision-seeking and new ideas. However, the workshop can only achieve the best results if all of its stages are taken into account and if all those involved in the problem, including investors and the general public, are involved (Ažman Momirski, 2019).

Accordingly, the idea grew that workshops, which have been an extracurricular activity, can be used as a tool for curricular renovation and flexibility because they complement the design studio program. Based on these considerations, the Faculty of Architecture prepared the EU Tempus project Restructuring the Main Course in Architectural Education (coordinator: Lucija Ažman Momirski), the goal of which was to develop intensive short-term courses for improving the regular main studio course and its curriculum. In addition, the project involved developing undergraduate teaching methods at the Faculty of Architecture, including the development and adaptation of teaching aids and materials, and staff and student mobility. The problem addressed was the varying quality of the main architecture courses at the Faculty of Architecture because in many cases the supervisors in the studio course highlighted the personality of the supervisor (the supervisor's charisma) as the leading educational motivation for students. Through this funding, we introduced workshops as an obligatory course in the faculty curriculum, which occurred in 2001.

In the following period, workshops complemented the studio program. To update the current course, short-term courses regulate both the dynamics of needs of the built environment and professional expectations. The advantage of introducing workshops into design studio education is that the professional subject changes every year depending on the current events taking place in the surroundings and the profession, and, in comparison to the compulsory curriculum, this dynamic component of studying links students and practice. During the workshop, the students have to focus their thoughts, work, and results in a short period. This allows them to contemplate current events and also to assess both their individual capabilities and what they have learned through regular study and extending the intuitive and intellectual learning process.

Workshops are an opportunity to bring together scholars and professionals from Slovenia and abroad to address critical and complex problems in contemporary architecture and urban design. Their lectures address current technical, social, and cultural developments, and inform students of the latest professional issues. Consequently, they offer a new dimension of constant sharing of ideas related to design, and they extend the intuitive and intellectual learning process in which students transform their experiences into design. The short-term courses cover various topics, adding a range of architectural and urban tasks, including housing, public buildings, buildings and the environment, public space, city planning, and regional planning.

Workshops give a design studio the opportunity to position itself in the framework of all design studios at the faculty and elsewhere, and therefore the studio gains a permanent instrument for its own quality control. Such an approach substantially raises the standard of architectural education in design studios.

Through workshops, teachers and students in studios are encouraged and offered the opportunity for exchange. Workshops also offer students the opportunity to participate in international developments in their field of study and to have supervisors review their teaching methods and material. The presentation of outside views, issues, and solutions is a stimulus to education. These short-term courses are not tied to any particular year of the program; instead, they are attended by a mix of students from all years.

The main disadvantage of urban design workshops is that only by completing all phases of a workshop will participants have the best results from every perspective.

METHODOLOGICAL APPROACH OF THE DESIGN STUDIO: NO LIMITS TO THE DIVERSITY OF STUDIO TOPICS

In the design studio we introduce a different task each year (Design Studio Ažman, 2022). For example, during the COVID pandemic we focused on various new questions considering design that were never the case before—for example, How can the layout of a primary school be changed so that education can take place during COVID? What is the post-COVID architecture of healthcare facilities? Do the design and layout of housing for the more vulnerable and physically challenged need to change during an epidemic? What do development history models teach us, and can we replicate them? How adaptable are contemporary paradigms of sustainable construction? Do architectural and urban design neglect the sensitization of residual housing issues during epidemics?

After the COVID pandemic, we were freer to travel into the countryside, and we selected some locations for new design interventions there. The karst landscape has unique landforms and landscape features, and it is known for its caves and areas with extremely permeable rocks. Pre-Hellenistic Greek urban planning and architectural practice already combined the design of a consciously structured city and buildings and steep, terraced terrain into a synthesis of convincing spatial interventions (as for example in Priene, Turkey). Greek builders did not adopt archaic spatial approaches because of the topographical conditions at such sites. The central challenge of the seminar work was therefore to sharpen the sensitivity to the fundamental conditions of space, while being aware of contemporary design trends, themes, materials, geometries, requirements, and so on. In parallel, the diversity of the program encouraged innovation, bearing in mind that we live in a multicultural society; that is, a society of people of all ages, ethnicities, genders, sexual orientations, and religious beliefs.

Under more demanding site conditions, such as steep banks or the edge of the sea near the coast, the concept of stair architecture and the landscape also changes the design of its basic cell: the house or building. The architectural proposals included a variety of activities: a biological sea station, a hotel, an intergenerational center, a fire station, and other concepts.

We have challenged the students with the question of what will the world look like in 2084. Can we even predict how architecture and urban planning will change in this future time, and how new technologies will influence spatial design: drones, hyperloops, 3D printing, tokamak reactors, and so on? Drones will transport people and goods, and inspect and monitor construction sites and urban areas. They will operate autonomously and unmannedly, equipped with sensors and cameras for real-time surveying, 3D mapping, and thus rapid and accurate surveying of land for construction and urban planning. Urban planning will be transformed by hyperloop technology, a high-speed transport system. A network of sealed pipes with flows of people and goods will allow a much more efficient use of space. This will also be supported by new logistics technologies such as autonomous vehicles and robots. Energy efficiency and alternative energy sources are already key issues in modern times. Tokamak reactors as part of nuclear fusion technologies could provide a clean and reliable source of energy in the future, not only for powering autonomous vehicles and drones but also for more sustainable building designs. 3D printing of buildings, structures, fillers, fixtures, and furniture will change the way we build and therefore design. Traditional building materials will be largely abandoned. Artificial intelligence will enable fast and accurate data processing, more efficient plans and spatial visions, and predictive analyses for the design of buildings.

A unique experience was a studio dealing with living on the Moon and in space. The topics and tasks of the studio were chosen in such a way that the students had to think unconventionally and from a different perspective during the planning process.

Moon and Space Studio Content

During the design studio, in which the students developed their concepts of architecture on the Moon and in space, students were exposed to the basics of extensive interdisciplinary work, which is impossible to cover within the confines of their studies with such a demanding starting point. Not only was it necessary to study reference material within architecture as a discipline, but it was also necessary to gain insight into the fundamental assumptions of life-support systems and to search in the hard sciences for what people experience in a virtually inanimate environment. Such a project in itself gives rise to initiatives for livelier and more curriculum-oriented cooperation between the various spheres of the university. The individual units—a greenhouse, a hospital, an observatory, dwellings, a solar power plant, a mining complex, and so on—create a new rethinking for real living on Earth's natural satellite and in space. Most of the projects are conceptually located at the Moon's south pole, where, in addition to relatively good solar irradiation, there are also thought to be some ice reserves. Almost every functional formation has its own autonomous living area. For living in orbit, the starting points of living, working, producing, and recreating on Earth that are taken for granted are completely transformed in the utterly different spatial and environmental conditions of the two locations. The project solutions are based on ergonomic, structural, technical, and material details.

Lunar Greenhouse

The lunar greenhouse (Figure 1) is a field of constantly moving units that either sink into the ground or allow specific vegetation to circulate according to the path of the Sun's rays. It is intended for basic food production, utilizing photosynthesis, and consequently an oxygen supply and crucial water metabolism. Many questions arise regarding the crops that the student highlighted in her plans as essential: tomatoes, cucumber, potatoes, lettuce, peppers, beans, peas, broccoli, cabbage, carrots, zucchini, pumpkins, garlic, onions, rice, wheat, corn, basil, oregano, rosemary, bay, thyme, parsley, apples, bananas, oranges, tangerines, grapes, cherries, lemons, peaches, and strawberries.

Beyond the Planetary Architecture

Figure 1. Lunar greenhouse

Lunar Hospital

The hospital is actually a narrower concept for a modular building (Figure 2) that provides all life-support functions and is not only a hospital. The modular structure makes it easy to add new wards as required, with the large, crisscrossing circular passageways at the edges of the building becoming giant windows that act like the observation dome on today's International Space Station (Figure 3).

Figure 2. Lunar hospital: Plans and sections

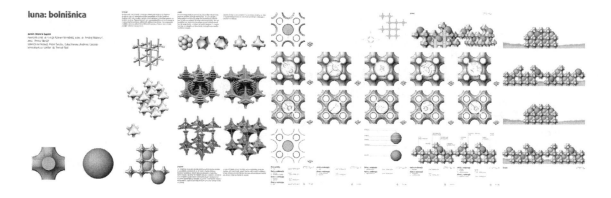

Figure 3. Lunar hospital: A view

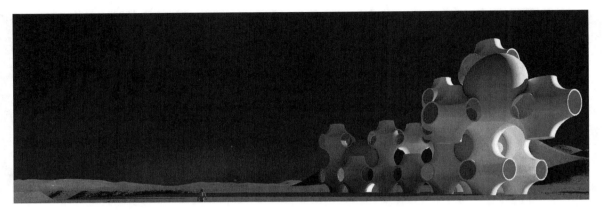

Lunar Mining Colony

This self-contained spatial hybrid of a helium-mining settlement combines residential space with production and warehousing facilities (Figure 4). Several separate diggers of regolith, a weathered overburden of rock, can be combined in different formations to comb the surface together.

Figure 4. Lunar mining colony

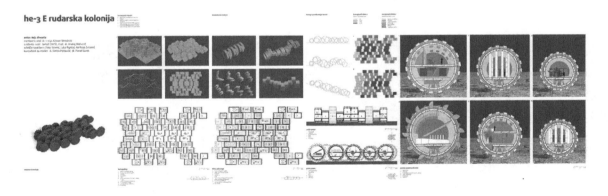

Lunar Eye

The lunar eye places the main emphasis on the large telescope systems at the top of the luster tower (Figure 5). The lower part of the building is surrounded by a protective ice mantle.

Figure 5. Lunar eye

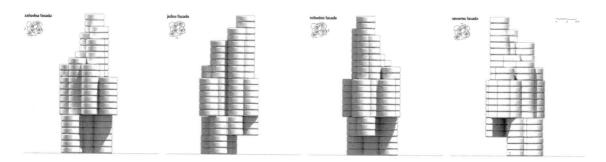

Lunar Solar Power Plant

The solar power plant consists of heliostats and solar cells arranged in concentric circles, which move along their vertical axes according to the best use of solar energy (Figure 6). Above them, obliquely, a large light collector dominates the extended arm of the building's perimeter, giving it the appearance of a giant sundial. The entire structure (Figure 7) moves about three meters a day, starting a new cycle every lunar month; that is, every 28 days.

Figure 6. Lunar solar power plant

Figure 7. Lunar solar power plant: Plans and sections

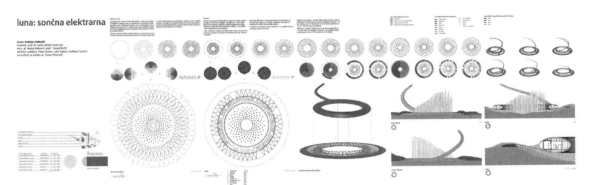

Space Power Plant

This small solar power plant is placed in the stratosphere to generate electricity (Figure 8). A solar power plant in space can be an inexhaustible source of clean energy for humans, so that the sun's energy is converted into electricity, and microwave or laser beams are used to transmit it to earth. The photovoltaic cells are suspended in fan-shaped wings attached to a spiral backbone, through which the supply and servicing takes place.

Figure 8. Space power plant

Multimedia Space Centre

The interactive multimedia center (Figure 9) allows visitors to experience presentations in zero gravity. The interactive module, using various technology and techniques, allows users to experience the transformation of a visual message into music and the change of the shape of the space: even a film score is translated into sound and movement, which the visitor experiences in a space adapted for this purpose.

Figure 9. Multimedia space centre

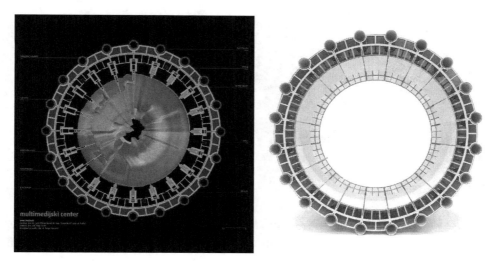

Space Debris Bin

Debris in space is becoming a pressing problem, and it can damage spacecraft and satellites when they collide. There are currently more than half a million pieces of potentially harmful debris orbiting the Earth. Space agencies usually return the debris to Earth on special missions and at high cost. A space garbage truck is a space structure that is able to grab the debris orbiting the Earth in several ways and process it at the same time. In doing so, the object adapts to the size of the garbage being processed, expanding and contracting as it does so (Figure 10). The space debris bin also uses or recycles some of the captured debris for its own growth.

Figure 10. Space debris bin

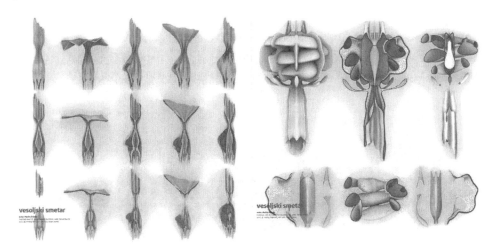

Space Greenhouse

During a prolonged stay in space, one of the most important questions is how to provide fresh and healthy food for the inhabitants of the space station. The space greenhouse is a garden in orbit that provides room for residents to cultivate and study plant growth in zero gravity. The spiral-shaped structure is also a place of socialization and an interaction area, which improves residents' quality of life (Figure 11).

Figure 11. Space greenhouse

DISCUSSION

The methodology of the studio work is based on getting to know the selected space, starting with an explicit brainstorming phase that brings many ideas to the table before settling on one, discussing the problems identified in space and in the program, analyzing known solutions to the problems identified, considering sectoral data, developing variant solutions, and presenting the selected project. When it is finished, it starts all over again: the design studio participants are joined by students and supervisors that were previously not part of the studio. Using new methods (film, photography, texts, and models) and through discussion, they evaluate the original solutions, which are supplemented by the newcomers.

The design of living spaces in space and on the Moon still has to put people at the center, while presenting possibilities for human coexistence in new environments and demonstrating whether and how architectural principles and strategies need to be changed when applying design to the extreme conditions of the Moon and space. Such concepts can present new paths for the future of design in general.

An architectural design is a synthesis and not the natural sum of all the requirements it is supposed to fulfill. A well-thought-out design is even more than that, and this is precisely why it can be surprising and significant. It is, therefore, necessary for students to articulate their views and perceptions, and their visions of the directions towards resilient and inspiring design and healthy environments. This means that the design process is not always linear or formulaic, but rather requires a creative integration of various factors. A design's ability to withstand challenges and inspire others is closely linked to the creative and personal contributions of those involved in the design process. It encourages students to bring their unique individuality and vision to the design process, which can help create a more impactful and meaningful outcome.

CONCLUSION

Alongside design visions, values play an essential role in design. Incorporating cultural and intellectual diversity to improve the quality of students' ideas and the adaptability of creative processes in design studios aims to increase students' sense of responsibility in their design actions. Exploring values promotes continuous learning for both students and supervisors, who share what they have learned with themselves, their educational institutions, and the wider community.

REFERENCES

Ažman Momirski, L. (2019). Urban design workshops in the education curriculum: advantages and disadvantages. In *IOP conference series, Materials science and engineering,* Vol. 471, 1–9. *3rd World Multidisciplinary Civil Engineering, Architecture,Urban Planning Symposium (WMCAUS 2018).* IOP. 10.1088/1757-899X/471/10/102048

Ažman Momirski, L., & Dimitrovska Andrews, K. (1997). Urbanistične delavnice: orodje v prostorskem planiranju = Urban design workshops: a planning tool. *Urbani Izziv*, 30–31(30-31), 40–47, 121–125. 10.5379/urbani-izziv-1997-30-31-005

Compilation of References

. Asanowicz, A. (2004). Computer, Creativity and Unpredictability. *Digital Design Methods*, 350-354.

. Lu, H., Yang, G., Fei, N., Huo, Y., Lu, Z., Luo, P., & Ding, M. (2023). *VDT: General-purpose Video Diffusion Transformers via Mask Modeling.*

Abdelbaky, L., Elfiki, S., & Barakat, H. (2022). The Impact of Furniture Arrangement upon Experiential Learning in Architectural Design Studios, with Reference to Cairo, Egypt. *Civil Engineering and Architecture*, 10(7), 3028–3045. 10.13189/cea.2022.100718

Abdelhameed, W. A. (2017). Creativity in the initial phases of architectural design. *Open House International*, 42(1), 29–34. 10.1108/OHI-01-2017-B0005

Abdelmonem, M. G. (2014). Transcending boundaries of creativity: Active learning in the design studio. *International Journal of Architectural Engineering Technology*, 1(1), 38–49. 10.15377/2409-9821.2014.01.01.5

Abioye, S. O., Oyedele, L. O., Akanbi, L., Ajayi, A., Delgado, J. M. D., Bilal, M., & Ahmed, A. (2021). Artificial intelligence in the construction industry: A review of present status, opportunities and future challenges. *Journal of Building Engineering*, 44, 103299. 10.1016/j.jobe.2021.103299

Abu Alatta, R. T., Momani, H. M., & Bataineh, A. M. (2023). The effect of online teaching on basic design studio during COVID-19: An application of the technology acceptance model. *Architectural Science Review*, 66(6), 417–432. 10.1080/00038628.2022.2153791

Achten, H. H. (2003). New design methods for computer aided architectural design methodology teaching. *International Journal of Architectural Computing*, 1(1), 72–91. 10.1260/147807703322467441

ACSA. (2018). *ACSA White Paper on Architectural Education Research and STEM*. Association Of Collegiate Schools Of Architecture, Washington, D.C.

Agrest, D. (2000). Representation as Articulation between Theory and Practice. In Stan Allen, *Practice: Architecture, Technique and Representation* (pp. 163-178). Routledge.

Ahn, J. N., Hu, D., & Vega, M. (2019). "Do as I do, not as I say": Using social learning theory to unpack the impact of role models on students' outcomes in education. *Soc Personal Psychol Compass*. 10.1111/spc3.12517

Ahn, J. N., Luna-Lucero, M., Lamnina, M., Nightingale, M., Novak, D., & Lin-Siegler, X. (2016). Motivating Students'. *Stem Learning Using Biographical Information, IJDL*, 7(1), 71–85.

Akalın, A. (2018). Architectural Design Education as a Context Related Mimetic Discipline, *Dicle University 1st International Architecture Symposium: From Environment to Space*. Dicle Üniversitesi.

Akcan, E. (1994). Sanatın ve mimarlığın göreli özerkliği / özgürlüğü üzerine. *Mimarlık*, 257, 21–22.

Akçayır, G., & Akçayır, M. (2018). The flipped classroom: A review of its advantages and challenges. *Computers & Education*, 126, 334–345. 10.1016/j.compedu.2018.07.021

Akdeniz, H., & Aksel, E. (1989). Güzel Sanatlar Fakültelerinde Temel Sanat Eğitimi Üzerine Düşünceler Ve Bir Bakış Açısı [Reflections on Basic Art Education in Fine Arts Faculties: A Perspective], *Güzel Sanatlar Fakültelerinde Temel Sanat Eğitimi Semineri*. Hacettepe Üniversitesi Güzel Sanatlar Fakültesi Yayınları. Ankara.

Akoury, C. (2020). Apprehending the creative process through drawing in the foundation design studio. *International Journal of Art & Design Education*, 39(1), 113–125. 10.1111/jade.12223

Aksu, A. (2016). "Dur Bir Mola Ver": Dünyayı Değiştirmeye İhtiyacın Var. In *Mimarlık Eğitiminde Pedagoji ve Pratik Arasında Var Olmak Symposium Book* (pp. 1-10). İstanbul Kemerburgaz University, İstanbul.

Aksu, A., Küçük, İ., & Çağlar, N. (2011). *Mimari Tasarım Eğitimi Söylemleri 2: Bütünleşme*. In YTU 2th National Symposium, İstanbul.

Aksu, A., & Yılmaz, İ. (2019). *Mimarlığın İcadı Mimarın İnşası, Mimarlık Okullarında Tasarım Stüdyoları: Farklı Denemeler*. Yem Yayın.

Al Maani, D., Alnusairat, S., & Al-Jokhadar, A. (2021). Transforming learning for architecture: Online design studio as the new norm for crisis adaptation under COVID-19. *Open House International*, 46(3), 348–358. 10.1108/OHI-01-2021-0016

Alexander, C. (2018). *A pattern language: towns, buildings, construction*. Oxford university press.

Alkin, M. C., & Christie, C. A. (2002). Teaching Evaluation, The Use Of Role-Play in Teaching Evaluation. *The American Journal of Evaluation*, 23(2), 209–218. 10.1177/109821400202300210

Alnusairat, S., Al Maani, D., & Al-Jokhadar, A. (2021). Architecture students' satisfaction with and perceptions of online design studios during COVID-19 lockdown: The case of Jordan universities. *Archnet-IJAR: International Journal of Architectural Research*, 15(1), 219–236. 10.1108/ARCH-09-2020-0195

Altomonte, S., Cadima, P., Yannas, S., De Herde, A., Riemer, H., Cangelli, E., Lopez De Asiain, M., & Horvath, S. (2012) *Educate!Sustainable Environmental Design in Architectural Education and Practice*. Proceedings of PLEA2012 - 28th Conference. Research Gate.

Alvarez, B. (2012). Flipping the classroom: Homework in class, lessons at home. *Education Digest*, 77(8), 18.

Alyn Griffiths (2014). *Hospital for rural chinese community fetureas a ramp that slopes up to the roof*. Dezeen. https://www.dezeen.com/2014/09/29/angdong-rural-hospital-rural-urban-framework-china/

Al-Zahrani, A. M. (2015). From passive to active: The impact of the flipped classroom through social learning platforms on higher education students' creative thinking. *British Journal of Educational Technology*, 46(6), 1133–1148. 10.1111/bjet.12353

American Institute of Architects (2006). Ecological Literacy in Architecture Education. *COTE Report and Proposal*. AIA.

Apaydın, Y. (1998). In *İlmihal: İman ve İbadetler* (v.1). İstanbul: DİVANTAŞ, 273.

Arendt, H. (1961). *Between past and present*. The Viking Press.

Arkiv. Katılımcı, Cami Mimarisi Üzerine Fikir Projesi Yarışması. Internet Arkiv. https://www.arkiv.com.tr/proje/katilimci-cami-mimarisi-uzerine-fikir-yarismasi-projesi/2380?lang=en, Last accesed: 03.08.2022.

Asanowicz, A. (1996). Teaching and learning-full brainwash. In *Education for Practice-14th Conference on Education in Computer Aided Architectural Design in Europe (eCAADe)* (pp. 51-54). Lund: eCAADe. 10.52842/conf.ecaade.1996.051

Asanowicz, A. (2008). How to Find an Idea?-Computer Aided Creativity. In *Architecture in Computro [26th ECAADe Conference Proceedings]* (pp. 735-742). Research Gate.

Compilation of References

As, I., Pal, S., & Basu, P. (2018). Artificial intelligence in architecture: Generating conceptual design via deep learning. *International Journal of Architectural Computing*, 16(4), 306–327. 10.1177/1478077118800982

Atölye Z ile 'Beden ve Mekan Halleri'. (2021, May 21). Arkitera. https://www.arkitera.com/haber/atolye-z-ile-beden-ve-mekan-halleri/

Atölye Z ile 'Çağdaş Mimarinin Kodları' Dizisi. (2020, June 20). Arkitera. https://www.arkitera.com/haber/atolye-z-ile-cagdas-mimarinin-kodlari-dizisi/

Attoe, W., & Mugerauer, R. (1991). Excellent studio teaching in architecture. *Studies in Higher Education*, 16(1), 41–50. 10.1080/03075079112331383081

Aybek Özdemir, D., & Akalın, A. (2024). Mimetic Teaching Strategy in Design Education: Relationship Between Students' Learning Style and Creativity. *DEPARCH Journal of Design Planning and Aesthetics Research*, 3(1), 24–55. 10.55755/DepArch.2024.26

Aycı, H. & İlerisoy, Z.Y. (2018). Mimarlık Eğitimi Meslek Pratiğinin Simulasyonu Olmalı mı?: Akademi, Büro ve Şantiye Alanlarında Yarı Yapılandırılmış Mülakat Yöntemi ile Bir Değerlendirme. *Online Journal of Art and Design, 6*(5).

Aydemir, Z. A., & Jacoby, S. (2020). *Design research and a shift in architectural education and practice*. EAAE-ARCC International Conference & 2nd VIBRArch: The architect and the city, Valencia, Spain.

Aydınlı, S. & Kürtüncü, B. (2018). Paradigm shift in studio culture. *ITU A/Z, 15*(3), 91-108.

Aydınlı, S. (2007). "Awareness" as a Design Paradigm. In Gulsun Saglamer (Ed.), *The Design Studio: A Black Hole* (pp. 113-136). Yem.

Aydınlı, S. (2016). Tasarım Eğitiminde Yapılandırıcı Paradigma: 'Öğrenmeyi Öğrenme'. [Constructivist Paradigm in Design Education: 'Learning to Learn']. *Tasarım + Kuram, 11*(20), 1-18.

Aydınlı, S. (1993). *Mimarlıkta Estetik Değerler*. İTÜ Mimarlık Fakültesi Baskı Atölyesi.

Azamfirei, L. (2016). Knowledge Is Power. *The Journal of Critical Care Medicine, 2*(2), 65-66. 10.1515/jccm-2016-0014

Ažman Momirski, L. (2019). Urban design workshops in the education curriculum: advantages and disadvantages. In *IOP conference series, Materials science and engineering,* Vol. 471, 1–9. *3rd World Multidisciplinary Civil Engineering, Architecture, Urban Planning Symposium (WMCAUS 2018)*. IOP. 10.1088/1757-899X/471/10/102048

Ažman Momirski, L., & Dimitrovska Andrews, K. (1997). Urbanistične delavnice: orodje v prostorskem planiranju = Urban design workshops: a planning tool. *Urbani Izziv*, 30–31(30-31), 40–47, 121–125. 10.5379/urbani-izziv-1997-30-31-005

Azzurra Ferraris (2019). *Fantastic Greenhouse Challenge*. URL-6: https://www.cgboost.com/challenges/fantastic-greenhouse-challenge, Last accesed: 03.08.2022.

Bal, B. (2017). Gordon Matta-Clark'ın kadavralarında mimari tanı[mlama]lar. *XXI, 2*. https://xxi.com.tr/i/gordon-matta-clarkin-kadavralarinda-mimari-tanimlamalar

Bal, W., Czałczyńska-Podolska, M., & Nieścior, M. (2023). The Importance of Architectural Icons of the City of Szczecin for the Transformation of Landscape Identity and Promotion of the City's Image. *Sustainability (Basel)*, 15(11), 8648. 10.3390/su15118648

Barkley, E. F., & Major, C. H. (2020). *Student engagement techniques: A handbook for college faculty*. John Wiley & Sons.

Barrett, B. (2018). When a country's towns and villages face extinction. *The Conversations*. https://theconversation.com/when-a-countrys-towns-and-villages-face-extinction-88398

Bashier, F. (2014). Reflections on architectural design education: The return of rationalism in the studio. *Frontiers of Architectural Research*, 3(4), 424–430. 10.1016/j.foar.2014.08.004

Baudrillard, J. (1998). *The Consumer society*. SAGE Publications.

Bauman, Z. (1988). *Freedom*. University of Minnesota Press.

Bayazıt, N. (1994). *Endüstri Ürünlerinde ve Mimarlıkta Tasarlama Metodlarına Giriş*. Literatür Yayıncılık.

Bayazıt, N. (2004). *Endüstriyel Tasarımcılar için Tasarlama Kuramları ve Metotları*. BirsenYayınevi.

Baydar, G. (2012). *Osmanlı-Türk Mimarlarında Mesleklesme*. Mimarlar Odası Yayınları.

Belluigi, D. Z. (2011). Intentionality in a creative art curriculum. *Journal of Aesthetic Education*, 45(1), 18–36. 10.5406/jaesteduc.45.1.0018

Benjamin, W. (1983). *Charles Baudelaire: A Lyric Poet in the Era of High Capitalism* (Zohn, H., Trans.). Routledge.

Benton, M. (2007). Reading Biograph. *Journal of Aesthetic Education*, 41(3), 77–88. 10.2307/25160239

Berger, J. (1972). *Ways of Seeing*. Penguin.

Bergström, A. (2014). Architecture and the rise of practice in education. *Architectural Theory Review*, 19(1), 10–21. 10.1080/13264826.2014.894604

Berrett, D. (2012). How 'flipping the classroom can improve the traditional lecture. *The Chronicle of Higher Education*, 12(19), 1–3.

Bhagat, K. K., Chang, C.-N., & Chang, C.-Y. (2016). The impact of the flipped classroom on mathematics concept learning in high school. *Journal of Educational Technology & Society*, 19(3), 134–142.

Białecki, T. (1992). *Historia Szczecina*.

Bickford, D. J., & Wright, D. J. (2006). Community: The Hidden Context for Learning. In Oblinger, D. G. (Ed.), *Learning Spaces*. Educause. https://www.educause.edu/ir/library/pdf/pub7102.Pdf

Biggs, J. (1999). What the student does: Teaching for enhanced learning. *Higher Education Research & Development*, 18(2), 57–75. 10.1080/0729436990180105

Billings, K., & Akkach, S. (1992). A study of ideologies and methods in contemporary architectural design teaching: Part 1: Ideology. *Design Studies*, 13(4), 431–450. 10.1016/0142-694X(92)90171-6

Bösner, S., Pickert, J., & Stibane, T. (2015). Teaching differential diagnosis in primary care using an inverted classroom approach: Student satisfaction and gain in skills and knowledge. *BMC Medical Education*, 15(1), 1–7. 10.1186/s12909-015-0346-x25879809

Boucharenc, C. G. (2006). Research on basic design education: An international survey. *International Journal of Technology and Design Education*, 16(1), 1–30. 10.1007/s10798-005-2110-8

Boyacıoğlu, E. (2021). THEME: 'Distance' Learning: Online Possibilities, Limits, Challenges [1] Interviews. *Arredamento Mmarlık*, 346, 57–59.

Boym, S. (2017). *The Off-Modern*. Bloomsbury Publishing. 10.5040/9781501328961

Bozdoğan, S. (2008). *Architecture Profession in Pre-Modern/Pioneer Chicago: 1871-1909, Vienna-Chicago: Metropolis and Architecture*. Bilgi University Press.

Compilation of References

Brook, I. (2001). In Warwick, F. (Ed.), *Can 'Spirit of Place' Be a Guide to Ethical Building? Ethics and the Built Environment* (pp. 139–151). Routledge.

Burkett, I. (2012). *An Introduction to Co-Design.* Knode: Sydney. https://www.yacwa.org.au/wp-content/uploads/2016/09/An-Introduction-to-Co-Design-by-Ingrid-Burkett.pdf

Çağlar, N., & Uludağ, Z. (2004). Vertically structured design studio: Developing critical concepts on conceptualization and organization of social space in urban context. In S. Constantin & M. Voyatzaki (Eds.), *Monitoring architectural design education in European schools of architecture* (pp. 211-223). EAAE Transactions on Architectural Education Series.

Çağlar, N., & Aksu, A. (2017). *Tenekeden Mimarlık.* Şevki Vanlı Yayınları.

Çağlar, N., & Aksu, A. (2021). *Mimarlığı Öğrenmek, Yapmak, Yazmak Üzerine Spekülasyonlar, 1919-2019 Samsun Yüzüncü Yıl Mimarlık Konuşmaları.* TMMOB Mimarlar Odası Samsun Şubesi Yayınları.

Can, A. (2017). Gordon Matta-Clark. *Manifold, 8.* https://manifold.press/gordon-matta-clark

Cangelli, E. (2018). Work on the informal city. Restoring the environmental balance of cities from their outskirts. *Journal of TECHNE vol. 01 (Special Issue),* 150-157. FU Press. https://oaj.fupress.net/index.php/techne/article/view/5098/5098

Cangelli, E., Arbizzani, E., Daglio, L., Baratta, A., Ottone, F., & Radogna, D. (2021). *Architettura e Tecnologia per l'Abitare. Upcycling degli edifici ERP di Tor Bella Monaca a Roma.* Santarcangelo di Romagna, Maggioli Editore.

Cansever, T. (2010). *Kubbeyi Yere Koymamak. İstanbul:Timaş Yayınları, 17.*

Casakin, H. (2004). Assessing the use of metaphors in the design process. *Environment and Planning. B, Planning & Design, 33*(2), 253–268. 10.1068/b3196

Casakin, H., & Goldschmidt, G. (1999). Expertise and the use of visual analogy: Implications for design education. *Design Studies, 20*(2), 153–175. 10.1016/S0142-694X(98)00032-5

Casakin, H., & Wodehouse, A. (2021). A systematic review of design creativity in the architectural design studio. *Buildings, 11*(1), 31. 10.3390/buildings11010031

Cennamo, K. S. (2016). What is studio? In *Studio Teaching in Higher Education* (pp. 260–271). Routledge.

Ceylan, S., Şahin, P. et al. (2024). The contribution of digital tools to architectural design studio: A case study. *Ain Shams Engineering Journal.*

Ceylan, S., Şahin, P., Seçmen, S., Somer, M. E., & Süher, K. H. (2021). An evaluation of online architectural design studios during COVID-19 outbreak. *Archnet-IJAR: International Journal of Architectural Research, 15*(1), 203–218. 10.1108/ARCH-10-2020-0230

Ching, F. (2011). *İç Mekan Tasarımı* (Çev: B. Elçioğlu),Yem Yayınevi, İstanbul.

Christian Richters (2010). *Roosendaal Pavilion.* URL-2: https://www.e-architect.com/holland/roosendaal-pavilion, Last accesed: 03.08.2022.

Christopher, M. J. L. (2015). Global, regional, and national disability-adjusted life years (DALYs) for 306 diseases and injuries and healthy life expectancy (HALE) for 188 countries, 1990-2013: quantifying the epidemiological transition. *The Lancet.* https://www.thelancet.com/journals/lancet/article/PIIS0140-6736(15)61340-X/fulltext

Christopher, J. J. (1970). *Design Methods; seeds of human futures.* John Wiley and Sons.

Ciravoğlu, A. (2014). Notes on architectural education: An experimental approach to design studio. *Procedia: Social and Behavioral Sciences, 152,* 7–12. 10.1016/j.sbspro.2014.09.146

Clough, G. (2004). *The Engineer of 2020: Visions of Engineering in the New Century*. National Academy of Engineering Washington. The National Academies Press.

Connell, E. (1997). *Teaching Intuition: Ways of Knowing for Begining Design Students*, the 14th Conference on the Begining Design Students, Pittsburgh, Pennsylvania, April 3-6.

Coorey, J. (2016). Active learning methods and technology: Strategies for design education. *International Journal of Art & Design Education*, 35(3), 337–347. 10.1111/jade.12112

Costa, E. N. P., & Sánchez, J. (2022). Flipped classroom for teaching structures in architecture courses. In *Structures and Architecture A Viable Urban Perspective?* (pp. 1011–1017). CRC Press. 10.1201/9781003023555-121

Coyne, R., Lee, J., & Petrova, D. (2017). Re-visiting the flipped classroom in a design context. *Journal of Learning Design*, 10(2), 1. 10.5204/jld.v10i2.281

Coyne, R., Snodgrass, A., & Martin, D. (1994). Metaphors in the Design Studio. *Journal of Architectural Education*, 48(2), 113–125. 10.1080/10464883.1994.10734630

Croce, B. (2017). *Aesthetic: As science of expression and general linguistic*. Routledge.

Crowther, P. (2013). Understanding the signature pedagogy of the design studio and the opportunities for its technological enhancement. *Journal of Learning Design*, 6(3), 18–28. 10.5204/jld.v6i3.155

Czałczyńska-Podolska, M., & Sochacka-Sutkowska, E. (2016). *Landscape values of the embankment of the Odra River in Szczecin and the degree of their use for building the city's identity*. Space & Form.

Czarnecki, B., & Chodorowski, M. P. (2021). Urban Environment during Post-War Reconstruction: Architectural Dominants and Nodal Points as Measures of Changes in an Urban Landscape. *Land (Basel)*, 10(10), 1083. 10.3390/land10101083

Dash, B., & Sharma, P. (2022). Role of artificial intelligence in smart cities for information gathering and dissemination (a review). *Academic Journal of Research and Scientific Publishing, 4*(39).

David Pereira (2011). *More Photographs of Champalimaud Centre for the Unknown*. URL-11: https://www.archdaily.com/147761/more-photographs-of-champalimaud-centre-for-the-unknown-charles-correa-associates, Last accesed: 03.08.2022.

de Graaff, E., & Kolmos, A. (2003). Characteristics of problem-based learning. *International Journal of Engineering Education*, 19(5), 657–662.

De Graaf, R. (2020). Padroni dell'Universo. *Journal of Domus*, 1042, 9–13.

Debrah, C., Chan, A. P., & Darko, A. (2022). Artificial intelligence in green building. *Automation in Construction*, 137, 104192. 10.1016/j.autcon.2022.104192

Dedekargınoğlu, C., Kutluoğlu, O., & Şumnu, U. (2023). *Ankara Palas'ın Merdivenleri*. Çizgilerle Modern Türkiye Mimarlığı Serisi, Karakarga Yayınları.

Deleuze, G., & Parnet, C. (2008). The Actual and the Virtual. In *Dialogues* (pp. 177–185). Flammarion.

Deleuze, G. (1994). *Difference and Repetition, Trans*. Columbia University Press.

Deleuze, G. (2001). *Empiricism and Subjectivity*. Columbia University Press.

Derya Gursel (2012). 3. Ödül, Halide Edip Adıvar Külliyesi Ulusal Mimari Proje Yarışması. URL-8: https://www.arkitera.com/proje/3-odul-halide-edip-adivar-kulliyesi-ulusal-mimari-proje-yarismasi/, Last accesed: 03.08.2022.

Dewey, J. (1958). *Art As Experience*. Capricorn Books, G. P. Putnam's Sons.

Compilation of References

Dewey, J. (1963). *Experience and education*. Collier Books.

Dewey, J. (1986). Experience and Education. *The Educational Forum*, 50(3), 241–252. 10.1080/00131728609335764

Distance Studio Consultant (2014). *Gymnasium*. URL-19: https://www.behance.net/gallery/69481259/Gymnasium, Last accesed: 03.08.2022.

Duniewicz, A., & Magdziak, M. (2022). Typology of Tactile Architectural Drawings Accessible for Blind and Partially Sighted People. *Sustainability (Basel)*, 14(13), 7847. 10.3390/su14137847

Dutton, T. A. (1987). Design and Studio Pedagogy. *Journal of Architectural Education*, 41(1), 16–25. 10.1080/10464883.1987.10758461

Edelson, D. C., Pea, R. D., & Gomez, L. (1996). Constructivism in the Collaboratory. In *Constructivist Learning Environments: Case Studies in Instructional Design* (pp. 151–164). Educational Technology Publications Inc.

EDUCATE Project Partners. (2012) *Sustainable Architectural Education*. (White Paper). EDUCATE Press/University of Nottingham.

Elrayies, G. M. (2017). Flipped Learning as a Paradigm Shift in Architectural Education. *International Education Studies*, 10(1), 93–108. 10.5539/ies.v10n1p93

Enomoto, K., Warner, R., & Claus Nygaard, C. (2022). *Active learning in higher education: Student engagement and deeper learning outcomes*. Libri Publishing Ltd.

Epstein, D. C., Jain, I., Wang, O., & Zhang, R. (2023). Online detection of ai-generated images. In *Proceedings of the IEEE/CVF International Conference on Computer Vision* (pp. 382-392). IEEE.

Erkök, F., Eren, C., Uz Sönmez, F., & Aydınlı, S. (2005). A paradigm shift in the first-year design education. *ITU A|Z*, 2(1/2), 62-78.

Ersine Masatlıoğlu C. S. and Balaban, Ö. C. (2024). Reflective thinking and self-assessment: A model for the architectural design studio. *Journal of Design for Resilience in Architecture and Planning, 5*.

Eşmeli, İ. (2018). Dinlerde mabed-ibadet ilişkisi (yahudilik örneği). *Pamukkale Üniversitesi İlahiyat Fakültesi Dergisi*, 6(11), 24–43.

European Commission. (2020). EU Recovery Instrument Next Generation EU. EC. https://eur-lex.europa.eu/EN/legal-content/summary/eu-recovery-instrument-nextgenerationeu.html

Farrelly, L. (2011). *Mimarlığın Temelleri* (Çev. Neslihan Şık). Literatür Yayınları, Akademik Temeller Dizisi 01, İstanbul.

Filiz, S. (2010). *Konut Tasarımına Yönelik Sürdürülebilirlik ve Teknoloji Bağlamında Bir Gelecek Tahmin Modeli*. Doctoral Thesis, Istanbul Technical University Graduate School.

Fross, K., Winnicka-Jasłowska, D., Gumińska, A., Masły, D., & Sitek, M. (2015). Use of qualitative research in architectural design and evaluation of the built environment. *Procedia Manufacturing*, 3, 1625–1632. 10.1016/j.promfg.2015.07.453

Galiana, M., & Seguí, L. (2016). Implementing flipped classroom in the School of Architecture. ICERI2016 Proceedings, Galway, L. P., Corbett, K. K., Takaro, T. K., Tairyan, K., & Frank, E. (2014). A novel integration of online and flipped classroom instructional models in public health higher education. *BMC Medical Education*, 14, 1–9.

Gallardo Architects Design Firm (2015). *Beijing National Stadium*. URL-4: http://gallardoarchitects.com/beijing-national-stadium/, Last accesed: 03.08.2022.

George, B. H., & Walker, A. (2017). Social learning in a distributed environment: Lessons learned from online design education. *Educational Media and Technology Yearbook*, 40, 53–66. 10.1007/978-3-319-45001-8_4

Glasser, D. E. Reflections on Architectural Education. *Journal of Architectural Education, 53*(4).

Goldschmidt, G., Hochman, H., & Dafni, I. (2010). The design studio "crit" teacher-student communication. *Artificial Intelligence for Engineering Design, Analysis and Manufacturing*, 24(3), 285–302. 10.1017/S089006041000020X

Gołębiewski, J. I. (2018). Perspektywy rewitalizacji Międzyodrza w Szczecinie przy zastosowaniu tymczasowych interwencji przestrzennych, Teka Zachodniopomorska 5/2018, Szczecin.

Gómez Puente, S. M., Eijck, M. v., & Jochems, W. (2013). Empirical Validation of Characteristics of Design-Based Learning in Higher Education. *International Journal of Engineering Education*, 29(2), 491–503.

González-Gómez, D., Jeong, J. S., Airado Rodríguez, D., & Cañada-Cañada, F. (2016). Performance and perception in the flipped learning model: An initial approach to evaluate the effectiveness of a new teaching methodology in a general science classroom. *Journal of Science Education and Technology*, 25(3), 450–459. 10.1007/s10956-016-9605-9

Graham, E. M. (2003). *Studio Design Critique: Student and Faculty Expectations and Reality.* [Doctoral dissertation. Louisiana State University]. Electronic Thesis & Dissertation collection.

Gray, J. A., & DiLoreto, M. (2016). The effects of student engagement, student satisfaction, and perceived learning in online learning environments. *The International Journal of Educational Leadership Preparation*, 11(1), n1.

Gren, L. (2020). A flipped classroom approach to teaching empirical software engineering. *IEEE Transactions on Education*, 63(3), 155–163. 10.1109/TE.2019.2960264

Grennan, S., & Lus Arana, L. M. (2024). Comics in the design studio. On the use of graphic narrative as a tool to represent, narrate, and rethink architectural space. In Colonnese, F., Grancho, N., & Schaevebeke, R. (Eds.), *Approaches to Drawing in Architecture and Urban Design*. Cambridge Scholars.

Griffin, A. (2020). *The Rise of Academic Architectural Education: The Origins and Enduring Influence of the Académie d'Architecture*. Routledge, Newyork.

Gross, M. D., & Do, E. Y. (1997). The design studio approach: Learning design in architecture education. In J. Kolodner & M. Guzdial. (Eds.), *Design Education Workshop: EduTech/NSF, College of Computing* (pp. 208-221). London: Brill.

Güngör, C., & Özkan Üstün, G. (2022). *The Importance of Working with Architectural Mock-Ups in Architectural Project Atelier Lessons: Comparison of Applications During and After the Pandemic Period*. 7th International "Başkent" Congress on Physical, Social, and Health Sciences, Ankara, Turkey

Hacihasanoglu, O. (2019). Architectural Design Studio Culture. *Journal of Design Studio*, 1(1), 5–15.

Hancock, J. E. (1987). Continuity, Change and the "Edges" of Architecture. *Journal of Architectural Education*, 40(2), 26–28.

Harapan, A., Indriani, D., Rizkiya, N. F., & Azbi, R. M. (2021). Artificial Intelligence in Architectural Design. [INJUDES]. *International Journal of Design*, 1(1), 1–6. 10.34010/injudes.v1i1.4824

Hasol, D. (2004). *Mimarlık ve Teknoloji*. Cumhuriyet Gazetesi Mimarlık Eki, Web Sitesi. https://xxi.com.tr/i/teknoloji-etkisi

Hawkes, D. (1995). The Centre and the Periphery: Some reflections on the nature and conduct of architectural research. Arq-architectural. *Research Quarterly*, 1(01), 8–11. 10.1017/S1359135500000051

He, K., Zhang, X., Ren, S., & Sun, J. (2016). Deep residual learning for image recognition. In *Proceedings of the IEEE conference on computer vision and pattern recognition* (pp. 770-778). IEEE.

Hettithanthri, U., & Hansen, P. (2022). Design Studio Practice in the Context of Architectural Education: A Narrative Literature Review. *International Journal of Technology and Design Education*, 32(4), 2343–2364. 10.1007/s10798-021-09694-2

Heynen, H. (1999). *Architecture and modernity; a critique*. Massachusetts Institute of Technology Press.

Higher Education Widening Participation. (n.d.). Department for the Economy online. https://www.economy-ni.gov.uk/articles/higher-education-widening-participation

Homeworlddesign. *House with Panoramic Ocean View in Okinawa*. URL-7: http://homeworlddesign.com/house-panoramic-ocean-view-okinawa-clair-archi-lab/, Last accesed: 03.08.2022.

Hou, H. T. (2011). A case study of online instructional collaborative discussion activities for problem-solving using situated scenarios: An examination of content and behavior cluster analysis. *Computers & Education*, 56(3), 712–719. 10.1016/j.compedu.2010.10.013

Huang, Y.-N., & Hong, Z.-R. (2016). The effects of a flipped English classroom intervention on students' information and communication technology and English reading comprehension. *Educational Technology Research and Development*, 64(2), 175–193. 10.1007/s11423-015-9412-7

Hyde, R. (2012). *Future Practice*. Routledge. 10.4324/9780203100226

Iavarone, A. H., & Birer, E. (2020). The concept of limits in architecture as an instructional tool for design education. *Journal of Design Studio*, 2(2), 111–130. 10.46474/jds.814390

Ibrahim, N. L. N., & Utaberta, N. (2012). Learning in Architecture Design Studio. *Procedia: Social and Behavioral Sciences*, 60, 30–35. 10.1016/j.sbspro.2012.09.342

IIDj. (n.d.). *DesignFactors*. Institute for Information Design Japan. https://www.designfactors.com/DesignAtCommunities

Ince, A. (2021). *Understanding contemporary contextualism: the relationship between designer approach and user perception in sancaklar mosque*. [Master Thesis, Gazi University, Ankara].

Internet Arkiv. (2012). *Katılımcı (Manço Mimarlık), Şişli Halide Edip Adıvar Külliyesi Ulusal Mimari Proje Yarışması*. Internet Arkiv. https://www.arkiv.com.tr/proje/katilimci-manco-mimarlik-sisli-halide-edip-adivar-kulliyesi-ulusal-mimari-proje-yarismasi/2386?lang=en,

Iranmanesh, A., & Onur, Z. (2021). Mandatory virtual design studio for all: Exploring the transformations of architectural education amidst the global pandemic. *International Journal of Art & Design Education*, 40(1), 1–17. 10.1111/jade.12350

Istek, C., & Schneider, A. (2020). *MURA - A Place for Design Practice: CO-Design Workshop 2019-2020*. Osaka University, CiNii Books. https://ci.nii.ac.jp/ncid/BC04874273?I=en

Itten, J. (1965). The foundation course at the Bauhaus. In Kepes, G. (Ed.), *Education of vision* (pp. 104–121). George Braziller, Inc.

Iwan Baan (2020). *Musee Atelier Audemars Piguet*. URL-5: https://www.archdaily.com/938537/atelier-audemars-piguet-museum-big, Last accesed: 03.08.2022.

Januszkiewicz, K., Paszkowska-Kaczmarek, N., Aduna Duguma, F., & Kowalski, K. G. (2020). *Living in the "Age of Humans". Envisioning CAD Architecture for the Challenges of the Anthropocene—Energy, Environment, and Well-Being*, MDPI Energies.

Johnson, D. W., & Johnson, T. R. (2018). Cooperative learning: The foundation for active learning. In Brito, S. M. (Ed.), *Active learning - beyond the future*. IntechOpen.

Jonassen, D. H. (1991). Objectivism Versus Constructivism: Do We Need a New Philosphical Paradigm? *Educational Technology Research and Development*, 39(3), 11–12. 10.1007/BF02296434

Jones, D., & Lotz, N. (2021). Design education: Teaching in crisis. *Design and Technology Education: An International Journal*, 26(4), 4–9.

Kalakoski, I., & Thorgrimsdottir, S. (2023). Learning from the secondary: Rethinking architectural conservation through 'barn architecture'. *Journal of Material Culture*, 28(2), 199–220. 10.1177/13591835221123953

Kaufman. (1965). The visual world today. In J. J. Hausman (Ed.), *Report of the commission on art education* (pp. 13-34). Washinigton, DC.: National Art Education Association.

Kember, D. (2009). Nurturing Generic Capabilities Through a Teaching and Learning Environment Which Provides Practise in Their Use. *Higher Education*, 57(1), 37–55. 10.1007/s10734-008-9131-7

Kemper, T. D. (1968). Reference groups, socialization and achievement. *American Sociological Review*, 33(1), 31–45. 10.2307/20922385644338

Khanova, J., Roth, M. T., Rodgers, J. E., & McLaughlin, J. E. (2015). Student experiences across multiple flipped courses in a single curriculum. *Medical Education*, 49(10), 1038–1048. 10.1111/medu.1280726383075

Khansari, M. G. (2015). Defining "Center and Edge" Concepts and Their Relationship with Durability and Dynamism in Architecture. *Armanshahr Architecture & Urban Development*, 8(14), 13–22.

Khogali, H. (2020). The effect of COVID-19 corona virus on sustainable teaching and learning in architecture engineering. *Modern Applied Science*, 14(8), 44–58. 10.5539/mas.v14n8p44

Kierkegaard, S., & Marino, G. (2013). *Fear and trembling and the sickness unto death*. Princeton University Press.

Kılıçaslan, H., & Kalaycı, P. D. (2021). A Joint Manifesto for Design Studios Based on Residuals and Experiences. *Periodica Polytechnica Architecture*, 52(1), 66–74. 10.3311/PPar.16758

Kim, N. (2006). A history of design theory in art education. *Journal of Aesthetic Education*, 40(2), 12–28. 10.2307/4140227

Kinsella, V. (2018). The use of activity theory as a methodology for developing creativity within the art and design classroom. *International Journal of Art & Design Education*, 37(3), 493–506. 10.1111/jade.12147

Kinzie, J. (2005). *Promoting Student Success: What Faculty Members Can Do*. (Occasional Paper No. 6). National Survey of Student Engagement.

Kirci, N. (2013). *20. Yüzyıl Mimarlığı, Nobel Yayın Dağıtım, Ankara, TR. 20th Century Architecture*. Nobel Publication.

Kłosek-Kozłowska, D. (2010). Strategiczny plan rewitalizacji Bilbao, gdzie architektura podąża za urbanistyką, [in:] Walczak B. M. (red.), *Modele rewitalizacji i ich zastosowanie w miastach dziedzictwa europejskiego*. Łódź.

Koester, R. J. (2006). Centers for regenerative studies: Graduate studio experiences in education for sustainable design. *Proceedings of PLEA2006 - The 23rd Conference on Passive and Low Energy Architecture*, (pp. 659-664). Research Gate.

Kolb, D. A. (1984). *Experiential Learning: Experience as the Source of Learning and Development*. Prentice-Hall.

Kolodner, J. L., Camp, P. J., Crismond, D., Fasse, B., Gray, J., Holbrook, J., Puntambekar, S., & Ryan, M. (2003). Problem-based learning meets case-based reasoning in the middle-school science classroom: Putting Learning by DesignTM into practice. *Journal of the Learning Sciences*, 12(4), 495–547. 10.1207/S15327809JLS1204_2

Compilation of References

Komarzyńska-Świeściak, E., Adams, B., & Thomas, L. (2021). Transition from physical design studio to emergency virtual design studio. Available teaching and learning methods and tools—A case study. *Buildings*, 11(7), 312. 10.3390/buildings11070312

Kömez-Dağlıoğlu, E., Pınar, E., Gursel-Dino, I., Yoncaci-Arslan, P., & Bas-Butuner, F. (2020). Teaching Architectural Design Studio Remotely: The Introduction to Architectural Design Course at METU. *Journal of Design Studio*, 2(2), 143–147. 10.46474/jds.820352

Köseoğlu, F., & Tümay, H. (2013). *Bilimde yapılandırıcı paradigma: Teoriden öğretim uygulamalarına*. Pegem Akademi Yayınları.

Kotla, R. (2008). *Rozwój techniczny i przestrzenny zespołu portowego Szczecin-Świnoujście na tle stosunków handlowych*.

Kregor, J. (2015). *Program music*. Cambridge University Press. 10.1017/CBO9781139506397

Kruglyk, V., Bukreiev, D., Chornyi, P., Kupchak, E., & Sender, A. (2020). Discord platform as an online learning environment for emergencies. *Ukrainian Journal of Educational Studies and Information Technology*, 8(2), 13–28. 10.32919/uesit.2020.02.02

Küçük, İ., & Aksu, A. (2023). Rethinking the Pedagogical Fiction of the Architectural Design Studio. Periodica Polytechnica. *Architecture (Washington, D.C.)*, 1–10.

Kuhn, S. (2001). Learning from the architecture studio: Implications for project-based pedagogy. *International Journal of Engineering Education*, 17(4/5), 349–352.

Kuloğlu, N. (2014). Mevcut Çevrede Tasarım: Stüdyo Deneyimleri. Mimari Güncellemeler, Şengül Öymen Gür (Editör), Nobel Yayın Dağıtım, İstanbul,.

Kurokawa, K. (1998). *From machine age to the age of life*. Book Art Ltd.

Ladousse, G. P. (1987). *Role-play*. Oxford University Press.

Lai, C.-L., & Hwang, G.-J. (2016). A self-regulated flipped classroom approach to improving students' learning performance in a mathematics course. *Computers & Education*, 100, 126–140. 10.1016/j.compedu.2016.05.006

Lave, J., & Wenger, E. (1991). *Situated Learning: Legitimate Peripheral Participation*. Cambridge University Press. 10.1017/CBO9780511815355

Lawson, B. (1990). *How Designers Think, The Design Process Demystified*. The Architectural Press Ltd.

Legeny, J., Spacek, R., & Morgenstein, P. (2018). Binding architectural practice with education. *Global Journal of Engineering Education*, 20(1), 6–14.

Leim, A. (2012). Teaching Strategic and Systems Design to Facilitate Collaboration and Learning. *Formakademisk*, 5(1), 29–48. 10.7577/formakademisk.374

Lekesiz, G., & Gürer, E. (2022). An overview of the architectural design studio in the conceptual framework of complex systems. JCoDe. *Journal of Computational Design*, 3(2), 1–26. 10.53710/jcode.1135984

Lerner, F. (2005). Foundations for design education: Continuing the Bauhaus Vorkurs vision. *Studies in Art Education*, 46(3), 211–226. 10.1080/00393541.2005.11650075

Liu, L. (2019). Face-to-face teaching in the flipped classroom supported by visualisation tools–Taking the course of "Architectural Design of Housing" as an example. *International Journal of Emerging Technologies in Learning*, 14(3), 220. 10.3991/ijet.v14i03.10106

Lizondo Sevilla, L., Bosch Roig, L., Ferrer Ribera, M. C., & Alapont-Ramón, J. L. (2019). Teaching architectural design through creative practices. *Journal of the Faculty of Architecture*, 36(1), 41–59.

Lukovich, T. (2023). Artificial Intelligence and Architecture Towards a New Paradigm. *YBL Journal of Built Environment*, 8(1), 30–45. 10.2478/jbe-2023-0003

Maldonado, T. (1970). *La speranza progettuale*. Einaudi Torino.

Market And Music School In Son Servera. URL-14: http://www.matoscastillo.com/index.php?/proyectos/mercado-y-escuela-de-musica-en-son-servera/, Last accesed: 03.08.2022.

Martin, B. O., Kolomitro, K., & Lam, T. (2013). Training Methods: A Review and Analysis. *Human Resource Development Review*, 13(1), 11–35. 10.1177/1534484313497947

Marvin, S., Luque-Ayala, A., & McFarlane, C. (2016). *Smart Urbanism, Utopian Vision or False Dawn?* Routledge.

Marx, D. M., & Ko, S. J. (2012). Superstars "like" me: The effect of role model similarity on performance under threat. *European Journal of Social Psychology*, 42(7), 807–812. 10.1002/ejsp.1907

Marx, D. M., & Roman, J. S. (2002). Female role models: Protecting women's math test performance. *Personality and Social Psychology Bulletin*, 28(9), 1183–1193. 10.1177/01461672022812004

Masdéu, M., & Fuses, J. (2017). Reconceptualizing the design studio in architectural education: Distance learning and blended learning as transformation factors. *Archnet-IJAR*, 11(2), 6. 10.26687/archnet-ijar.v11i2.1156

Masuda, H. (2014). *Chihō shōmetsu – Tōkyō ikkyoku shūchū ga maneku jinkō kyūgen* [Local extinctions: Rapid population decline due to the concentration in Tokyo]. Chuokoron-Shinsha Publishers.

Matthieu Gafsou. *Barozzi veiga clad monolithic art museum in lausanne with vertical brick fins*. URL-15: https://www.designboom.com/architecture/barozzi-veiga-mcba-art-museum-lausanne-switzerland-06-14-2019/, Last accesed: 03.08.2022.

McDonnell, J. (2016). Scaffolding practices: A study of design practitioner engagement in design Education. *Design Studies, 45*(Part A), 9-29.

McKercher, K. A. (2021). *Beyond sticky notes. Doing co-design for Real: Mindsets*. Methods, and Movements, Kindle Edition.

Merriam, S., & Cafferella, R. (1999). *Key theories of learning. Learning in adulthood: A comprehensive guide* (2nd ed.). Jossey Bass.

Merrill, B. (2015). Determined to stay or determined to leave? A tale of learner identities, biographies and adult students in higher education. *Studies in Higher Education*, 40(10), 1859–1871. 10.1080/03075079.2014.914918

Moonen, S. P. G., & Veeger, T. T. (2014). Preparing students towards the complexity of today's practice: startup in a multidisciplinary assignment. In Ö. Dincyürek, S. Hoskara, & S. M. Vural (Eds.), *International conference unspoken issues in architectural education*(UIAE'14), (pp. 299-319). Eastern Mediterranean University Press. https://research.tue.nl/nl/publications/preparing-students-towards-the-complexity-of-todays-practice-star

Moonen, S. P. G., & Veeger, T. T. (2016). Evaluation assessment carrousel: providing feedback in different stages of a problem-based learning-assigment. In S. Emmitt (editor), *Building our Future: Proceedings of the Integrated Design Conference*. University of Bath https://research.tue.nl/nl/publications/evaluation-assessment-carrousel-providing-feedback-in-different-s

Compilation of References

Moonen. S.P.G., & Veeger, T.T. (2013a). *Organization and assessment of a multidisciplinary project.* Proceedings, Project Approaches in Engineering Education: Closing the gap between university and industry, Eindhoven, the Netherlands. https://research.tue.nl/nl/publications/organization-and-assessment-of-a-multidisciplinairy-project

Moonen. S.P.G., & Veeger, T.T. (2013b). *Evaluation assessment carrousel for multidisciplinary design projects.* Proceedings, 11th International Detail Design in Architecture (DDiA), Kaohsiung, Taiwan. https://adk.elsevierpure.com/ws/portalfiles/portal/59224404/OHI_Vol.40_No.2.pdf

Morgenroth, T., Ryan, M. K., & Peters, K. (2015). The motivational theory of role modeling: How role models influence role aspirants' goals. *Review of General Psychology*, 19(4), 465–483. 10.1037/gpr0000059

Morin, E. (1986). *La Connaissance de la connaissance. Anthropologie de la connaissance* (Vol. 3). Seuil.

NAAB. (2020). *Conditions for Accreditation* (202nd ed.). National Architectural Accrediting Board.

Nagakura, T. (2017). Acadia 2017 Disciplines & Disruption. *Proceedings of the 37th Annual Conference of the Association for Computer Aided Design in Architecture.* Acadia Publishing Company.

Nancy, J. L. (1993). *The Experience of freedom.* Stanford University Press.

Nanda, U., Pati, D., Ghamari, H., & Bajema, R. (2013). Lessons from neuroscience: Form follows function, emotions follow form. *Intelligent Buildings International*, 5(sup1), 61–78. 10.1080/17508975.2013.807767

Navasa & Partners (2021). Tod's Omotesando Building. URL-3: https://www.archdaily.com/966848/i-am-always-inside-the-architecture-that-i-design-in-conversation-with-toyo-ito?ad_medium=gallery, Last accesed: 03.08.2022.

Nguyen, B., Yu, X., Japutra, A., & Chen, C.-H. S. (2016). Reverse teaching: Exploring student perceptions of "flip teaching". *Active Learning in Higher Education*, 17(1), 51–61. 10.1177/1469787415616727

Noel, L. A. (2020). "A Time for Change: Reimagining Design Education", Dialogues. *The Intersection of Emerging Research and Design for Learning*, (04), 14–15.

Norberg-Schulz, C. (1980). *Genius Loci: Towards a Phenomenology of Architecture.* Rizzoli.

Norberg-Schulz, C. (1996). In Nesbitt, K. (Ed.), *The Phenomenon of Place, Theorizing a New Agenda for Architecture: An Anthology of Architectural Theory 1965-1995* (pp. 414–428). Princeton Architectural Press.

Nose Town Office. (2018). *Asoberu Nose: Nose Town Promotion Project.* [Video]. Youtube. https://www.youtube.com/watch?v=miuwLbHeuP8

Nose Town Office. (2021). *Reiwa 3 nen jūmin kihon daichō jinkō [2021 Basic Registered Resident Population].* Nose Town Office. http://www.town.nose.osaka.jp/material/files/group/7/202103.pdf

Nose Town Office. (n.d.). *Ōsakadaigaku to hōkatsu kyōtei o teiketsu shimashita [Nose Town has concluded a comprehensive cooperative agreement with Osaka University].* Nose Town Office. http://www.town.nose.osaka.jp/kurashi/kyodo_machi/daigaku/1700.html

Nose Town Tourism Association. (n.d.). *Nose Note: Nose Town Tourism and Local Products.* Nose Town Tourism Association. https://www.town-of-nose.jp/

Odagiri, T. (2016). *Atarashī kokudo keisei keikaku no tokuchō [Characteristics of the new national land formation plan]. Tochi Sōgō Kenkyū [Comprehensive Land Research].* Land Institute of Japan.

Odile Decq (2014). *Fangshan Tangshan National Geopark Museum / Studio Odile Decq* [digital image]. URL-1: https://www.archdaily.com/771367/fangshan-tangshan-national-geopark-museum-studio-odile-decq, Last accesed: 03.08.2022.

Öğüt, S. (2008). Saf. In *TDV İslâm Ansiklopedisi* (c. 35, s. 435-436). Ankara: TDV İslâm Araştırmaları Merkezi.

Önkal, A. ve Bozkurt, N. (1993). Cami. In *TDV İslâm Ansiklopedisi* (c. 7, s. 46-56). Ankara: TDV İslâm Araştırmaları Merkezi.

Onur, D., & Zorlu, T. (2017). Tasarım Stüdyolarında Uygulanan Eğitim Metotları ve Yaratıcılık İlişkisi. *The Turkish Online Journal of Design, Art and Communication, 7*(4).

OPEN. (2021). *Osaka University Vision 2021*. OPEN. https://www.osaka-u.ac.jp/en/guide/strategy/OUvision2021/open2021/top

Ortony, A. (1993). *Metaphor and thought*. Cambridge University Press. 10.1017/CBO9781139173865

Özden, Y. (2013). *Eğitimde yeni değerler*. Pegem Akademi Yayınları.

Özel, A. (2002). Kıble. In *TDV İslâm Ansiklopedisi* (c. 25, p. 365-369). Ankara: TDV İslâm Araştırmaları Merkezi.

Ozenen, G. (2023). Self-Assessment and Learning Outcome Evaluation of Interior Architecture Students Using Flipped Versus Traditional Classroom Education Models. *SAGE Open, 13*(4), 21582440231209891. 10.1177/21582440231209891

Özkan Yazgan, E., & Akalın, A. (2019a). Metaphorical reasoning and the design behavior of "pre-architects". *International Journal of Technology and Design Education, 29*(5), 1193–1206. 10.1007/s10798-018-9485-9

Özkan Yazgan, E., & Akalın, A. (2019b). The comprehension of place awareness in a historical context: Metaphors in architectural design education. *METU Journal of The Faculty of Architecture, 36*(1), 183–202. 10.4305/METU.JFA.2019.1.7

Özkar, M. (2017). *Rethinking Basic Design in Architectural Education: foundations past and future*. Routledge. 10.4324/9781315740003

Öztürk, M. N., & Türkkan, E. E. (2006). The Design Studio as Teaching/Learning Medium—A Process-Based Approach. *International Journal of Art & Design Education, 25*(1), 96–104. 10.1111/j.1476-8070.2006.00472.x

Özüm İtez (2020). Yiwu Kültür Merkezi. URL 17: https://www.arkitera.com/proje/yiwu-kultur-merkezi/, Last accesed: 03.08.2022.

Paez, R., & Valtchanova, M. (2022). Art and Design: How Artistic Practices Enrich Design Education. In Cunha, M. F., & Franco, J. R. G. (Eds.), *Handbook of Research on Active Learning and Computational Thinking in Engineering Education* (pp. 38–55). IGI Global., 10.4018/978-1-7998-7865-0.ch001

Pallasmaa, J. (2009). *The Thinking Hand: Embodied and Existential Wisdom in Architecture*. Wiley and Sons.

Pallasmaa, J. (2011). *The Embodied Image: Imagination and Imagery in Architecture*. John Wiley and Sons.

Pallasmaa, J., & Zambelli, M. (2020). *Inseminations: Seeds for Architectural Thought*. Wiley.

Pasha, Y. N., Adnan, S., & Ahmed, N. (2020). Positioning historical evidences in architectural education: Review of methods and contents. *Open House International, 45*(4), 481–507. 10.1108/OHI-05-2020-0032

Pasick, A. (2014). Japan is rapidly losing population and half the world is about to join it. *Quartz*. https://www.qz.com/162788/japan-is-rapidly-losing-population-and-half-the-world-is-aboutto-join-it/

Pasin, B. (2017). Rethinking the design studio-centered architectural education. A case study at schools of architecture in Turkey. *The Design Journal, 20*(sup1), S1270-S1284.

Paszkowska N. E. (2014). Muzeum Tadeusza Kantora. Nowa Cricoteka w Krakowie. *Archivolta, 4*(64).

Compilation of References

Paszkowski Z. & Gołebiewski J. I. (2020). Heritage protection in the education of the modern architect. *World Transactions on Engineering and Technology Education*. World Institute for Engineering and Technology Education.

Paszkowski, Z. (2004). *City planned in the city without the masterplan*. Wydawnictwo Politechniki Krakowskiej.

Paszkowski, Z. (2008). Restrukturalizacja miasta historycznego jako metoda jego współczesnego kształtowania na przykładzie Starego Miasta w Szczecinie. hogben, Szczecin.

Paszkowski, Z. (2011). Miasto idealne w perspektywie Europejskiej i jego związki z urbanistyką współczesną. Universitas Kraków.

Paszkowski, Z., & Gołębiewski, J. I. (2020). International design workshops as an intensive form of architectural education. *World Transactions on Engineering and Technology Education*. World Institute for Engineering and Technology Education.

Paszkowski, Z. (1997). *Tradycja i innowacja w twórczości architektonicznej*. Politechnika Szczecińska.

Paszkowski, Z. (2003). *Transformacja przestrzeni śródmiejskich na przykładach miast europejskich*. Walkowska Wydawnictwo.

Paszkowski, Z. (2005). *Wizja rozwoju przestrzennego Szczecina*. Space & Form.

Paszkowski, Z. (2015). *Is there any sense of Port landscape protection in Szczecin?* Space & Form.

Pavlo Kryvozub (2012). *Community Center.* URL-10: https://www.behance.net/gallery/5272859/Community-Center, Last accesed: 03.08.2022.

Peikoff, L. (2018). *Teaching Johnny to Think: A Philosophy of Education Based on the Principles of Ayn Rand's Objectivism*. Blackstone Publishing.

Peimani, N., & Kamalipour, H. (2022). The future of design studio education: Student experience and perception of blended learning and teaching during the global pandemic. *Education Sciences*, 12(2), 140. 10.3390/educsci12020140

Pekdemir, Ş. (2016). In *Fıkhın Cami Mimarisine Etkisi. Çağımızda Cami Mimarisinde Arayışlar Sempozyumu bildiriler kitabı* (p. 187-195). Giresun: Giresun Üniversitesi İslami İlimler Fakültesi Yayınlari.

Peng, F., Kueh, C., & Cetinkaya Sendas, M. (2022). Design pedagogy in a time of change: Applying virtual flipped classroom in design higher education. *Journal of Design. Business & Society*, 9(1), 41–56.

Peterson, M., & Tober, B. (2014). Institutionalising the Vertical Studio: Curriculum, Pedagogy, and the Logistics of Core Classes with Mixed-Level Students. *Proceedings of AIGA Connecting Dots Conference*. AIGA.

Petry, E. (2002). *Architectural Education: Evaluation and Assessment*. 32nd ASEE/IEEE Frontiers in Education Conference, Boston, MA. 10.1109/FIE.2002.1158116

Piotr Zelaznowski. Westerplatte Memorial Museum. URL-21: https://www.behance.net/gallery/25547309/Westerplatte-Memorial-Museum-Gdansk

Po, R., Yifan, W., Golyanik, V., Aberman, K., Barron, J. T., Bermano, A. H., & Wetzstein, G. (2023). *State of the art on diffusion models for visual computing*. arXiv preprint arXiv:2310.07204.

Porter, T. (2004). *Archispeak: an illustrated guide to architectural terms*. London: Spon Press (an imprint of the Taylor & Francis Group). 10.4324/9780203643150

Proveniers, A., & Westra, J. (2009). The Evaluation Carrousel: an Assessment Tool for Interdisciplinary Science Innovation Education. in Education. in Kouwenhoven. W. (Ed.) *Advances in Technology, Education and Development*. Springer.

QUB. (n.d.). A Timeline of the Queen's Story. *QUB 175 Celebration online*. https://www.qub.ac.uk/about/175-celebration/timeline/

Rabbani, M., Bashar, A., Atif, M., Jreisat, A., Zulfikar, Z., & Naseem, Y. (2021). Text mining and visual analytics in research: Exploring the innovative tools. In *2021 International Conference on Decision Aid Sciences and Application (DASA)* (pp. 1087-1091). IEEE. 10.1109/DASA53625.2021.9682360

Rand, A. (1971). *The Romantic Manifesto*. Penguin.

Rand, A. (2005a). *[1943]. The Fountainhead*. Plume.

Rane, N. (2023). Role of ChatGPT and Similar Generative Artificial Intelligence (AI) in Construction Industry. *SSRN* 4598258. 10.2139/ssrn.4598258

RIBA. (2014). *RIBA procedures for validation and validation criteria for UK and international courses and examinations in architecture*. RIBA. <https://www.architecture.com/-/media/GatherContent/Validation-Procedures-and-Criteria/Additional-Documents/ValidationProcedures2011SECONDREVISION2MAY2014pdf.pdf>

RIBA. (2015). *RIBA Education Review May 2016 Update*. Royal Institute of British Architects.

RIBA. (2020). *The Way Ahead: An introduction to the new RIBA Education and Professional Development Framework and an overview of its key components*. Royal Institute of British Architects.

Rich, P. J., West, R. E., & Warr, M. (2015). Innovating how we teach collaborative design through studio-based pedagogy. *Educational Media and Technology Yearbook*, 39, 147–163. 10.1007/978-3-319-14188-6_11

Rodríguez-Ardura, I., & Meseguer-Artola, A. (2016). What leads people to keep on e-learning? An empirical analysis of users' experiences and their effects on continuance intention. *Interactive Learning Environments*, 24(6), 1030–1053. 10.1080/10494820.2014.926275

Rodriguez, C., Hudson, R., & Niblock, C. (2018). Collaborative learning in architectural education: Benefits of combining conventional studio, virtual design studio, and live projects. *British Journal of Educational Technology*, 49(3), 337–353. 10.1111/bjet.12535

Roland Halbe. Louvre Abu Dhabi's giant dome creats a 'rain of light'. URL-18: https://thespaces.com/louvre-abu-dhabis-giant-dome-creates-a-rain-of-light/, Last accesed: 03.08.2022.

Ross, W., & Glăveanu, V. (2023). *The constraints of habit: craft, repetition, and creativity*. Phenom Cogn Sci., 10.1007/s11097-023-09902-5

Rostand, E. (1942). *Cyrano de Bergerac* (Siyavuşgil, S. E., Trans.). Maarif Matbaası.

Rowan, H. (2016). Rethinking the age-old question of youth. *The Japan Times*. https://www.japantimes.co.jp/news/2016/07/16/national/science-health/rethinking-age-old-question-youth/

Rudewicz J. (2021). *Spatial and functional transformations of post-port areas in Szczecin in the context of classical city-port models*. Studies of the Industrial Geography Commission of the Polish Geographical Society.

Ruiz-Montiel, M., Boned, J., Gavilanes, J., Jiménez, E., Mandow, L., & Pérez-de-la-Cruz, J.-L. (2013). Design with shape grammars and reinforcement learning. *Advanced Engineering Informatics*, 27(2), 230–245. 10.1016/j.aei.2012.12.004

Russell, B. (2020). *In praise of idleness: And other essays*. Routledge. 10.4324/9781003059493

Rutherford, S. (2020). Engaging students in curriculum development through design thinking: A course design case. *International Journal of Designs for Learning*, 11(3), 107–125. 10.14434/ijdl.v11i3.25359

Compilation of References

Ryce-Paul, R. *Waterfront revitalisation: profitability vs social equity strategies shaping the urban waterfront*, [Thesis at Columbia State University, USA]. https://www.academia.edu/27040058/WATERFRONT_REVITALISATION _PROFITABILITY_VS_SOCIAL_EQUITY_STRATEGIES_SHAPING_THE_URBAN_WATERFRONT?email_work _card=view-paper

Rylander Eklund, A., Navarro Aguiar, U., & Amacker, A. (2022). Design thinking as sensemaking: Developing a pragmatist theory of practice to (re) introduce sensibility. *Journal of Product Innovation Management*, 39(1), 24–43. 10.1111/jpim.12604

Saghafi, M. R., Mozaffar, F., Moosavi, S. M., & Fathi, N. (2015). Teaching methods in architectural design basics. *Ciência e Natura*, 37, 379–387. 10.5902/2179460X20868

Saint-Exupéry, A. (1943). *Le petit prince [The little prince]*. Verenigde State van Amerika: Reynal & Hitchcock (US), Gallimard (FR).

Salama, A. (1995). *New trends in architectural education: Designing the design studio*. [Doctoral dissertation]. Raleigh NC: Tailored Text & Unlimited Potential Publishing.

Salama, A. (2010). Design Education. *ArchNet-IJAR: International Journal of Architectural Research, 4*(2).

Salama, A. M., & Osbourne, L. (2009). Unveiling the experiential dimension of field/work in architectural pedagogy.

Salama, A. (1995). *New Trends in Architectural Education: Designing the Design Studio*. Arti-arch.

Salama, A. M. (2007). Introduction: Legacies for the Future of Design Studio Pedagogy. In Salama, A. M., & Wilkinson, N. (Eds.), *Design Studio Pedagogy: Horizons for the Future* (pp. 2–8).

Salama, A. M. (2015). *Spatial Design Education: New Directions for Pedagogy in Architecture and Beyond*. Routledge.

Salem-Gur, O., & Dundar, M. (2019). Re-thinking Basic Design Course in Architectural Education in Turkey. *Intercultural Understanding*, 9, 7–14.

Sanders, E. B. N. (2002). From user-centered to participatory design approaches. In J. Frascara (Ed.), Design and the Social Sciences. Taylor & Francis. https://www.researchgate.net/publication/235700594_From_user-centered_to_participatory _design_approaches10.1201/9780203301302.ch1

Sanders, E. B. N., & Stappers, P. J. (2008). Co-creation and the new landscapes of design. *CoDesign*, 4(1), 5–18. https://www.tandfonline.com/doi/full/10.1080/15710880701875068 10.1080/15710880701875068

Santos, C. M., Franco, R. A., Leon, D., Ovigli, D. B., & Colombo, D. (2017). Interdisciplinarity in Education: Overcoming Fragmentation in the Teaching-Learning Process. *International Education Studies*, 10(10), 71–77. 10.5539/ies.v10n10p71

Sartre, J. P. (2007). *[1948]. Existentialism is a Humanism*. Yale University Press.

Schön. (1987). *Educating the Reflective Practitioner: Toward a New Design for Teaching and Learning in the Professions*. Jossey-Bass.

Schön, D. A. (1984). The architectural studio as an exemplar of education for reflection-in-action. *Journal of Architectural Education*, 38(1), 2–9. 10.1080/10464883.1984.10758345

Schubert, D. (2001). *Hafen und Uferzonen im Wandel*. Leue Verlag.

Seels, B. (1995). *Instructional Design Fundamentals: A Reconsideration*. Educational Technology Publications.

Şentürer, A. (1995). *Mimaride Estetik Olgusu: Bağımsız-Değişmez ve Bağımlı-Değişken Özellikler Açısından Kavramsal, Kuramsal ve Deneysel Bir İnceleme*. İTÜ Mimarlık Fakültesi Baskı Atölyesi.

Shane, G. (1976). Contextualism. *Architectural Design*, 46(11), 676–679.

Shearcroft, G. (2021). The joy of architecture: Evoking emotions through building. *Architectural Design*, 91(1), 108–117. 10.1002/ad.2660

Shulman, L. S. (1987). Knowledge and learning: Foundations of the new reform. *Harvard Educational Review*, 57(1), 1–22. 10.17763/haer.57.1.j463w79r56455411

Silva Pacheco, C. (2020). Art education for the development of complex thinking metacompetence: A theoretical approach. *International Journal of Art & Design Education*, 39(1), 242–254. 10.1111/jade.12261

Simamora, R. M. (2020). The Challenges of online learning during the COVID-19 pandemic: An essay analysis of performing arts education students. *Studies in Learning and Teaching*, 1(2), 86–103. 10.46627/silet.v1i2.38

Skivko M., Korneeva E., & Bisakayeva N. (2023). City ports as a place for iconic architecture and the meeting point for sustainable ideas: the cases of Antwerp and Hamburg. *E3S Web of Conferences 458*, 07028.

Slutskaya, N. (2006), Creativity and Repetition. Creativity and Innovation Management, 15: 150 156. 10.1111/j.1467-8691.2006.00384.x

Smatanová, K., Gregor, P., & Šeligová, A. (2020). Pros and cons of the vertical and horizontal design studios in architects' education. *Global Journal of Engineering Education*, 22(3).

Smith, C. (2022). Socio-constructivist pedagogy in physical and virtual spaces: the impacts and opportunities on dialogic learning in creative disciplines'. *Architecture_MPS 22*, 1.

Smith, D., & Kolb, D. (1996). User Guide for the Learning Style Inventory: A Manual for Teachers and Trainers. Boston: MA McBer(Mc Berand Company).

Smith, J. D. (2013). Student attitudes toward flipping the general chemistry classroom. *Chemistry Education Research and Practice*, 14(4), 607–614. 10.1039/C3RP00083D

Soliman, A. M. (2017). Appropriate teaching and learning strategies for the architectural design process in pedagogic design studios. *Frontiers of Architectural Research*, 6(2), 204–217. 10.1016/j.foar.2017.03.002

Steenson, M. W. (2022). Architectural intelligence: How designers and architects created the digital landscape. *MIT Press*.

Stouffs, R. (2018). Implementation issues of parallel shape grammars. *Artificial Intelligence for Engineering Design, Analysis and Manufacturing*, 32(2), 162–176. 10.1017/S0890060417000270

Stouffs, R., & Rafiq, Y. (2015). Generative and evolutionary design exploration. *Artificial Intelligence for Engineering Design, Analysis and Manufacturing*, 29(4), 329–331. 10.1017/S0890060415000360

Swagten, J. P. M., Moonen, S. P. G., & Wennekes, I. (2010). *The proof of the pudding is in the eating. Engineering Education 2010: Inspiring the next generation of engineers*. Birmingham UK Higher Education Academy Engineering Subject Centre, Loughborough University.

Taber, K. S. (2011). Constructivism as Educational Theory: Contingency in Learning, and Optimally Guided Instruction. *Educational Theory*. Nova. https://www.merriam-webster.com/dictionary/genius%20loci#h1

Tanalı, Z. (2000). Sadeleştirmeler. *Ankara: Alp*.

Tanyeli, U. (2007). *Mimarlığın Aktörleri, Türkiye 1900-2000*. Garanti Galeri.

Tanyeli, U. (2017). *Yıkarak yapmak: Anarşist bir mimarlık kuramı için altlık*. Metis Yayınları.

Compilation of References

Taş, M. (2003). *Osmanlı'dan Günümüze Yapı Üretiminde Mimarlık Meslek Örgütlenmesinin Gelişimi*. Uludağ Üniversitesi Mühendislik-Mimarlık Fakültesi Dergisi.

Taussig, M. (1993) Mimesis and Alterity. Routledge, London. In Slutskaya, N. (2006)

Terzidis, K. (2006). *Algorithmic Architecture*. Architectural Press. 10.4324/9780080461298

Teymur, N. (1992). *Architectural Education: Issues in Educationl Practice and Policy*. ?uestion Press.

Teymur, N. (2002). *Re-Architecture: themes and Variations*. ?uestion Press.

The Human Mortality Database. (2002). The University of California, Berkeley, USA and the Max Planck Institute for Demographic Research, Germany. https://www.mortality.org

Theories of Architecture. URL-13: https://kfynm.wordpress.com/2017/09/26/context-vs-building/, Last accesed: 03.08.2022.

Triyason, T., Tassanaviboon, A., & Kanthamanon, P. (2020). Hybrid classroom: Designing for the new normal after COVID-19 pandemic. Proceedings of the 11th international conference on advances in information technology,

Turkish Chamber of Architects. (2020). *Turkey Architectural Education Policies (Türkiye Mimarlık Eğitimi Politikası)*. TMMOB Mimarlar Odası.

Türkiye Mimarlık ve Eğitim Ortamıyla İlgili Bilgiler. (2017). *TMMOB Mimarlar Odası*.

Turrin, M., Von Buelow, P., & Stouffs, R. (2011). Design explorations of performance driven geometry in architectural design using parametric modeling and genetic algorithms. *Advanced Engineering Informatics*, 25(4), 656–675. 10.1016/j.aei.2011.07.009

UIA. (2017). Charter for Architectural Education: Revised 2017 Edition. UNESCO-UIA Validation Council For Architectural Education, International union of architects.

Uludağ, Z. (2016). Re-Thinking art and architecture: An Interdisciplinary experience. In Uludağ, Z., & Güleç, G. (Eds.), *Rethinking art & architecture: A Challenging interdisciplinary ground* (pp. 2–11). Nobel Academic Press.

Uludağ, Z., & Güleç, G. (2018). Reinterpreting city as a critical ground in atelier 1 projects: Some prospects and projections on Ankara. [IJADE]. *International Journal of Art & Design Education*, 37(3), 413–425. 10.1111/jade.12144

Uludağ, Z., Güleç, G., & Gerçek Atalay, N. (2018). *Criticism as a Design Method in Architectural Education: Criticizing City and Culture in Atelier 1. Architectural episodes 01: Educational pursuits and experiences*. İstanbul Kültür University Publications.

Uluoğlu, B. (1990). *Mimari Tasarım Eğitimi:Tasarım Bilgisi Bağlamında Stüdyo Eleştirileri*, [Doctoral dissertation, Istanbul Technical University].

Uluoğlu, B. (2000). Design knowledge communicated in studio critiques. *Design Studies*, 21(1), 33–58. 10.1016/S0142-694X(99)00002-2

Uluoğlu, B. (2011). *İTÜ Mimarlık Fakültesi'nin Kuruluş Yılları: Holzmeister, Bonatz, Diğerleri ve Mimarlık Eğitiminin Örgütlenmesinde Orta Avrupalı İzler, Bauhaus: Modernleşmenin Tasarımı, Türkiye'de Mimarlık, Sanat, Tasarım Eğitimi ve Bauhaus içimde*. İletişim Yayınları.

Ünal, F. C. (2013). Tasarım Sürecinin Saydamlaştırılmasında Hesaplamalı Tasarım Yöntemlerinin Kullanılması. In *VII MSTAS Conference Proceedings*. Research Gate.

UNESCO/UIA. (2011). *Charter For Architectural Education Revised Edition*. UIA General Assembly, Tokyo. www.uia-architectes.org

Uraz, T. U. (1993). *Tasarlama, Düşünme, Biçimlendirme*. İTÜ Mimarlık Fakültesi.

Uysal, Y. Y. (2011). *ODTÜ Mimarlık Fakültesi Mimarlık Bölümü'nde 1956-1980 Yılları Arası Eğitim Sistemi, Bauhaus: Modernleşmenin Tasarımı, Türkiye'de Mimarlık, Sanat, Tasarım Eğitimi ve Bauhaus içimde*. İletişim Yayınları.

van Bruinessen, T., Hopman, J. J., & Smulders, F. E. H. M. (2013). Towards a different view on ship design the development of ships observed through a social-technological perspective. Proceedings, ASME 2013 32nd International Conference on Ocean, Offshore and Arctic Engineering, Nantes, France 10.1115/OMAE2013-11585

Varinlioğlu, G., Pasin, B., & Clarke, H. D. (2018). Unconventional formulations in architectural curricula: An atelier on design for outer space architecture. In *Proceedings of the 15th International Conference on Engineering and Product Design Education (E&PDE)* (Vol. 15, pp. 93-105). Research Gate.

Vosniadou, S., & Ortony, A. (1989). Similarity and analogical reasoning: A synthesis. In Vosniadou, S., & Ortony, A. (Eds.), *Similarity and analogical reasoning* (pp. 1–18). Cambridge University Press.

Vural-Cutts, A. (2018). *Teknoloji Etkisi*. XXI Dergisi. http://www.doganhasol.net/mimarlik-ve-teknoloji.html

Vygotsky, L. S. (1978). *Mind in Society: Development of Higher Psychological Processes*. Harvard University Press.

Wahyuningsih, E., & Baidi, B. (2021). Scrutinizing the potential use of Discord application as a digital platform amidst emergency remote learning. [JEMIN]. *Journal of Educational Management and Instruction*, 1(1), 9–18. 10.22515/jemin.v1i1.3448

Wang, T. (2010). A New Paradigm for Design Studio Education. *International Journal of Art & Design Education*, 29(2), 173–183. 10.1111/j.1476-8070.2010.01647.x

Wanner, T., & Palmer, E. (2015). Personalising learning: Exploring student and teacher perceptions about flexible learning and assessment in a flipped university course. *Computers & Education*, 88, 354–369.

Want, S. C., & Harris, P. L. (2001). Learning from Other People's Mistakes: Causal Understanding in Learning to Use a Tool. *Child Development*, 72(2), 431–443. 10.1111/1467-8624.0028811333076

White, R. (2000). *The Student-Led 'Crit' as a Learning Device, Changing Architectural Education: Towards a New Professionalism*. London: E and fN Spon.

Wijnen, W. H. F. W. (2000). *Towards Design-Based Learning*. Eindhoven University of Technology Educational Service Centre.

Williamson, T., Radford, A., & Bennetts, H. (2003). *Understanding Sustainable Architecture*. Spon Press.

Xie, C., Wang, Y., & Cheng, Y. (2022). Does artificial intelligence satisfy you? A meta-analysis of user gratification and user satisfaction with AI-powered chatbots. *International Journal of Human-Computer Interaction*, 1–11.

Yen, Y.-C., Hou, H.-T., & Chang, K. E. (2015). Applying role-playing strategy to enhance learners' writing and speaking skills in EFL courses using Facebook and Skype as learning tools: A case study in Taiwan. *Computer Assisted Language Learning*, 28(5), 383–406. 10.1080/09588221.2013.839568

Yılmaz, İ. (2018). *Rethinking Design Space in Architecture*. [Doctoral dissertation, Gazi University.

Yorgancıoğlu, D., Aman, D. D., & Şat, B. (2023). Inquiring the generative capacity of urban abstraction and mapping for first-semester basic design studio. *IDA: International Design and Art Journal*, 5(1), 42–56.

Compilation of References

Young, G. (2002). 'Hybrid' Teaching Seeks to End the Drive Between Traditional and Online Instruction. *The Chronicle of Higher Education*.

Youssef, K. A. (2014). Horizontal Design Studio versus Vertical Design Studio: A Tale of Two Architecture Schools. *7th International Conference of Education, Research and Innovation (ICERI2014)*, Seville, Spain.

Yücel, A. (2007). Çoğulculuk İş Başında: Türkiye'nin Bugünkü Mimarlık Manzarası. *Modern Türk Mimarlığı 1900-1980 içinde* (Holod, R., Evin, A., & Özkan, S., Eds.). TMMOB Mimarlar Odası.

Yürekli, H. (2007). The Design Studio: A Black Hole. In Gülsün Sağlamer (Ed.), *The Design Studio: A Black Hole* (pp. 17-34). Yem.

Yurtsever, B., & Polatoğlu, Ç. (2020). Mimari Tasarım Eğitiminde 'Aktif Stüdyo' Deneyimleri. *Megaron, 14*(3). https://www.artsteps.com/view/602a1bec9cb19b786ac5bb26/

Zaremba, P., & Orlińska, H. (1965). *Urbanistyczny rozwój Szczecina*. Wydawnictwo Poznańskie, Poznań 1965.

Zarzar, K. M. (2008). The use of architectural precedents in creative design. In Zarzar, K. M., & Guney, A. (Eds.), *Understanding meaningful environments, architectural precedents and the question of identity in creative design* (pp. 7–21). Delft University Press.

Zenter, Ö. (2018). *Kinetik Biyomimetik Yaklaşımların Mimari Tasarımda İşlevsel Esneklik Amaçlı Kullanılması*. MSc. Thesis, Gazi University Graduate School of Natural and Applied Sciences.

Zenter, Ö., Özmen, F., & Yıldırım, T. (2024). Deprem Sonrası Çocuk Özel Eğitim Yerleşkesi Mimari Tasarım Deneyimi. *Journal of Architectural Sciences and Applications*, 9(Special Issue), 270–292. 10.30785/mbud.1334865

Zuk, W., & Clark, R. H. (1970). *Kinetic Architecture*. Van Nostrand Reinhold Company.

About the Contributors

Pınar Dinç Kalaycı graduated from the Department of Architecture, Gazi University, Ankara as she received PhD from the same institue. Her research interests involve design studio teaching, AI use in design studio, criticism in architecture, theory of architecture, design competitions, design awards, building programming, building assessment, environmental psychology, qualitative and quantitative methodologies in architectural inquiry. She lectured in design studio in Antwerp as a visiting lecturer, and in Ljubljana and Rome as Erasmus mobility staff. She was jury member in World Architecture Festival, Inspirelli Awards, ReThinking the Future Awards and uni.xyz competitions. She coordinates StudioThinkImagine and her students received several awards in international student design competitions.

***

Aysu Akalın received her B.Arch from Gazi University Faculty of Architecture in 1986, in restoration from Middle East Technical University in 1991 and her Ph.D. in architecture from the University of Manchester School of Architecture in 1996. She has been working at Gazi University Department of Architecture since 1988, and as Prof. since 2011. Some of her research interests include environmental psychology, meaning of space, regionalism, place identity, contextual reasoning in architectural education.

Abdullah Al Mahmud is a design researcher who works at the intersection of design and health. His research interests include co-design, child-computer interaction, and designing with and for marginalised communities living in low-resource regions. He has been the deputy chair of the Department of Architectural and Industrial Design since 2023.

Doğa Aman is a landscape architect who graduated from Istanbul Technical University (ITU) with a diploma prize in 2011. She completed her doctorate in ITU on public open space and disaster relief in 2019. During her doctoral studies, she continued her research at Wageningen University (2016). She worked as a research assistant in ITU between the years 2011-2019. She participated in national and international competitions in professional categories and received first prizes. Her research focuses on urban landscape planning, green urbanism, hazard mitigation and climate adaptive design. She currently works as Assist. Prof. in Ozyegin University Department of Architecture.

Szymon Andrejczuk is a member of the research team of the Faculty of Architecture at Bialystok University of Technology. Szymon Andrejczuk as a wheelchair user, specializes in the use of modern technological solutions in the aid of the physically disabled, as well as the use of artificial intelligence in digital art and conceptual design of everyday objects. Having experience in management and digital tools in marketing and brand management, Mr. Andrejczuk strives to improve his skills in the introduction of experimental and open source tools in the improvement of the quality of life of the physically disabled and to further expand the use of AI tools in general design pipelines.

Mehmet Emre Arslan is currently working as assistant professor at the department of interior architecture and environmental design, faculty of architecture at Istanbul Kultur University, Turkey. He received his master's degree from Istanbul Technical University in 2006 and PhD from Istanbul Technical University in 2013. He has published articles in international refereed journals and conference papers. His research interests are architectural design, wellness architecture, history of Turkish modernity. He is also a practicing architect who has many finished and built architectural designs.

Hilal Aycı has been teaching architectural design, theory, contemporary architecture and city-identity courses in the Gazi University Department of Architecture since 2005. After studying architecture in the Gazi University Department of Architecture, she graduated in 2005 with her MSc degree (2009) and her PhD degree (2017) from the same department. In the 2011-2012 Fall Semester, she conducted doctoral research in Henry van de Velde in Antwerp, Belgium. She has various academic and architectural design competition awards. She has been published in journals and books both nationally and internationally.

About the Contributors

Semra Aydınlı received her bachelor's and master's degree from ITU Faculty of Architecture and completed her doctoral thesis at the same institution. Semra Aydınlı, who continued her academic studies as a professor at ITU Faculty of Architecture since 2004, retired in April 2014. She has publications in the fields of design theories, architectural criticism, aesthetic experience, architecture and phenomenology, design culture and philosophy, paradigm shift in architecture architectural education and creativity, pedagogical approach to studio culture, ethics in design. She did two research projects about post occupancy evaluations on housing with two different research teams: first project was about a holistic approach to housing problems supported by TOKİ and the second project was about housing and its meaning of inside and outside living environments supported by ITU Research Fund. In addition to several professional projects, she attended urban and architectural design competitions with different teams and received 2 awards and 2 honorable mentions. She was invited as a visiting scholar for teaching first year design studio at Clemson University in the USA (1999-2000 academic year), and invited as a guest lecturer at Westminster University, London (2010 Spring), and invited as a co-tutor critic for Istanbul Studio at Wentworth Institute of Technology, Boston (2011 Fall), invited as the doctoral jury member of Delft technical University in the Netherlands (2015 Fall) and as a guest lecturer at Chalmers University of Technology, Sweden (2016 Spring) She took part in architectural education accreditation studies as a board member and board chairman at MIAK. She completed the supervision of 14 doctoral students and many theses of graduate students. She has 4 books, chapters in 10 international books, chapters 6 national books and many articles in various international and national periodicals.

Lucija Ažman Momirski, PhD, holds the position of Associated Professor of architecture and urban design since 2010. She served as Vice Dean of science and research at the Faculty of Architecture in Ljubljana from 2005 to 2007, and is involved in practice (a registered architect and urban planner since 1988), education (an associate professor of urban design since 2010, the chair of Technology, Computer Design and (Urban) Management at the Faculty of Architecture University of Ljubljana from 2012 to 2018) and research. Besides she has been working on the topic of conflicts of interest in space and spatial planning for at least 25 years, which can be measured by the many workshops (25) she has conducted on urban planning topics. Her international cooperation (at the Graz University of Technology, University of Zagreb, TU Delft, in Italy, Germany, the Netherlands, Spain, Liechtenstein and Turkey) has added to the wealth of experience on the proposed research topic.

Figen Beyhan completed her undergraduate education at KTU Faculty of Engineering and Architecture, Department of Architecture in 1989, and received her master degrees in 1994 and doctorate degrees in 1999 from the Department of Architecture of the Institute of Science and Technology at KTU. She worked as a research assistant at the Department of Architecture at KTU between 1995-2000, as a lecturer at the Department of Interior Architecture at KTU between 2001-2002, as an Assistant Professor at the Department of Architecture at KTU between 2003-2008, and as Associate Professor between 2009-2011 at the Department of Architecture, KTU. She continued her research as a visiting professor at the University of New South Wales-Faculty of Building Environment-Sydney between 2003-2004. Between 2008-2011, She served as Head of the Department of Building Sciences at KTU and as Deputy Head of the Department of Architecture at KTU in 2009. Between September 2010 and February 2011, she worked as a faculty member at Eskişehir Osmangazi University, Faculty of Engineering and Architecture, Department of Architecture with Farabi Exchange Program. She started to work as an Associate Professor at Gazi University, Faculty of Architecture, Department of Architecture in November 2011, and received the title of Professor in January 2015. She carried on as the Head of the Interior Design Department between 2011-2016 and was a member of the Faculty Senate between 2017 and 2020 at the Gazi University. She is continuing her research at Gazi University. She has served as the Head of the Forensic Architecture Commission in Forensic Science Foundation since 2016. She gave many vocational pieces of training, took part in workshops, and contributed to competition juries in corporation framework with ministries, foundations, and companies in the building sector. She has national and international articles, research projects, books, and papers on fire safety in buildings, energy-efficient building design, sustainable architecture, and forensic architecture within the scope of Architectural Design and Building Physics, which are her fields of study. She is a lecturer at Studio V since 2011 and, the coordinator of Studio V since 2012.

Burçin Mızrak Bilen has obtained her B.Arch. degree in 2009, from Middle East Technical University Faculty of Architecture Department of Architecture; and completed her M.Sc. in Architecture study in 2012, with her thesis called "Where We Grow Up Does Really Matter: Child Friendly Cities And A Proposal For Tarlabasi Istanbul" from Milan Technical University School of Architecture and Construction Engineering Architecture Program. She has received her Ph.D. in Architecture degree in 2018, with her doctoral thesis named "A Power-Centered Approach to the Capitalization of Climate Change in Property Sector and Strategic Limitation" from Bauhaus-Weimar University Faculty of Architecture and Urbanism. Between the years 2009-2012, she worked in small-scale interior design studios in Milan. And between the years of 2013-2018, she worked as a research and teaching assistant at Yildiz Technical University in the Department of Architecture. Her researches focused on child friendly spaces, sustainable architecture and the valuation of intangibles in architectural design.

Esin Boyacıoğlu received her BArch degree from ADMMA Turkey. MArch and PhD from Gazi University, Institute of Natural and Applied Sciences. She is retired from Gazi University Department of Architecture, taught architectural design, contemporary architecture and housing courses. She took part in many architectural design competitions and has awards/honorary mentions from several. Boyacıoğlu has authored various presentations, articles and chapters in books on the history and theory of modern architecture.

About the Contributors

Eliana Cangelli, associate professor of Architectural Technological Design, President of the Architectural and Urban Quality Committee of the Municipality of Rome, and Vice President of the European Board of EUROsolar - European Association for Renewable Energy. Former coordinator of the Doctoral Programme in Environmental Design at the Sapienza, since 1993 she has been conducting scientific research and planning experiments on the topics of technological and environmental design applied urban and rural space management, public heritage enhancement and recovery, and social housing.

Salih Ceylan is currently an associate professor in the department of architecture, faculty of architecture and design at Bahçeşehir University, Turkey. He received his master's degree from Istanbul Technical University in 2007 and PhD from Yıldız Technical University in 2017. He has published articles in international refereed journals, book chapters, and conference papers. His research interests are virtual reality in architecture, digital representation techniques, architectural education, sustainability, energy efficiency in architectural design, Space architecture and retail design.

Gizem Efendioğlu received her bachelor's degree from Istanbul Bilgi University, Department of Architecture in 2015 and her Master's from Yıldız Technical University, Computer-Aided Design. She is continuing her PhD in Architectural Design Computing Program at Istanbul Technical University. Her research areas focus on creativity, design cognition, and design process.

Merve Ertosun Yildiz received her Ph.D in 2023 from the Gazi University. She is a lecturer of Studio V since 2014. Her research interest focuses on a transdisciplinary that merges architecture with machine learning (MC) for forecasting the energy consumption of buildings. She is interested in energy-efficient building design, and sustainable architecture. She also studied about the assessment of construction-demolition waste in the context of sustainability. She completed her undergraduate education at Karadeniz Technical University-Department of Architecture in 2013.

Bengi Su Ertürkmen-Aksoy completed her undergraduate studies at the Department of Architecture of Gazi University. She received her PhD from Gazi University. Her academic career as a Research Assistant at the Department of Architecture at Gazi University started in 2012 while working on her master thesis. Her architectural and urban history research mainly focuses on modernity and daily life in late Ottoman and early Republican Turkey. She was awarded, together with her colleagues, the VEKAM Research Award in 2021. Apart from her academic research, she has various degrees in architectural design competitions.

Neva Gerçek Atalay is research assistant in the Department of Architecture at Gazi University, Ankara, Turkey. She graduated from the Department of Architecture at Karadeniz Technical University, where she also received her MA. She is currently studying on her PhD in the same department at Gazi University.

Jakub I. Gołębiewski, Ph.D. Civil engineer architect graduated in 2009 from the Faculty of Architecture and Urban Design at the West Pomeranian University of Technology in Szczecin. Currently, he is an assistant professor in the Department of History and Theory of Architecture at the Faculty of Architecture, the West Pomeranian University of Technology in Szczecin. In his scientific activity, he deals with the revitalization of post-industrial spaces and waterfronts; heritage protection, art in public space, and temporary architecture. He is the author of many scientific articles in Polish and foreign publications and a speaker at scientific conferences. As a tutor, he participated in many national and international architectural and urban workshops. In architectural practice, he is the co-author of many architectural concepts, completed projects, and competition concepts that received awards.

Gülşah Güleç is associate professor in the Department of Architecture at Gazi University, Ankara, Turkey, where she also received her MA and PhD. She graduated from the Department of Architecture at Eskisehir Osmangazi University. She has published on architectural theory, architectural design, architectural education, contemporary architecture and design theories.

Can Güngör was Born in Ankara in 1977. He graduated from TED Ankara College Foundation Private High School, Ankara, Turkey, in 1994. He completed his Undergraduate Degree at Yildiz Technical University, Faculty of Architecture, Department of Architecture, Istanbul, Turkey in 1999. He achieved his postgraduate degree at Gazi University, Institute of Natural And Applied Sciences, Department of Architecture, Ankara, Turkey in 2002. He achieved his Doctorate Degree at Gazi University, Institute of Natural And Applied Sciences, Department of Architecture, Ankara, Turkey in 2007. Has has worked at Gazi University, Faculty of Architecture Department of Architecture as Lecturer Dr. From 2009 to 2023. He has been the Deputy Head of the Department of Architecture at Gazi University Faculty of Architecture, Department of Architecture from 2010 to 2022. He earned his Associate Professor Degree in 2023. He has been the Vice Dean of the Faculty of Architecture since August 2023. He specializes in Architecture, Architectural Design, Accessibility, Universal and barrier-free design.

Ayşegül İnce received her B.Arch in architecture from International University of Sarajevo (2010-2015). Earned her MSc. Degree in architecture from the Gazi University (2021). She is currently a PhD student at Gazi University and works as a Research Assistant at the same university. Major research interests include architectural design, modern mosque architecture, sembolism in architecture, user perception in architecture.

About the Contributors

Cihangir Istek is specialized in the areas of Architecture, Design, Design Management and Education. He has held several teaching and leadership positions in design education, worked as an architect and design consultant in Japan, Europe, Turkey, Southeast Asia, and the United Kingdom. Between 2015-2017, he served as vice president on the board of ICoD: International Council of Design, representing designers and creators. Currently, he is Visiting Professor at Osaka University's Center for Global Initiatives and Istanbul Bilgi University's Department of Communication Design and Management. He teaches and researches on design and implementation in collaboration with professional and local communities.

Adam Jakimowicz is the Director of the Augmented Reality Laboratory and Vice-Dean for Development and Cooperation at the Faculty of Architecture of Bialystok University of Technology, Adam Jakimowicz has focused his works on the implementation of unconventional methods of teaching design and the use of technologies in the early stages of the process of architectural design. Prior to teaching at the current faculty, Adam has had past experience with teaching at other European universities such as KU Leuven, Sint-Lucas School of Architecture, as well as more current experience with Erasmus+ programme mobilites, international research projects throughout the eCAADe association and the OIKONET research network. In addition, he is the founder and one of the chief organizers of the annual East Design Days in Bialystok, Poland.

Gul Kacmaz Erk, with work/life experience in Ireland, Netherlands, Turkey, UK and USA, they conduct research on 'architecture and cinema'. Before joining Queen's Architecture in 2011, she worked as a licenced architect in Istanbul/Amsterdam, researched at University of Pennsylvania, University College Dublin, and ZK/U Berlin, and taught at Philadelphia (Thomas Jefferson) University, TUDelft and IUE. She holds BArch (METU), MArch (METU) and PhD (ITU) degrees in Architecture, directs CACity Research Group, organises Walled Cities film festivals, and conducts urban filmmaking workshops. She is an associate professor at Queen's University Belfast in Northern Ireland, UK.

Bilge Beril Kapusuz-Balcı has been a researcher at Gazi University Department of Architecture since 2012, where she teaches architectural design and photography. Her research fields include 20th-century theory and criticism of architecture and visual arts, architectural representation focusing on the history of architectural photography, and exhibition histories. She received her BArch at Gazi University in 2009; her MArch at Middle East Technical University in 2012. In 2018, she completed her PhD in Architecture with her dissertation based on her research in the historical archives of the Venice Biennale. Currently, as a fellow of The Scientific And Technological Research Council of Turkey, she is pursuing her postdoctoral research at the Iuav University of Venice on the critical pedagogies of architectural photography.

Mert Zafer Kara obtained Bachelor's degrees in Architecture and Interior Design from Istanbul Technical University in 2019. He spent a semester of his undergraduate education at Università IUAV di Venezia. During 2019-2021, he worked as an exhibition designer in various museum and gallery exhibitions. He continues his education at Istanbul Technical University in the Architectural Design Master's program. Since 2021, he has been working as a Research Assistant. His research interests focus on representation, memory, archive, and imagination in architectural design.

Nazan Kırcı received her B. Arch, M.A., and Ph. D. from KTU. She has teaching design studio since 1992. She carries out duties related to architectural education and accreditation within MIAK. She teaches 20th-century architectural theories, history of architecture, contemporary architecture, environmental ethics and aesthetics, and architectural design studios. She is the author of "20th Century Architecture", "First Step to Architecture", "a Guide to Architecture", "How the Student Learns and How the Tutor Assesses in a Design Studio".

İrem Küçük completed her undergraduate studies at Gazi University Faculty of Engineering and Architecture in 2009. She completed her master's thesis on "Editing the Architectural Design Studio Through Experimental Architecture Concept" in 2013, simultaneously at Gazi University Faculty of Architecture and IAAC. She completed her Ph.D. thesis on "Rethinking the Design Space in Architecture" at Gazi University in 2018. She has been teaching at the architectural design studio since 2009 and has developed various studio fictions with an experimental approach to design. She has been working as a coordinator at atelierz since 2014, producing experimental works that question what architecture is and who the architect is in the context of diverse thematic content. In addition to her research studies on design contexts, design tools, design products, design processes and design education in architectural design studios, she continues her professional studies with academic studies investigating and researching design space in different thematic frameworks. Design theories, architectural design, architectural design education, experimental design pedagogy, design space are her areas of expertise.

Ece Kumkale Açıkgöz, an architectural researcher, explores the intersection of architecture, digital design, and data management. Her focus lies in creative thinking and conceptualization within architectural education. She conducts research on Building Information Modeling (BIM), emphasizing collaboration, process management, data handling, and design research. Additionally, she redefines tools and methods used in architectural education. With degrees from Middle East Technical University (ODTÜ), she has held academic positions at various universities.

About the Contributors

Arzu Özen Yavuz received her B.A in 2001, Master's Studies in 2005, and was granted PhD in 2011 at Gazi University Faculty of Architecture. She is continuing her academic career as an Associated Professor at Gazi University Department of Architecture where she began her career as a Research Assistant in 2002. Ozen-Yavuz is the head of first year design studios including Basic Design Studio and Architectural Project II while also serving as a Department Vice Chair at Gazi University Department of Architecture. Her research is structured around architectural design and primary design education in the first-year architectural design studios. Her expertise lies in formation embedded design in architecture, the use of computational and computer-aided design technologies including parametric, generative and algorithmic designstrategies and their uses in architectural design and education.

Gizem Özkan Üstün was born in Ankara in 1991. She received her master's degree in 2017 and her doctorate from Gazi University Faculty of Architecture with her doctoral thesis titled 'Understanding World Architecture in the Fluid Age: A Discussion of Four Examples' in 2024. She worked as an assistant at StudioThinkImagine between 2017 and 2024 and finished her job at Gazi University in 2024. She continues to work on world architecture and architects. Her research interests are architectural design, design education, architectural theory, and philosophy.

Fulya Özmen graduated from Galatasaray Hihgschool (1980), holds a Professional degree in architecture from Mimar Sinan University (1985) and a Ph.D. from Gazi University (2003). She is an academic member of Gazi University Faculty of Architecture since 1988, focusing on building technologies, building and construction management systems, building and environmental qualities, mass-housing techniques and problems, hotel buildings and architectural education. Her Ph. D. title is "Quality Management Evaluation Model in Building Production: The Example of Hotel Buildings' Post Occupancy Process". She has coordinated two international workshops series under the Erasmus founds (Ewta 2009-2011 and Ewuq-Port 2013-2014); took part in several workshops as a member of organisation committee and participated as a studio leader to several workshops both national and international levels.

Zbigniew W. Paszkowski, Prof. PhD Architect, professor at the Department of Architecture of the Andrzej Frycz Modrzewski Kraków University, graduated 1979 from the Architecture Faculty of the Technical University in Cracow, member of the Committee of Architecture and Urban Planning of the Polish Academy of Sciences, the member of SARP, ICOMOS, ISOCARP, founder of the Urbicon Ltd. architectural design office, author of numerous scientific papers and books on architecture, urban renewal and planning, as the architect author of several realized architectural big-scale projects in Poland. His scientific work mainly deals with urban transformations, revitalization, urban renewal, heritage protection, and theoretical approaches to the discipline of architecture and spatial planning. He developed the international links of the Faculty of Architecture to other European universities, gave lectures and participated in many conferences and workshops worldwide.

Maciej Poplawski is a technical research assistant and facilitator of novel technologies, Maciej Poplawski promotes the use of unique and abnormal digital tools in architectural design teaching, conceptual architectural design and experimental graphic design. Being experienced in IT development, Mr. Poplawski has unique skills in the use of several Python frameworks, front end development and backend server maintenance, which greatly supports the mission of the design studio and the faculty as a whole. By providing personalized solutions for teaching tools, and by introducing IT developer tools to architects and designers, Mr. Poplawski has proven his ground as a valuable member of the team.

Zümrüt Şahin obtained her bachelor's degree from Istanbul Technical University Department of Architecture in 2020 as the 2nd highest ranked graduate of her class. She received her master's degree from Istanbul Technical University Architectural Design Master Program in 2023 with her thesis titled "The Production and Transformation of Space: Dismantling the Space of Artistic Production". In 2022, she studied at Vienna Technical University as an exchange student of the Erasmus+ Program. She is a PhD student at Istanbul Technical University Architectural Design Program. Her research interests include space time body relations in architectural theory and the intersection of art and architecture.

Beyza Şat graduated B.Sc. with an honorary degree from Istanbul University, Landscape Architecture Department in 1999, then orderly obtained M.Sc. in 2002, and Ph.D. in 2009 from Science Institute of Istanbul University. She is expertise on Landscape Analysis and Ecological Planning subjects. Over a span of twenty years, she has taught on ecology and sustainability related issues both in state and private universities. She had worked in Toledo University, (U.S.) as visiting scholar in 2014 with a research proposal award. She has been working as an associate editor in a prestigious journal of Springer Open, Ecological Processes since 2017.

Andreas Schneider is one of the founding members of the Institute for Information Design Japan – IIDj, where he has been involved in planing, designing, and editing of publications on Information Design, Urbanism, Architecture, and Mobility since 1999. He has been teaching as full-time faculty at the University of the Arts Berlin, Tama Art University Tokyo and the Institute for Advanced Sciences Arts and Media – IAMAS, in Gifu prefecture Japan. Over the years, he has been invited as a visiting professor, lecturer and curator of symposia and workshops by the National Institute for Design and JK Lakshmipat University in India, Asian Creative Academy in Korea, Helwan University in Egypt, Kadir Has University and Istanbul Bilgi University in Turkey, Aalto University in Finland, Kyushu University, Osaka University, and Waseda University in Japan, among others. He has a long-standing interest in developing tools for structured thinking that support practice and lifelong learning.

About the Contributors

Bartosz Sliwecki is a researcher at the AURELA laboratory at the Architecture Faculty of Bialystok University of Technology, specializing in virtual reality architectural design, user generated architectural design in online social platforms, FFF 3D printing, optical 3D scanning and virtual reality design research. Having joined the academic community in 2017, Bartosz Sliwecki had previous experience with 3D rapid prototyping and 3D scanning through works with the Bialystok Museum of Warfare and the creation of blind oriented historical exhibitions. In the past, has participated in numerous research and didactics grants of the European Union, such as with the use of gamification and virtual reality for novel teaching methods. His PhD thesis has been awarded at the 38th international ECAADE conference PhD Workshops, in Berlin, Germany. Bartosz Sliwecki has participated in research projects revolving around the use of virtual reality in the assessment of concept stage furniture designs and the collection of view tracking of target groups.

Zeynep Uludağ is professor in the Department of Architecture at Gazi University, Ankara, Turkey. She graduated from the Department of Architecture at Middle East Technical University, where she also received her MA and PhD. She has published on architectural theory, architectural design, urban landscape, semiotics and architectural education.

Mehmet Yildirim graduated from Selçuk University, employed in construction sector abroad Russia, S. Arabia and Turkey for Holiday Village, Hotel, Border Center, Office, Shopping Mall, Housing projects. Completed M. Sc. in Gazi University, Ph. D. study in Istanbul Technical University. He worked in Gazi University Department of Architecture between 1992-2023. Designed elemantary school in Yozgat, Gazi Campus Gate, Ankara University Congress Center, attended to many winter school events as instructor and roving critic in Ankara and Lisboa during that period. Working on topics of Design Methods, Morphological Analysis, Advences in Design.

Senem Yildirim is an architectural historian working as a Research Assistant, PhD at Gazi University Faculty of Architecture since 2012. She completed her Master's studies at Middle East Technical University in 2013, and was granted a PhD in 2020 at Middle East Technical University, Graduate Program of History of Architecture. During her dissertation research, she worked as a Visiting Scholar at Columbia University-Harriman Institute in 2018 and currently conducting research as a Post-Doctoral Fellow at New York University, Graduate School of Arts & Sciences, The Department of Russian and Slavic Studies with Prof. Boris Groys. Yildirim-Evsen's research is structured around visuality and architectural history, spatial representations in alternative forms of art and underrepresented art movements, as well as spatiality of artists' spaces. Her expertise lies in Cold War Architecture and its visual cultures. Her latest work is published in the edited volume "Appropriated Interiors" by Routledge Press.

Derya Yorgancıoğlu holds a B.Arch. (2000) degree from YTU Department of Architecture (2000), and M.Arch. (2004) and Ph.D. (2010) degrees in architecture from METU Department of Architecture, Turkey. She conducted research studies at Queen's University of Belfast, Center for Educational Development (CED) in 2017 and Indiana University, Bloomington, Center for Innovative Teaching and Learning in 2018 as a visiting researcher. She is currently working at Özyeğin University Department of Architecture and teaching basic design and architectural design studios. Her research interests cover theory and research in architecture, architectural education, design studio pedagogy, scholarship of teaching and learning in higher education.

Özge Zenter completed her undergraduate education at Karabük University Department of Architecture in 2014. She studied at Universita degli Studi di Sassari-Italy in 2013 as part of Erasmus student mobility. She completed her master's thesis titled "Biomimetic Approaches in Architectural Design Use for Functional Flexibility" at Gazi University Department of Architecture in 2018. She worked as an architect at 2K Group Architecture and Engineering company between 2014-2015. She has been working as a research assistant at Gazi University Department of Architecture since 2016 and continues her research. Her research interests are architectural design, current developments in design, flexibility, biomimicry and kinetic architecture.

Index

Symbols

3D Modelling 127

A

Animation 114, 117, 127, 187, 189
Architectural Design 2, 34, 35, 36, 37, 48, 59, 61, 62, 63, 65, 66, 75, 77, 78, 80, 101, 103, 109, 111, 113, 114, 117, 120, 124, 127, 132, 133, 134, 137, 142, 143, 144, 145, 146, 147, 148, 154, 156, 157, 158, 159, 160, 161, 162, 163, 164, 165, 166, 169, 170, 172, 173, 174, 175, 176, 177, 178, 179, 180, 182, 189, 191, 203, 219, 220, 221, 222, 232, 233, 234, 235, 237, 239, 240, 241, 242, 243, 247, 257, 272, 274, 282, 292, 293, 297, 310, 333
Architectural Design Education 35, 37, 62, 77, 101, 111, 113, 142, 148, 257, 310
Architectural Design Studio 35, 36, 59, 61, 62, 63, 66, 75, 132, 133, 165, 178, 179, 182, 189, 191, 219, 237, 239
Architectural Design Studios 2, 34, 36, 37, 109, 142, 144, 178, 180, 219, 222, 240, 242, 272, 292, 293, 310
Architectural Education 1, 2, 6, 16, 34, 35, 37, 54, 59, 62, 63, 65, 66, 74, 75, 77, 80, 98, 111, 114, 127, 129, 130, 135, 138, 140, 142, 144, 145, 146, 147, 152, 153, 156, 159, 162, 164, 165, 169, 172, 174, 178, 179, 180, 188, 189, 191, 202, 203, 204, 206, 217, 219, 220, 221, 222, 232, 233, 235, 236, 237, 238, 239, 240, 241, 253, 254, 273, 275, 276, 277, 278, 281, 282, 283, 284, 285, 286, 287, 288, 289, 290, 291, 293, 294, 309, 310, 321, 322, 324, 325
architectural practice 147, 165, 253, 276, 287, 288, 290, 325
Architecture 1, 2, 6, 9, 10, 14, 15, 34, 35, 37, 38, 39, 41, 42, 47, 48, 50, 59, 61, 62, 63, 64, 65, 66, 67, 68, 71, 72, 74, 75, 77, 78, 79, 80, 84, 87, 90, 97, 98, 99, 100, 103, 104, 109, 111, 112, 113, 114, 115, 117, 118, 120, 123, 124, 127, 129, 130, 131, 132, 133, 134, 135, 137, 138, 140, 141, 142, 144, 146, 147, 153, 154, 155, 156, 157, 158, 159, 160, 163, 164, 165, 167, 168, 169, 170, 173, 174, 175, 176, 177, 178, 179, 180, 182, 183, 184, 185, 187, 188, 189, 190, 191, 192, 193, 194, 195, 202, 203, 205, 206, 209, 216, 217, 219, 220, 221, 222, 223, 227, 233, 234, 236, 237, 238, 239, 240, 241, 242, 253, 254, 255, 256, 257, 258, 263, 269, 270, 272, 273, 274, 275, 276, 277, 278, 279, 280, 281, 282, 283, 284, 285, 286, 287, 288, 289, 290, 292, 293, 294, 295, 296, 298, 299, 303, 304, 306, 309, 310, 311, 312, 313, 314, 321, 323, 324, 325, 326, 334
architecture education 98, 203, 237, 256, 257, 276, 277, 279, 283, 286, 287, 289, 292
architecture profession 254
Artificial Intelligence 37, 50, 162, 163, 165, 168, 169, 172, 174, 175, 176, 177, 201, 289, 321, 326
Atelier 1 61, 62, 63, 65, 66, 74, 75, 77

B

basic design 63, 64, 66, 192, 194, 201, 219, 220, 221, 222, 223, 224, 225, 226, 232, 233, 234, 235, 237, 238, 240, 242, 269, 272, 281
Being Earthian 1, 2, 8
blended learning 35, 59, 256, 274

C

CAAD 156, 157, 158, 161, 162, 164, 165
Cinematic Analysis Methods 114, 117, 118, 120, 123, 124
City Film 114, 117, 127
Co-Design 17, 18, 31, 32
Collage 114, 117, 123, 124, 129, 194, 196, 198, 199
Communities 18, 19, 21, 22, 23, 30, 31, 80, 81, 86, 165, 230, 232, 293
Complexity 9, 10, 19, 36, 63, 79, 81, 83, 88, 117, 135, 138, 142, 144, 161, 168, 169, 206, 211, 215, 241, 304, 312, 320, 321
Concept Film 114, 117, 124, 127
Contexts 18, 19, 167, 184, 187, 193, 205, 227, 293, 297, 298, 301, 309
contextual reasoning 100, 101, 102
Covid 19 pandemic 221
Creative Practices 176, 256
Creative Process 157, 162, 165, 170, 181, 216, 217
Critical Design 61, 63, 65, 74, 75

D

design education 2, 35, 36, 37, 62, 63, 65, 77, 101, 111, 113, 129, 130, 142, 144, 145, 148, 162, 177, 179, 191, 193, 194, 201, 202, 204, 210, 214, 216, 217, 218, 219, 220, 221, 222, 225, 233, 237, 240, 254, 256, 257, 273, 283, 290, 310
Design process 3, 35, 36, 38, 62, 63, 64, 65, 66, 68, 72, 74, 75, 78, 79, 80, 84, 91, 100, 101, 102, 109,

110, 111, 117, 125, 127, 138, 142, 143, 144, 145, 146, 147, 148, 152, 154, 159, 163, 169, 172, 173, 174, 177, 198, 199, 204, 211, 213, 216, 241, 259, 298, 301, 324, 333

design studio 1, 2, 7, 8, 12, 17, 18, 34, 35, 36, 37, 38, 59, 61, 62, 63, 64, 65, 66, 75, 77, 79, 87, 88, 89, 90, 96, 97, 111, 114, 130, 132, 133, 136, 157, 159, 160, 161, 162, 164, 165, 169, 174, 178, 179, 182, 183, 189, 190, 191, 192, 193, 194, 195, 196, 197, 198, 200, 201, 207, 212, 217, 219, 220, 221, 222, 225, 226, 236, 237, 239, 240, 242, 253, 254, 255, 258, 269, 270, 272, 273, 274, 283, 284, 286, 287, 289, 290, 310, 311, 321, 322, 323, 324, 325, 326, 333

E

Education 1, 2, 3, 5, 6, 10, 14, 15, 16, 17, 31, 34, 35, 36, 37, 39, 52, 54, 59, 62, 63, 65, 66, 68, 69, 74, 75, 77, 80, 98, 101, 109, 110, 111, 113, 114, 116, 117, 121, 123, 124, 127, 129, 130, 132, 134, 135, 138, 140, 142, 143, 144, 145, 146, 147, 148, 152, 153, 156, 159, 162, 164, 165, 169, 172, 174, 175, 177, 178, 179, 180, 187, 188, 189, 191, 193, 194, 201, 202, 203, 204, 206, 210, 214, 216, 217, 218, 219, 220, 221, 222, 225, 227, 232, 233, 234, 235, 236, 237, 238, 239, 240, 241, 253, 254, 255, 256, 257, 272, 273, 274, 275, 276, 277, 278, 279, 281, 282, 283, 284, 285, 286, 287, 288, 289, 290, 291, 292, 293, 294, 299, 302, 306, 309, 310, 311, 312, 316, 320, 321, 322, 324, 325, 334
Emancipation 61, 64, 65, 66, 74, 75
Encourage 63, 162, 174, 195, 196, 197, 203, 204, 222, 223, 225, 226, 228, 235, 240, 242, 253
Experimental Design 173, 179

F

Filmmaking Practices 114, 117, 123, 127
first-year architectural education 220, 221, 232, 236, 240
Flipped classroom 256, 257, 262, 269, 270, 271, 272, 273, 274

G

Generative Design 37, 163

H

Heritage Protection 140

higher education 3, 15, 129, 130, 132, 175, 201, 227, 255, 256, 272, 273, 274, 275, 288, 310, 321, 322
Housing 12, 13, 43, 78, 80, 81, 83, 84, 85, 86, 87, 89, 90, 91, 92, 93, 96, 138, 143, 226, 257, 274, 302, 318, 319, 325

I

Image Generation 163
Integrated design 312, 321

L

learning by doing 5, 78, 80, 129, 192, 193, 194, 195, 196, 198, 200, 222
learning by experience 194, 196, 198, 200
Legendary Architects 1, 2, 6, 7, 9, 14

M

mimesis 5, 15, 100, 109
modern mosque 100, 102, 104
Montage 114, 117, 123, 124, 125, 129, 196, 198, 199
moodPaint 114, 117, 123, 124
Moon 326, 333
Motivation 4, 6, 14, 193, 197, 203, 204, 208, 256, 324

O

Organization 26, 36, 63, 77, 91, 93, 147, 187, 199, 230, 278, 302, 321

P

Practice 1, 6, 14, 17, 18, 19, 27, 29, 30, 31, 32, 35, 73, 79, 83, 96, 98, 117, 118, 123, 127, 129, 130, 132, 147, 162, 165, 172, 175, 179, 189, 200, 218, 219, 226, 234, 247, 253, 256, 262, 269, 274, 275, 276, 280, 282, 283, 284, 285, 286, 287, 288, 289, 290, 292, 293, 295, 298, 306, 312, 321, 323, 324, 325
Project-based Learning 259

R

Revitalisation 141

S

Sensible Design 216
Site film 114, 117, 124, 127
space 9, 10, 14, 26, 28, 35, 39, 46, 47, 48, 59, 65, 66, 73, 74, 77, 100, 102, 103, 104, 109, 111, 117,

123, 124, 135, 136, 138, 140, 143, 145, 147, 157, 158, 165, 177, 178, 179, 181, 182, 183, 185, 187, 188, 190, 191, 192, 193, 195, 199, 200, 207, 211, 212, 215, 220, 222, 223, 224, 225, 226, 227, 232, 233, 235, 240, 241, 243, 246, 256, 259, 261, 286, 302, 319, 325, 326, 327, 328, 330, 331, 332, 333
Stable Diffusion 164, 165, 167, 168, 169, 170, 172, 174
Storyboard 114, 117, 123, 124
Studio culture 8, 35, 59, 120, 201
studio teaching 35, 175, 271, 272, 323
Suburbs of Rome 81
Sustainability 9, 35, 48, 65, 78, 79, 80, 84, 85, 87, 91, 93, 96, 97, 140, 143, 146, 147, 175, 259, 289, 292, 293, 294, 296, 297, 309
Szczecin 132, 133, 134, 135, 136, 138, 140, 141

T

Teaching Method 78, 83, 257, 271, 306, 309
Technical Visit 298, 299, 300, 301, 306
Technological and Environmental Design 78, 79, 81
Threshold Studio 240, 253
transformative learning 198

V

value 21, 43, 104, 132, 137, 146, 172, 257, 298, 306, 309, 317
vision 1, 17, 32, 98, 124, 175, 176, 203, 217, 237, 317, 324, 333

W

Walkthrough 127
Waterfront 132, 133, 134, 135, 136, 137, 138, 141
Workshop 23, 27, 29, 32, 45, 75, 237, 258, 259, 260, 261, 262, 263, 269, 270, 271, 277, 319, 324, 325
workshops 13, 18, 19, 23, 27, 66, 135, 140, 168, 183, 255, 258, 271, 281, 287, 306, 323, 324, 325, 334

Publishing Tomorrow's Research Today

Uncover Current Insights and Future Trends in
Education
with IGI Global's Cutting-Edge Recommended Books

Print Only, E-Book Only, or Print + E-Book.
Order direct through IGI Global's Online Bookstore at www.igi-global.com or through your preferred provider.

ISBN: 9781668493007
© 2023; 234 pp.
List Price: US$ 215

ISBN: 9798369300749
© 2024; 383 pp.
List Price: US$ 230

ISBN: 9781668486467
© 2023; 471 pp.
List Price: US$ 215

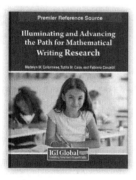

ISBN: 9781668465387
© 2024; 389 pp.
List Price: US$ 215

ISBN: 9781668475836
© 2024; 359 pp.
List Price: US$ 215

ISBN: 9781668444238
© 2023; 334 pp.
List Price: US$ 240

Do you want to stay current on the latest research trends, product announcements, news, and special offers?
Join IGI Global's mailing list to receive customized recommendations, exclusive discounts, and more.
Sign up at: **www.igi-global.com/newsletters**.

Scan the QR Code here to view more related titles in Education.

www.igi-global.com   Sign up at www.igi-global.com/newsletters   facebook.com/igiglobal   twitter.com/igiglobal   linkedin.com/igiglobal

Ensure Quality Research is Introduced to the Academic Community

Become a Reviewer for IGI Global Authored Book Projects

 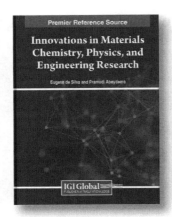 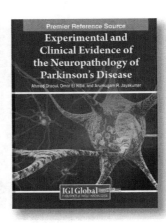 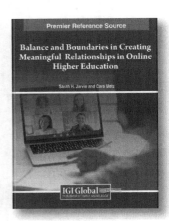

The overall success of an authored book project is dependent on quality and timely manuscript evaluations.

Applications and Inquiries may be sent to:
development@igi-global.com

Applicants must have a doctorate (or equivalent degree) as well as publishing, research, and reviewing experience. Authored Book Evaluators are appointed for one-year terms and are expected to complete at least three evaluations per term. Upon successful completion of this term, evaluators can be considered for an additional term.

If you have a colleague that may be interested in this opportunity, we encourage you to share this information with them.

www.igi-global.com

Publishing Tomorrow's Research Today
IGI Global's Open Access Journal Program

Including Nearly 200 Peer-Reviewed, Gold (Full) Open Access Journals across IGI Global's Three Academic Subject Areas: Business & Management; Scientific, Technical, and Medical (STM); and Education

Consider Submitting Your Manuscript to One of These Nearly 200 Open Access Journals for to Increase Their Discoverability & Citation Impact

| Web of Science Impact Factor **6.5** | Web of Science Impact Factor **4.7** | Web of Science Impact Factor **3.2** | Web of Science Impact Factor **2.6** |

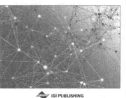  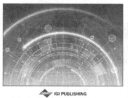 

Journal of Organizational and End User Computing — *Journal of Global Information Management* — *International Journal on Semantic Web and Information Systems* — *Journal of Database Management*

Choosing IGI Global's Open Access Journal Program Can Greatly Increase the Reach of Your Research

Higher Usage
Open access papers are 2-3 times more likely to be read than non-open access papers.

Higher Download Rates
Open access papers benefit from 89% higher download rates than non-open access papers.

Higher Citation Rates
Open access papers are 47% more likely to be cited than non-open access papers.

Submitting an article to a journal offers an invaluable opportunity for you to share your work with the broader academic community, fostering knowledge dissemination and constructive feedback.

Submit an Article and Browse the IGI Global Call for Papers Pages

We can work with you to find the journal most well-suited for your next research manuscript.
For open access publishing support, contact: journaleditor@igi-global.com

Recommended Titles from our e-Book Collection

Innovation Capabilities and Entrepreneurial Opportunities of Smart Working
ISBN: 9781799887973

Advanced Applications of Generative AI and Natural Language Processing Models
ISBN: 9798369305027

Using Influencer Marketing as a Digital Business Strategy
ISBN: 9798369305515

Human-Centered Approaches in Industry 5.0
ISBN: 9798369326473

Modeling and Monitoring Extreme Hydrometeorological Events
ISBN: 9781668487716

Data-Driven Intelligent Business Sustainability
ISBN: 9798369300497

Information Logistics for Organizational Empowerment and Effective Supply Chain Management
ISBN: 9798369301593

Data Envelopment Analysis (DEA) Methods for Maximizing Efficiency
ISBN: 9798369302552

Request More Information, or Recommend the IGI Global e-Book Collection to Your Institution's Librarian

For More Information or to Request a Free Trial, Contact IGI Global's e-Collections Team: eresources@igi-global.com | 1-866-342-6657 ext. 100 | 717-533-8845 ext. 100

Are You Ready to Publish Your Research?

IGI Global offers book authorship and editorship opportunities across three major subject areas, including Business, STM, and Education.

Benefits of Publishing with IGI Global:

- Free one-on-one editorial and promotional support.
- Expedited publishing timelines that can take your book from start to finish in less than one (1) year.
- Choose from a variety of formats, including Edited and Authored References, Handbooks of Research, Encyclopedias, and Research Insights.
- Utilize IGI Global's eEditorial Discovery® submission system in support of conducting the submission and double-blind peer review process.
- IGI Global maintains a strict adherence to ethical practices due in part to our full membership with the Committee on Publication Ethics (COPE).
- Indexing potential in prestigious indices such as Scopus®, Web of Science™, PsycINFO®, and ERIC – Education Resources Information Center.
- Ability to connect your ORCID iD to your IGI Global publications.
- Earn honorariums and royalties on your full book publications as well as complimentary content and exclusive discounts.

Join Your Colleagues from Prestigious Institutions, Including:

- Australian National University
- MIT – Massachusetts Institute of Technology
- Johns Hopkins University
- Tsinghua University
- Harvard University
- Columbia University in the City of New York

Learn More at: www.igi-global.com/publish

or Contact IGI Global's Aquisitions Team at: acquisition@igi-global.com

Printed in the United States
by Baker & Taylor Publisher Services